INSIDERS' GUIDE® TO THE MONTEREY PENINSULA

HELP US KEEP THIS GUIDE UP TO DATE

Every effort has been made by the authors and editors to make this guide as accurate and useful as possible. However, many things can change after a guide is published—establishments close, phone numbers change, facilities come under new management, etc.

We would love to hear from you concerning your experiences with this guide and how you feel it could be improved and be kept up to date. While we may not be able to respond to all comments and suggestions, we'll take them to heart and we'll also make certain to share them with the authors. Please send your comments and suggestions to the following address:

The Globe Pequot Press
Reader Response/Editorial Department
P. O. Box 480
Guilford, CT 06437

Or you may e-mail us at:

editorial@GlobePequot.com

Thanks for your input, and happy travels!

INSIDERS'GUIDE®

INSIDERS' GUIDE® SERIES

INSIDERS' GUIDE® TO THE
MONTEREY PENINSULA

FOURTH EDITION

TOM OWENS AND MELANIE BELLON CHATFIELD

INSIDERS'GUIDE®

GUILFORD, CONNECTICUT
AN IMPRINT OF THE GLOBE PEQUOT PRESS

The prices and rates in this guidebook were confirmed at press time. We recommend, however, that you call establishments before traveling to obtain current information.

Publications from the Insiders' Guide® series are available at special discounts for bulk purchases for sales promotions, premiums, or fund-raisings. Special editions, including personalized covers, can be created in large quantities for special needs. For more information, please contact The Globe Pequot Press at (800) 962–0973.

INSIDERS' GUIDE®

Text design by LeAnna Weller Smith
Maps by XNR Productions Inc. © Morris Book Publishing, LLC

ISSN 1540-1758
ISBN 978-0-7627-2970-8

Manufactured in the United States of America
Fourth Edition/Second Printing

CONTENTS

CONTENTS

Directory of Maps

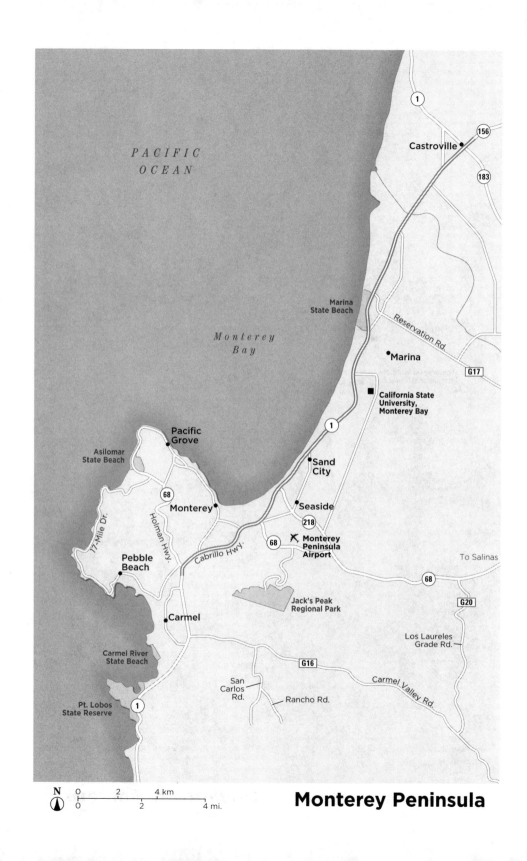

Monterey Peninsula

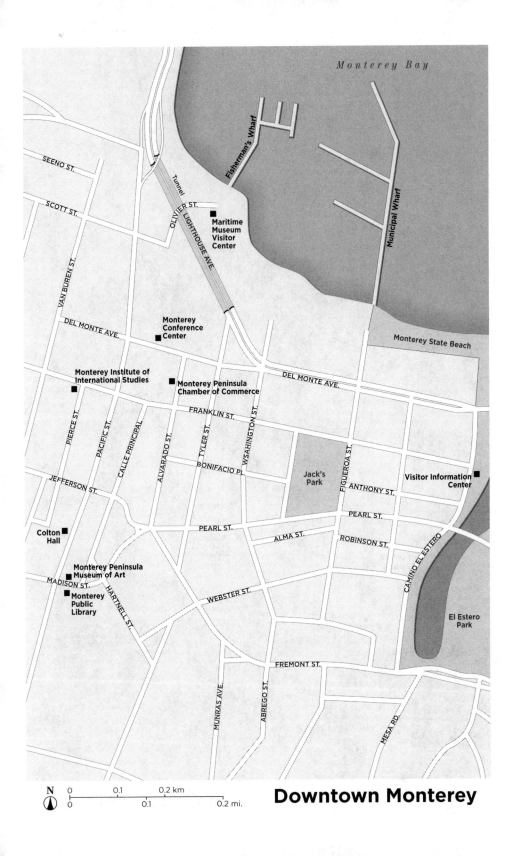

Downtown Monterey

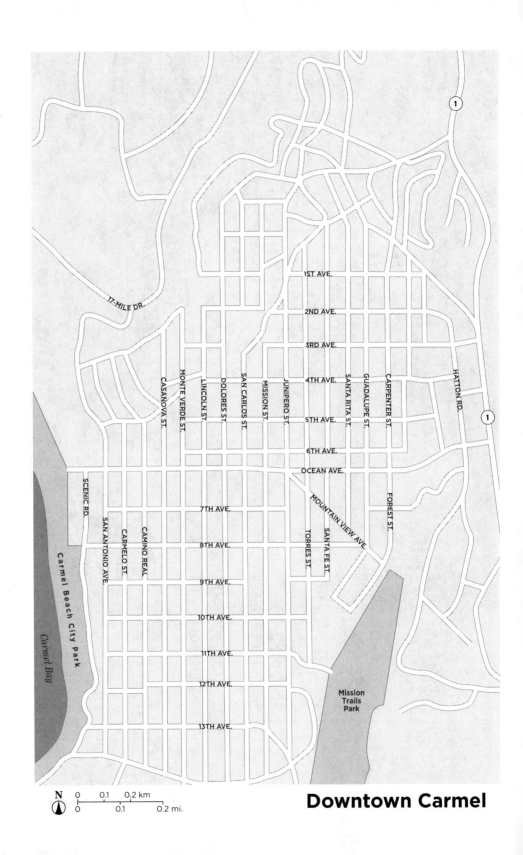

Downtown Carmel

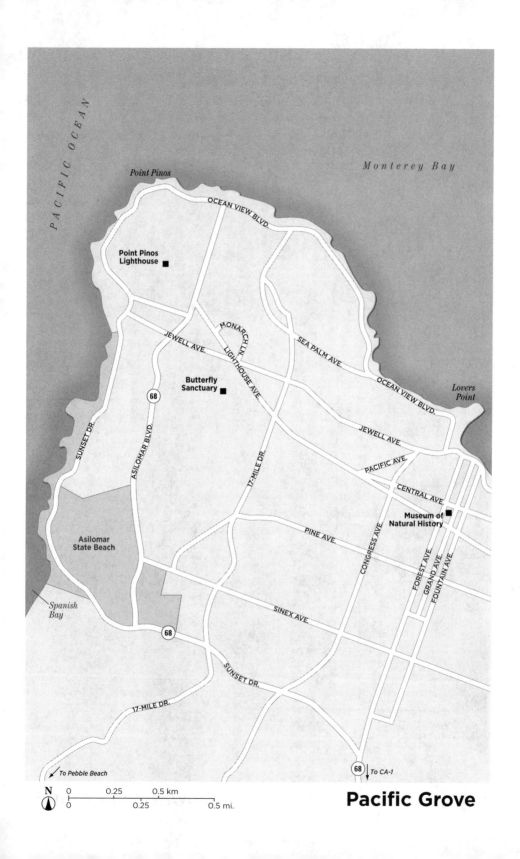

PACIFIC OCEAN

Monterey Bay

Point Pinos

OCEAN VIEW BLVD.

**Point Pinos
Lighthouse** ■

MONARCH LN.

JEWELL AVE.

LIGHTHOUSE AVE.

SEA PALM AVE.

OCEAN VIEW BLVD.

Lovers
Point

**Butterfly
Sanctuary** ■

68

SUNSET DR.

ASILOMAR BLVD.

17-MILE DR.

JEWELL AVE.

PACIFIC AVE.

CENTRAL AVE.

**Museum of
Natural History** ■

PINE AVE.

CONGRESS AVE.

FOREST AVE.

GRAND AVE.

FOUNTAIN AVE.

Asilomar
State Beach

Spanish
Bay

68

SINEX AVE.

SUNSET DR.

17-MILE DR.

→ To Pebble Beach

68 ↓ To CA-1

N
⊕

0   0.25   0.5 km

0   0.25

0.5 mi.

Pacific Grove

PREFACE

Welcome to the Monterey Peninsula! The natural splendor and scenic wonders of our area are magical and inspirational. If you are looking for a place to relax, unwind, and slow down for just a little while, you've chosen the ideal location. Sit on the beach and watch the sparkling waves, or listen to the sacred silence in one of our many forested parks. Feel the tranquility of your surroundings. The magnetic environment of this particular stretch of California coast has attracted and encouraged world-class writers, artists, photographers, and performers, due in part to the continual inspiration provided by the incredible beauty of the Monterey Peninsula.

But the spectacular scenery is only one of the Monterey Peninsula's many attractions. The Monterey Bay Aquarium is internationally famous for its stunning exhibits and informative tours. Our wine region rivals Napa County in wine production; many of these local wineries have tasting rooms and tours open to the public. Our art galleries offer an unbelievable variety of art styles, and many specialize in the works of regional artists. Recently, the opening of several fabulous spas has added one more entry to our never-ending list of things to see and do while visiting the area. Many of our festivals and special events draw a returning crowd each year: auto races at Laguna Seca, major golf events at Pebble Beach, the Monterey Jazz Festival, the Monterey Blues Festival, the Carmel Bach Festival, the list goes on and on . . . .

Each town in our fascinating Peninsula has a distinctive character and unique appeal. Though close in proximity, the types of activities, style of architecture, and layout of the land vary from one town to the next. Monterey, as California's first state capital, is steeped in history and filled with historic buildings including California's First Theater and the oldest building in California, the Royal Presidio Chapel. Pebble Beach, though not a city but a planned community, is in the midst of the Del Monte Forest and is known the world over for its luxury resorts, estates, and famed golf courses. Carmel is famous for its wide sandy beaches, numerous art galleries, high-end shopping, and quaint cottages. Pacific Grove is a seaside Victorian village with a beautiful ocean drive, many shops and restaurants, and its famed Monarch butterfly sanctuary.

In addition to the usual information you would expect to find in a tourist guide (accommodations, restaurants, shopping, attractions), you will also find chapters highlighting relocation information, such as education, worship, media, health care, and retirement. Visitors to the Peninsula will find the guide especially useful, and even longtime residents who read the Insiders' Guide will discover something new about the Monterey Peninsula.

It is with an unending respect and appreciation for our beloved home that we encourage you to use this publication to fully enjoy the sights and delights of the Monterey Peninsula. In this, our fourth edition, we have done our best to give you an accurate representation of the wonder and majesty of our magnificent area. Enjoy!

ACKNOWLEDGMENTS

Where to start is easy. Dear Emily, thank you for covering for my mental and physical absence while I whiled away the hours on the road and on my laptop. Your strength, support, and understanding made this all possible. I love you. And thanks to my pride and joys, Kate and Anna, for forgiving Dad who wasn't always there nights and weekends because he had homework of his own. I love you two, too, and am so proud of both of you.

And to my coauthor, Melanie, it has been an adventure, hasn't it? Exploring our hometown as if we didn't live here. I appreciate your talent, your effort, your humor, and your support.

For my day tripping buddies, thank you. Thanks to my family again for that great long and winding road south through Big Sur. Thanks to Leslie and Em for Salinas Valley and all that wine. To Martha, for a smile-filled day traversing the roads of Carmel Valley. For Dan and Gena for wonderful hospitality (and needed shoulder massages) in San Francisco.

Thanks to my editors Joshua Rosenberg and Amy Hrycay, for direction, understanding, forgiveness, patience, great talent, and support. For all you others at Insiders' Guide and The Globe Pequot Press, thank you for this opportunity and your efforts. I know what it takes.

Many thanks to all of you other friends and good sports out there who helped me through this project with your words, guidance, answers, kindness, encouragement, and support in getting this done.

And to my wonderful mother, who understood that her son had a commitment to keep and maybe didn't phone or drive down to L.A. as often as he should. I love you, Mom. And you, too, sisters one and two. Ciao, Cyn and Deb.

Finally, I dedicate this effort to my father, who passed away just before I started the first edition of this book. He taught me the quiet dedication and perseverance needed to complete the job. Thanks Pops.

—Tom Owens

As in any dynamic environment, many changes, updates, closures, openings, and new twists occurred that required a great deal of checking, double-checking, and rewriting. My husband Michael, a skilled writer in his own right, not only put up with my long hours staring into the manuscript and at my computer screen but also worked with me to gather the reams of data that go into a new edition. He is also responsible for the beautiful photographs that grace many of the chapters.

My brother Skip fuels my drive with his confidence in and pride of me. I've never met another human being who has set such an example of courage, passion for life, and love of family. Thanks to Skip and his wife, Kathy, I can enjoy children, niece Megan and nephew Dalton, without having to go through the pain of childbirth or the expense of providing for college educations. I love you!

Loving thanks to my father for giving me the support, encouragement, and freedom to grow as a person and as a professional writer. And to my dearest friends—Susan, Carolyn, Jan, Kathy, Jane, Jackie, Cynthia, and Marcia (my stepmom)—I think you know how important you are to me.

Thanks also to The Globe Pequot Press and my editors, Joshua Rosenberg and Amy Hrycay.

—Melanie Bellon Chatfield

HOW TO USE THIS BOOK

From the beginning of this project, we wanted to write a friendly book. We wanted to write a useful book that would paint a true picture of our home (through only slightly rose-colored glasses) so you could better plan your stay. We wanted to write a book that you'd keep by your side during your travels on the Monterey Peninsula and that would help you make the most of your time here. And we wanted to write a book that, if you lived here or dreamed of living here, gives you insight into everyday life on the Monterey Peninsula.

Eight months later (only slightly less time-consuming than bearing a child), we thought we had written a pretty darn good first edition of that book we envisioned. And with the subsequent editions, we corrected our mistakes, updated what had changed, and polished our prose. We have dug deep to uncover what we feel is the best our neck of the woods has to offer. We organized the chapters by subject matter so you can easily access the information you need. We used bold headings and individual listings to make it easy for you to skim through the chapters and pinpoint exactly what you're looking for. We included in-depth descriptions to allow you to get the inside scoop when you need it. Plus, we have tried to make this book fun and interesting reading, in the event you want to sit down for a while, at home or on one of our many gorgeous beaches, and get a good taste of this place.

We hope by the end of your stay on the Monterey Peninsula that this book is torn, dog-eared, marked up, smelling of the sea, and stained with wine, coffee, or some of the many other good things our home has to offer. Then we will know we did our job and you put this book to good use. We also hope you discover your own favorite places and tell us about them. We trust you'll let us know if you found our descriptions incorrect or off base. The information we gathered here is based on our combined decades living on the Peninsula and the best research we human beings could gather, arrange, and compile within our allotted time. Please take the time to let us know your thoughts and comments by writing to: Insiders' Guides, The Globe Pequot Press, P.O. Box 480, Guilford, CT 06437-0480.

HOW THIS BOOK IS ORGANIZED

Insiders' Guide® to the Monterey Peninsula provides extensive coverage to the cities of Monterey, Pacific Grove, Carmel, and Pebble Beach. Geographically, these communities make up all of the Monterey Peninsula proper and spill a mile or so farther inland and up and down the California coast at the southern end of Monterey Bay. We have also included a day trip section, which will provide overviews of outlying areas, including Big Sur, Carmel Valley, and Salinas Valley. In fact, we take you all up and down the California central coast from San Francisco to San Luis Obispo.

The subject matters covered are outlined in the table of contents. We suggest you fold or tab the corner of that page for repeated reference. A detailed index in the rear of the book is especially helpful for finding particular places and specific things by name. Within most of our chapters you will find an introductory description followed by individual entries categorized by subject and listed alphabetically. Whenever the number of entries warrants (as with accommodations and attractions), we also divide categories by locale in the following sequence: Monterey, Pacific Grove, Carmel, and Pebble Beach.

Close-ups provide additional information about people, places, and things of note. For helpful advice and interesting notes designed to make your visit more enjoyable. You'll find insiders' tips—(shhh!) local secrets—designated with an [i].

When writing this book, we found that the lines of distinction were not always clear for some of our entries. For instance, many of the finest restaurants in the area are also some of its hottest spots for nightlife. Thus, you'll see numerous places listed more than once, with cross-references throughout the book to help you find just the information you are looking for.

The area code for the Monterey Peninsula is 831. Our day trip chapter does venture outside the county, and neighboring area codes are given where appropriate.

Finally, we look forward to revisiting this book for subsequent editions, hearing your comments, and gaining from your perspective on the Monterey Peninsula. We hope you enjoy this book, and we know you'll enjoy your time in our own backyard. Do us a favor, will you? Look at our smiling faces on the About the Authors page. Then if you happen to see either of us walking through the streets of Pacific Grove, sitting along the beach in Carmel, or strolling along Fisherman's Wharf in Monterey, say hello. We'd love to welcome you personally to the Monterey Peninsula.

AREA OVERVIEW

The Monterey Peninsula, one of the most picturesque spots in North America, if not the world, is a can't-miss destination for anyone traveling in and around the state of California. Yet miss it is exactly what explorer Juan Rodriguez Cabrillo did in 1542, sailing his galleon right past the Peninsula and Monterey Bay as he headed up the coast of this newfound continent. It wasn't until nearly 60 years later that Captain Sebastian Vizcaino came ashore on this rocky headland at "El Puerto de Monterey," which he named in honor of the Viceroy of New Spain, Count de Monte Rey.

The Monterey Peninsula sits 125 miles south of San Francisco, 345 miles north of Los Angeles. It's 17 miles west of Salinas, which is the largest city in the agricultural region of Monterey County known as the Salad Bowl of the World. To the north of the Peninsula is the spectacular Monterey Bay, a National Marine Sanctuary with abundant sea life and an undersea canyon deeper than the Grand Canyon. With its rich harvest of seafood, the Bay has long been the source of livelihood for Peninsula residents. Today, it attracts as many fishers of tourism dollars as it does fishers of fish. To the west is the Pacific Ocean, creating spectacular meetings of land and sea as waves crash along the rugged shoreline in Pacific Grove, Carmel, and Pebble Beach.

Today the Monterey Peninsula proper, a compact landmass of fewer than 25 square miles, is made up of three incorporated cities—Monterey, Carmel, and Pacific Grove—and an unincorporated area of Monterey County known as Pebble Beach. Immediately east of the Peninsula are the bedroom communities of Seaside and Del Rey Oaks and the small industrial/retail town of Sand City. To the southeast is sunny Carmel Valley, with its oak-covered hills and Western-style flair.

Farther south is the spectacular Big Sur Coast, a 90-mile stretch of unrivaled scenic beauty. Up the coast lie Marina, Castroville (Artichoke Capital of the World), Watsonville, and, at the northern tip of Monterey Bay, Santa Cruz with its famous Beach Boardwalk.

Approximately 125,000 residents populate the Monterey Peninsula and the immediate surrounding communities. They are host to more than two million annual visitors who arrive year-round to enjoy the natural beauty, world-class accommodations, and historic attractions.

WEATHER AND CLIMATE

Geographically, the Peninsula features a mix of rocky coastlines, gentle sand dunes, and native forests of Monterey pine and cypress. After more than a century of development, the forests have been cut back significantly within the city limits of Pacific Grove and Monterey, but substantial wooded areas remain in Pebble Beach and the northern end of Carmel. This seaside forest environment is the direct result of a mild, ocean-influenced climate that envelops the Peninsula.

Many "California-Dreaming" tourists arrive on the Peninsula during the summer with suitcases full of shorts and tank tops only to scurry to a local clothier for long pants and a sweater. While the Peninsula's temperature occasionally reaches into the 80s and infrequently hits 90, the average summer temperature is only a daytime high of 68 and a nighttime low of 51. The average winter temperature is a slightly cooler high of 61 and low of 44.

Why the mild summers in a Golden State known for its warm sun, sand, and surf? During the summer, as the inland California Central Valley swelters beyond

Nature's power and beauty take center stage all across the Monterey Peninsula. MONTEREY COUNTY CONVENTION AND VISITORS BUREAU

100 degrees, air rises, pulling the cool marine air above the cold waters of the Pacific over the Peninsula. This effect can engulf the Monterey Peninsula in fog, sending temperatures plunging. If you don't like bundling up in blankets and sweaters during those foggy days of July or August, a 10-minute drive inland to Carmel Valley or toward Salinas usually finds warm, if not hot, sunshiny weather. Insiders suggest dressing in layers that may need to be peeled off and put back on repeatedly throughout your stay.

The warmest and most pleasant months of the year are September and October, the only months when average highs exceed 70 degrees. May and June are also nice, typically dry, and in the mid-60s. The rainy season runs from November to April, with January and February the wettest months. Average seasonal rainfall is 18 inches, but rarely is there an "average" year. The Peninsula tends to go through cycles of heavy rain and drought, often influenced by the ocean current phenomena El Niño and La Niña.

This unpredictable rainfall plays havoc with the area's freshwater supply. Not connected to the elaborate California aqueduct system that irrigates the arid southern part of the state, the Peninsula depends on local groundwater and on area rainfall gathered behind small dams up the Carmel River. If you arrive during one of the periodic droughts, be prepared to experience water rationing at the hotels, inns, and restaurants. Locals have learned to live with the on-again, off-again water restrictions (repeatedly voting down measures to build new, larger dams), and they appreciate the cooperation of visitors in their water-preservation efforts.

COMMERCE AND INDUSTRY

Tourism is by far the leading industry in the area. Fishing remains prevalent, but much of the commercial activity has moved north up the Bay to Moss Landing. Squid, or calamari, not sardines, is now the silver harvest of the Bay. The agriculture industry is huge in Monterey County but not on the Peninsula. The limited land is just too valuable to be used for growing crops. A once-large military presence was scaled down dramatically with the closure of the Fort Ord Army Base in the mid-1990s. Still, the armed forces retain a significant presence with the United States Naval Postgraduate School, the United States Army Defense Language Institute (the largest foreign-language school in the country), and a United States Coast Guard Station.

Educational facilities also play a key part of the Peninsula makeup, with California State University Monterey Bay (located on the former site of Fort Ord), Monterey Peninsula College, the Monterey Institute of International Studies, and other small colleges and private prep schools.

A recent trend finds small high-tech and service companies discovering the attractions of the Monterey Peninsula and relocating from Silicon Valley and San Jose, just 70 miles to the north. With advancements in Internet technology, firms are realizing they no longer have to be physically located next to their clients or suppliers and can run their businesses in any locale they want to live in.

For those who can afford it, the Monterey Peninsula isn't a bad choice as a place to set up shop. The cost of living on the Peninsula is high, much like the San Francisco Bay Area to the north. Homes on the Peninsula proper begin at around $300,000, and that's for a small one-bedroom, one-bath fixer-upper without an ocean view. A standard three- or four-bedroom home is likely to be in the $600,000 to $800,000 range, and from there, the sky's the limit. You can read more about homes and home prices in our Relocation chapter.

But along with those high costs of living come some perks that are standard equipment on the Monterey Peninsula. Locals enjoy daily walks on spectacular beaches; strolls through native forests along narrow trails that only Insiders know

about; fantastic restaurants of all sizes, shapes, and ethnicities; cultural richness in the fine and performing arts; a mild climate free of the extremes of snowstorms or humid heat waves; decent to top-rated schools; and a low to moderate crime rate.

CRIME

While we're on the subject of crime, burglary represents the biggest threat of misdeed to visitors on the Monterey Peninsula. As in any tourist area, a certain criminal element preys on the fact that motel rooms and parked cars full of valuables are left vacated for hours while visitors are out having a wonderful time. Valuables left clearly visible from the outside are likely targets. Simple precautions, such as keeping locks locked and valuables stored out of sight or in a hotel safe, go a long way toward preventing you from becoming a victim. It may seem like paradise, but keep alert when carrying valuables.

THE NEIGHBORS

As you get out and about and mix with the natives, you'll find that most Peninsula neighborhoods are involved communities, each with great pride in its particular city or area. Each community also has a distinct personality, and Montereyans, Carmelites, and Pagrovians can be very different animals, as can the residents of Pebble Beach. We'll get more into that a bit later in this chapter. Ethnically, the Peninsula is a diverse community. Spaniards, Mexicans, Italians, Chinese, Japanese, Portuguese, Filipinos, and Caucasian and African-American descendants

Alvarado Street in Monterey is home to the Old Monterey Market Place, which offers fresh produce, local artwork, good food, and live music every Tuesday from 3:30 to 7:00 P.M.

from the dust bowl era (a la the Joad family in Steinbeck's *The Grapes of Wrath*) make up a patchwork of cultures that have arrived at various periods of Monterey's history and left their marks on the Peninsula. Each has brought along the riches of its culture, as evidenced by the many popular ethnic festivals and other celebrations that take place throughout the year.

Visitors will likely find the Peninsula a diverse, accommodating community. Most local citizens realize how fortunate they are to live here, and they are happy to share their corner of the world with visitors who equally enjoy and—importantly—respect the spectacular beauty of the place.

Now let's take a little closer look at the four unique communities that make up the Monterey Peninsula.

THE PENINSULA TOWNS
Monterey

Rich in history that dates back prior to the pilgrims' landing at Plymouth Rock, Monterey is a multifaceted city that seeks to preserve its long, rich heritage while at the same time thriving in the 21st century. Culturally diverse Monterey is a true ethnic melting pot that reflects the city's storied past. You'll find, for instance, two and three generations of Italian fishing families still playing a central role in community leadership and still gathering to play some serious bocce ball down at the Custom House Plaza every week. Mixed with that rich heritage is a new generation of Montereyans, many of whom have relocated from Los Angeles and other hectic urban areas and fallen in love with the city's laid-back, almost Mediterranean lifestyle. The local foreign-language schools, which have led to Monterey's designation as a "language capital of the world," add a dash of international flavor to the city.

The heart of Monterey remains Alvarado Street, the longtime business district of the city. Today a potpourri of shops, restaurants, and local businesses, Alvarado Street reflects a blend of Monterey's old-town stability and vibrant new life. This area provides an ample supply of coffeehouses, juice bars, movie theaters, sports bars, and nightclubs and is a popular gathering spot for students, the military, and other young adults. For locals, it's where it's happening within the overall scope of the rather docile Monterey Peninsula. Visitors likely find it low-key by urban standards, but it's about the only game in town.

The downtown area surrounding Alvarado Street is home to most of Monterey's splendid adobes and other historic highlights, including Fisherman's Wharf, Custom House Plaza, and Colton Hall. It's truly a town to discover on foot (see the Monterey Path of History in our Attractions chapter), so leave the car in one of the many parking garages and take a walk.

The largest of the Peninsula's cities with a population of approximately 30,000, Monterey spreads out in all directions from the downtown area and covers almost 9 square miles. Due north is Fisherman's Wharf and Monterey State Beach, great for a relaxing day on the Bay. To the east toward Seaside are the greenbelts of El Estero Park, Monterey Peninsula College, the Naval Postgraduate School, and Old Del Monte Golf Course. Northwest toward Pacific Grove is the Presidio of Monterey, and beyond that is the residential area of town known as New Monterey, with small businesses along Lighthouse Avenue, and historic Cannery Row. Southwest toward Pebble Beach lie the Skyline Forest and Jack's Peak areas of pastoral hillside homes, and the Community Hospital of Monterey Peninsula. To the southeast, out along the Highway 68 corridor east toward Salinas, lie the Monterey Peninsula Airport and the Ryan Ranch Business Park, a modern light-industry center.

Monterey Harbor is home to an active group of local sailors and fishermen. TOM OWENS

Pacific Grove

Pacific Grove goes by two monikers: "Butterfly Town USA" and "The Last Hometown." The former name is earned as a result of P.G.'s famous stands of pines, cypress, and eucalyptus trees to which the Monarch butterfly returns like clockwork every fall and winter for the Peninsula's mild climate. The latter name reflects the pride of the city's 15,500 inhabitants and their determination to keep Pacific Grove a safe refuge for a family lifestyle reminiscent of days gone by. A more appropriate name these days might be "The Last Second-Home Town," considering the number of P.G. houses that are purchased as vacation homes by out-of-towners.

The stately Victorian homes and turn-of-the-century architecture create a proper setting for this bit of Americana. But it is the steadfast citizenry who make sure "progress" is kept in check and treas-

ured values are retained. Nothing is more evident of this mind-set than a not-too-distant hoopla over the proposed introduction of a new Taco Bell fast-food restaurant into Pacific Grove. City ordinances were passed a decade or two back prohibiting any new fast-food establishments within city limits. The prospective new franchisee, however, took the ordinance head-on, arguing that his proposed business was actually a sandwich shop, which the ordinance didn't cover. City Hall became a hotbed of debate as forces pro and con debated whether or not a taco was a sandwich and whether the new franchise was really a threat to all that Pagrovians hold dearest. In the end, the fast-food franchisee tucked his tail between his legs and abandoned his plans. And all was right again in Pacific Grove.

Kidding aside, preservationists deserve a lot of credit for keeping the character of Pacific Grove as special as it is. A trip through the downtown district on Lighthouse Avenue quickly takes you back to a time when Main Street USA was a way of life. The huge Holman Building, a former family department store that now houses an antiques mall, stands proudly near the town entrance, its magnificent stained-glass butterfly window celebrating our special winter guests.

Leave your butterfly nets at home. In Pacific Grove it's against the law to harass Monarch butterflies.

Victorian storefronts line both sides of the street and are occasionally interrupted by more modern architecture, but they're still prevalent enough to retain the town's overall character. Stately Queen Anne–style homes pepper the town, with many now serving as restaurants or bed-and-breakfast inns rather than private residences.

Downtown Pacific Grove has experienced quite a revival in the last few years. It wasn't too long ago that the Holman's Building stood vacant, a victim of America's preference for mega-shopping malls over stand-alone department stores. The local five-and-dime and other longtime merchants also closed down as Peninsula residents chose to do their buying in the new discount shopping centers surrounding the larger cities of Monterey and Salinas.

Today, Pacific Grove is reinventing itself as a home and garden design mecca. Antiques shops, interior design studios, plant boutiques, and stores of similar ilk are attracting attention from all over Monterey County and beyond. Suddenly there's more to do in Pacific Grove than simply enjoy the serenity and scenery.

Despite the revival, P.G. is still the quiet side of town, even by Peninsula standards. Visitors looking to simply relax and get away from it all will have a hard time finding anything to beat this tranquil locale. Check in at a quaint bed-and-breakfast inn or family-run motel and kick your shoes off. Stroll along the beach and boardwalk on the spectacular Asilomar coastline. Take in a meditative afternoon at the Monarch Butterfly Sanctuary. Or picnic at Lovers Point or one of the many secluded coves along Ocean View Boulevard. Ask a local for a restaurant recommendation and you'll likely obtain a host of choices for breakfast, lunch, or dinner. And don't miss the beach sunsets with the Point Pinos Lighthouse pulsating gently in the background.

Carmel

To some it's Carmel-by-the-Sea. To most Insiders, however, it's simply Carmel. But whatever you call it, this lovely seaside village and artists colony is just about as storybook as it gets. Picture Hansel and Gretel on Rodeo Drive. That's Ocean Avenue, the main shopping and dining thoroughfare through downtown Carmel. Then for two to three blocks east and west of Ocean Avenue and down most of its north-south length are streets and streets of quaint shops, hideaway restaurants, charming inns, and almost secret courtyards that contain their own hidden treasures.

Despite a population of only 4,100 and an area of only 1 square mile, Carmel is truly a tale of two cities. First there's the bustling Carmel commercial shopping district of art galleries, clothiers, specialty shops, and exceptional restaurants most visitors become familiar with. Its quaint village character has been preserved by strict building codes and regulations that prohibit neon signs, parking meters, souvenir shops, and high-rise structures. Then there's the picturesque residential Carmel of neither sidewalks nor streetlights, where the inhabitants largely conduct their daily lives away from downtown.

Carmel Beach is a favorite spot for couples to watch the sunset after a busy day of shopping, golf, or sight-seeing. TOM OWENS

You'll immediately notice that Ocean Avenue and its environs are not designed to meet the day-to-day needs of locals. How many sweaters can you wear, paintings can you hang, or figurines can you dust? Ocean Avenue is for the visitor, who can find the perfect outfit or the special piece of artwork to capture the memory of a magical moment. Yes, there are a few markets and stores that can provide some of the necessities of life. But if you need staples like milk, bread, and toilet paper, it's often less of a hassle to head on over to the more resident-friendly mouth of Carmel Valley or even into Monterey or Pacific Grove.

Still, there's a strong local culture in downtown Carmel, made up of resident artists, writers, shopkeepers, gallery and restaurant owners, and other longtime Carmelites. Part of that local culture is spawned at the Carmel Post Office, where citizens gather to collect their daily mail and exchange the latest news and gossip. There's no mail delivery in most of Carmel proper, which is good for the mailcarrier

Bring your flats to Carmel: An ordinance still on the books outlaws high heels in order to protect the city from liability lawsuits for trips and falls on the town's uneven streets.

because there aren't any street addresses either.

If a local is giving directions to his or her home, it usually goes something like this: "It's the stone house on the beach side of Ocean View between Bay View and Stewart." Or the house may enjoy its own personal name, such as "Knot Very Lodge" or "The Holly House." The same thing goes for most Carmel shops, galleries, and restaurants. "Ocean between Mission and Junipero" or "Sixth between Lincoln and Dolores" is about as specific as addresses get. But with a street map in hand, even first-time visitors find Carmel easily navigable on foot. And the key words here are "on foot." Parking has

Monterey Peninsula Vital Statistics

Mayors:
> Monterey: Dan Albert
> Carmel: Sue McCloud
> Pacific Grove: Morrie Fisher

California governor: Arnold Schwarzenegger

Area (square miles): 24.5 miles

Nickname/motto:
> Monterey: California's first capital
> Pacific Grove: Butterfly Town USA
> Carmel: A city in a forest

Average temperatures:
> July (high/low) 68/51
> January (high/low) 60/43

Average rainfall/days of sunshine: 19.29 inches/298 days

Cities founded: Monterey, 1850; Pacific Grove, 1889; Carmel, 1916

Major university: California State University Monterey Bay

Important dates in history:

1542: La Bahía de los Pinos (Bay of Pines) was first discovered by Juan Rodriguez Cabrillo.

1602: Sebastian Viscaino officially named the port Monterey, in honor of the Viceroy of New Spain.

1770: Gaspar de Portolá and Franciscan Father Junipero Serra came to Monterey to establish a mission.

1776: Spain named Monterey as the capital of Baja (lower) and Alta (upper) California. Captain Juan Bautista de Anza arrived from Sonora with the first settlers for Spanish California.

1818: Argentinean revolutionary privateer Hippolyte Bouchard arrived and burned the compound at the Royal Presidio Chapel in an effort to destroy Spain's attempt to colonize California.

1822: Mexico seceded from Spain, bringing Monterey and all of California under the rule of Mexico.

1842: The United States established a consulate in Monterey, and Thomas Larkin was appointed first consul to Mexico.

1846: Commodore John Drake Sloat's flagship arrived in Monterey Bay, and the American flag was raised.

1848: Treaty of Guadalupe Hidalgo was signed, making California part of the United States. In Monterey, Chaplain Walter Colton, U.S. Navy, was appointed as Monterey's first American alcalde, a position defined as mayor and judge. He established *The Californian,* California's first newspaper. Colton Hall was built to serve as a public school and town meeting hall.

1849: Colton Hall was chosen as the site for the convention where delegates drafted and signed California's first state constitution.

1850: California becomes 31st state to enter the Union.

1875: Pacific Grove was settled as a Methodist retreat.

1897: Del Monte golf course opened, first course west of the Mississippi.

1906: San Francisco earthquake occurred; artists began to move to Carmel.

Major area employers: County of Monterey; The United States Government (U.S. Navy, U.S. Army); Community Hospital of the Monterey Peninsula; Pebble Beach Company

Famous sons and daughters: John Steinbeck, author; Edward Weston, photographer; Ansel Adams, photographer; Robinson Jeffers, poet; Clint Eastwood, actor; Leon Panetta, politician; Alan Funt, television personality; Hank Ketcham, cartoonist; Mary Austin, author; Doris Day, actress; Emily Fish, Point Pinos Lighthouse lightkeeper

State/city holidays: New Year's Day; Martin Luther King Day; Presidents' Day; Easter; Memorial Day; Independence Day; Labor Day; Thanksgiving Day; Christmas Day

Chamber of commerce:

Monterey Peninsula Chamber of Commerce

380 Alvarado Street

Monterey, CA 93940

(831) 648-5360

Fax: (831) 649-3502

www.mpcc.com

Major airports/interstates: Monterey Peninsula Airport (Monterey), San Jose International Airport (San Jose); Highway 1, Highway 68, U.S. Highway 101

Public transportation: Monterey-Salinas Transit (bus); Amtrak (train)

Military bases: Naval Postgraduate School; Defense Language Institute (Presidio of Monterey); United States Coast Guard Station

Driving laws: Seat belts must be worn by all passengers; right turns permitted on red; speed limit is as posted; maximum speed is 65 on interstates.

Alcohol laws: Legal drinking age is 21 years; blood/alcohol level of 0.8 or higher is a DWI; it is unlawful to drive with an open container of alcohol in the car.

Daily newspaper: The Monterey County Herald

Sales tax: 7.25 percent city/state taxes on all retail sales

always been and likely always will be a problem in Carmel, particularly during the peak summer tourist season. So, should you find that rarest of all species, an available parking space on Ocean Avenue, grab it and milk it for all it's worth.

Carmel is truly a shopper's and art lover's paradise. Its rich cultural history, embodied in the Sunset Cultural Center since its founding in 1964, adds an air of elegance to this remarkable town. The white sandy beach at the end of Ocean Avenue can be absolutely spectacular on a perfect day, and the picturesque residential cottages off the beaten path elicit thoughts of a quaint English village. World-class hotels, inns, and restaurants are the topper for an enchanting stay.

Pebble Beach

It's known worldwide as an exclusive address. Its seashore villas are home to the rich and famous. (Robin Leach could have shot a season's worth of episodes along 17-Mile Drive alone.) Visitors must pass through guarded gates to gain admittance. If you're dropping in just for a quick look-see, it will cost you an $8.00 entry fee. If you're staying for a round of golf at The Links, Spyglass Hill, Poppy Hill, or Spanish Bay, the price of admission just got considerably higher—if you can get a tee time. Stay a few days at The Lodge or The Inn at Spanish Bay, and you may have to bring more than your American Express.

Pebble Beach is the geographic heart of the Monterey Peninsula. The widely held image of wealth and exclusivity conjured at the mention of the name is accu-

rate, at least along the coastal route of 17-Mile Drive and surrounding the famous Lodge. But not every home is a mansion and not every one of the approximately 6,000 residents is a movie star, oil baron, or silver-spoon-fed millionaire. In fact, some abodes in the Del Monte Forest might even be called rustic or modest by Peninsula standards. And some residents are hardworking stiffs just trying to make ends meet.

Beyond being a famous resort destination, Pebble Beach is also a company town. Not being an incorporated city, there's no mayor, no city council, and no police department. Instead there's the Monterey County Sheriff and The Pebble Beach Company, which owns much of the property and serves largely as lord and master over the forest.

As ruler over this prime primeval real estate, The Pebble Beach Company (now owned by an investment group that includes Clint Eastwood, Arnold Palmer, and other celebrities) often finds itself in a somewhat awkward position. It constantly finds itself trying to balance its role as a responsible corporate citizen (its community work and monetary contributions to good causes are legendary) and profitable corporate entity. On the one hand, The Pebble Beach Company is expected by residents and neighbors to preserve and protect what remains of the undeveloped forest, providing whatever maintenance and tending is deemed necessary to keep pest and pestilence away. On the other hand, the company is called to task by preservationists whenever it tries to recoup its shareholders' considerable investment by further developing its valuable land holdings. It's an age-old battle that continues daily behind the scenic scenes.

Such rumblings remain largely inaudible to the casual visitor, and that's the way it should be. Your senses should be overwhelmed with the sights of awe-inspiring natural beauty, the smells of pine

The 200- to 300-year-old Lone Cypress, one of California's most famous landmarks, is a copyrighted symbol of The Pebble Beach Company.

Pine trees, ocean views, and golf are trademarks of beautiful Pebble Beach. TOM OWENS

forests and salty ocean air, the sounds of squawking sea gulls and barking seals, the feel of ribbed seashells and smooth ocean pebbles, and the taste of delectable meals served in delightful surroundings. If you're fortunate enough to stay at The Lodge or The Inn at Spanish Bay, take full advan-tage of the amenities that await you. Even if you're just driving through, an hour or two perusing the shops or sampling the food and drink is an unforgettable taste of the good life.

GETTING HERE, GETTING AROUND

To travel to the scenic Monterey Peninsula you have several choices—by air, by roads, and by sea. Once here, the choices continue; rental cars are readily available at the airport if you choose to drive, but taxicabs and public transportation are also options. Many locals and visitors alike prefer to explore Monterey, Carmel, and Pacific Grove on foot; don't forget to pack your walking shoes! Biking, in-line skating, or walking along the bike path is a great way to get around and provides up-close views of beautiful Monterey Bay.

The daily rise and fall in temperature in the coastal areas call for a mixture of layered clothing. Early mornings and late afternoons tend to be cooler and windier than the midday, which in September and October can be quite mild and pleasant. A warm sweater or light jacket is recommended, especially if you will be spending a lot of time enjoying the area's spectacular beaches or tide-pooling along the rocky coast.

BY AIR
Commercial Flights

Monterey Peninsula Airport
200 Fred Kane Drive, Suite 200,
Monterey
(831) 648–7000
www.montereyairport.com
The Monterey Airport is small, friendly, and centrally located, providing easy access to all cities within the county. The airport

Direct flights to major air hubs—
Los Angeles, San Francisco, and Phoenix—
are offered daily from Monterey Peninsula
Airport.

offers about 50 conveniently scheduled daily arrivals and departures with connecting flights to anywhere in the world. The following airlines currently serve the airport: America West Express, American Airlines/American Eagle, and United/United Express. Ask your travel agent about fares from your home city to Monterey. Sometimes the fare is only a few dollars more than flying into San Francisco or San Jose airports.

There is one restaurant at the airport, the Golden Tee. A snack bar and coffee cart can provide something quick if you're in a rush. Five major car rental companies operate out of the airport: Avis, Budget, National, Enterprise, and Hertz. (For more on rental cars, see our "Ground Transportation" section in this chapter.) Ground transportation service, including taxis and Monterey-Salinas Transit (city bus), is offered in front of the airport.

Other Options

You can fly into San Francisco International Airport or San Jose International Airport via most major airlines. From there you can rent a car and drive to Monterey or take the Monterey-Salinas Airbus (see our "By Bus" section in this chapter). The San Francisco airport is approximately 100 miles from Monterey, and San Jose is about 70 miles away. Follow the signs from either airport to U.S. 101 South to the Salinas and the Monterey Peninsula exits.

If you own your own plane, you can fly into the Monterey Airport by utilizing Million Air, (831) 373–4151; Del Monte Aviation-East, (831) 373–3201; and Monterey Jet Center, (831) 373–0100. These companies are at the airport and offer tie-down service, hangars, fuel, and repairs for various types of planes.

Charter Flights

Three charter companies serve the Monterey Peninsula area. Rates for their service depend on the type of aircraft, the destination, and wait time for the pilot. You can expect to pay a rate starting at $200 an hour up to $4,500 per hour or more depending on the type of aircraft.

Million Air Monterey
100 Sky Park Drive, Monterey
(831) 373-4151
www.millionairmonterey.com
Million Air Monterey, a division of Del Monte Aviation, offers premier charter flights in the private plane of your choice to your desired destination. Services for pilots include aircraft fuel, cleaning and maintenance of aircraft, hangar space and tie-down rental, comfortable terminal and pilots' lounge, and air shares and aviation sales.

The Monterey Airplane Company
514 Airport Way, Monterey
(888) 843-7031
www.flymac.com
The Monterey Airplane Company provides aircraft charter and air ambulance services. When flying commercial is not an option, their fleet of two Astra 1125 jets and a Rockwell Turbo Commander turboprop provide on-demand service to domestic and international destinations. MAC also has an aircraft management service. Customers can add their aircraft to the Monterey Airplane Company fleet, providing cost reduction in flight crews and maintenance. Your plane can also be leased to other customers when you are not using it.

Monterey Jet Center
Airport Road, Monterey
(831) 373-0100
www.montereyjetcenter.com
The Jet Center offers charter service to the location of your choice as well as air shares and aircraft sales. It also provides aviation fuel services, cleaning and maintenance of aircraft, hangar and tie-down rental, and pilots' lounge.

BY SEA

Monterey Bay, a broad 20-mile-wide, open roadstead, is between Point Pinos and Point Santa Cruz. The shores vary. Some are low with sandy beaches backed by dunes or low, sandy bluffs; others are rocky with heavy surf. Salinas Valley, the lowland extending eastward from about the middle of the Bay, is prominent from seaward as it forms the break between the Santa Lucia Range southward and the high land of the Santa Cruz Mountains northward.

The Bay is free of dangers and has a 10-fathom curve lying at an average distance of 0.7 mile offshore. The tidal currents in the Bay are weak. The submarine Monterey Canyon heads, near the middle of the Bay at a depth of more than 50 fathoms, lie about 0.5 mile from the beach near Moss Landing. Shelter from southwesterly winds is afforded at Monterey Harbor off the southern shore.

When arriving by boat, you will find Monterey Harbor, a compact resort harbor with some commercial activity and fishing, 3 miles east of Point Pinos.

Prominent landmarks include the granite Presidio Monument on the brow of a barren hill and a radio tower 0.6 mile north of the monument. A large red-roofed building is conspicuous on a bluff above the shore 4 miles northeastward from the breakwater. Two radio towers just inshore from the sand dunes at Marina, 6 miles northeastward from the breakwater, are conspicuous in the southern part of Monterey Bay. An aero light at Monterey Peninsula Airport is 2.2 miles southeastward of Monterey Harbor breakwater light.

A breakwater extends from the foot of Spence Street in an easterly direction for about 1,700 feet. This affords excellent protection in northwesterly weather. The outer end is marked by a light and in the daytime usually by the loud barking of sea lions. A Coast Guard Station is near the inner end.

For seafaring visitors, Monterey's Municipal Marina offers a safe and welcoming harbor.
MICHAEL CHATFIELD

The outer harbor and entrance offer depths of more than 20 feet, and the small-boat basin is 8 to 10 feet deep. There are many sport-fishing landings here, and the small-craft basin provides good shelter for about 350 vessels.

Transients should report to the harbor office at the head of Municipal Wharf #2 for berth assignments. The harbormaster can be contacted on channel 5 or 16. Quarantine, customs, and immigration services are handled by representatives from San Francisco, (831) 373-1155.

The easterly municipal wharf is 1,600 feet long and 86 feet wide at the outer end. Depths alongside the outer east and west sides are 24 feet. Freight and supplies are trucked directly to the wharf, and a 10-ton hoist is available. There is a fog signal on the northern end of the wharf.

Monterey Bay Boatworks/Breakwater Cove Marina
32 Cannery Row, Monterey
(831) 373-7857
www.montereybayboatworks.com
Restoration, repairs, and fabrication are provided for both motor and sail vessels to 70 tons. A special keel lift is available for wood vessels. Spray painting and welding are also available.

Monterey Marina
Del Monte Avenue, Monterey
(831) 646-3950
www.monterey.org/harbor
The Monterey Marina is between Fisherman's Wharf and Wharf #2. Gasoline, diesel, oil, water, and ice are available at

---

i *Shining since 1855, the Point Pinos Lighthouse in Pacific Grove is the oldest active lighthouse on the West Coast. Free tours are offered daily.*

Breakwater Cove. Several machine shops operate in Monterey, and marine supplies are readily available.

BY LAND

Three major highways lead to the Monterey Peninsula: U.S. 101/156 west/Highway 1 from the north and from the south; and Highway 68, also known as the Monterey-Salinas Highway, from the east.

Highway 1 is the most direct route to the Monterey Peninsula. It was appointed one of six All-American Roads by the Federal Highway Administration. If you are coming from the Bay Area or farther north, take the Highway 1 south/Pacifica exit and wind your way down a breathtaking stretch of the Pacific Coast until you reach the Monterey/Highway 156 west exit. Once in Monterey, Highway 1 cuts across the Peninsula, north to south, providing easy access to Carmel, Carmel Valley, and farther south to Big Sur. From Southern California, take Highway 1 north at Santa Barbara and enjoy an equally inspiring drive north until you see the signs for Monterey. Highway 1 is by far the most scenic route, not necessarily the fastest. If time is an issue, take U.S. 101.

U.S. 101 can take you to the Monterey area from the north or south as well. If you are coming from the north, take U.S. 101 south until you reach Salinas and the Monterey Peninsula exit. This exit connects you to Highway 68, or the Monterey-Salinas Highway, which traverses west to Monterey Peninsula cities. The directions are the same for Southern California, except of course, you will be traveling on U.S. 101 North until you arrive at Salinas.

Highway 68 originates in Salinas and, after a short diversion onto Highway 1, travels across the Peninsula, ultimately providing access to Pebble Beach and Pacific Grove, the westernmost point on the Peninsula.

Ground Transportation

RENTAL CARS

Five major car rental companies serve the area, most with offices at the Monterey Peninsula Airport. Rental rates vary based on the length of rental and time of year. The airport is a short drive from Peninsula hotels and attractions. Advance reservations are strongly recommended.

Avis Rent A Car
Monterey Peninsula Airport, Monterey
(831) 647-7140, (800) 831-2847
www.avis.com

Budget Rent A Car
Monterey Peninsula Airport, Monterey
(800) 527-0700
www.budget.com

Enterprise Rent-A-Car
1178 Del Monte Avenue, Monterey
(831) 649-6300, (800) RENTACAR
www.enterprise.com

Hertz Rent A Car
Monterey Peninsula Airport, Monterey
(831) 373-3318, (800) 654-3131
www.hertz.com

National Rent A Car
Monterey Peninsula Airport, Monterey
(831) 373-4181, (800) 227-7368
www.nationalcar.com

Monterey Rent-A-Roadster
229 Cannery Row, Monterey
(831) 647-1929
www.rent-a-roadster.com
Travel around the Peninsula in style by renting a reproduction of a 1929 Mercedes, Model A, or Phaeton roadster. These specialty cars are fun and easy to drive, making any occasion a memorable one. Hourly rates start at around $30. Monday through Friday you get three hours for the price of two. Reservations are required.

TAXI AND LIMOUSINE SERVICE

If you don't drive your own vehicle or haven't rented a car, there are several other options including taxis, limousines, shuttles, and motor coaches. Cab fees vary depending on the destination, but the starting fee is $2.00 followed by a mileage rate of $2.00. Limousine and shuttle services vary a great deal depending on the number of people, the amount of luggage, the destination, and driver waiting time. These vehicles also have a three-hour minimum. Limousine rentals range from $45 to $85 per hour, and minivans cost about $50 to $60 per hour. Motor coaches require a four-hour minimum, and the price range is from $60 to $80 per hour. For specific price information, call the company directly. The following companies currently serve the Monterey Peninsula area:

A-1 Chartered Limousine Service
(831) 899-2707

Cypress West
(831) 626-1234

Joe's Taxi
(831) 624-3885

Marina Taxi Co.
(831) 384-3894

Monterey Limousine Service
(831) 646-9635

Yellow Cab Company
(831) 646-1234

Your Maitre d' Limousines
(831) 624-1717

BUS SERVICE

Greyhound
1042 Del Monte Avenue, Monterey
(831) 373-4735
19 West Gabilan Street, Salinas
(800) 231-2222
www.greyhound.com
Bus service to anywhere in the continental United States is available from the Monterey and Salinas terminals. Eight buses leave daily, four northbound and four southbound. Services at the station include restrooms, snacks, and a delivery service for packages.

Monterey-Salinas Transit
1 Ryan Ranch Road, Monterey
(831) 899-2555
www.mst.org
Monterey-Salinas Transit (MST) covers the entire Peninsula area from Watsonville to the north, Big Sur to the south, Salinas to the east, and Pacific Grove to the west. Buses run from 6:00 A.M. to 11:00 P.M. Monday through Saturday and from 7:00 A.M. to 7:40 P.M. on Sunday. Fees vary depending on distance. Exact change is required on all MST buses. Special-rate passes are available. Wheelchair lift buses are available, and the use of the bike racks is free on all MST routes.

Monterey/Salinas Airbus
Monterey
(831) 883-2871, (800) 291-2877
www.montereyairbus.com
The bus arrives and departs at the Monterey Transit Plaza in Monterey at the corner of Pearl and Alvarado Streets. There are 11 departure/arrival times, the first at 4:00 A.M. From Monterey the route continues to the Amtrak station before departure to San Jose airport (approximately two hours) or the San Francisco airport (approximately three hours). A prepaid one-way fare is around $30. Holiday schedules vary, and reservations are recommended.

Waterfront Area Visitors Express
(The WAVE)
1 Ryan Ranch Road, Monterey
(831) 899-2555
www.mst.org
The WAVE is a free shuttle that operates from 10:00 A.M. to 7:00 P.M., Memorial Day weekend through Labor Day. The quaint buses, which look like cablecars, start their

route every 10 to 12 minutes at the Monterey Transit Plaza at Munras and Tyler Streets and continue to the Monterey Bay Aquarium, stopping at the Conference Center, Fisherman's Wharf, and Cannery Row along the way. The WAVE also stops at several public parking garages.

TRAINS

Amtrak
11 Station Place, Salinas
(800) 872–7254
www.amtrak.com
Amtrak provides service from Monterey to 39 points on the West Coast on its Coast Starlight route. Amtrak Thruway Bus Service is the easy, convenient way to reach cities where Amtrak trains do not stop. Amtrak offers coordinating connecting schedules, guaranteed connections through ticketing and thoroughfares, and direct service to and from the Amtrak rail station. From Monterey the service includes nine trains and buses. The Monterey Marriott, Monterey Hyatt, the Monterey Bay Aquarium, Monterey Travelodge, and the Monterey Transit Plaza serve as departure points from Monterey.

Parking

Parking in Pacific Grove is usually not a problem. Street parking is not metered, and most spaces have a 90-minute limit. Pacific Grove has two large public parking lots, one in front of Fandango restaurant (between 16th and 17th Streets) and the other behind Lighthouse Cinema (between Fountain Avenue and 15th Street).

Parking spaces in Carmel generally have a 90-minute limit, although there are quite a few spaces with shorter time allotments, so be sure to check the signs and the curb for the exact parking time limit for each available space. There is no metered street parking, and the only lot is the garage beneath Carmel Plaza (between Ocean and Seventh Avenues). A tight blend of residential and commercial real

One way to avoid high parking costs when visiting the Monterey Peninsula is to park at Del Monte Center on Munras Avenue near Highway 1. Buses to all points in the area stop here every few minutes.

estate, Carmel can present a challenge in terms of finding a free parking space. Be persistent; the quaint architecture, great shopping, diverse selection of art galleries, and excellent food are worth it.

There are 31 parking facilities in Monterey, ranging from 10-space parking lots to a 1,000-space, state-of-the-art, award-winning parking garage. These facilities total 3,504 off-street parking spaces. Lots are located throughout the city and are affordable, safe, and clean.

In addition to off-street parking, there are 3,312 metered on-street spaces in the downtown, Cannery Row, and Lighthouse Avenue areas.

PUBLIC GARAGES

Cannery Row
Foam Street, Monterey
This 1,000-space garage is between Hoffman and Prescott Streets. It provides the best parking for Cannery Row, the Aquarium, and the recreation trail.

East Custom House
Washington Street, Monterey
This parking garage, between Franklin Street and Del Monte Avenue, has 590 spaces. There is a ticket dispenser that accepts cash or credit cards. It is close to Fisherman's Wharf and the marina and is the best spot to park in downtown Monterey.

West Custom House
Tyler Street, Monterey
This 229-space garage is between Franklin Street and Del Monte Avenue. It is close to Fisherman's Wharf, the marina, and downtown Monterey. The first hour is free.

Calle Principal Garage
Calle Principal, Monterey
Between Franklin and Jefferson Streets, this 124-space metered garage provides nearby parking for Colton Hall Museum, Monterey Peninsula Museum of Art, downtown Monterey, and City Hall.

PARKING LOTS

Waterfront Lot #1
Del Monte Avenue, Monterey
The 479-space lot, between Washington Street and Fisherman's Wharf, is close to the Wharf, the marina, and the recreation trail. Bus and RV parking is available.

Waterfront Lot #2
Del Monte Avenue, Monterey
This lot, between Washington Street and Fisherman's Wharf, contains 235 spaces and provides ample parking for Fisherman's Wharf, the marina, and the recreation trail. Trailer parking is available in this lot.

Lot #21
Foam Street, Monterey
Lot 21 is between Cannery Row and Reeside Avenue and provides 79 spaces for parking for Cannery Row, the recreation trail, and San Carlos Beach Park. Trailer and RV parking is allowed here.

Coast Guard Lot
Cannery Row, Monterey
This 77-space lot is by the Coast Guard Pier at the south end of Cannery Row, providing the best parking for Cannery Row and the recreation trail. Trailer and RV parking is allowed, and shower facilities are available.

Jacks Peak County Park offers miles of hiking trails that afford spectacular view of Monterey Bay, Carmel Bay, and Carmel Valley. Avoid the entrance fee by parking in the lower parking lot and walking in.

Cannery Row Lot 7
David Avenue, Monterey
This 103-space lot, between Foam and Wave Streets, is close to the Aquarium and Cannery Row.

ALTERNATIVE TRANSPORTATION

Bicycle and Moped Rentals

Adventures by the Sea
299 Cannery Row, Monterey
201 Alvarado Mall, Monterey
Lovers Point Park, Pacific Grove
(831) 372-1807
www.adventuresbythesea.com
Kayak tours and rentals, bicycle and surrey rentals, fully catered themed group events on the beach for up to 1,000 people or indoors for up to 350 with entertainment . . . . is there anything these guys don't do? The oldest business of its kind on the Monterey Peninsula has something for everybody from the casual day-tripper wanting to see the sights from the recreation trail to the hard-core kayak trekker wanting to get up close and personal with the marine life of the Monterey Bay Marine Sanctuary. Kayaks are rented for a full day and include all gear and a safety and paddling orientation. That nemesis of the bicycling user of the recreation trail, the two- or four-person surrey, can be rented by the hour. Serenely pedaling past dozing sea lions and feeding sea otters is a lovely way to spend an afternoon in paradise.

Monterey Moped Adventures
1250 Del Monte Avenue, Monterey
(831) 373-2696
Exploring the Monterey Peninsula on a moped can be an exciting alternative. Monterey Moped Adventures has single- and double-seated mopeds, motorcycles, and bicycles available for rent. Helmets and area maps are available at no extra charge. They even rent baby strollers and

carriages to go with bicycles so the little ones can tag along.

Moped drivers must be at least 18 years old (unless accompanied by a parent) and possess a driver's permit or driver's license. Call for hours and pricing information.

Wheel Fun Rentals @ Bay Bikes
99 Pacific Street/Fisherman's Wharf,
Monterey
(831) 655–8687
585 Cannery Row, Monterey
(831) 646–9090
www.baybikes.com
This well-known business has 21-speed bikes, wide-tire bicycles, and four-wheel surreys. It carries men's, women's, and children's frames in addition to child trailers, baby seats, and trunk racks. Bikes can be delivered to your hotel by calling (831) 659–BIKE. Their brochure has a map to guide you to some of the best cycling around. Call for hourly, daily, and weekly rates.

Bike Trails

A recreation trail runs along the coastline from Pacific Grove to Marina. Most of the other Peninsula cities offer a bike lane for two-wheeled travelers. Caution should be taken since the trail is popular with cyclists as well as those traveling on foot, on in-line skates, or by surrey.

Sharing Rides

Rideshare
(831) 422–POOL
www.ambag.org/sharing.html
Call or visit the Web site for information on carpools, vanpools, and other alternative commute options. The carpool lot is at the corner of Laureles Grade and Highway 68. The lot has 20 parking spaces for autos, but no bike lockers.

The Association of Monterey Bay Area Governments (AMBAG) offers electric bicycles for lease to people who live or work in Monterey County as part of its Commute Alternative Program. For more details call (831) 883–3750 or visit www.ambag.org/sharing.html.

Special Needs

RIDES
(831) 373–1393
www.mst.org
RIDES is a transit service for seniors or special-needs riders. It offers curb-to-curb service anywhere in the county for $1.00 each way. Hours of operation are from 5:00 A.M. to 7:00 P.M. daily. It is best to reserve your ride 24 hours in advance to ensure service.

On Foot

The Monterey Peninsula is an area where walking is not only possible but also very pleasant. The cities of Monterey, Pacific Grove, and Carmel are especially suited to exploration on foot. Each city provides ample sidewalks with crosswalks at major intersections.

In addition, the recreation trail provides a path for walking from Lovers Point in Pacific Grove to Canyon Del Rey Road in Seaside. The trail is shared also by skaters and bicyclists in Monterey, so caution is recommended.

If you are interested in a guided or self-guided walking tour, the Monterey Path of History Tour, (831) 649–7118, and Carmel Walks, (831) 642–2700, are two organizations designed to provide you with specific area information to discover while walking your way through town.

HISTORY 🏛

The history of the Monterey Peninsula area is rich and sustaining; many historic events happened right here in the "Cradle of California History." The tales of each of the early cities are as unique and diverse as the individuals who settled Monterey, Carmel, Pacific Grove, and Pebble Beach. The Peninsula's history is a collection of adventures that starts with the first Native Americans and continues to the present-day residents. This area has been called home by the practical and the posh, from cannery workers and fishermen to celebrities and government leaders. Today, the Peninsula includes other lively and growing communities—Seaside, Sand City, Del Rey Oaks, and Marina—however, we've chosen to highlight the earlier settlements in these pages.

MONTEREY

Monterey's earliest Spanish settlers can be traced back to June 3, 1770, with the arrival of Gaspar de Portolá and Father Junipero Serra. Wishing to secure the area north of Mexico before other nations could lay claim, Spain's King Charles III established 21 missions in California. Father Serra, leader of the California missions, oversaw the founding of the first nine, including those in Monterey, Carmel, and the Presidio of Monterey.

Monterey was named capital of Alta (upper) and Baja (lower) California in 1777.

Since the September 11, 2001, terrorist attacks, the Presidio of Monterey has been closed to the public. As a result, a shortcut from Monterey to Pacific Grove has been eliminated, making Lighthouse Avenue and Highway 68 the only routes available between the two cities.

Felipe de Neve, the new Spanish governor, developed a code of laws that regulated both civil and military affairs. He is also credited for the improvement of the Presidio by converting it to an adobe structure.

Mexico granted the pueblo lands to Monterey in 1830 and set territorial boundaries. Fourteen *ranchos* existed in Monterey County in 1834. The ranchos, with Spanish names like Aguajito, Laguna Seca, El Pescadero, and Cañada la Segunda, were huge tracts of land. The Punta de Pinos *ranchero* encompassed the entire Monterey Peninsula. During this time, the human population of 2,000 was greatly outnumbered by nearly 140,000 head of cattle. After Mexico's independence from Spain in 1822, the nonmilitary citizens living near the Presidio headquarters were organized into the "Pueblo de Monterey" or village of Monterey.

Monterey continued to serve as the capital of Alta California under the Mexican government until 1846, when relations with Mexico began to break down. The United States had two allies in California during this time, Mr. Larkin, a consul and confidential agent of the United States who resided in Monterey, and Captain John C. Frémont, an officer in the U.S. Army.

Larkin was instructed to bring about, if possible, a nonviolent penetration of American citizens into California. He also was to support Californians in asserting and maintaining their independence from Mexico.

Frémont, the son-in-law of U.S. Senator Thomas Hart Benton, had set out to defeat Mexican power in California of his own accord. His idea was to establish a military presence in California, though he apparently was under no authorization from President Polk or the United States War Department. He arrived in Monterey with a ragtag band of 24 Americans, among

The first brick house built in California has been preserved as a museum in Monterey's Heritage Harbor, near downtown and Fisherman's Wharf. MICHAEL CHATFIELD

them Kit Carson. He eventually left Monterey and gained control of Sonoma, where he established the Bear Flag Republic.

U.S. Commodore John Drake Sloat arrived in Monterey Harbor on July 2, 1846, carrying with him instructions from the U.S. government to capture all California ports and hold them in the event of a war between the United States and Mexico. He sent for Larkin and learned of the Bear Flag Republic and Captain Frémont's participation in it. On July 7, he sent four of his officers ashore with a demand to the Mexican commandant to surrender the port of Monterey with all its troops, arms, and other public property. The commandant replied that he had neither troops nor arms to surrender. Upon receipt of this message, Sloat disembarked and declared American freedoms for the Californians and that "henceforth California will be a portion of the United States."

Troubled, weary, and in poor health, Sloat turned over his command to Commodore Robert F. Stockton, who had arrived in Monterey a few days earlier. Stockton was more of a militant, uncompromising executive who sought to immediately conquer all of California. Frémont, who heard the news and came to Monterey to confer with Sloat, related to Stockton easily and planned an attack to the south to drive the Mexican authorities from the region. Frémont and his battalion were taken into the naval service, and he was made major in command. The whole contingent sailed to San Diego to seal off California from further invasion by Mexico.

From the beginning Monterey seemed destined to become known as a place of "firsts." In California, Monterey was the site of the first newspaper, theater, library, post office, and real estate transaction.

The discovery of gold in the Sierras, in

The Presidio of Monterey Museum leads visitors through the rich military history of the Monterey Peninsula. Call (831) 646-3456 for hours and directions.

1848, nearly made a ghost town out of Monterey and several other California cities. Despite the exodus of those seeking a fast fortune, Monterey was finally declared a city on June 10, 1889.

David Jacks, owner of the 3,323-acre Rancho Aguajito, was one of the most influential people in Monterey County. Jacks, born in the town of Crieff in Perthshire, Scotland, came to the United States in 1841. He worked for a few years in New York, and in April 1849 he came to California, traveling immediately to the Sierra gold mines. Not liking what he saw there, he went to San Francisco in 1850 and worked in a grocery and dry goods store. He moved to Monterey a year later and became a herdsman for government horses and sheep on Rancho San Francisquito. Later, Jacks was employed by a fellow Scotsman, James McKinley, in his grocery and dry goods store.

Mr. Jacks became the Monterey County Treasurer in 1852. He began acquiring land through direct purchase, buying up tax-delinquent tracts, exchanges, and foreclosures. His land holdings in Monterey County totaled more than 70,000 acres. His purchase of 30,000 acres of Monterey city land made David Jacks the most hated and feared man in the county. Jacks acquired the property by foreclosing on city lands for a debt Monterey owed his attorney. The city was forced to auction its land in order to satisfy the debt. Jacks and his attorney were apparently the only two bidders at the auction.

From that point on Jacks became almost a marked man. He always traveled with a bodyguard, especially if he left the Monterey area. He was so despised, local legend has it, that someone placed a curse on him to prevent his family name from surviving another generation. In spite of his bad reputation, Jacks was a God-fearing man who taught Sunday school. He generously donated property and funds to the Methodist Church for the establishment of a summer camp in Pacific Grove.

For nearly a century Monterey was a sleepy little ranch community. Its citizens lived in adobes, spoke Spanish, and maintained Latin customs. The arrival of the Southern Pacific Railroad to the Peninsula, in 1880, signaled a rapid change. Tourism, recreation, fishing, and agriculture became new industries drawing thousands to Monterey County.

Monterey didn't have a Gold Rush but made up for it with the Silver Rush, a dramatic increase in the harvest of sardines from the Bay. Sardines had always been caught in the Bay, but after 1900 the sardine catch became an industry.

The birth of the industry actually began in 1909 when Frank Booth set up a tiny plant near the present-day Fisherman's Wharf to can salmon. Impressed by the large schools of silver-sided sardines, he began canning them in small tins. At that time the fish were caught in gill nets strung in the path of a school of sardines. The nets caught only a small percentage of the fish, and many of those slipped away as the fish were passed from sailboats to the cannery in wire baskets. The fish were then cut by hand and cooked in wire baskets that were pushed through troughs of boiling oil. After the cooking process they were hand-packed in tins and hand-soldered. This method allowed for the production of only 400 cans per day.

When Booth's plant burned down, he established another at the foot of Alvarado Street. Proximity to the Bay was important because the fish had to be transported to the cannery from the ship. Booth hired Knute Hovden, a young Norwegian who had graduated from National Fisheries College in his country. He also hired Pietro Ferrante, a Sicilian immigrant whose family was involved in the fishing industry. Coupled with the introduction of the *lampara* net by Pietro Ferrante and the streamlining

California's first constitution was drafted in Colton Hall when Monterey was the capital of Alta California. In continuous use since its completion in 1849, the building has been used as Monterey's City Hall, a public school, and police offices. Today it is a museum.
MICHAEL CHATFIELD

of the processing and canning of the fish by Knute Hovden, Monterey was geared up for the making of a legend.

By 1918 the canneries were producing little one-pound oval cans from the 50,000 tons of sardines caught in the Bay. The invention of purse seiners in the 1920s replaced the lampara nets. These vessels bore huge nets, with the depth of a 10-story building, encircling an area the size of a football field. In the years that followed, more than 70 seiners, with seasonal catches soaring to 215,000 tons, fished Monterey Bay. For 30 years Cannery Row was the "Sardine Capital of the World." In its heyday, it had 30 canneries employing 2,500 full-time workers and thousands of part-timers.

For years Ed Ricketts, a marine biologist and longtime Cannery Row resident, urged officials to adopt a conservation program. (Ricketts was immortalized by John Steinbeck as Doc, in *Cannery Row*.) His warnings continued to fall on deaf ears, and the sardine catch of 1948 was the worst ever. It rebounded in 1950 to 132,000 tons, but by the next season it was all over. The sardine canning industry, sustained only a half-century, was gone for good. Life on the Row ground to a halt, and the canning machinery was sold off to foreign buyers.

A remnant of this bygone era started the revival of Cannery Row; the Hovden Cannery, built in 1916, became the nucleus for the new Monterey Bay Aquarium. The opening of the aquarium in 1984 laid the cornerstone for new vitality on Cannery Row. Today the Monterey Bay Aquarium is recognized as one of the world's premier aquariums.

The legend of Cannery Row continued

At the corner of Drake and Wave Streets in Monterey, there is a bust of Ed Ricketts, better known as Doc of John Steinbeck's Cannery Row. *It was at this intersection that Ricketts met his death in a collision with the Del Monte Express, the train that connected the Peninsula with San Francisco at that time. Locals see to it that there is always a bouquet of fresh flowers in Doc's hand.*

as other businesses were quickly established. Today visitors stroll through several blocks of gift and specialty shops and art galleries. New restaurants, many with unobstructed ocean views, continue to breathe new life into this historic district.

The arrival of the railroad was the genius of Charles Crocker, one of four rail barons who owned Southern Pacific Railroad. Crocker envisioned Monterey as a resort and lost no time in erecting a magnificent Victorian castle at the site of the Naval Postgraduate School. Crocker spent $1 million building the Hotel Del Monte in a mere 100 days.

When the doors opened in 1880, the hotel was an immediate success. It was built in a parklike setting, and no expense was spared to provide guests every possible amenity. Each room had a telephone, and the bath was equipped with hot and cold running water, both rarities in the late 1800s.

Tragedy struck on March 31, 1887, when the "Queen of American Watering Places," as the hotel had become known, was completely destroyed by fire. Although no lives were lost in the flames, the hotel was reduced to ashes.

The following year the Hotel Del Monte was rebuilt in a Gothic-Victorian architectural style and was even more sumptuous. It covered 16 acres and could lodge 700 guests. The spacious dining room, with four fireplaces, seated up to 750 people.

The hotel grounds boasted a 15-acre lake, lawn tennis courts, archery ranges, exotic gardens, and miles of walking paths. An immaculate stable and carriage house held the surreys used to transport guests to the Del Monte Forest for picnics on the pebbled beach. A beachfront bathing pavilion, the largest in the world at the time, was also built. It contained 210 dressing rooms and four swim tanks, each tank measuring 70 by 170 feet. Three of the pools were heated to different temperatures. This allowed swimmers to prepare for a dip in the chilly bay by moving from pool to pool.

A second fire in 1924 again destroyed the hotel, and it was rebuilt in a Mediterranean style with a fireproof red-tile roof. The third Hotel Del Monte, the one that exists today, was even larger and more elaborate than the other two. Unfortunately it never quite regained its previous status as a luxury hotel because the Great Depression curbed travel and extravagance for even the elite.

Monterey's culture and history is revisited through the many festivals and events that take place throughout the year (see our chapter on Annual Events), and many historic buildings in Old Monterey have been preserved. The promotion of economic growth while maintaining the historic quality of Monterey is of great concern to city officials, business owners, and residents. For example, Monterey's Alvarado Street has successfully blended a variety of hotels, shops, service-oriented businesses, and eating establishments with charming adobe buildings of historical significance.

PACIFIC GROVE

The first development in Pacific Grove was the installment of a lighthouse that began operating at Point Pinos in 1855. The lighthouse served as a guide to mariners entering Monterey Bay. The lighthouse keeper, Captain Allen Luce, received authorization in 1874 to cut a trail through the forest

The Custom House, located at the foot of Fisherman's Wharf, is the oldest public building still standing in California. It contains an interactive historical display of its days as a busy customs office. MICHAEL CHATFIELD

from Point Pinos to Monterey. This trail became what is now known as Lighthouse Avenue.

Pacific Grove is located where the Pacific Ocean meets the waters of the Monterey Bay. This area was formerly Rancho Punta de Pinos, one of the great *ranchos* of the Spanish/Mexican era in California history. Methodist Church officials founded Pacific Grove in 1875 as a religious and cultural retreat. The retreat consisted of 100 acres of dense pine forest.

Reverend Ross, a Methodist minister, convinced the Bishop of the Methodist Church to purchase headlands northwest of Monterey, owned by David Jacks, for a summer camp. At a meeting in San Francisco on June 1, 1875, a new organization, the Pacific Grove Retreat Association, met and formed the first Board of Trustees.

With the donation of the land and the financial assistance of David Jacks, the association laid out the first lots for tenting in 1875.

The first camp meeting officially opened August 8, 1875, and became the forerunner of the summer religious meetings and Chautauquas that followed. The Chautauqua, a religious camp meeting consisting of sermons, educational lectures, family get-togethers, and the singing of Psalms, originated on the East Coast. The first West Coast meeting of the Chautauqua Scientific and Literary Society was held in Pacific Grove in 1879. A large tent was set up for group meetings on present-day Forest Avenue.

Every year the summer retreat groups grew larger. Eventually tents were set up on 30-by-60-foot lots, each selling for $50.

A large meeting place, Chautauqua Hall, was completed in 1881. The building seated about 1,500 people.

The last Pacific Grove Chautauqua was held on August 7, 1926. Changes in lifestyle brought an end to nearly five decades of the religious camp meetings that led to the development of Pacific Grove.

In 1881 David Jacks sold 7,000 acres of ranch land on the Peninsula to the Southern Pacific Railroad, the sister company of the Pacific Improvement Company. He also sold several thousand acres of the Pescadero and Point Pinos *ranchos* to the Pacific Improvement Company in 1881 and 1883. The sale of the property eventually led to the religious retreat becoming more of a secular location as more and more people, some uninterested in religion, came to Pacific Grove. All parties agreed that the Pacific Grove Retreat Association would maintain control over the grounds. In 1919 Samuel F. B. Morse and other investors purchased the holdings of the Pacific Improvement Company; the new company, called Del Monte Properties, was formed with Morse serving as its president.

In the early 1850s a community of Chinese immigrants began settling in the area where Hopkins Marine Station stands today. It wasn't long until the population of Chinatown grew to about 500. They built wooden cottages perched above the water on stilts and rocks; some cottages included balconies. The Chinese were industrious, hardworking people who prospered by cultivating the area's natural resources. Some grew vegetables in little gardens, while others set up shell stands along 17-Mile Drive.

The truly ambitious relied on the ocean for their livelihood. By day they fished for rockfish, cod, halibut, red and bluefish, yellowtail, mackerel, and sardines. Nighttime would find them bobbing along the Bay amongst a fleet of about 30 junkets and sampans. A fire of pitch logs laid out on wire racks attached to the stern of their boats attracted squid to the water's surface. By early morning the nightly catch was spread out to dry on the ground; the potent odor of the drying squid was not fully appreciated by the residents of Pacific Grove. In addition, the Italian fishermen from Monterey grew increasingly threatened by the Chinese presence in the Bay.

On the night of May 16, 1906, Pacific Grove's Chinatown was completely destroyed by fire. Flames roared through the village, quickly burning the wooden cottages. Those who fled the disaster watched in horror as the deadly blaze destroyed their homes and all of their earthly possessions. The fire was especially tragic for the San Francisco Chinese, who had recently come to the Peninsula in hopes of building a new life after losing everything six weeks earlier in the great earthquake.

The settlement burned to the ground as firefighters worked desperately to get water in and quench the flames. It was later discovered that the fire hose connected to the 2-inch water main had been cut when the fire first started. Although authorities suspected the fire was not accidental, no further investigation took place. Once in motion, the rumor mill produced stories that implicated the Pacific Improvement Company. The rumors stemmed from the fact that Pacific Grove was continually growing and the demand for housing was becoming greater. The waterfront property where Chinatown stood was now prime real estate, and the company had previously considered evicting the Chinese.

To further fan the flames, after the fire the Pacific Improvement Company fenced in the former village and prohibited the Chinese from entering. This thwarted the efforts of the Chinese, who wanted to rebuild their homes. A small Chinese village was established at McAbee Beach near the present-day Steinbeck Plaza. It should be noted that the Chinese played a great part in establishing Monterey as a fishing port, ranking second only to San Francisco.

On July 16, 1889, Pacific Grove was incorporated as a city. Mr. O. S. Trimmer was appointed as the first president of the Board of Trustees. Pacific Grove became a chartered city on April 22, 1927. This resulted in the calling of a general election for a mayor and city council.

The quality of life in Pacific Grove attracted people who were not necessarily interested in religion. The leaders of the retreat drew a dim view of these outsiders. In the early 1900s blue laws were put into effect in order to maintain the lifestyle of the Methodists.

Not only was the use of liquor against the law, but also the sale of alcoholic beverages was strictly prohibited within the city limits. (Pacific Grove remained a "dry" town until 1969 when the city council adopted an ordinance repealing prohibition. Voters enthusiastically approved the repeal of the ordinance, which legalized the sale of alcoholic beverages.) Curfew laws went into effect stating that residents were required to keep their window shades up until 10:00 P.M. At that time, the shades were to be pulled down and all lights turned off.

Around 1915 it was determined that it was in the best interest of the city to own its own waterfront. Provisions were made to curtail development on the waterfront without the approval of Pacific Grove's residents.

The city of Pacific Grove purchased Lovers Point from the Pacific Improvement Company in 1902 to develop a park. Lovers Point and its beaches have been a focal point since the early days of Pacific Grove. The protected waters and white sand on the main beach were a very popular place. Gatherings such as prayer meetings, band concerts, and festivals were held there.

Lovers Point was the original site of Hopkins Marine Station. In those days it was called the Hopkins Seaside Laboratory. In 1891 Timothy Hopkins, the adopted son of Mark Hopkins (one of the "Big Four" rail barons of the Southern Pacific Railroad), established this important laboratory.

After visiting Dr. Anthony Dohrn's Zoological Station in Naples, Italy, Timothy approached several professors at Stanford University about opening a laboratory in Pacific Grove. With the help of the Pacific

Improvement Company, a large two-story building was constructed. By the early 1900s the lab needed a larger facility and moved to Cabrillo Point where the Chinese village had once been.

After the move, the lab became known as the Hopkins Marine Station of Stanford University. Over the years it has become a well-known and esteemed research facility, gaining the respect of scientists throughout the world.

No history of Pacific Grove would be complete without mentioning Asilomar, the "Refuge by the Sea." This beautiful facility came into existence in 1913 with a gathering of girls from the Young Women's Christian Association (YWCA). Architect Julia Morgan, who developed Hearst Castle, designed the early plans for the grounds and original structures. The original 30-acre site was a gift of the Pacific Improvement Company.

From 1936 to 1941 Asilomar was leased and operated as a public resort. During WWII the National Youth Authority used it as a training facility. The YWCA resumed its normal operations there in 1946. In 1956 the YWCA offered to sell the property, now 60 acres, to the state of California providing it be used for a state park. The state purchased the property and added to it another 34 acres, renaming it Asilomar State Beach and Conference Grounds.

The name Pacific Grove was appropriate for the area because in the early days there was nothing but a grove of trees here. The city became known by various other names including the Christian Seaside Retreat, Methodist Episcopal Encampment Grounds, Pacific Grove Retreat, Piney Paradise, the Grove, and the Retreat. It was also know as Chautauqua-by-the-Sea, the City of Churches, and the City of Homes. Today, Pacific Grove is called "P.G." by Peninsula residents and other Insiders. The town is promoted outside the area as Butterfly Town USA and America's Last Hometown.

Today, Pacific Grove still maintains its small-town atmosphere. Residents are active in the community and take a strong interest in local politics. The people who

i *When Father Junipero Serra first set foot on the Monterey Peninsula, he held mass under a huge oak tree. A large fragment of the tree has been preserved at the Royal Presidio Chapel on Church Street.*

live and work in P.G. are proud of their business district, which has seen a revival in the past several years. The opening of the historic Holman building as an antiques mall and the arrival of several new businesses have filled long-vacant large retail sites, giving locals and visitors an added incentive to shop Pacific Grove.

CARMEL

Present-day Carmel received its name in 1602 from two Carmelite friars traveling with Don Sebastian Vizcaino. Upon entering Monterey Bay they noticed a valley beyond the hills to the south of Monterey and named it Carmello.

Father Junipero Serra founded the Mission and Presidio of San Carlos Borroméo de Monterey in 1770. The following year it was determined that the land was more fertile to the south, so the mission was moved, and San Carlos Borroméo de Carmelo was established to provide for the agricultural needs of the new community.

The restoration of the mission was undertaken in 1883, with the financial support of Mrs. Leland Stanford. A new, steep-pitched, shingle roof was added, and the mission grounds were restored.

The area surrounding the mission was desolate, but with its restoration, it was hoped the area could be developed. The aesthetic quality of the land wasn't enough to attract real estate buyers in 1886. What mattered to most buyers was if the land was good for raising crops and cattle or if it contained timber or mineral resources. Carmel had little to offer because the dunes, scrub oaks, twisted pines, and high chaparral rendered it useless in the development of

these industries.

The idea of promoting the mission as a tourist attraction was developed in 1888 by Santiago J. Duckworth, a Monterey real estate dealer, and his brother, Belisario E. Duckworth. Their idea was to develop the area into a Catholic summer resort, somewhat like that of Pacific Grove's Methodist retreat. They purchased 234 acres of the Las Manzanitas ranchero, where Carmel now stands. With no reliable water source except a Pacific Improvement Company water line across the bottom end of the property, the land was considered worthless.

A map of Carmel City was filed in May 1888 after a survey by W. C. Little, the city engineer of Monterey. By July of that same year, 200 lots were sold. The price of these lots, located east of Junipero, was an astounding $20 for inside lots and $25 for corner lots.

The Duckworths planned to sell $50 lots where the current business district is located, turning the money over to Catholic Societies of California for use in building convention halls and establishing a school or college. The brothers firmly believed that Southern Pacific Railroad would reach the mission in the near future, but this never happened. An insufficient water supply further complicated development plans. Most of the water was still hauled in barrels from the Pacific Improvement Company's pipeline. A windmill pump managed by Carmel Waterworks proved inadequate for the needs of a growing population.

About 10 families were established in Carmel at this time. Even though the Duckworths gave up their plan in 1894, most of these families stayed on. There were also three cabins (one of which was around prior to any development by the Duckworths) that housed a tiny Mexican community.

Two developers, Frank Powers and James Devendorf, with the formation of the Carmel Development Company, established Carmel-by-the-Sea in 1902. Frank Powers was a real estate developer with subdivisions near San Jose, Stockton, Morgan Hill, and Gilroy. Powers exchanged his Stockton properties for Carmel. Before long M. J. Murphy came to the little city. Murphy built his first house at age 17 and went on to build much of Carmel.

Carmel owes a debt to Powers and Devendorf, who were largely responsible for planting the trees that created the wooded village valued by residents today. In the early 1900s Carmel was practically barren, but beginning in 1904, Devendorf began planting thousands of trees each winter. Up to that time Ocean Avenue was a wide dusty strip in summer and muddy bog each winter. Planting the trees and installing a boardwalk helped to rectify the situation.

Since the beginning, the area has attracted creative people such as artists, writers, musicians, and educators. The beauty of Carmel attracted them, inspired them, and captivated them: Many decided to set up permanent residence here. Carmel became appealing to several Bohemian writers and artists in the 1920s; among these early residents were George Sterling, Mary Austin, Upton Sinclair, William Rose Benét, Sinclair Lewis, and Robinson Jeffers. These six artists laid the foundation for the arts community in Carmel, which still is an active and vibrant part of the charm of Carmel. Approximately 90 art galleries catering to a wide range of tastes and styles form the majority of the town's businesses.

Carmel is also referred to as Carmel-by-the-Sea. Picturesque houses have whimsical or romantic names such as "Frivolity" or "Song of the Sea." Photogenic gates, doorways, and secret gardens are reminiscent of a tiny English village. The architecture of the houses is fascinating—from tiny, thatched-roof cottages to palatial estates.

In many ways Carmel has stuck to its early, small-town traditions by prohibiting the use of neon lighting, high-rises, and parking meters. From its very beginnings Carmel was free of racial prejudice, and, in fact, there was quite a cosmopolitan air about the place. This impression still carries today. Each year thousands of visitors from all socioeconomic levels meander through the streets and wander down Ocean Avenue to Carmel's gorgeous beach.

It might have been the absence of trees in early Carmel that has fueled an obsession with them today. The city of Carmel has gone above and beyond the call of duty in preserving trees. Winding, narrow streets are built around the trees. Architectural plans for houses and businesses incorporate trees, a tradition started by James Devendorf. The center strip of trees in the middle of Ocean Avenue, planted by Devendorf, still stands in beautiful tribute to his vision.

Carmel is home to scores of art galleries, specialty shops, and exceptional restaurants, all compactly located within a square mile radius of "downtown." Walk around this picturesque section of the Peninsula and appreciate the natural beauty, the slower pace, and quaint character of Carmel-by-the-Sea.

PEBBLE BEACH

In 1840 Pebble Beach was part of a rancho owned by Maria del Carmen Garcia Barreto Madariaga. Maria, a widow, inherited the ranch after her husband's death. Being more of a city girl, she felt lonely and isolated on the ranch. In 1846 she sold the entire estate, over 4,000 acres, for $500 and purchased an adobe in Monterey. The ranch passed through a series of owners and 16 years later fell into the hands of David Jacks, who purchased the property at a sheriff's sale for 12 cents an acre.

In 1868 Jacks leased the area now known as Stillwater Cove to the China Man Hop Company. By 1888 this Chinese village had more than 30 residents. When 17-Mile Drive opened in the early 1900s, Chinese entrepreneurs set up shell stands along the drive, selling polished abalone shells to the tourists. Due to the stiffening of immigration laws, changes in the fishing industry, and the development of the surrounding land, the last Chinese villager left Pebble Beach in 1912.

Who Invented Monterey Jack Cheese?

The mystery of who invented Monterey Jack cheese and how it got its name has raged on the Peninsula for many years. The U.S. Food and Drug Administration officially sanctioned the name "jack" cheese in 1955, but it had long been in use.

Most common are theories that involve early landowner David Jacks, who indeed was in the dairy business, but there is disagreement. Granted, he did own 14 dairy ranches. But it appears that he stole the idea and marketed the cheese as "Jack's Cheese," which by one account was changed because people began asking for the cheese made by "Monterey Jack."

Records show that cheese had been commercially manufactured here as early as 1859. Domingo Pedrazzi of Carmel Valley created a cheese-making process that required the application of pressure, using a "housejack." His cheese became known as "Pedrazzi's Jack Cheese" and, later, "Del Monte Cheese."

Another theory is that the method for making Jack cheese came to California with the Franciscan friars in the 1700s. When the Franciscans arrived to establish their famous missions, they brought with them the secret to making a descendant of the semisoft Italian cheeses that Rome had used to feed its armies.

Whichever theory is correct, the name "Monterey Jack" is known throughout the world and has added to the mystique and fame of the Monterey Peninsula.

Pebble Beach, the resort and community in Del Monte Forest, began in 1907 when Charles Crocker purchased the land from David Jacks for $5.00 an acre. Crocker was a member of the "Big Four," a group including Leland Stanford, Collin Huntington, and Mark Hopkins. The Big Four were rail barons of the Central Pacific Railroad and also owned the Pacific Improvement Company. Crocker, who thought Pebble Beach would make a good summer resort, also owned the luxurious Hotel Del Monte in Monterey.

Development in Pebble Beach began in 1908 when Crocker built a log cabin where The Lodge now stands. As little as it was, the presence of the cabin led to the opening of the first Pebble Beach post office on October 4, 1909. Charles Fahl served as the first postmaster. Crocker's cabin provided a comfort stop for people traveling through the Del Monte Forest. The cabin was destroyed by fire in 1917, but two years later it was replaced with the elaborate Del Monte Lodge, under the direction of Samuel F. B. Morse.

Samuel Finley Brown Morse, the nephew of the inventor of the telegraph, came to the Peninsula in 1915. Morse, who eventually became known as "The Duke of Pebble Beach," was hired to manage the Pacific Improvement Company.

During his first year with the company, Morse laid out the Pebble Beach Golf Course using all but 4 percent of the property's shoreline for the course. Construction on the course began in 1916 when Morse hired Douglas Grant and John F. Neville. Grant was a student of architecture, and both gentlemen were amateur golf champions.

The course, named Pebble Beach Links, was dedicated on February 2, 1919. It was only a matter of time before the Links became the world's most celebrated golf course. In 1919 Samuel F. B. Morse, with other investors, bought the holdings of the Pacific Improvement Company for a reported $1.3 million.

Having completed the Links and the Del Monte Lodge, today known as The Lodge at Pebble Beach, Morse turned his attention to the completion of 17-Mile Drive. He also laid out more than 100 miles of bridle paths, and some of these riding trails are still in use today. It was Morse's dream to see Pebble Beach become one of the world's most fashionable resorts.

Though fashionable, the Del Monte Lodge was a boring place throughout the 1920s, except when an orchestra played dance tunes on Saturday nights. More than anything, the Lodge was meant to serve as a watering hole for the small, exclusive circle of Pebble Beach residents and for golfers who played the Links.

What the Lodge lacked in excitement, the residents of the Forest made up for by entertaining the "beautiful people" at private parties in their lavish Pebble Beach mansions. The parties were quite spirited in spite of the subdued mood in the rest of the country brought on by Prohibition. Some say illegal aqua vitae was frequently brought in, throughout the 1920s, by boats that landed in the Point Lobos area.

The devastating effect of the stock market crash finally touched the elite of Pebble Beach in 1933. Nearly 85 percent of all hotels in the United States went into receivership, including San Francisco's Mark Hopkins, The Fairmont, and the Clift Hotel. Although this wasn't the fate of The Pebble Beach Lodge or the Del Monte Hotel, during the Great Depression Samuel F. B. Morse reported losses of more than $300,000. In the early 1930s, Pebble Beach real estate sales fell from more than a million dollars to nothing.

Throughout its history, Pebble Beach has been the home of many events including the Bing Crosby Golf Tournament (now the AT&T National Pro-Am), which opened in 1947. Every year, in February, the AT&T Tournament brings together celebrities with professional and amateur golfers for a week of golf that raises millions of dollars for local charities. Another world-renowned event, the Concours d'Elegance, a premier competition of classic and vintage cars, began in 1950 and was the brainchild of Gwenn Graham. Today, it remains one of the classiest and best-attended events on the Peninsula.

Samuel F. B. Morse died in 1969 but not before he saw the realization of his dream: Pebble Beach did indeed become one of the most highly acclaimed resorts in the world. The beautiful scenery that first attracted the wealthy to Pebble Beach continues to draw visitors from around the globe. The area is also a magnet for movie directors who use Pebble Beach as a backdrop for films set in the French or Italian Riviera, Isle of Capri, or parts of Britain. Recently, several famous residents, including the former mayor of Carmel, Clint Eastwood, purchased the Pebble Beach Company, returning it once again to local ownership.

The renowned 17-Mile Drive, which, incidentally, is now only 12 miles, remains a toll road. Meandering along the drive today, motorists or cyclists pass several championship golf courses. The Links at Spanish Bay; Poppy Hills, home of the Northern California Golf Association; Spyglass Hill, ranked one of the top 40 courses in the United States; the world-famous Pebble Beach Links; and the nine-hole Peter Hay course are all open to the public. In 2001 the Pebble Beach Company hosted the 100th anniversary of the U.S. Open. Sam Morse's dream continues to expand and grow long after its initial inception.

HOTELS AND MOTELS

It's hard for locals to imagine that there could be enough visitors to fill all the available rooms on the Monterey Peninsula. Yet on many of the special-event weekends, finding a room on the Peninsula can be as difficult as finding a Saturday morning tee time at Pebble Beach. Drive into town during the Monterey Jazz Festival, the Concours d'Elegance, or a big weekend racing event at Laguna Seca, and you may have trouble finding a room for the night. That's nearly always the case if you have your heart set on a room with a view along the Pacific Grove coastline, near Cannery Row, or in central Carmel or Pebble Beach. (This is especially true for bed-and-breakfast inns, which we cover in our next chapter.)

Despite an abundance of accommodations of all types and price ranges, the key phrases to remember are "special-event weekend" and "advance reservations." If you've read our Annual Events chapter, you'll know that festivals and other special events occur throughout the year on the Monterey Peninsula. If you're planning to attend a major event, it isn't out of line to be thinking about reserving your room up to a year in advance. For any nonevent weekends during the summer or holidays, it's still a good idea to make your reservations two to six months in advance if you want to make sure you'll get into your choice of locations. Even during the off-season, a month's advance planning is recommended at the most popular hotels and motels. That's not to say you can't pull into town without reservations and find a great room, especially on a weeknight. Cancellations and other strokes of good fortune do happen. Just don't expect to have a wide choice of prime locations.

Also be aware that many of the hotels and motels on the Peninsula have two- or three-night minimum stays during all peak-season, special-event, and holiday weekends. Peak season is generally June through September. Some of the most popular establishments impose the two-night weekend minimum year-round. But again, exceptions to these restrictions are made if the hotel or motel has unexpected vacancies.

Amenities offered at the hotels and motels vary widely. However, you'll find that a great majority of the establishments offer both smoking and nonsmoking rooms, cable television (many with premium movie and sports channels and/or VCRs with videotape rentals), and in-room telephones. Most accept major credit cards such as Visa, MasterCard, Discover, and American Express. Unless the listings in this chapter note otherwise, you can safely assume that these conveniences are provided. Sorry, pets are probably not allowed unless we note otherwise. Where they are OK, be sure to call in advance to confirm any room fees, deposits, and restrictions. Virtually all hotels and motels, except for a few historic inns, are wheelchair accessible, but inquire about your specific needs.

PRICE CODES

Prices for accommodations on the Monterey Peninsula cover a wide range, from less than $60 per night to more than $1,000. In fact, the very same room may cost you twice as much or more during the peak season (June through September) or a special-event weekend than it does on a weekday during the quiet off-season. These codes represent the average price of a double-occupancy room during the peak season, taxes not included. This average may represent a wide range of room prices, with added amenities and ocean views hiking up the price of a standard room. Be sure to confirm the current rates and available methods of payment when making your reservation.

$	Less than $90
$$	$90–130
$$$	$131–190
$$$$	More than $190

WHERE TO STAY

So where should you stay during your time on the Monterey Peninsula—Monterey, Pacific Grove, Carmel, or Pebble Beach? That will depend on your preferences and your pocketbook. Below, we describe the types of accommodations found in each of the four locales and then list some specific establishments representing your range of choices.

Monterey

For hotels and motels, Monterey is by far your best bet for finding a full range of accommodations representing all price ranges. From budget motels to luxury hotels, Monterey has it all. And you'll find that particular sections of town are home to particular types of accommodations. Generally speaking, the farther away from the water and major attractions you get, the less expensive your night's stay will be.

If you're simply looking for a clean, inexpensive room and don't particularly give a darn about a great ocean view or being within walking distance to the major attractions, try the stretch of motels along Fremont Boulevard east of Highway 1. Here you'll find a choice of rooms for about $70 to $80 a night, which is just about as inexpensive as it gets in these parts during peak seasons. This stretch of Fremont Boulevard is near the Monterey Fairgrounds, home of the Monterey Bay Blues Festival and Monterey Jazz Festival. Rates seem to mysteriously skyrocket at most of these establishments during these

Take advantage of the Web site listings for Monterey Peninsula hotels and motels. Some allow you to make your reservations online; others provide pictures or virtual tours of the accommodations.

two weekends in June and September (see our Annual Events chapter).

Another great spot for motels is Munras Avenue, just off Highway 1 near the Del Monte Shopping Center. The south side of the street is a virtual motel row; many of the establishments are of 1960s vintage with heated pools. Expect to pay anywhere from $80 to $120 here, depending on season and amenities. Note that weekend rates at some of these motels can be substantially higher than weekday rates, so weekenders are often able to find a nicer, quieter spot in, say, Pacific Grove, for about the same price.

If you prefer larger hotels complete with restaurants, lounges, pools, and exercise rooms, downtown Monterey should be your cup of tea. Centrally located and within walking distance of Fisherman's Wharf and Cannery Row, the downtown hotels are typically $100 and up a night. That also includes the smaller hotels and inns that populate the historic downtown Monterey area. The Cannery Row area has its share of upscale hotels and motels as well. Again, you're likely to find rooms in the $100-plus range, but the views and easy access to the Monterey Bay Aquarium and the Monterey Peninsula Recreation Trail make this area a great choice for a special family vacation.

Following is a selection of hotels and motels in the city of Monterey, representing all of the areas mentioned above and even a few more. The list is far from exhaustive but offers a good range of choices.

Bay Park Hotel   **$$$**
1425 Munras Avenue, Monterey
(831) 649-1020, (800) 338-3564
www.bayparkhotel.com

Nestled among the pines at the top of Munras Avenue between Highway 1 and the Del Monte Shopping Center, the Bay Park Hotel offers 80 clean and comfortable rooms in a central location providing easy freeway access. Many of the rooms in this full-service hotel have bay or wooded hillside views to enjoy from your patio or balcony. A full-size outdoor pool, a whirlpool spa with a brick patio, and a rustic gazebo add to an enjoyable stay. The Bay Park Hotel is home to the Crazy Horse Restaurant, which features an exceptional salad bar and hearty fare, as well as the Safari Club lounge for evening cocktails. Locally owned and operated by Kurt Lang, the Bay Park Hotel is known for its friendly, long-term staff, many of whom have welcomed visitors here for more than 10 years. Pets OK.

The Beach Resort $$$
2600 Sand Dunes Drive, Monterey
(831) 394-3321, (800) 528-1234
www.montereybeachresort.com
The Beach Resort by Best Western has perhaps the best ocean view of any hotel in the area. Right on a long stretch of sandy beach east of the Peninsula proper, the hotel looks across Monterey Bay toward the Monterey Harbor, Cannery Row, and the Pacific Grove coastline. Both day and night views are breathtaking, and sunsets can be downright awesome. The hotel has 196 rooms, an outdoor pool, a whirlpool spa, and a fitness center. A comfortable lounge with a fireplace and baby grand piano is a great spot to enjoy the complimentary afternoon hors d'oeuvres, and the Cafe Beach restaurant on the fourth floor offers a spectacular vantage point from which to enjoy your breakfast, lunch, or dinner. The Sandals Lounge has live entertainment Thursday through Saturday evenings. Pets OK.

Cannery Row Inn $$$
200 Foam Street, Monterey
(831) 649-8580, (800) 385-2299
www.canneryrowinn.com
Just a block above Cannery Row, this inn

offers 32 nonsmoking rooms, most with fireplaces. You can chose from king- or queen-size beds in the ample rooms. Eight specialty rooms offer great bay views from private balconies. In-room coffeemakers and pastries are provided. An inviting hot tub is just the thing after a day of walking Cannery Row.

Carmel Hill Lodge $$
1374 Munras Avenue, Monterey
(831) 373-3252, (888) 551-4455
www.carmelhilllodge.com
Situated across Munras Avenue from Del Monte Shopping Center, the Comstock-style Carmel Hill Lodge offers comfortable beds and affordable rooms and friendly service. The 38 units are nothing fancy, but the good-sized outdoor pool will be a hit with the kids.

Casa Munras Garden Hotel $$$
700 Munras Avenue, Monterey
(831) 375-2411, (800) 222-2558
www.casamunras-hotel.com
Casa Munras Garden Hotel is a historic 4.5-acre adobe property near downtown Monterey. The hotel is built around the original hacienda of Don Esteban Munras, the last Spanish diplomat to California.

Its 166 rooms are situated in an idyllic garden setting reminiscent of old Monterey. The rooms are pleasantly furnished with comforters, armoires, shuttered windows, and other warm touches. Selected rooms have fireplaces and balconies, and spacious specialty suites are available. A large heated outdoor pool is a great spot to while away the day. The Casa Cafe & Bar serves a varied menu for breakfast, lunch, and dinner. The happy hour with live entertainment draws a local crowd. Casa Munras is a good choice for first-time visitors looking for a taste of old Monterey.

Clarion Hotel Monterey $$
1046 Munras Avenue, Monterey
(831) 373-1337, (800) 821-0805
www.clarionhotelmonterey.com
Groovy is the word to describe this

1960s-style, 52-unit motel operated by Clarion Hotels. Executive suites have king-size beds, full kitchens, and fireplaces. The honeymoon suite has an in-room spa and private patio. Family units are also available. All guests can enjoy the only indoor heated pool on Munras Avenue. Continental breakfast and in-room coffee is available to all guests. A little kitsch, the Clarion Hotel Monterey will bring back memories of '60s vacations.

The Colton Inn $$$
707 Pacific Street, Monterey
(831) 649-6500, (800) 848-7007
www.coltoninn.com

If a motel on a quiet corner along a meandering creek sounds appealing, try The Colton Inn. Situated on Pacific Street a few blocks north of the downtown area, this inn offers 50 amply sized rooms, many with special amenities such as wood-burning fireplaces, whirlpool tubs, kitchenettes, microwave ovens, and refrigerators. A honeymoon suite is fully equipped with these and other extras, including a great sound system. A private dry sauna and a sundeck with a barbecue grill are available to guests. A continental breakfast of fresh-made muffins, Danish rolls, and coffee is included in the room price.

Cypress Gardens Resort Inn $$
1150 Munras Avenue, Monterey
(831) 373-2761, (877) 922-1150
www.cypressgardeninn.com

On the site of a former Monterey nursery, the Cypress Gardens Inn is an Insiders' favorite, with 46 good-sized rooms in a lush garden setting. Many of the private balconies overlook the garden and the 55-foot heated outdoor pool (Monterey's largest) and hot tub. Each room has its own refrigerator, and a continental breakfast is available in the lobby. Pets are allowed in some rooms. A special two-story town house features a full kitchen, large fireplace, dining room, and queen bedroom up a spiral staircase.

Cypress Tree Inn $
2227 North Fremont Street, Monterey
(831) 372-7586, (800) 446-8303
www.cypresstreeinn.com

One of the true bargains in Monterey, Cypress Tree Inn offers 55 clean rooms and amenities such as hot tubs, fireplaces, kitchenettes, sauna, barbecue patio, coin-operated laundry, and even an on-site bake shop. Divers will appreciate the dip tanks and hanging area for their gear. There are even RV hookups. Yes, you are east of Highway 1, away from the beaches and major attractions, but for the price you'll be hard-pressed to find a better stay in the area. The Cypress Tree Inn is also a favorite of jazz and blues festival fans, so book your room for those events far in advance.

Del Monte Pines $$
1298 Munras Avenue, Monterey
(831) 375-2323, (800) 633-6454

Directly across Munras Avenue from the Del Monte Shopping Center is the Del Monte Pines Motel. This cozy two-story complex of 19 rooms has a heated outdoor pool, and some of the rooms include fireplaces and hot tubs. Family suites are available. A continental breakfast is served each morning in the lobby, and all rooms have coffeemakers.

DoubleTree Hotel $$$$
2 Portola Plaza, Monterey
(831) 649-4511, (800) 222-8733
www.doubletreemonterey.com

The large, 380-room DoubleTree Hotel lies in the heart of Monterey. Just steps from Custom House Plaza and Fisherman's Wharf on one side and facing downtown's Alvarado Street on the other, it's centrally located, allowing guests to enjoy most of Monterey's attractions on foot. The hotel itself features a heated outdoor pool, hot tub, and complete fitness room. The Spa on the Plaza offers massage, facials, and yoga classes. The California Grill restaurant serves breakfast, lunch, and dinner and is noted for its fine salad bar and excellent steak dinners. Some upper-story rooms have great bay vistas, and the large rooftop two- and three-bedroom suites enjoy spectacular views. For nightlife, the DoubleTree has a lobby bar and is also home to Peter B's microbrewery, which serves up many fine local brews as well as delectable light fare. The Monterey Conference Center is adjacent to the hotel.

El Adobe Inn $$
936 Munras Avenue, Monterey
(831) 372-5409
www.el-adobe-inn.com
El Adobe Inn provides clean and comfortable rooms at a reasonable price. The 26 units are nicely decorated, and the service is friendly. A secluded hot tub provides a great place to relax. In-room coffeemakers and refrigerators are available. A complimentary continental breakfast is served in the lobby. Pets are welcome in the smoking rooms only.

Embassy Suites $$$
1441 Canyon Del Rey, Seaside
(831) 393-1115, (800) EMBASSY
www.embassy-suites.com
Located in the neighboring community of Seaside, the 12-story Embassy Suites deserves your consideration when visiting the Monterey Peninsula. Each of the 225 suites has a separate bedroom and living area, including a queen-size sleeper sofa. A refrigerator, microwave, and coffeemaker make quick snacks a snap. The indoor heated swimming pool (kept at a constant 85 degrees), whirlpool, and fitness center provide for relaxation and recreation. All guests receive a complimentary full breakfast each morning and a complete choice of beverages during a two-hour manager's reception each evening. The Pacifica Cafe specializes in steaks, pasta, and seafood, and the Cypress Lounge is a great place to relax at the piano bar and enjoy the 1,000-gallon saltwater aquarium. Friday at happy hour, the Cypress Lounge at Embassy Suites typically presents the best free live jazz and blues in the area.

Hilton Monterey $$$$
1000 Aguajito Road, Monterey
(831) 373-6141, (800) 774-1500
www.monterey.hilton.com
The 204-room Hilton Monterey is becoming a favorite of both business and vacation travelers alike. Amenities include an outdoor pool, an indoor whirlpool spa, his and hers saunas, a fitness room, two tennis courts, a putting green, table tennis, and shuffleboard. The Pacific Grille restaurant serves coastal California cuisine, and all guests can enjoy a private patio and in-room coffeemakers. A few of the larger suites have kitchen facilities.

Hotel Pacific $$$$
300 Pacific Street, Monterey
(831) 373-5700, (800) 232-4141
www.hotelpacific.com
Planning a weekend getaway, California style? Hotel Pacific pays homage to Old Monterey with 105 magnificent adobe-style suites that take you back to an earlier time in the Golden State. Rooms include Spanish-tile floors, fireplaces, impressive wooden furniture, feather beds, vaulted ceilings, wet bars with minifridges, and 500 square feet of space so you can stretch out. Nice touches include Aveda bath products, bathrobes, and in-room CD players. In the two gardens you'll find whirlpool spas, decorative fountains, and bright and colorful plantings. In historic downtown Monterey, Hotel Pacific treats guests to continental breakfast and afternoon refreshments in the salon. Truly an experience to remember, the Hotel Pacific is built for the romantic at heart.

Hyatt Regency Monterey $$$
1 Old Golf Course Road, Monterey
(831) 372-1234, (800) 824-2196
www.hyatt.com
The largest hotel complex in Monterey, the 575-room Hyatt Regency Monterey offers amenities such as two heated outdoor pools, two whirlpool spas, six tennis courts, a fitness club, massage services, a game room, and a hair salon. Plus, it's on the Pebble Beach Company's Del Monte

Golf Course, the oldest 18-hole course west of the Mississippi. Hotel guests enjoy discounted greens fees. Camp Hyatt for Kids provides arts, crafts, and other activities for kids ages three to 15. The Peninsula Restaurant and Cafe Monterey offer a wide choice of entrees for breakfast, lunch, and dinner, while Knuckles Historical Sports Bar features drinks, light fare, and plenty of sports on television in a fun-filled setting. Regency Club members receive complimentary breakfasts and other extras.

Merritt House $$$
386 Pacific Street, Monterey
(831) 646-9686, (800) 541-5599
www.merritthouseinn.com
Want a real taste of Monterey history? Here's your chance to stay in an authentic Monterey adobe (circa 1830), the former home of County Judge Josiah Merritt. The home is divided into three suites, each decorated in 19th-century style. Twenty-two additional units surround the adobe. All suites have fireplaces, and some have private balconies overlooking the historic home and its grand old fig tree and courtyard rose garden. A complimentary sit-down continental breakfast is included in the room package. Merritt House is centrally located near historic downtown Monterey and is along the Monterey Path of History.

Monterey Bay Inn $$$$
242 Cannery Row, Monterey
(831) 373-6242, (800) 424-6242
www.montereybayinn.com
Right on the water at historic Cannery Row, the Monterey Bay Inn offers spectacular views and special amenities for active vacationers. Large sliding glass doors and private balconies take full advantage of this prime bayfront location. Binoculars are provided! A soak in the rooftop whirlpool spa at sunset is a moment to remember. All 47 units feature king-size feather beds and honor bars, and guests can lounge in plush terry cloth robes while listening to their in-room CD player. Some rooms have cozy fireplaces. Spa services are available. Enjoy a continental breakfast brought right

to your room, or feel free to enjoy your pastries, fruit, and coffee on the second-floor outdoor garden patio. Divers will appreciate the handy scuba facilities, including lockers and rinse-off showers, and the inn has an exercise room. The Monterey Bay Inn is a nonsmoking facility.

The Monterey Fireside Lodge $$
1131 10th Street, Monterey
(831) 373-4172, (800) 722-2624
www.montereyfireside.com
This comfortable hotel features gas fireplaces in each of its 21 rooms. It also has an outdoor whirlpool spa. Family units have kitchenettes and refrigerators, and all guests enjoy complimentary continental breakfasts. Near Lake El Estero off Camino Aguajito, this hotel is just off Highway 1. Pets OK.

The Monterey Hotel $$$
406 Alvarado Street, Monterey
(831) 375-3184, (800) 727-0960
www.montereyhotel.com
The pride of Alvarado Street, the Monterey Hotel is a historic Victorian inn that was renovated from top to bottom in 1996. The 1904 building is simply charming, including its two-story atrium, second-floor lobby with carved crown molding and gallery railing, and the original Hammond elevator with gilt-edged molding and bevel leaded glass. The 45 rooms are all exquisitely furnished with reproduction hand-carved furnishings, ceiling fans, and plantation shutters. Master suites have harbor views, fireplaces, and oversized tubs in the marble-floor bathrooms. Guests are treated to a continental breakfast, afternoon tea, and milk and cookies at bedtime. Lovers of historic European-style hotels shouldn't miss this 100 percent nonsmoking facility.

Monterey Marriott Hotel $$$$
350 Calle Principal, Monterey
(831) 649-4234, (800) 228-9290
www.marriott.com/mryca
Dominating the downtown Monterey skyline, the 363-room Monterey Marriott is a modern luxury hotel with all the amenities.

Overlooking the Monterey Harbor, it's close to Fisherman's Wharf and adjacent to the Conference Center, making the Marriott popular among both the vacation and business set. A heated outdoor pool, day spa, and 24-hour health club provide ample opportunity for relaxation and recreation. The Three Flags Cafe prepares buffet breakfast and lunch, while Characters Sports Bar and Grill dishes up all-American food and drinks as well as plenty of sports programming and memorabilia for the avid fan.

Monterey Plaza Hotel & Spa $$$$
400 Cannery Row, Monterey
(831) 646-1700, (800) 368-2468
www.montereyplazahotel.com

If you're looking for luxury on Cannery Row, the Monterey Plaza Hotel has it. Built right on the edge of Monterey Bay, the hotel affords spectacular views from the bayside rooms. Lobbies are replete with Italian marble and rich Brazilian teakwood. Luxury penthouse suites have bayfront balconies and are exquisitely appointed with Biedermeier-style armoires and writing desks. Plush terry cloth robes invite visitors to lounge to their hearts' content. A European-style health spa and fitness room provide a place to work off those extra ounces you may have put on at the Duck Club Restaurant or Schooners Bistro on the Bay. The Monterey Plaza Hotel is a good choice for an anniversary or other special occasion.

Padre Oaks Motel $
1278 Munras Avenue, Monterey
(831) 373-3741, (888) 900-6257

Here's one of the best bets for motel fans who like quaint, well-maintained, and modestly priced properties. This small 19-room motel is pleasantly decorated and landscaped and provides a heated outdoor pool. A continental breakfast and in-room coffee are included. Some rooms have private decks.

Sand Dollar Inn $$
755 Abrego Street, Monterey
(831) 372-7551, (800) 982-1986
www.sanddollarinn.com

A good value, the Sand Dollar Inn is a modern 63-unit motel complex near the historic district of downtown Monterey. Amenities include a large heated pool and outdoor spa, guest laundry facilities, continental breakfast, and in-room coffeemakers and minifridges. Deluxe rooms have fireplaces, wet bars, and private balconies or patios. A two-bedroom family suite is also available. The Sand Dollar Inn is located just off the Monterey Path of History, and it's a great walk down to Fisherman's Wharf and Cannery Row (see Attractions chapter).

Spindrift Inn $$$$
652 Cannery Row, Monterey
(831) 646-8900, (800) 841-1879
www.spindriftinn.com

A favorite among honeymooners, Spindrift Inn combines life in the heart of Cannery Row with luxurious accommodations. The 42 rooms in this classic small hotel include antique decor, hardwood floors with Oriental rugs, half-canopied goose-down feather beds with down comforters and pillows, marble baths, hand-tiled floors, wood-burning fireplaces, honor bars, and window seats or balconies. Imagine: all of these creature comforts available in a European-style hotel that's right on the beach of Cannery Row, with breathtaking bay views in many rooms. Complimentary continental breakfast is brought to your room on a silver tray. Afternoon tea includes pastries, wine, and cheese. Enjoy the rooftop garden and private beach as well as turndown service each night. The Spindrift Inn is a truly memorable place for those who want a real taste of the romantic side of Monterey.

[Facing page] *If you're looking for a historic hotel smack dab in the middle of downtown Monterey, it's hard to beat the Monterey Hotel.* TOM OWENS

Travelodge, Monterey Downtown $$
675 Munras Avenue, Monterey
(831) 373-1876, (800) 578-7878
www.montereytravelodge.com
You'll find no surprises here. You get every-
thing you've come to expect in a Trav-
elodge motel, including a clean room, a
comfortable bed, and an outdoor pool. The
special feature here is location—51 rooms
right downtown in historic Monterey, within
walking distance of most major attractions.

Victorian Inn $$$
487 Foam Street, Monterey
(831) 373-8000, (800) 232-4141
www.victorianinn.com
A short block from Cannery Row, the Victorian Inn offers 68 well-appointed rooms.
Each room has a marble fireplace, honor
bar, and either a private patio, balcony, or
window seat. Deluxe suites feature bay
views, feather beds, jetted tubs, CD players, and microwave ovens. Family suites
have kitchenettes and dining nooks. All
guests can enjoy the garden courtyard
hot tub. Continental breakfast and afternoon wine and cheese are served in the
parlor of the 1907 Victorian home that
serves as the lobby and office. Pets OK.

Way Station Monterey $$
1200 Olmstead Road, Monterey
(831) 372-2945, (800) 858-0822
www.waystationmonterey.com
The affordable Way Station Monterey is near
the Monterey Airport off Highway 68. That
makes it convenient for air travelers as well
as those attending events out at Laguna
Seca Raceway. About five minutes from
downtown Monterey, the Way Station has 46
rooms including luxury suites with fireplaces,
wet bars, and refrigerators. Most rooms have
private decks overlooking a parklike setting.
Continental breakfasts are provided.

Services such as Monterey Peninsula
Reservations, (888) 655-3424, can
assist you in finding just the right
accommodations for your needs.

Pacific Grove

Is your trip to the Monterey Peninsula one
of those I-just-want-to-get-away-from-it-
all-and-relax kinds of vacations? Then
consider Pacific Grove for your accommo-
dations. The rates for a simple room are
equivalent to those of the motels on the
major thoroughfares of Fremont and
Munras in Monterey, but the locale is
much more peaceful. Spend a bit more
and you'll have your choice of beachfront
motels, forest cottages, historic hotels,
and stately Victorian mansions (see our
Bed-and-Breakfast Inns chapter). A few of
the accommodations are in and around
downtown Pacific Grove, but the great
majority are farther north out the Penin-
sula toward Point Pinos. Most of the
motels down Lighthouse Avenue are tra-
ditional family-style establishments. Those
out Asilomar Boulevard are more cottage-
like and situated beneath tall Monterey
pines. All are in easy walking distance of
the spectacular Pacific Grove coastline,
and all are (fellow visitors permitting)
quiet, quiet, quiet. Be prepared for cool,
maybe foggy weather out here on the
point—just the ideal climate for a brisk,
bundled-up walk along the sand dunes
and rugged coast.

Andril Fireplace Cottages $$
569 Asilomar Boulevard, Pacific Grove
(831) 375-0994
www.andrilcottages.com
For a week in a woodland cottage by the
seaside, think Andril Fireplace Cottages.
You'll find 16 separate cottages set under
tall pines in a quiet corner of P.G. Each
unit has a full kitchen and wood-burning
fireplaces. For larger groups, the Ranch
House has five bedrooms, while Casa
Linda has four. Barbecues and table tennis
add to the fun. From June through September, Andril's has a standard five-night
minimum stay. (But Insiders know that,
depending on how reservations book up,
you might be able to squeeze your way in
for just a couple of nights.) Daily rentals

are available in the off-season. Enjoy amenities such as VCRs with free tape rentals. Pets OK.

Anton Inn $$$
1095 Lighthouse Avenue, Pacific Grove
(831) 373–4429, (888) 242–6866
www.antoninn.com

A longtime favorite of Pacific Grove visitors, the Anton Inn (formerly the Feather Bed Inn) recently enjoyed a refreshing face-lift. Window treatments, Italian-tile floors, paint, and artwork have livened up the place, but it still provides an affordable and homey stay. The 12 nonsmoking units present a variety of accommodation choices, including suites with formal bedrooms and rooms with kitchenettes, fireplaces, Jacuzzi tubs, and outdoor verandas or patios. Continental breakfast is provided in the lobby, and it's a short walk to the beach or the Monarch Grove Sanctuary (see our Attractions chapter).

Asilomar State Beach and Conference Grounds $$
800 Asilomar Boulevard, Pacific Grove
(831) 372–8016
www.visitasilomar.com

The Asilomar Conference Grounds, on 105 beautiful acres of pine forests and rolling sand dunes on the northern end of the Monterey Peninsula, is part of the California State Park system. The original buildings were designed by noted California architect Julia Morgan and opened in 1913, providing a spectacular yet rustic setting ever since for the many conferences that are held here year-round. For vacationers, the Asilomar Conference Center provides very affordable accommodations on a space-available basis. The staff recommends calling no more than 90 days in advance of your planned date of arrival to check on room availability. Guests are treated to a complimentary full breakfast and can also have lunch and dinner in Crocker Dining Hall for an additional charge. (Listen for the meal bell, which is rung on the meal hour.) Several of the rooms have fireplaces, some have private

decks, and a few have kitchenettes. Cottages sleep up to seven. The 313 rooms don't have televisions or phones, but there are plenty of pay phones throughout the grounds. You can take advantage of recreational facilities, such as a heated outdoor pool, Ping-Pong, pool tables, and volleyball courts as well as partake in evening barbecues and bonfires. A winding boardwalk provides a direct path to the beach through rolling dunes. Asilomar Conference Center is a nonsmoking facility.

Beachcomber Inn $$
1996 Sunset Drive, Pacific Grove
(831) 373–4769, (800) 634–4769

Location, location, location: The Beachcomber Inn has it. There is nothing special about the accommodations themselves, but look out back from one of the private patios, and you're sitting right on the edge of Spanish Bay and Asilomar Beach. The 26-room motel is a nonsmoking establishment with an outdoor heated pool and sundeck protected from the wind by a glass enclosure. Complimentary bicycles are available for exploring the Asilomar area. Speaking of location, right next door is the highly acclaimed Fishwife seafood restaurant, a locals' favorite for lunch or dinner. If your idea of an ideal weekend is surfing the wild Pacific or combing the Pacific Grove beaches, the Beachcomber Inn isn't a bad choice for a clean and comfortable bed.

Bide-A-Wee Motel and Cottages $$
221 Asilomar Boulevard, Pacific Grove
(831) 372–2330
www.bestlodging.com

If you're looking for a quiet and quaint motel setting, consider the Bide-A-Wee. Located near Point Pinos and a quick stroll from the beach, this 11-unit and nine-cottage charmer is no-frills but provides a great hideaway. You'll enjoy a continental breakfast and in-room coffeemakers. Most of the cottages have kitchens and living rooms; one has a fireplace. Pets OK. And how could you not like the name?

Borg's Ocean Front Motel $$
635 Ocean View Boulevard, Pacific Grove
(831) 375-2406

Owned by the Borg family for more than 50 years, this motel right on the waterfront has some of the best oceanview rooms on the Peninsula, many with great balconies for taking in Lovers Point and the Bay beyond. Borg's has 60 rooms and four feature kitchenettes. No in-room coffee- makers are available, but you can get hot beverages in the lobby. There's nothing fancy about the accommodations, but the rooms with a view (be sure to ask for one) are a great place from which to enjoy the beauty of the Bay.

Butterfly Grove Inn $$$
1073 Lighthouse Avenue, Pacific Grove
(831) 373-4921, (800) 337-9244
www.bflyinn.qpg.com

For a true feel of Pacific Grove, consider a stay at the Butterfly Grove Inn during the Butterfly Parade weekend in October (see our Annual Events chapter). The 28 one- and two-bedroom units (including family units in a large Victorian home) are right next door to the Monarch Grove Sanctuary (see our Attractions chapter). That makes it a good spot for both summer and winter visits. You'll find a heated outdoor pool, hydrojet spa, shuffleboard, croquet, volleyball, continental breakfast, and an in-room refrigerator and coffeemaker. A few units have kitchenettes with microwaves and fireplaces. Upstairs rooms offer peeks at the ocean. Divers will appreciate the outdoor wash lines. Pets OK.

Lighthouse Lodge & Suites $$$
1150 and 1249 Lighthouse Avenue, Pacific Grove
(831) 655-2111, (800) 858-1249
www.lhls.com

On both sides of the northern end of Lighthouse Avenue, the Lighthouse Lodge and Suites are actually two separate facilities. The Lodge is a comfy motel with 68 units. Guests can enjoy a heated outdoor pool, whirlpool spa, and sauna. A deluxe continental breakfast is served, and summer poolside barbecues are held for guests when weather permits. Some rooms have fireplaces, and pets are welcome. The 31-unit Lighthouse Suites across the street provide Cape Cod–style luxury accommodations that include king-size beds, down pillows, fireplaces, whirlpool tubs, terry robes, honor bars, and kitchenettes. For the ultimate in a group vacation, the Executive Residence sleeps six adults and has three bathrooms, three marble fireplaces, a gourmet kitchen, laundry facilities, a fully fenced backyard, and a rooftop deck. All guests at the Lodge enjoy a full chef-prepared breakfast and an evening hospitality reception of wine and hors d'oeuvres.

Pacific Gardens Inn $$$
701 Asilomar Boulevard, Pacific Grove
(831) 646-9414, (800) 262-1566
www.pacificgardensinn.com

Situated across from the Asilomar Conference Center, the Pacific Gardens Inn offers 28 rooms under a canopy of pines. Guests can enjoy two outdoor hot tubs, a buffet continental breakfast, wood-burning fireplaces, and complete kitchens with refrigerators and popcorn makers (nice touch!). A two-bedroom cottage with living room and deck is available. Wine and cheese are served in the evening.

Rosedale Inn $$$
775 Asilomar Boulevard, Pacific Grove
(831) 655-1000, (800) 822-5606
www.rosedaleinn.com

A great place to unwind, the Rosedale Inn features in-room Jacuzzi tubs, wet bars, fireplaces, fridges, sinks, coffeemakers, microwaves, VCRs, and cathedral ceilings with fans in the 19 units. Complimentary extended continental breakfasts are served each morning. Sofa beds and pri-

Planning to visit the Peninsula during the off-season? Always ask about special vacation packages. They can save you big bucks!

vate patios on some suites add to the pleasure. If you're looking for nothing more rigorous than a walk on the beach, this is a nice choice for some serious R and R. An added feature is the Rosedale Inn's own gallery which features hand-thrown pottery and Tibetan wool rugs.

Sea Breeze Inn and Cottages   **$$**
1101 Lighthouse Avenue, Pacific Grove
(831) 372-7771, (800) 525-3373
The Sea Breeze Inn and Cottages offers affordable and comfortable lodgings. It's conveniently located close to the Monarch Grove Sanctuary (see our Attractions chapter), the beach and tide pools, Point Pinos Lighthouse, and downtown Pacific Grove. There are 67 rooms including private cottages, as well as an outdoor pool and Jacuzzi. A simple complimentary continental breakfast is served. The Sea Breeze Inn and Cottages is nothing fancy, but for an inexpensive family stay in one of the most beautiful parts of the Peninsula, it's just right.

Sunset Inn   **$$**
133 Asilomar Boulevard, Pacific Grove
(831) 375-3936, (800) 525-3373
www.montereyinns.com
Built in 1939, the Sunset Inn has a long history of providing a quaint and quiet place to stay near Point Pinos. A half-million dollar renovation brought this charming 20-unit motel back to its former glory. Each room has a cozy fireplace, some wood-burning, some gas. The remodeled interiors with high ceilings provide a classic atmosphere. Some rooms have in-room two-person spas, and all have refrigerators. An outdoor spa and continental breakfast add to the enjoyment. If you've enjoyed your stay here in the past, you won't believe the love and attention given to this Pacific Grove landmark.

The Wilkie's Inn   **$**
1038 Lighthouse Avenue, Pacific Grove
(831) 372-5960, (866) 372-5960
www.wilkiesinn.com
Another moderately priced family motel in Pacific Grove, The Wilkie's has 24 units,

with peeks of the ocean from some upstairs rooms. There's a complimentary continental breakfast and in-room coffee. Two units have full kitchens. Be sure to visit The Butterfly Shop, which sells just about anything you can think of that's about or in the shape of a Monarch butterfly. Proceeds support the Friends of the Monarch, a local environmental group. The motel is a short stroll from the Monarch Grove Sanctuary.

Carmel

How do you spell romance? Around these parts, it's C-A-R-M-E-L. And that's especially true when you're talking about accommodations. While families of four or five are likely to find Monterey to their liking, parties of two owe it to themselves to give Carmel an extra-close look. Known for its quaint inns, charming cottages, and splendid hotels, Carmel boasts some of the most unique and memorable accommodations you'll find anywhere. Prices won't be cheap, yet some are surprisingly reasonable during the off-season. Here's a sample representation of what you'll find in the village of Carmel.

Candle Light Inn   **$$$$**
San Carlos Street and Fifth Avenue, Carmel
(831) 624-6451, (800) 433-4732
www.innsbythesea.com
This 20-unit Tudor-style inn provides a nice heated outdoor pool, picnic-basket breakfast with a newspaper, and in-room coffee. Some rooms provide wood-burning fireplaces, whirlpool spas, and kitchenettes. All rooms have refrigerators and loveseat-size sofa hideaway beds. Friendly, attentive service is a hallmark of the Candle Light Inn.

Carmel Country Inn   **$$$**
Dolores Street and Third Avenue, Carmel
(831) 625-3263, (800) 215-6343
www.carmelcountryinn.com
This small 12-room, nonsmoking inn is a real

country-style charmer with many modern amenities. All but one of the one- and two-bedroom suites have a fireplace, and some provide private decks. Kitchenettes with refrigerators and tables are also available. A generous continental breakfast and afternoon sherry are served, and off-street parking is provided. Pets OK.

Carmel Mission Inn $$$
3665 Rio Road, Carmel
(831) 624-1841, (800) 348-9090
www.carmelmissioninn.com

This 165-room hotel near the mouth of Carmel Valley has some of the least expensive weekday rooms in town as well as some large specialty suites. An outdoor heated pool and two spas are relaxing spots to enjoy the sunshine, while the Villa Carmel Restaurant and Beethoven's Bar & Grill provide fun places to recall your day's adventure. In-room coffeemakers and private decks are among the amenities. Although outside of downtown Carmel, the Carmel Mission Inn is conveniently located near the Barnyard and Crossroads shopping centers. Pets OK.

Carmel Oaks Inn $$$$
Mission Street and Fifth Avenue, Carmel
(831) 624-5547, (800) 266-5547
www.carmeloaksinn.com

This California-country-style inn prides itself in providing the little extras that make a visit to Carmel something special. Start the day with an in-room picnic-basket breakfast you can enjoy on your private deck. Later, sample the homemade candies that are a Carmel Oaks specialty. Wine in the evening tops your splendid day. This is an all nonsmoking, 17-room establishment that provides in-room refrigerators. One room has a kitchenette. There's plenty of off-street parking to make your stay in Carmel hassle-free.

Carriage House Inn $$$$
Junipero Street and Eighth Avenue, Carmel
(831) 625-2585, (800) 433-4732
www.innsbythesea.com

The Carriage House Inn is well known as a favorite honeymoon spot in Carmel. Secluded and quiet, it's a great spot to cuddle under a down comforter in front of a wood fire and enjoy a late-morning, made-to-order continental breakfast that's delivered right to your door. Among the 13 rooms, special suites include whirlpool spas and baths. Walk a couple of short blocks down Junipero, and you're at the trendy Carmel Plaza shopping center. In the evening enjoy wine and hors d'oeuvres in the library. Three is definitely a crowd at the Carriage House Inn.

Casa de Carmel Inn $$$
Monte Verde Street and Ocean Avenue, Carmel
(831) 624-7738, (800) 262-1262
www.casadecarmel.com

This cute two-story inn has only seven guest rooms, making for an intimate setting. It's a quiet and comfortable place without a lot of extras, but fresh-cut flowers are always on hand to brighten up your day. A continental breakfast and off-street parking are provided. This is a nonsmoking inn.

Coachman's Inn $$$
San Carlos Street and Seventh Avenue, Carmel
(831) 624-6421, (800) 336-6421
www.coachmansinn.com

With a European decor of Old World timber and stucco, the Coachman's Inn provides a quiet stay in downtown Carmel. The 30 rooms include queen, king, and family units, some with kitchens, whirlpool tubs, and wet bars, and a few with fireplaces. Complimentary continental breakfast is provided each morning, and coffee, tea, and hot chocolate are available to guests throughout the day. Evening sherry is also on the house. Enjoy the outdoor patio with hot tub and dry sauna. All rooms have in-room coffeemakers. Off-street parking is provided.

Cypress Inn $$$$
**Lincoln Street and Seventh Avenue,
Carmel**
(831) 624-3871, (800) 443-7443
www.cypress-inn.com
A Carmel landmark since 1929, this fabulous
Moorish Mediterranean-style hotel with a
Spanish-tile roof offers the best in elegant
comfort. Walk in the ornate entrance to find
a spacious living room lobby with a large
fireplace. Down the hall is the Library Bar, a
cozy cocktail lounge that is a popular
happy hour spot with Insiders. The 33
rooms themselves are one of a kind. Some
have fireplaces, whirlpool tubs, private
verandas, intimate sitting rooms, and stylish
wet bars. Guests can enjoy afternoon tea
and hors d'oeuvres in the lounge. Co-owner
and animal lover Doris Day probably has
something to do with the fact that this
small luxury hotel accepts up to two pets
per room, and pet-sitting service is available. Continental breakfast is served in a
sunny breakfast room and secluded courtyard garden. *Note:* Cypress Inn underwent a
major expansion to add 10 deluxe rooms
and a full workout facility. At the time of this
writing, the estimated completion date was
June 2004.

Dolphin Inn $$$
**San Carlos Street and Fourth Avenue,
Carmel**
(831) 624-5356, (800) 433-4732
www.ibts-dolphininn.com
Accommodations at the Dolphin Inn are
friendly and comfortable with pleasant
touches such as fresh flowers, a picnic-
basket continental breakfast brought to
your door, in-room coffee and refrigera-
tors, and a nice heated outdoor pool.
Many rooms have gas fireplaces; specialty
rooms include the two-bedroom, two-
bath family suite and the deluxe suite with
living room, whirlpool tub, and fireplace.

Highlands Inn $$$$
120 Highland Drive, Carmel
(831) 620-1234, (800) 682-4811
www.highlands-inn.com
South of Carmel, about 15 minutes down
Highway 1, lies the Highlands Inn, a Park
Hyatt Hotel. At the gateway to Big Sur,
this spectacular 142-room inn is world
famous for its California coastline views,
its superb restaurants, and its hosting of
the Masters of Food and Wine festival
each spring. The inn features one- and
two-bedroom suites as well as 37 guest
rooms with unsurpassed coastal views. A
heated outdoor pool, three outdoor spas,
and two great restaurants provide more
reasons to not set foot off the property.
Most suites have wood-burning fireplaces;
some have view decks, double spa baths,
and fully equipped kitchens. Expect to
find terry bathrobes and binoculars in
your room. Special amenities such as
massages and complimentary bicycles are
also provided. The elegant Pacific's Edge
restaurant offers a 180-degree panoramic
view, great food, and a 28,000-bottle
wine cellar that was one of fewer than 100
to win *Wine Spectator* magazine's Grand
Award (see our Restaurants chapter). The
more casual California Market offers a
variety of fares for breakfast, lunch, or
dinner, enjoyable from inside the restau-
rant or outside on the breathtaking cliff-
side deck. The Sunset & Lobos Lounge
provides a spectacular afternoon and
evening view over Point Lobos State
Reserve while you sip your favorite bever-
age and listen to a live jazz trio. Pets OK.

Hofsas House $$
San Carlos and Fourth Avenue, Carmel
(831) 624-2745, (800) 221-2548
www.hofsashouse.com
You might think you're spending a summer in the Bavarian Alps, perched on a
hillside overlooking a green forest. But
that's the Pacific Ocean beyond and
you're at Hofsas House, the big pink
Carmel landmark near Carmel Woods.
Each of the 38 rooms is unique, including
the popular Bridal Suite and King Cottage.
Some have wood-burning fireplaces, sun-
decks, and/or kitchenettes; most have
ocean views. Continental breakfast is
served in the lounge, and deluxe rooms
have coffeemakers. Guests can enjoy the

heated outdoor pool and dry saunas. Pets OK in a few rooms.

Horizon Inn and Ocean View Lodge $$$
Junipero Street and Third Avenue, Carmel
(831) 624-5327, (800) 350-7723
www.horizoninncarmel.com

These two properties, across Junipero Street from each other, provide a choice of accommodations. The Horizon Inn has 21 smartly redecorated rooms, most with gas fireplaces and some with kitchenettes and in-room whirlpool baths. The more expensive Ocean View Lodge offers six minisuites with separate living rooms, wood-burning fireplaces, and some private balconies with nice ocean views. Rooms at Ocean View Lodge have either a full-size Jacuzzi tub or a fully equipped kitchen. Each establishment offers access to a heated outdoor pool, a picnic-basket continental breakfast delivered to your room, and in-room coffeemakers.

Lamp Lighter Inn $$$
Ocean Avenue and Camino Real Street, Carmel
(831) 624-7372 $225 · 3

Hansel and Gretel could live here. With the official title of "The most photographed inn in Carmel," The Lamp Lighter Inn consists of five turn-of-the-century baby-blue cottages set in a fairy-tale garden, complete with elves. All cottages are nonsmoking and have private baths, Dutch doors, and quilts on the beds. A kitchen and fireplace are available in the renovated Hansel & Gretel Cottage. The Lamp Lighter has performed the commendable task of developing an inn that can please both honeymooners and families with small children. While lovers snuggle in the cozy Treetop House, kids will be fascinated by the special kid's bedroom in the Bluebird Cottage. Pets OK. In-room coffee is provided.

La Playa Hotel $$$$
Eighth Avenue and Camino Real, Carmel
(831) 624-6476, (800) 582-8900
www.laplayahotel.com

Originally a private Carmel mansion built for a member of San Francisco's famous Ghirardelli chocolate family, La Playa Hotel is a true classic. Noted Norwegian-born painter Christopher Jorgensen, who was inspired by the stone and heavy beam of the nearby Carmel Mission, designed the original home in 1902. Much of the mansion has been expertly preserved as part of the current 80-room La Playa (a charter member of the Historic Hotels of America). In 1983 the Cope family of San Francisco (owners of the city's prestigious Huntington Hotel) purchased and fully refurbished La Playa and its large award-winning garden with a wrought-iron gazebo to create a magical atmosphere. You'll find a few rooms with fireplaces, others with great ocean views. A heated outdoor pool provides recreation and relaxation, and a menu of on-site spa treatments is available. The popular Terrace Grill restaurant serves up excellent California cuisine for breakfast, lunch, dinner, and Sunday brunch, either indoors or alfresco on the heated open-air terrace. La Playa also offers five storybook cottages with full kitchens, wood-burning fireplaces, private patios, and extras such as wet bars and stereo systems.

Mission Ranch Lodging $$
26270 Dolores Street, Carmel
(831) 624-6436, (800) 538-8221

A truly unique experience at a very reasonable price, the Mission Ranch is unlike any other lodge in Carmel. Built on ranchlands behind the Carmel Mission, it consists of 11 buildings ranging from the rustic to the sublime, with 31 guest rooms available. The grounds include an 1850s farmhouse and enchanting fields of grazing sheep, with wetlands, Carmel Bay, and Point Lobos as the backdrop. Complimentary continental breakfast and in-room coffee are provided in this fully nonsmoking facility. Most rooms have fireplaces, and the higher-end ones feature carved-wood beds with handmade quilts, whirlpool tubs, and breathtaking views from your private deck. The Mission

The pastoral splendor of Mission Ranch in Carmel makes it a great choice for a romantic weekend. TOM OWENS

Ranch restaurant, an Insiders' favorite, serves up delectable California cuisine. Six championship tennis courts and a workout room are available. Did we forget to mention that Clint Eastwood is the proprietor? If you're really lucky, you might even find Clint tickling the ivories one evening in the Mission Ranch piano bar within the restaurant. Make your reservations well in advance for this very popular spot.

Normandy Inn $$$$
Ocean Avenue and Monte Verde Street, Carmel
(831) 624-3825,
(800) 343-3825 (Calif. only)
www.normandyinncarmel.com
Looking for an Old European-type inn in the center of downtown Carmel? The Normandy Inn is a charming 45-room hotel and three cottages suites, each with three bedrooms and two baths. All feature French-country decor and cozy feather beds; some have fireplaces. On Ocean Avenue only blocks from the beach, this nonsmoking establishment has beautifully landscaped gardens. Guests can enjoy a heated outdoor pool, continental breakfast, in-room coffee, and afternoon sherry.

Pine Inn $$$
Ocean Avenue and Monte Verde Street, Carmel
(831) 624-3851, (800) 228-3851
www.pine-inn.com
Built in 1889, the Pine Inn was the first Carmel inn. Originally a few blocks away, it was moved to its current location in 1903. Enter the plush red and dark wood interior, and you're immediately hit with the inn's warm, sophisticated elegance. The decor reflects that of a world traveler, with European and Far East influences coming together most effectively. With 49 nonsmoking rooms, the Pine Inn has everything from simplicity to opulence, with amenities such as whirlpool tubs, fireplaces, and private entrances. For dinner, enjoy Il Fornaio, a cozy Italian restaurant on the premises.

Quail Lodge Resort & Golf Club $$$$
8205 Valley Greens Drive, Carmel
(831) 624-2888, (888) 828-8787
www.quaillodge.com

Recently reopened after a $25 million reno-
vation, Quail Lodge is the ultimate in rustic,
upscale elegance. The Lodge is situated on
850 acres within usually sunny Carmel Valley. Beautifully landscaped grounds, tranquil
lakes, rolling hills, and an 18-hole championship golf course provide the setting for
the 100 luxurious guest rooms. You'll enjoy
four tennis courts, two outdoor heated
pools, a soothing redwood hot tub, miles of
jogging and hiking trails, and a complete
workout facility. There's refined dining with
European and Mediterranean cuisine at the
award-winning Covey at Quail Lodge
restaurant (see our Restaurants chapter)
and enjoyable breakfast and lunch at the
casual Country Club dining room. All guest
rooms are stylishly furnished and feature
private decks or patios, fresh fruit baskets,
and in-room coffee as well as plush terry
cloth bathrobes. Most have minifridges, and
some have fireplaces. Twelve cottages are
available with up to five rooms each, and
the Executive Villa offers the ultimate in privacy and luxury. Guests enjoy a favorable
rate when playing at the Golf Club at Quail
Lodge. One pet per room is allowed, and
pet-sitting services are available. Quail
Lodge is truly a five-star experience.

Sandpiper Inn $$$
2408 Bay View Avenue, Carmel
(831) 624-6433, (800) 633-6433
www.sandpiper-inn.com

Fewer than 100 yards from the white
sands of Carmel Beach, the Sandpiper Inn
is an excellent choice for those who want
to get away from it all and enjoy the
sights and sounds of the open sea. This
romantic 1929 California-style country inn
has 17 rooms, several with ocean views
and some with fireplaces. But you'll find
neither in-room televisions nor in-room
phones. (Sounds pretty good, doesn't it?)
A fine continental breakfast is served, and
you can enjoy a good book all snug in the
library nook or in front of the Carmel
stone fireplace in the lounge. Award-
winning gardens provide the perfect
surroundings for a most restful stay.

Sundial Lodge $$$
Monte Verde Street and Seventh Avenue,
Carmel
(831) 624-8578
www.sundiallodge.com

Here's a great European-style inn right in
the heart of downtown Carmel. The 19 nonsmoking rooms surround a beautiful brick
courtyard full of brightly colored plants. The
rooms are tastefully furnished in wicker,
English Victorian, or French Country, and
the private baths have plenty of brass and
marble. All rooms include a refrigerator, and
some have kitchenettes. Guests enjoy a
deluxe continental breakfast, afternoon
sherry or port, and evening tea and cookies.

Svengaard's Inn $$$
San Carlos Street and Fourth Avenue,
Carmel
(831) 624-1511, (800) 433-4732
www.innsbythesea.com

Country decor and a beautiful garden setting are the hallmarks of the 35-room
Svengaard's Inn. You can enjoy the heated
kidney-shaped pool and quiet garden
courtyard. In-room continental breakfast
and morning paper arrive daily. Many
rooms have fireplaces, kitchenettes, and
Jacuzzi tubs.

Tally Ho Inn $$$
Monte Verde Street and Ocean Avenue,
Carmel
(831) 624-2232, (800) 652-2632
www.tallyho-inn.com

Across Monte Verde Street from the Pine
Inn is the Tally Ho Inn, run by the same
owners. Here in the former residence of cartoonist Jimmy Hatlo (creator of Little
Iodine), you'll find 12 lovely rooms and
patios with an English-countryside atmosphere. Most rooms have fireplaces and private decks, some have marble tubs,

whirlpool spas, and ocean views. An expanded continental breakfast is served, and room service is available from Il Fornaio, the Italian restaurant across the street at Pine Inn.

Tickle Pink Inn $$$$
155 Highland Drive, Carmel
(831) 624-1244, (800) 635-4774
www.ticklepink.com

South of Carmel approximately 10 minutes down Highway 1 is the legendary Tickle Pink Inn. Long a favorite spot for honeymooners and the romantic at heart, the inn is on the hills of Carmel Highlands and has some of the most breathtaking views of the California central coast you'll ever find. The 35 rooms include 12 suites, all of which have fireplaces and private decks. A few units have full kitchens. The secluded Senator's Cottage (the site of the former home of state senator Edward Tickle) features two bedrooms, a kitchenette, and private patio. A continental breakfast and in-room coffee are provided in all rooms, and an outdoor hot tub is sure to please any pair of lovebirds. An evening wine and cheese reception in the Terrace Lounge or on the outdoor Cliffside Deck provides the opportunity to get acquainted with your fellow guests.

The Village Inn $$$
Ocean Avenue and Junipero Street, Carmel
(831) 624-3864, (800) 346-3864
www.carmelvillageinn.com

The Village Inn offers 48 rooms right on Ocean Avenue at the entrance to downtown Carmel. Lovely landscaped gardens and the post-adobe construction create a warm atmosphere. Complimentary continental breakfast and in-room coffee are provided. Five suites feature fireplaces, living rooms, and full kitchens. There is plenty of off-street parking. If you enjoy being at the head of the action, The Village Inn is for you.

For more lodging options, check out www.monterey.com, www.gomonterey.com, or www.monterey2000.com

Wayside Inn $$$
Mission Street and Seventh Avenue, Carmel
(831) 624-5336, (800) 433-4732
www.innsbythesea.com

One of the better spots for families in Carmel, the 22-unit Wayside Inn offers suites with full kitchens and extra bedrooms or queen-size sofa hideaway beds. Pets are welcome at no extra charge, although it's preferred that you not leave them alone in the room. On a quiet corner of Carmel, the Wayside Inn is a cozy place with lots of wood-burning fireplaces and a few private balconies and patios. There's no pool on the grounds, but guests can use an outdoor pool at one of the other sister properties in Carmel owned by Inns By The Sea. A complimentary picnic-basket breakfast is provided.

Pebble Beach

For many an avid golfer, a stay at one of the Pebble Beach resorts is a lifelong dream. And since you may only live once, we suggest that you golfers live out your dream. Sure, it's expensive. But how can you put a price on walking up to the 18th green at Pebble Beach Golf Links? Even when you're not out on the course, the ambience of these world-class resorts is a memorable experience. Here's a quick snapshot of what you can expect.

Casa Palmero $$$$
1518 Cypress Drive, Pebble Beach
(831) 647-7500, (800) 654-9300

The newest of the Pebble Beach resorts, Casa Palmero is a luxurious 24-room estate overlooking the first and second fairways of the Pebble Beach Golf Links. It's the feel of a private old-world estate with an emphasis on personal service. Casa Palmero features well-appointed estate rooms and studios, spa rooms and courtyard suites with private patios and whirlpools, and the opulent Palmero Suite, replete with living room, fireplace, wet bar, guest powder room, oversize bath, four-poster bed, sitting area, outdoor courtyard, and whirlpool spa. Complimentary continental breakfast and an evening cocktail and hors d'oeuvres reception are included, and you're a spectacular stroll away from the world-class restaurants at the Lodge at Pebble Beach. Access to the Beach and Tennis Club and other Pebble Beach amenities are also available. It's one of the most expensive choices you have for a stay on the Monterey Peninsula, but for that very special occasion, Casa Palmero is hard to beat.

The Inn at Spanish Bay $$$$
2700 17-Mile Drive, Pebble Beach
(831) 647-7500, (800) 654-9300
www.pebblebeach.com
Overlooking the 18-hole Links at Spanish Bay and the Pacific Ocean beyond, The Inn at Spanish Bay is a splendid Old Monterey and Spanish California-style resort. Of its 270 guest rooms, 145 enjoy ocean views, while the rest overlook the Del Monte Forest. Each room has two queen- or one king-size bed, a living room, fireplace, dressing area, private deck or patio, and a large bathroom with Italian marble and brass decor. Sixteen special suites provide additional luxurious amenities.

Guests receive special rates for the inn's linksland golf course and any of the other Pebble Beach Company golf courses. You can also take advantage of the Spanish Bay Club with heated outdoor pool, spas, steam rooms, and a complete fitness center. The Tennis Pavilion has eight outdoor tennis courts, one stadium court designed for tournaments, a pro shop, lockers, and expert instruction. There are also excellent walking and jogging trails along the boardwalk and sandy beaches. Plus, don't forget to indulge at the Spa at Pebble Beach, a complete health resort near The Lodge and available to guests at Spanish Bay.

For full meals or quick snacks, Spanish Bay provides some excellent choices. Roy's at Pebble Beach presents great breakfasts, lunches, and "Euro-Asian" dinners from the menu of world-famous chef Roy Yamaguchi (see our Restaurants chapter). Peppoli at Pebble Beach provides an intimate and elegant atmosphere for Northern Italian cuisine. Sticks is a sports memorabilia club that's popular among golfers looking for a hearty breakfast or lunch. Traps, an 80-seat lounge, is perfect for catching your favorite sporting event on TV or for an evening scotch. The Lobby Lounge serves refreshments and cocktails around a wood-burning fireplace, with live entertainment Thursday through Saturday. Retail shopping includes Breezes for fashion and the Ansel Adams Gallery for fine art.

The Inn at Spanish Bay has been honored with many awards, including the title of "Number One Mainland Resort," bestowed by *Condé Nast Traveler* Readers Choice Awards, and "Best North American Hotel," from *Travel & Leisure* magazine. The Inn at Spanish Bay is a stay to remember, with golf, fine dining, opulent accommodations, and a lone kilted Scotsman who serenades the sunset each evening with his bagpipe.

The Lodge at Pebble Beach $$$$
17-Mile Drive, Pebble Beach
(831) 624-3811, (800) 654-9300
www.pebblebeach.com
For golfers, it just doesn't get any better. Overlooking the Links at Pebble Beach with Carmel Bay and Point Lobos as your backdrop, The Lodge at Pebble Beach is a world-class experience. The 155 luxury rooms, five spa rooms, and one spa suite have a relaxed elegance that sets the tone for your stay in Pebble Beach. All but seven of the rooms (which average more than 560 square feet) have fireplaces, and many have balconies

Guests at the opulent Inn at Spanish Bay in Pebble Beach enjoy outdoor refreshments along with spectacular views of the golf links and the Pacific Ocean beyond. TOM OWENS

overlooking the seaside fairways.

Built in 1919, The Lodge provides a full range of activities to fill your day. In addition to receiving special rates to play Pebble Beach Golf Links, one of the most famous golf courses in the world, guests are provided privileges to Poppy Hill Golf Course, the Links at Spanish Bay, and the Del Monte Golf Course in Monterey. Then there's the great Beach and Tennis Club that offers 12 tennis courts and a heated pool right on the edge of Carmel Bay. The Spa at Pebble Beach offers such luxuries as therapeutic baths, body wraps, massages, and facials as well as healthy cuisine. The Pebble Beach Equestrian Center is only a few blocks away for an incredible trail ride through the forest and to the beach. For shopping enthusiasts, the Lodge offers a breezeway of 15 specialty shops with an emphasis on golf, fashion, accessories, and gifts to appease the jealous folks who had to stay back home.

For dining, the Lodge offers a great variety of choices. The Stillwater Bar & Grill serves a nice lunch and dinner with panoramic views of the 18th green and Carmel Bay. On the lower level, Club XIX is a perfect spot to enjoy a sandwich for lunch on the outdoor patio or have contemporary French cuisine for an intimate evening. The Tap Room has just the right friendly pub atmosphere for embellishing your latest round of golf and enjoying the memorabilia from "The Crosby." Finally, across from The Lodge is The Gallery, providing breakfast and lunch overlooking the first tee. Winner of numerous awards, including being named the "Best Resort in Northern California" by *San Francisco Focus* magazine, The Lodge at Pebble Beach will put a wide smile on your golfer's face. All rooms are nonsmoking, and small pets are accepted.

Many hotels and motels sell Monterey Bay Aquarium tickets right in the lobby.

BED-AND-BREAKFAST INNS

The Monterey Peninsula is world-famous for its bed-and-breakfast inns, particularly those in Pacific Grove and Carmel. From stately Victorian mansions to quaint cottages, you'll find a host of comfortable accommodations for a very special stay.

Before we highlight the individual inns, let's go over a few of the basics. It's no secret that most of the bed-and-breakfast inns are designed for romance, and you'll find many honeymooners, anniversary celebrators, and other romantic couples among your fellow guests. While some inns do accept children, it's a good idea to remind the kids that they need to be on their best behavior. Many of the inns are classic homes, some National Historic Landmarks, filled with delicate and breakable antiques. If your clan is subject to bed-jumping, tag-playing, noisemaking, and other hyperactive types of family vacation fun, consider a sturdier hotel or motel instead.

Breakfasts at these inns will vary from full sit-down meals to in-room deluxe continentals. City safety and health regulations limit the types of kitchens and therefore the types of meals that the small inns may provide in particular parts of the Peninsula. Therefore, you won't be able to find cooked meats, for example, at all of the establishments. But most bed-and-breakfast inns offer egg dishes, waffles or pancakes, baked goods, hot and cold cereals, and a variety of fresh juices, coffees, and teas.

Since most of the bed-and-breakfast inns have a small number of guest rooms available, last-minute cancellations can be especially hard on the innkeepers' pocketbooks. Therefore, be sure to ask about reservation and cancellation policies, which can be strict. Most inns accept major credit cards. If you pay by personal check, you may be required to submit a deposit weeks in advance of your stay. Smoking is typically prohibited and few inns accept pets, but ask about it when making reservations. Wheelchair access may be limited at some of these historic inns, so check in advance if it is important to you.

Most of the innkeepers we talked to recommend making your reservations at least two to three months in advance during the peak season (June through September) and for holiday weekends. Some special-event weekends may require bookings up to a year in advance. During the off-season, rooms can often be found up to the week of your stay, sometimes at great special rates. But if you have your heart set on a special room at a popular inn, avoid disappointment by reserving your accommodations as early as possible. With these caveats, let's take a look at some of the most popular of the Monterey Peninsula's bed-and-breakfast inns.

PRICE CODES

Prices for accommodations in a bed-and-breakfast on the Monterey Peninsula cover a wide range, from less than $90 per night to more than $1,000. In fact, the very same room may cost you twice as much during the peak season (June through September) or a special-event weekend than it does during the quiet off-season. These codes represent the average price of a double-occupancy room during peak season. This average may represent a wide range of room prices, with added amenities and ocean views hiking up the price of a standard room. Be sure to confirm the current rates and available methods of payment when making your reservations.

$	Less than $90
$$	$90–130
$$$	$131–190
$$$$	More than $190

Monterey

Del Monte Beach Inn $
1110 Del Monte Avenue, Monterey
(831) 649-4410

For a very reasonably priced small bed-and-breakfast hotel in the European tradition, try the Del Monte Beach Inn. This quaint 1929 beach hotel right across the street from the Bay was once home to whaling captains, cannery workers, and other merchants of the sea. Today, it is an 18-guest room bed-and-breakfast inn (nonsmoking) that offers no-frills but comfortable accommodations. An extended continental breakfast featuring hot baked goods and fresh fruit is offered buffet style on crisp linens in the downstairs dining room. The single television is in the library, and the phone is down the hall. Each room has a sink and vanity, but only two have full private baths. But fear not; the shared baths are kept clean and nicely decorated. One of those rooms is a suite that sleeps five and includes a kitchenette. (This is the only room that accepts children.) Pets OK. Divers will appreciate the rinse tank out back.

The Jabberwock $$$
598 Laine Street, Monterey
(831) 372-4777, (888) 428-7253
www.jabberwockinn.com

Situated in New Monterey on the hill above Cannery Row, The Jabberwock is a 1911 Craftsman-style home offering seven cozy guest rooms with goose-down pillows and comforters and a decidedly *Alice In Wonderland* theme. For 30 years, this splendid home served as a Victory Mission Sisters' convent and later as a church retreat. Since 1982, it has provided a serene haven for visitors who enjoy the spacious common areas and outdoor garden. Four of the rooms of this whimsical inn (The Brillig, The Mome Rath, The Toves, and The Borogove) have fireplaces, one (The Toves) has a secret garden, and five have bay views. The Mome Rath, Borogove, and Toves also have Jacuzzi tubs for fabulous soaks for two. All rooms also private baths. Complete breakfasts include fanciful specialties like Snackleberry Flumpsious (crème brûlée) and a surprise egg dish called Humpty Dumpty. Afternoon nibblers and evening homemade cookies and milk add to the bemusement. Sherry and hors d'oeuvres add a touch of elegance. Children older than 12 are welcome at this nonsmoking inn.

Old Monterey Inn $$$$
500 Martin Street, Monterey
(831) 375-8284, (800) 350-2344
www.oldmontereyinn.com

Though not as well known as some of its more famous bed-and-breakfast brethren in Pacific Grove and Carmel, the Old Monterey Inn is on par with the best on the Peninsula. In fact, it was recently named one of the top 12 inns by *Country Inns* magazine and made the *Condé Nast Traveler* Reader's Choice Gold List. Up a quiet residential neighborhood above Pacific Street, this 10-guest room, ivy-covered English Tudor-style country home is on one and a half wooded and garden acres. It was built in 1929 for the first mayor of Monterey, Carmel Martin. An inn

When inquiring about your stay at a bed-and-breakfast inn, be sure to ask specifically about the menus and dining arrangements, especially if you have special dietary needs or desires.

for more than 20 years, this property features private baths and sitting areas in all guest rooms, wood-burning fireplaces in most, and whirlpool tubs in three. A favorite among repeat guests is the Library Room with a private sundeck. Honeymooners fall in love with the Garden Cottage and the Chawton, a comfy and romantic room with a whirlpool tub for two, fireplace, and secluded garden entrance. A few in-room phones and televisions are available upon request. The innkeepers serve a full gourmet breakfast. Enjoy it in the dining room by the massive ironwork fireplace, out in the sunny English garden—or even in bed! The sunset wine hour is a great time to enjoy the wooded gardens, which afford many quiet sitting areas and hammocks for some serious R and R. In-room massage and day membership at the Monterey Sports Center are among the amenities offered. A true romantic getaway, the nonsmoking Old Monterey Inn allows children older than 12. However, the inn limits reservations to two guests per room.

Pacific Grove

The Centrella Inn $$$
612 Central Avenue, Pacific Grove
(831) 372-3372, (800) 233-3372
www.centrellainn.com
An 1889 National Historic Landmark, the Centrella Inn takes you back in time to turn-of-the-century Pacific Grove. The classic Victorian design and small but comfortable, high-ceilinged guest rooms are a real treat to behold. Located between downtown P.G. and the beach, the main hotel has 26 rooms. All rooms have in-room phones and private baths,

Some of the smaller bed-and-breakfast inns have strict payment policies. Make sure you ask about acceptable forms of payment and cancellation policies to avoid any unpleasant surprises.

many with claw-foot tubs, and a few rooms have ocean views, including the airy attic suites. A favorite among honeymooners is the Garden Room, with a Jacuzzi tub, potbelly stove, canopy bed, wet bar, and private entrance. Outside within a peaceful garden are five cozy cottages, each with a fireplace, wet bar, and private bath. All guests enjoy an extended sit-down continental breakfast (ask about the inn's famous waffles) and a light repast at the evening social hour. Children younger than 12 are allowed in the cottages only.

Gatehouse Inn $$$
225 Central Avenue, Pacific Grove
(831) 649-8436, (800) 753-1881
www.sueandlewinns.com
A picturesque Victorian home circa 1884, the Gatehouse Inn is one of the better-kept secrets among Pacific Grove's Victorians. While not right on the waterfront, it does boast some nice bay views from the upstairs rooms. Homey and cozy, this nine-guest room inn features private baths (most with claw-foot tubs), in-room phones (no TVs), and full gourmet breakfasts. Some rooms have fireplaces or wood stoves, others have private decks and porches. A favorite is the Langford Room (named after original owner Benjamin Langford, a California senator), with a sitting area, wood stove, ocean view, queen-size bed, and claw-foot tub. Gourmet breakfast is served in the dining room. An early-evening tea with wine and home-baked goodies allows you to visit with fellow guests by the fireplace in the parlor. And you can raid the cookie jar all day long! Some rooms will accommodate children.

Gosby House Inn $$$
643 Lighthouse Avenue, Pacific Grove
(831) 375-1287, (800) 527-8828
www.foursisters.com
Welcoming guests to downtown Pacific Grove for more than 100 years, Gosby House Inn is one of the most recognized landmarks in Butterfly Town USA. The

The Centrella Inn in Pacific Grove is an 1889 National Historic Landmark with 26 rooms in the main hotel and five cottages out back. TOM OWENS

stately Queen Anne Victorian mansion provides 22 antique-filled guest rooms plus two romantic carriage-house rooms with spa tubs, fireplaces, and private balconies. All but two of the mansion's guest rooms have private baths, and many have sitting areas, each of which has a fireplace, private patio entrance, and/or window seat from which to view the ocean or hometown scenery. Lavish breakfasts with homemade breads are a hallmark of the nonsmoking Gosby House, and afternoon teas with wine and sherry are a great way to meet fellow guests. For a small charge, you can even have champagne and truffles delivered to your room.

Grand View Inn   **$$$$**
557 Ocean View Boulevard,
Pacific Grove
(831) 372-4341
www.pginns.com
Elegant is the only word to describe this lovely 1910 Edwardian-style mansion, situated on the waterfront with a spectacular view of Lovers Point in Pacific Grove. The 22-guest room, nonsmoking Grand View Inn, originally home to noted marine biologist and P.G.'s first woman mayor Julia Platt, has been extensively renovated by its current owners and is now a showcase of the post-Victorian era. The dining room features oak columns, a marble fireplace, and exquisite antique furniture and has ocean views that will make your full breakfasts and afternoon teas simply unforgettable. Guest rooms feature marble-tiled private baths (plush bathrobes too), patterned hardwood floors, and striking antique furnishings. The two-bedroom Sea View Cottage offers a fireplace and a private dock and garden. There are no televisions or in-room phones, but who needs them? Well-behaved older children are welcome.

Green Gables Inn   **$$$**
104 Fifth Street, Pacific Grove
(831) 375-2095, (800) 722-1774
www.foursisters.com

And the Winner Is:
Green Gables Inn

Okay, so if we Insiders had to pick just one place to stay on the Monterey Peninsula for a warm, cozy, romantic night it would be—a difficult choice. But if push came to shove, our numero uno bed-and-breakfast inn would be the Green Gables Inn, at 104 Fifth Street, Pacific Grove.

First of all, we're partial to Pacific Grove with its quiet charm and home-town casualness. Second, a Queen Anne mansion sitting right on the edge of the Bay is pretty hard to beat. The Seven Gables Inn and the Grand View Inn, just down Ocean View Boulevard, probably have even more spectacular views, but their high-brow opulence and antiques don't bring the down-to-earth comfort level we'd be looking for to get that ultimate rest and relaxation.

And we Insiders are not alone in picking Green Gables Inn as the crème de la crème. In 1997, Green Gables Inn was voted North America's number one bed-and-breakfast inn by none other than the Official Hotel Guide's (OHG) travel-agent survey. (The annual OHG Readers' Choice Awards survey is based on responses from 20,000 subscribers who rated properties across 51 categories. OHG is said to be the world's largest supplier of information and services for the travel industry.)

A visit to the Green Gables Inn confirms that these travel agents know what they're talking about. The 1888 National Historic Landmark is a multi-gabled Queen Anne right on the waterfront at the corner of Fifth Street and Ocean View Boulevard. The 11-room mansion and carriage house are painted white with dark green trim. The windows, fixtures, and woodwork are all original features. Walk up the front steps into the warm and cozy living room of the main house, and you immediately feel at home. The six guest rooms in the main house feature English antiques, comfortable beds, and snuggly teddy bears to welcome you.

Each guest room has its own special touches. The Chapel Room features a rich mahogany interior, while the Gable Room has a sturdy ladder that takes you up to the cozy attic room in the main gable itself. Canopy bed aficionados will appreciate the aptly named Lacey Room. Rooms in the main house share baths (some consider this one of the few drawbacks), except for the two-room suite. Out back, the carriage house has five more rooms, each with a fireplace, queen bed, bath, and extra foldout sofa bed. Each guest room is tastefully decorated with romantic wallpaper and fabric. All guests enjoy a full breakfast each morning in the ocean-view dining room. Wine and hors d'oeuvres are served in the afternoon next to the parlor fireplace. Call (831) 375–2095 or (800) 722-1774 for reservations.

And our pick for the "Best Bargain" B&B in Pacific Grove: The Centrella Inn.

So if Green Gables Inn tops the charts in Pacific Grove, what about Monterey and Carmel? Again, there are many splendid choices and our top picks would vary depending on our mood. But for unbeatable B&Bs, try:

Green Gables Inn is a Pacific Grove landmark and our number-one bed-and-breakfast inn. MONTEREY COUNTY CONVENTION AND VISITORS BUREAU

Old Monterey Inn, Monterey, (831) 375-8284. This English Tudor-style inn is off the beaten path and secluded within lush wooded and garden acres. For a real Monterey getaway in plush surroundings, stay here (see listing).

Our "Best Bargain" in Monterey: **Del Monte Beach Inn, (831) 649-4410** (see listing).

The Green Lantern Inn, Carmel, (831) 624-4392. We pick the Green Lantern because it epitomizes what Carmel is all about. Quaint, charming, storybook cottages in a splendid garden setting, easy walking distance to the beach, and close to Ocean Avenue shopping (see listing).

Our "Best Bargain" in Carmel: **Happy Landing Inn, (831) 624-7917** (see listing).

The Gosby House Inn is a 1910 Edwardian-style mansion centrally located in downtown Pacific Grove. TOM OWENS

Perhaps the best-known Pacific Grove bed-and-breakfast (and a favorite of this Insider), the Green Gables Inn, an 11-guest room inn and carriage house, is right on the corner of Ocean View Boulevard and Fifth Street and affords warm and comfortable accommodations with spectacular waterfront views. See our Close-up on the Green Gables Inn in this chapter.

The Inn at 213 Seventeen
Mile Drive $$$
213 17-Mile Drive, Pacific Grove
(831) 642–9514, (800) 526–5666
www.innat17.com
This is the newest of the Pacific Grove bed-and-breakfast inns, welcoming its first guests in 1998. The main Craftsman-style house, built in 1925, features seven tasteful rooms, each with its own motif. Some have Asian influence in recognition of the area's rich Chinese heritage; others honor the Monarch butterfly or the area's nautical legacy. Each is named for a local seabird. Then there are seven more rooms

on the spacious grounds, including the Pelican cottage and the entirely redwood Guillemot loft. All rooms have private baths. An outdoor spa and fountain add to the tranquility. A large buffet breakfast and evening hors d'oeuvres and wine provide a great opportunity to mingle with your hosts and fellow guests. Innkeepers Tony and Glynis Greening are avid runners and kayakers and relish in sharing their favorite spots for each.

The Martine Inn $$$$
255 Ocean View Boulevard, Pacific Grove
(831) 373-3388, (800) 852-5588
www.martineinn.com
Perched on a small bluff overlooking the rocky coastline of Monterey Bay, The Martine Inn was built in 1899 and was originally the opulent home of Laura and James Parke of Parke-Davis Pharmaceuticals. Today, after many renovations, it is a striking 24-guest room inn with special touches that please the most discerning visitor, as evidenced by its place on a

number of travel magazine top-12 lists. Think elegant. Breakfast is served on Victorian china with old Sheffield silver and crystal goblets. Lunches and dinners are based on the 1880s "White House" cookbooks and are lengthy multicourse affairs that may even include Victorian spoon warmers. The furnishings are museum quality. Bedroom ensembles include the Malarin Estates mahogany suite exhibited in the 1893 Chicago Words Fair; an 1860 Chippendale Revival four-poster bed with canopy and side curtains; and Edith Head's bedroom suite complete with her early commissioned portrait. All rooms have private baths, some with claw-foot tubs, as well as in-room phones. Many guest rooms have wood-burning fireplaces, and smoking is allowed in these rooms only. You can enjoy a comfortable library, enclosed courtyard (where antique MG automobiles are on display), a garden conservatory with a hot tub spa, and a game room with a 1917 nickelodeon and an 1890 white oak pool table. At twilight the inn serves wine and hors d'oeuvres around the knabe reproducing Baby Grand Piano, where you can take in the spectacular bay view. Wine, champagne, and picnic-basket lunches can all be provided. The Martine Inn prides itself in hosting spectacular weddings, and an on-staff consultant will help organize and coordinate the entire event.

The Old St. Angela Inn $$$
321 Central Avenue, Pacific Grove
(831) 372-3246, (800) 748-6306
www.sueandlewinns.com
Formerly a rectory and later a convent, The Old St. Angela Inn is now a comfy Craftsman-style bed-and-breakfast inn. The circa-1910 inn may lack the opulence of some of Pacific Grove's more stately Victorian Queen Annes and Edwardians, but it offers a comfortable stay at a reasonable price. There are nine guest rooms, including the upstairs Whale Watch, with an ocean view from the private balcony, fireplace, and Jacuzzi tub. Each room has a private bath, and most have either a

fireplace or cast-iron stove. Breakfast is served in a bright redwood and glass solarium or in the oceanview dining room. Home-baked cookies and other treats are a specialty and can be enjoyed before the cut stone fireplace in the living room. Those scrumptious cookies are especially good with evening wine, tea, or coffee. A garden gazebo and spa add to the enjoyment. Some rooms accommodate children, and all are nonsmoking.

Pacific Grove Inn $$$
581 Pine Avenue, Pacific Grove
(831) 375-2825, (800) 732-2825
This 1904 Victorian mansion at the corner of Pine and Forest Avenues is a marvel in its detail. Carved oak walls, a round turret room with a 30-foot pointed ceiling, and antique Oriental carpeting are just a few of the highlights. In its main house and guest house, the nonsmoking Pacific Grove Inn has a total of 16 guest rooms, each with a private bath featuring a full-size tub and heated towel racks. All rooms have brass beds, fireplaces, minibars, televisions, VCRs, and phones; a few rooms feature extras like a whirlpool tub, an enclosed sundeck, or an open-air porch. The four-room, oceanview suite is perfect for families. Children of all ages are welcome. The large buffet breakfast includes waffles, eggs, baked goods, juices, six choices of coffee, and 14 kinds of tea. Hors d'oeuvres are served every afternoon.

Seven Gables Inn $$$$
555 Ocean View Boulevard,
Pacific Grove
(831) 372-4341
www.pginns.com
Like its sister Grand View Inn next door, the Seven Gables Inn offers a breathtaking view of Lovers Point and Monterey Bay that in itself is worth the price of a night's stay. But the classic inn, with its many gables, sun porches, beveled glass windows, and gilded and inlaid antique furniture, gives the ocean view a run for its money in both beauty and elegance.

The showy 1886 Victorian main house topped by the Breakers room, along with its guest house and cottages, offers 14 guest rooms, each with a full private bath and queen-size bed. Virtually all of the rooms have a spectacular view of the Bay, and one of the carriage-house rooms adds a cozy fireplace. The host Flatley family's eclectic collection of fine antiques adds both opulence and warmth. A full breakfast and elegant afternoon high tea are served in the grand Victorian dining room. The Seven Gables is a nonsmoking inn, and children younger than 12 are not allowed because of the low windows, sharp corners, and delicate furnishings. For sheer beauty indoors and out, it's tough to top the Seven Gables Inn.

Carmel

Carmel Wayfarer Inn $$$
Fourth Avenue and Mission Street, Carmel
(831) 624-2711, (800) 533-2711
www.wayfarerinn.com
Established in 1929, the nonsmoking Carmel Wayfarer Inn has 18 comfortable rooms, all with private baths, TVs, VCRs, coffeemakers, and refrigerators. Most rooms in this small hotel-like facility have fireplaces; some have kitchens, others enjoy ocean views. Rooms are situated around a quaint courtyard garden that has a cozy outdoor fireplace with plenty of fireside seating. An extended continental breakfast is served buffet style in a common dining area, with a menu of fresh fruits, baked goods, and other treats.

Cobblestone Inn $$$
Junipero Street and Seventh Avenue, Carmel
(831) 625-5222, (800) 833-8836
www.foursisters.com
This English-style country inn combines warm charm with modern amenities. Stone from the Carmel River covers the first level of this two-story inn and is also used in the fireplaces that grace every one of the 24

rooms. The slate courtyard in the center of the horseshoe-shaped building is a great place to enjoy a full gourmet breakfast during warm weather. When the fog rolls in, you can move into the enclosed dining room or have breakfast in bed. All rooms have refrigerators stocked with cold beverages, and wine and hors d'oeuvres are served each afternoon. A special honeymoon suite features a four-poster bed with a European cutwork canopy, a jetted tub and window seat. Use the complimentary bicycles to explore the back streets of Carmel. The large stone fireplace in the comfortable parlor is a great place to unwind at the end of the day.

The Green Lantern Inn $$$
Seventh Avenue and Casanova Street, Carmel
(831) 624-4392, (888) 414-4392
www.greenlanterninn.com
Of all the inns in Carmel, perhaps none epitomize English country charm as much as The Green Lantern Inn, established in 1926. The historic main house and five cottages, nestled in a quaint garden of roses, azaleas, and other flowers amid pine and oak trees, offer 18 guest rooms, each with an individual charisma. The Cedar room is a spacious room with queen bed and a private Carmel stone patio. The Holly has a hipped vestibule with a narrow stairway leading up to the "lighthouse" bedroom. The high-ceiling Cypress is a fireplace suite with a spacious loft and two queen beds. The Maple is roomy with two queen beds and a secluded redwood deck. You get the idea. Guests enjoy a buffet breakfast in the cozy fireside room or out in the courtyard. All rooms are nonsmoking and have private baths, some with full-size tubs. It's a short walk to the beach and downtown, if you can pull yourself away. Afternoon refreshments are served in the fireside room.

Happy Landing Inn $$
Monte Verde Street and Sixth Avenue, Carmel
(831) 624-7917

This storybook 1929 Comstock house has seven guest cottages, each with a cathedral ceiling, private bath, and stained-glass window. The two-room suite with fireplace is a favorite among repeat visitors. You'll find televisions but no phones in the rooms—a guest phone is available off the living room. Rooms look out over a lovely courtyard garden with a vine-covered gazebo, frog pond, and many, many flowers. The Happy Landing Inn serves a gourmet continental breakfast with a unique custom: In the morning, you pull up your window shade as a signal you're ready, and the staff brings the breakfast to your room. Feel free to enjoy your morning meal out in the garden gazebo. Evenings include tea and cookies served in the main house and in-room sherry. The Happy Landing Inn is a nonsmoking establishment that provides quiet comfort in residential Carmel and is just blocks from downtown and the beach.

Holiday House $$$
Camino Real and Seventh Avenue, Carmel
(831) 624-6267
Built in 1905 as a summer home for a Stanford University professor, the shingle-covered, Craftsman-style Holiday House has six guest rooms, two with ocean views. Dormer windows and quilted bedspreads add to a cozy atmosphere that makes you feel like you're part of the family. The emphasis here is on rustic simplicity. Although most rooms have private baths, only one has a television. And if you need to call home or the office, you'll have to use your cell phone or the coin phone in the lobby. A full breakfast is served buffet style in the dining room. Afterward, enjoy a relaxing moment in front of the living room's big wood-burning fireplace or cuddle up with a good book in the well-stocked library. A walk down the Carmel stone paths through the peaceful garden is a pleasantry before your afternoon sherry. The Holiday House, known as Carmel's oldest guest house, is a nonsmoking inn.

Monte Verde Inn $$$
Monte Verde Street and Ocean Avenue, Carmel
(831) 624-6046, (800) 328-7707
Built as an inn in 1900, the Monte Verde Inn has been welcoming guests to Carmel for nearly 100 years. The Mediterranean-style villa offers 10 nonsmoking guest rooms, two with fireplaces and a few with private balconies or decks. One large suite has two queen-size beds, a sitting room, and full kitchen. Another has an ocean view, a sitting room, and a balcony. A secluded brick patio provides a great place to enjoy the fresh ocean air. Guests receive an extended continental breakfast in the sunny dining room. All rooms have private baths, and there is ample off-street parking. The Monte Verde Inn is only a half-block from downtown and 3 blocks from the beach.

San Antonio House $$$
San Antonio Avenue and Ocean Avenue, Carmel
(831) 624-4334
www.carmelgardencourtinn.com
The five-guest room San Antonio House was built in 1927 and is one of the smallest bed-and-breakfasts in Carmel. Rooms have in-room televisions and phones, private baths, cozy fireplaces, breakfast patios, and their own entrances to heighten privacy. The secluded Treetop Suite atop the carriage house is a favorite among romantics. There is a quaint outdoor garden so you can enjoy the mild Carmel days. A gourmet continental breakfast of fruit, granola, yogurt, and pastries is delivered to your room. Accommodations are comfortable, with a cozy put-up-your-feet, don't-worry-about-the-furniture ambience. Plus, you can't get a room much closer to Carmel Beach than at the San Antonio House.

Sea View Inn $$
Camino Real and 11th Avenue, Carmel
(831) 624-8778
www.seaviewinncarmel.com

This turn-of-the-century, three-story Victorian offers eight nonsmoking guest rooms in quiet residential Carmel, about as far away from downtown as you can get. Antique accents and comfortable surroundings make this a great spot to sit back and relax in real peace and quiet. There are no in-room phones or televisions to distract you. Six rooms have private baths; two attic rooms share a bath. The large front porch and lush back garden make great spots for reading, writing, or just enjoying the moment. And you're only a few hundred feet from the sand beach—colorful towels provided. A full breakfast is served in the spacious dining room on weekend mornings, and generous continental breakfasts are offered on weekdays. Enjoy afternoon tea and evening wine and cheese before a crackling fire. Children 11 and older are welcome.

The Stonehouse Inn $$$
Eighth Avenue and Monte Verde Street, Carmel
(831) 624-4569, (877) 748-6618
www.carmelstonehouse.com

The Stonehouse Inn is a 1906 Carmel home that gets its name from the rugged stone exterior that was hand-shaped by local Native Americans. Among the guests of original owner, Josephine "Nanna" Foster (who had a penchant for inviting San Francisco writers and artists to her home for long conversations), were Jack London and Sinclair Lewis. Subsequent owners included cartoonist Gene Byrnes (of *Reg'lar Fellers* fame) and A. T. Hyde, of the Mentholatum fortune. Today, you enter The Stonehouse through a long glass-enclosed porch and walk into a large living room with an impressive stone fireplace—ask the innkeeper to show you the hidden vault! Each of the seven guest rooms has its own unique charm, but the big favorite is the upstairs suite with an ocean view and the George Sterling hand-carved canopy bed. Two of the light and airy rooms have private baths, the other four share. Amenities include cozy quilts, plenty of pillows, and a full sit-down breakfast in the sunny dining room. Breakfast includes omelets, bacon, fruit, juices, baked goods, and coffee or tea. Ever tried southern-style banana rice pancakes? Enjoy wine in the evening before the living room fireplace. A large backyard patio is a great relaxation spot on warm afternoons. Smoking is not permitted, and children must be 12 or older.

The Sunset House $$$
Camino Real and Ocean Avenue, Carmel
(831) 624-4884
www.sunset-carmel.com

If you're looking for a Carmel inn with all the special touches, The Sunset House may be just your cup of tea. With only four spacious guest rooms, all with private baths and some with great ocean views, this nonsmoking inn caters to your every need. Great breakfasts, delivered to your room by the innkeepers, feature hand-squeezed juices, freshly baked goods, specially made granola, and a special house-blend gourmet coffee. Floor-to-ceiling brick fireplaces in each room come complete with hand-split wood, expertly mixed to provide just the right heat, scent, and color of fire. Wet bars, kitchenettes, Jacuzzi tubs, hide-a-beds, sitting areas, and outdoor decks and patios are other available extras. Built in 1960, The Sunset House may not be a picturesque historic inn, but it has a charming fountain garden and all the modern conveniences. Plus, it's just a short walk from the beach or downtown Carmel.

Historic inns might have limited wheelchair access, narrow winding staircases, no in-room televisions or phones, and shared bathrooms. Check for details if these limitations are important to you or someone you're traveling with.

Vagabond's House Inn $$$
**Dolores Street and Fourth Avenue,
Carmel**
(831) 624-7738, (800) 262-1262
www.vagabondshouseinn.com
The Vagabond's House Inn was originally built in the 1940s as housing for officers at Fort Ord to the north of Monterey. Today, four English Tudor shingle-roofed cottages have been transformed into comfy rooms and suites situated in a horseshoe around a secluded cobblestone courtyard with waterfall pool, beautiful award-winning gardens, and a stately oak tree. There are 11 guest rooms and two suites in this nonsmoking inn, the favorites being rooms 1 and 11, which have great courtyard views. Each room is decorated in a unique theme or style, such as nautical or floral, with many antiques throughout the inn. Most rooms have fireplaces, coffee bars, and refrigerators, and all have private baths. Enjoy an elaborate continental breakfast in your room or in the courtyard. Complimentary wine and cheese are served each evening. Children 12 and older are welcome. Pets OK. Vagabond's House Inn was selected the 2003 Best Inn on the West Coast by *Arrington's Bed and Breakfast Journal.*

VACATION RENTALS

Visitors looking for a vacation rental on the Monterey Peninsula may be in for a bit of a surprise. Yes, there is an ample supply of single-family homes, apartments, and condominiums available to rent as vacation getaways. They range from small studios, cottages, and beach bungalows to expansive estates.

However, you might have to plan on an extended stay to be able to enjoy many of these homes. Ordinances in the cities of Monterey, Carmel, and Pacific Grove require a minimum of a 30-night stay in many vacation rentals. Why? Unlike most resort communities, the Monterey Peninsula does not have vicinities devoted to short-term vacation properties. Most of the vacation rentals here are second homes that owners live in part time and rent out the rest of the year through a property-management firm. These houses are primarily in residential neighborhoods, surrounded by the homes of full-time residents. Understandably, some of these residents object to having their quiet neighborhoods turned into a weekly merry-go-round of active new visitors. They took their complaints to the city governments, who established ordinances calling for 30-night minimum stays to establish some semblance of neighborhood stability.

That being said, there are still opportunities to find a vacation rental on the Peninsula for a weeklong stay. A seven-day minimum, not the 30-night ordinance, applies to the unincorporated areas of the Peninsula. That includes all of Pebble Beach and many neighborhoods commonly considered Carmel and Monterey but actually outside the boundaries of the incorporated cities. Some vacation rentals within Monterey, Carmel, and Pacific Grove commercial zones are also exempt from the 30-day minimum.

HOW TO FIND RENTALS

Vacation rentals can be found through a variety of sources. You can check the classified ads in the local newspapers for private owners who are renting their second homes. Some of the larger Monterey Peninsula real estate companies handle property rentals as well (see our Real Estate chapter). The primary source is a handful of property-management firms that specialize in vacation rentals. These are listed at the end of this chapter.

THE COST

How much can you expect to pay for a vacation rental? That will depend on the size and location of the property, the duration of your stay, and the time of year you're coming into town. At the low end of the price spectrum, small studios and one- or two-bedroom houses and condominiums start around $800 per week or $1,700 per month in the off-season. At the high end, large estates can run $5,000 or more per week and into the tens of thousands per month during the peak months. While it's difficult to pinpoint a typical rental price, you can expect to pay $1,500 to $2,500 per week or $3,500 to $5,000 per month during the peak summer season for a comfortable home in a nice location with ample room for a family of four to stretch out. Weekly rentals in unincorporated locales will also include a 10.5 percent occupancy tax.

WHAT YOU GET

If you deal with a specialist property-management firm, you'll likely get a fully furnished, clean home complete with bed and bath linens, glasses and dishes, cooking equipment, a telephone, a television,

Vacation rentals on the Monterey Peninsula are primarily located in quiet residential neighborhoods. TOM OWENS

and a VCR or DVD player as standard equipment. Many of these homes also have fireplaces (complete with a supply of wood), washers and dryers, a microwave oven, a deck or patio, and a barbecue grill. Some include stereo systems, pools, hot tubs, spas, fax machines, and even computers. In many cases, all you need is clothing and groceries. (Property-management firms may also provide faxes, copy machines, express mail, and other administrative services through their offices.)

Of course, for a price, extra amenities are always available. Maid service, grocery shopping, and catering as well as massages and baby-sitting can be arranged through the property-management firm or an independent contractor. Cribs, high chairs, rollaway beds, cars, bicycles, and other equipment can also be rented. Some firms will even arrange tee times at local golf courses. Just ask, and you can probably get it. Many vacation homes are nonsmoking properties, and pets are typically excluded. But exceptions can often

be made in exchange for an added cleaning fee and/or security deposit.

MAKING ARRANGEMENTS

Property-management firms recommend reserving vacation homes eight months to a year in advance for the peak seasons. That includes the summer months of June through August, the winter months of January through March, and the major holiday weekends. During the off-season, generally spring and fall, try to make your reservations three to six months in advance. Security deposits (typically $300 and more) are usually required to hold a property. Full payment is often due 30 days in advance of your stay. Still, don't be afraid of calling for a vacation property a week before your planned trip—or even dropping in on a property-management firm when you arrive in town. You never know what might be available due to an unusually slow week or a last-minute cancellation.

PROPERTY-MANAGEMENT FIRMS

Although a number of real estate agencies, private individuals, and property-management firms handle vacation homes on the Monterey Peninsula, the majority of the business is handled by four firms, each with a solid local reputation. Check out a variety of sources, but be sure to include these firms in your search for that perfect Monterey Peninsula vacation home.

Be a good neighbor. Your Monterey Peninsula vacation rental is likely in a residential area, so respect the requests of others and try to blend in with the neighborhood ambience.

Monterey Bay Property Management
816 Wave Street, Monterey
(831) 655-7840
www.montereyrentals.com
With 20 years of experience, Monterey Bay Property Management handles more than 100 fully furnished vacation rentals, ranging from small studio apartments and condominiums to luxury estates; from the quaint to the exotic. Properties are located throughout Monterey, Carmel, Pacific Grove, Pebble Beach, and Carmel Valley as well as the South Coast and other surrounding unincorporated areas. Weekly and monthly rentals are available from this agency that prides itself on its customer service. The firm also specializes in second-home purchases for out-of-area buyers.

Pine Cone Property Management
26613 Carmel Center Place, Carmel
(831) 626-8163
www.pineconerentals.com
From golf course country club homes to beachfront bungalows, Pine Cone Property Management offers a wide range of properties in Monterey, Carmel, Pacific Grove, Pebble Beach, and surrounding unincorporated areas. Most rental properties are nonsmoking, and pets are allowed only by prearranged permission with a deposit required. Pine Cone Property Management prefers not to give out a full list of available properties. Instead, you provide a description of your dream vacation home, and they present a selection of homes that make a good match. Cashiers checks are required on walk-in rentals.

San Carlos Agency
26358 Carmel Rancho Lane, Carmel
(831) 624-3846
www.sancarlosagency.com
With half a century in the business, San Carlos Agency is the oldest and largest vacation-property specialist on the Monterey Peninsula. Representing up to 150 vacation rental properties in Pebble Beach, Carmel, Pacific Grove, and surrounding unincorporated areas, the firm is a member of the Vacation Rental Managers Association, a national group. Visitors to the Peninsula can drop in to view photos of the properties. Rent a property, and you typically have first choice to rebook the home during the same period the following year. As a full-service real estate company, San Carlos Agency can also handle all types of residential and vacation-property sales and then provide continuing property-management services.

Vintage Property Management
San Carlos Street and Seventh Avenue, Carmel
(831) 624-2930
Owner-operated Vintage Property Management prides itself in being a full-service vacation-rental agency. It offers single-family vacation homes in Carmel, Pebble Beach, Pacific Grove, Carmel Valley, and surrounding unincorporated areas. Vintage does not handle condominiums or apartments, and all properties are nonsmoking and no-pet homes.

RESTAURANTS

The culinary selections on the Monterey Peninsula are as bountiful and satisfying as the glorious ocean that graces our coast and the fertile fields of the inland areas. Many of the innovative chefs in this area make use of the abundant fresh seafood, herbs, and vegetables available. Our proximity to the Salinas Valley for lettuces and vegetables, Castroville for artichokes, Gilroy for garlic, and the Pacific Ocean for crab, calamari, fish, and rock shrimp leads to the superb quality and freshness of area cuisine.

While many establishments pay homage to the Italian origins of many Peninsula residents, there is also an eclectic offering of international cuisine and cooking styles. From American comfort food to Thai and Indian fare, and representing just about every point on the globe, you'll find a place to indulge your culinary cravings.

Although we have by no means even scratched the surface of the Peninsula's dining and snacking options, our hope is to give you a small sampling of the range of possibilities. For your convenience we have organized the chapter by categories based on the type of food offered. Within each category, the selections are presented alphabetically.

Here are a few other guidelines to keep in mind. Reservations are not generally required. However, in most cases they are suggested, especially on weekends and during any of the area's many festivals and events. To avoid disappointment, it is best to call ahead. Smokers be warned that all restaurants and bars in California are, by law, nonsmoking establishments.

Although some national chain restaurants are located here, you won't find them among our listings. We prefer to focus on unique eating environments in the descriptions that follow. With few exceptions, we have not mentioned restaurants within hotels or shopping centers. If there is something you are looking for that we didn't have space to cover, you'll find a complete listing of restaurants in the local Yellow Pages. Newsstands, visitor centers, and the concierges of many hotels also have several publications to assist you in your dining discoveries. If you're looking for places the kids will enjoy, see our Kidstuff chapter. Buon appetito!

PRICE CODES

The following dollar-sign codes are designed to give you an idea of the approximate price range for each restaurant. The codes represent the price of dinner entrees for two, without cocktails or wine. We have not included tax and gratuity in our price code. Cash, travelers checks, and most major cards are the norm for payment—unless otherwise noted, you can expect major credit cards to be accepted at all restaurants listed. If you are concerned about which credit cards are accepted, just call ahead to check the restaurant's current policy.

$	Less than $25
$$	$25–40
$$$	$41–55
$$$$	More than $55

AMERICAN

Elli's Great American Restaurant $
1012 Del Monte Center, Monterey
(831) 372–5080
Although it's located at the Del Monte Center, an outdoor shopping mall, Elli's is anything but your typical mall food stop. Named for Ellis Island in the New York City harbor, the first stop for millions of

immigrants between 1892 and 1954, Elli's serves up a heaping portion of Americana along with breakfast, lunch, and dinner every day. In fact, you're greeted by a statue of Lady Liberty just inside the front doors. Portions are as large as the menu is extensive. Entrees and sandwiches are huge and inventive, spanning American classics and venturing into surprising territory with our favorite—the Cuban sandwich. If you're a true patriot, you'll save room for desserts like homemade apple pie or a good old-fashioned banana split.

Forge in the Forest $$
**Junipero Street at Fifth Avenue, Carmel
(831) 624–2233
www.forgeintheforest.com**

Welcome to the Forge, a unique collection of buildings, patios, and gardens that includes a blacksmith shop, an old-fashioned general store, a wine cellar, and a Gold Rush–era bar. Find a seat in the most appealing area to you and peruse the creative American menu. Lunch favorites are the baked onion soup, Caesar salad (with or without chicken), and the seared ahi tuna salad. A genuine deli selection of sandwiches, with authentic New York pastrami heading the list, is another lunch option. Six different kinds of steak, juicy baby back ribs, roasted duck, and several seafood and pasta entrees are some of the tantalizing dinner choices. Visit this Carmel landmark restaurant for lunch or dinner.

From Scratch Restaurant $
**The Barnyard Shopping Center, Lobos Barn, Carmel
(831) 625–2448**

From Scratch serves breakfast and lunch every day and dinner Tuesday through Sunday. As the name implies, the food here has a delightfully homemade, comfort-food feel with fresh ingredients and a creative approach. And although it's listed under American, the breakfast menu in particular draws from the globe—Belgian waffles, huevos rancheros, frittatas, and of course, good old American

grits. The offerings here are extensive and include meats, seafood, pastas, soups, salads, and a large selection of vegetarian items. Beer and wine are also served.

Red House Cafe $$
**662 Lighthouse Avenue, Pacific Grove
(831) 643–1060**

The Red House Cafe is located in a former residence (that's right, a little red house), giving one a sense of being at the home of a friend. The cuisine at breakfast, lunch, and dinner is best described as American with European influences and virtually everything is house-made. In one of their charming rooms or outside on the shaded front porch, you can sip a cappuccino, espresso, glass of wine, or a beer and feast on great omelets, lovely sandwiches and salads, and a changing menu of entrees that includes meats as well as vegetarian options. Closed Monday.

Tarpy's Roadhouse $$
**Highway 68 at Canyon Del Rey, Monterey
(831) 647–1444
www.downtowndining.com**

The historic vine-covered stone ranch house with indoor and outdoor seating sets the stage for a true roadhouse dining experience. The courtyard, with an arched entrance enclosed by the stone walls of the ranch house, offers delightful garden dining, weather permitting. Inside, the stone house has seven separate dining rooms, including perfect spots for a cozy meal in front of the fire. One intermittent drawback is the roadhouse's location under the flight path to the airport. Momentary pauses in conversation are a remedy, and the food and service are certainly worth it. Tarpy's is famous for its wood-burning grill that brings out the special flavors of vegetables, steak, wild game, and fresh seafood. Innovative salads, vegetarian selections, daily specials, and delectable dessert creations are additional specialties of the house. The award-winning wine list and full bar complement the food. Tarpy's is open for lunch and dinner.

A former residence, the Red House Cafe in Pacific Grove gives one the sense of dining at the home of a friend. The ample front porch sports a few tables where diners can enjoy their repast alfresco. MICHAEL CHATFIELD

Tinnery at the Beach $$
Lovers Point Park, 631 Ocean View Boulevard, Pacific Grove
(831) 646-1040
www.thetinnery.com

The Tinnery, a Pacific Grove landmark established in 1980, offers incredible views of Lover's Point and the Monterey Bay. Within the last year, The Tinnery has undergone a significant remodel of the interior as well as the breakfast, lunch, and dinner menus. The new menu includes pasta bowls, wraps and sandwiches, and gourmet pizzas in addition to American favorites. There's a full bar and live music on weekends. Their Sunday brunch buffet is a serious spread that includes made-to-order omelets and a carving station with ham and baron of beef.

Toasties Café $
702 Lighthouse Avenue, Pacific Grove
(831) 373-7543

This cozy cafe serves breakfast fare that includes homemade hash, eggs benedict, French toast, and pancakes. For lunch try the specialty sandwiches, yummy fresh salads, or the fajitas, if you're in the mood for something a little different. A partial listing of the dinner menu includes pork chops, chicken, and a steak and scampi combo. Desserts are all-American here too: You'll find both apple pie and chocolate cake. Home-style atmosphere and meals, reasonable prices, and friendly staff make this a great spot for breakfast, lunch, or dinner.

ASIAN

Barn Thai Restaurant $
1760 Fremont Boulevard, Seaside
(831) 394-2996

Tucked into a small strip mall off Fremont Boulevard in Seaside, Barn Thai is a true find for those who crave authentic Thai cuisine. Having returned from a few weeks in that exotic paradise, our search for the genuine article was in earnest, and we found it at the casual yet comfortable Barn Thai. All the classic soups, noodles, and rice dishes are found on the lunch and dinner menus, and they'll spice it up to your liking. We even found sticky rice and *som tom*—a crunchy, spicy salad that varies a little by chef but typically includes fresh green papaya, tiny dried shrimp, long beans, tomatoes, carrots, peanuts, garlic, lime, and Thai chilies. A meal here brings back memories for us and just may create them for you.

Ichi-Riki Japanese Restaurant $$
1603 Del Monte Boulevard, Seaside
(831) 394-9905

A long-standing favorite of locals and visitors from Japan, Ichi-Riki (sounds like EE-KEY-REE-KEY) has a sushi bar, two dining rooms, a Tami room for groups, and karaoke every Saturday night. Open every day starting at 11:00 A.M., Ichi-Riki specializes in that food/art form called sushi, and they have a lengthy menu of other Japanese standards such as teriyaki, tempura, and donburi. Vegetarians and seafood lovers alike will not be disappointed. For lunch they offer a solid bargain with a selection of combination boxes that include a choice of entrees plus rice, miso soup, and salad, most under $8.00 (add around $3.00 after 3:00 P.M.).

Mandarin Gourmet Restaurant $
1184-G Forest Avenue, Pacific Grove
(831) 373-7427

This little gem is tucked into a small grouping of shops and restaurants along Forest Avenue next to Trader Joe's. Lunch and dinner menus (closed on Tuesday) feature several styles of Chinese cuisine, including Mandarin, Szechwan, Mongolian, and Hunan with Singapore curry added for good measure. There's a lighter touch to traditional dishes here. Wonderfully absent are the obvious fats and oils that many Chinese establishments add in an effort to court the American palate. Vegetarians and carnivores will be equally pleased. A personal favorite is Evergreen—fresh broccoli, snow peas, and green beans stir-fried in a lovely sauce that they will gladly make spicy upon request. In fact, the proprietor, Paul, will graciously accommodate just about any request, and he'll likely remember your name if you introduce yourself just once. Lunch specials, take-out, or free delivery within geographic reason, and family-style meals are available. Beer and wine are served.

Na Ra Korean Restaurant $
420 Tyler Street, Monterey
(831) 333-0800

For us, one sign of a good Asian restaurant is its popularity with people of Asian heritage. It's the type of place where navigating the menu is an adventure, and you're pretty much assured of trying something new. Opened in 2003, Na Ra Korean Restaurant in downtown Monterey serves up the genuine article, including personal favorites bulgogi (grilled, thinly sliced marinated beef), galbi (grilled, marinated beef ribs), and kimchi (fermented vegetables, cabbage, and radish are common, in spicy red paste). The menu of noodles, soups, meats, fish, and vegetables is extensive, and Na Ra's owners are very accommodating and helpful. In fact, when we didn't see naeng myun—an ice cold soup with buckwheat noodles, pears, beef, and kimchi, on the menu and asked about it, they were happy to prepare it for us. Most entrees are served with rice and a selection of six to twelve small side dishes featuring various pickled and spiced vegetables and sometimes dried fish. Na Ra serves lunch and dinner Monday through Friday, dinner only on Saturday, and they're closed Sunday.

New Hong Kong Restaurant $
3046 Del Monte Boulevard, Marina
(831) 883-1818

Nary a Saturday goes by that we don't drop in to the New Hong Kong Restaurant for a bowl of *pho* (pronounced *far* with a soft r)—a Vietnamese beef noodle soup. Rice noodles are topped with delicately spiced beef broth and paper-thin slices of beef (or Asian-style meatballs). Pho is served with a plate of fresh basil, cilantro, jalapenos, bean sprouts, and lime for flavoring and spicing as you like. The fresh shrimp rolls are another favorite. There's plenty of other fare from which to choose for lunch and dinner every day. From 11:00 A.M. to 3:00 P.M. every day, you have your choice of nearly 30 Asian entrees served with soup, egg roll, steamed rice, hot tea, and fortune cookie, and all are under $6.00. The dinner menu is extensive and includes special meals for two or more people to share. You won't leave hungry or broke.

Sapporo Japanese Steakhouse &
Sushi $$
Fisherman's Wharf #2, Monterey
(831) 333-1616

This teppan grill-style restaurant makes the claim, "Where every meal is a performance," and they don't disappoint. Customers are seated around a large hibachi grill, set in a room with sweeping views of the Monterey Harbor. After choosing from a dizzying array of combinations of meat and seafood, a chef approaches the grill and the show begins. All flying knives and flailing food, the experience brings new meaning to the term "dinner theater." Particularly entertaining is the onion volcano, made by stacking sliced onions in a conical shape and lighting brandy sprayed inside. Each meal comes with soup and salad, a shrimp appetizer, rice, and vegetables. An adjacent sushi bar serves all the standard sushi fare. A full bar, beer, and wine are also available.

Thai Bistro II $$
159 Central Avenue, Pacific Grove
(831) 372-8700

From the outside, Thai Bistro looks like Grandma's house, all old-fashioned Americana. Upon entering, however, you'll find yourself in a pleasantly decorated Asian atmosphere where the walls are lined with pillowed benches and adorned with an eclectic mixture of Asian and local art. But make no mistake; the food is Thai through and through. They serve up good-size portions of traditional favorites such as chicken and beef *sa-tay* with peanut sauce for dipping, *phad thai,* and *tom kah kai*—a spicy coconut milk-based soup with lemongrass, fresh mushrooms, and chicken. A variety of noodles, rice dishes, curries, salads, and soups make Thai Bistro a great choice for lovers of Southeast Asian cuisine.

CALIFORNIAN

Montrio $$
414 Calle Principal, Monterey
(831) 648-8880
www.downtowndining.com

Montrio is in a richly restored 1910 historic firehouse in downtown Monterey. The menu is influenced by the foods of France, Italy, and America. The dining room is simultaneously sophisticated and casual with the feel of an upscale European bistro. The Dungeness crab cakes accompanied by a spicy remoulade are a house specialty. The grilled portobello mushroom with a ragout of vegetables is another excellent choice. Choose from grilled favorites such as rosemary garlic chicken or Black Angus rib eye cooked to perfection on the wood-burning rotisserie. Numerous side dishes, both unusual and delicious, are presented using beans, grains, and locally grown vegetables.

Desserts at Montrio look and taste like works of art. The excellent wine list includes a few French and Italian selections. A fully stocked bar is available.

Pacific's Edge $$$$
Highlands Inn-A Park Hyatt Hotel,
Highway 1, 4 miles south of Carmel
(831) 622-5445
www.highlands-inn.com
Quite possibly one of the most inspiring
spots on the California coast, the recently
remodeled Pacific's Edge affords breathtaking ocean views accented by a jagged
seacoast and windblown cypress trees.
The accolades from national and international food critics for the regional cuisine
at Pacific's Edge continue. The menu
changes with the seasons, incorporating
fresh ingredients from many regions of
the country. New menu items include
yellowfin tuna sashimi and seabean salad
with rice chips, and coriander-crusted ahi
tuna with orange citrus sauce. The *Wine
Spectator* Grand Award wine list is a perfect complement to the exquisite food. A
special four-course prix-fixe dinner menu
is available nightly; the menu changes
every two weeks. Indulge in sensational
food and wine. Pacific's Edge is open for
lunch, dinner, and Sunday brunch.

Rio Grill $$$
Highway 1 at Rio Road, Carmel
(831) 625-5436
www.downtowndining.com
For well over a decade, people have con-
sidered the Rio Grill an extraordinary place
to have fun and enjoy fine dining. There is
a Southwest influence in the preparation
of the California foods served here.
Entrees like smoked chicken served with
mild smoked chili butter and filet mignon
with wild mushroom and guajillo chile
salsa prove the point. If you want to have
something sweet afterward, you'll love the
ice cream sandwich with almonds, straw-
berries, and chocolate packed between
two cookie wafers. The creative, colorfully
presented food, impeccable service, and
festive atmosphere make the Rio Grill a
locals' favorite. The colorful artwork and
sculptures throughout the restaurant
enhance the artistic food presentations.
There is even a cup full of crayons and
butcher paper over each tablecloth to

encourage your own artistic inclinations.
The full bar offers cocktails, premium
liquors, and a selection of wines by the
glass. Rio Grill is open for lunch and dinner
and on Sunday for brunch.

Stokes Restaurant & Bar $$
500 Hartnell Street, Monterey
(831) 373-1110
www.stokesadobe.com
Stokes Restaurant & Bar, located in an
adobe structure built in 1833, has an
ambiance that speaks well of the friendly
people and casual atmosphere that define
Monterey. You'll feel comfortable socializ-
ing with friends while lingering over a
splendid meal. Country Mediterranean cuisine in both small and large plate portions
create the menu. The innovative culinary
presentations include grilled lavender-
infused pork chop with leek-lemon bread
pudding and plum chutney. Relax and
enjoy a charming setting and wonderful
food. Choose from a specially selected
variety of wines from California, France,
and Italy. Stokes serves lunch and dinner.

Tillie Gorts Café $
111 Central Avenue, Pacific Grove
(831) 373-0335
Long known as the premier vegetarian
restaurant on the Peninsula, the menu at
Tillie Gorts also features beef and turkey
burgers, chicken entrees, sandwiches,
soups, and salads. The cafe also features
pasta, including a rich spinach and cheese
lasagna, spinach ravioli, or fettuccine
served with fresh vegetables and your
choice of Alfredo or marinara sauce. Sample one of the homemade desserts after
dinner. Tillie's serves beer and wine. It is
open for breakfast, lunch, and dinner.

ENGLISH PUBS

The Crown & Anchor $
150 West Franklin Street, Monterey
(831) 649-6496
www.crownandanchor.net
Open from 11:00 A.M. to 2:00 A.M., the

Crown & Anchor is a lively gathering, conversation, and dining place that serves up quite a range of pub-style food until midnight every day. English Fish and Chips, George III Steak and Mushroom Pie, Sovereign's Lamb Shanks, Cutty Sark's Curries, Bounty's Bangers and Mash, and Shannon's Corned Beef and Cabbage are but a few of the headliners. Wash it all down with a chilled pint—they have 20 beers on draft. They also carry a wide selection of single malt scotches, vintage ports, aged bourbons, and California wines by the glass or bottle. Whether at the handsome bar, in one of the cozy booths, or out on the heated patio, don't be surprised to find yourself drawn into a spirited conversation. It's the kind of place where you feel at home, and that's the intended effect.

London Bridge Pub $
Fisherman's Wharf #2, Monterey
(831) 655-2879
This traditional English pub serves up fish and chips made with true Atlantic cod. Other dishes include cottage pie, bangers and mash, seafood salads, and a ploughman's lunch. Stop in anytime for cream tea, coffee, or specialty drinks. In the English manner, join friends for afternoon tea accompanied by scones, cream, and jam. The pub features live entertainment in the evenings, but most people show up for the beer. There's an impressive selection of more than 60 international beers, all served with good cheer at Monterey's only waterfront pub. You'll have a jolly good time at lunch or dinner.

EUROPEAN/MEDITERRANEAN

Anton & Michel $$$
Mission Street between Ocean and
Seventh Avenues, Carmel
(831) 624-2406
www.carmelsbest.com
A fine dining spot for both lunch and dinner, Anton & Michel has been a favorite of locals, restaurant critics, and visitors since 1980. The setting is sublime, an elegant and romantic interior with original oil paintings, soft colors, and dramatic windows. Outside on the patio are gracious gardens and two soothing fountains. The well-crafted menu showcases a highly acclaimed rack of lamb in addition to grilled lamb medallions with mint pesto sauce. The catch of the day and other seafood creations are magnificent. Even the most discriminating wine lover will appreciate the award-winning wine list with a good showing of California wines from Napa Valley and Monterey County. The regions of Burgundy and Bordeaux have a prominent place on the wine list as well. Exquisite flaming desserts include bananas Foster and crepes Suzette. The wonderfully dark cocktail lounge is a good meeting place for pre-dinner libations. Lunch and dinner are served.

Fandango $$
223 17th Street, Pacific Grove
(831) 372-3456
www.fandangorestaurant.com
If you're hungry for a taste of the continent, the proprietors serve it up with style at Fandango. Even the building, a larger version of a country French stone cottage, oozes European charm. The house special, paella, is but one example of the authentic ethnic dishes featured at Fandango. Whether here for lunch or dinner, one can't help but relax and soak in the aromas and the ambience. A three-course prix fixe lunch, at $11.95, inspires memories of a meal the U.S. dollar used to buy in Europe, pre-Euro. On Sunday lunch is replaced by a lovely brunch. Fandango has a full bar and a wine list that is more than 1,500 vintages long.

Petra $
477 Lighthouse Avenue, Pacific Grove
(831) 649-2530
For 20 years, family-owned Petra has provided a pleasant, casual setting inside or on the patio for enjoying delicious Mediterranean and Greek cuisine. As with most restaurants of this ilk, vegetarians will

Outdoor Dining on and Near the Peninsula

Dining alfresco on the Monterey Peninsula is increasingly popular. Although some would think it a natural offering in sunny California, it takes a little more effort in this area, which enjoys a temperate climate and almost daily periods of fog. Whether it's cool and cloudy, sunny and clear, or, most often, all of the above in any given three-hour period, creative restaurateurs employ a range of implements including heaters, panels that block the wind, and the use of a protected courtyard. Opportunities range from full-fledged outdoor dining rooms to a couple of tables and a few chairs sprinkled along the sidewalk,

driveway, or on a small patio. Breakfast, lunch, and dinner as well as appetizers, dessert, or drinks can be enjoyed in the great out-of-doors. Here, where we talk less about the food and more about the outdoor accommodations, are just a few of our favorite outdoor dining options. It's best to call ahead for information on hours and menus.

Lighthouse Bistro, 281 Lighthouse Avenue, Monterey; (831) 649–0320. A cozy neighborhood place, Lighthouse Bistro is located in a remodeled house just a few blocks uphill from Cannery Row in New Monterey. The outdoor patio, which is glassed in from busy

The white patio umbrellas mark the location of Schooners Bistro on the Bay in the Monterey Plaza Hotel, one of the many spectacular outdoor dining venues on the Monterey Peninsula. MICHAEL CHATFIELD

Lighthouse Avenue, is comfy, snug, and pleasant, especially on a warm autumn evening.

Schooners Bistro on the Bay, in the Monterey Plaza Hotel, 400 Cannery Row, Monterey; (831) 646-1700; www.montereyplazahotel.com. Schooners is on a deck one floor below the courtyard of the Monterey Plaza Hotel. Just above the water and sheltered from the ocean breezes, it's almost like being on a ship—although a very stable one. Overhead heaters mean Schooners can be enjoyed year-round.

Frank's 17th Street Grille, 617 Lighthouse Avenue (corner of 17th), Pacific Grove; (831) 373-5474. The little establishment took what used to be a parking lot and turned it into an interesting urban patio. In downtown Pacific Grove, the 17th Street Grille is a ringside seat for people- and classic automobile-watching.

Forge in the Forest, Fifth and Junipero, Carmel; (831) 624-2233; www.forgeintheforest.com. The Forge is a wonderful, casual, and spacious alfresco dining option on the edge of downtown Carmel. Strategically placed heaters and fireplaces ward off the chill Carmel evenings, and lovely vine-covered trellis create a countryside feel.

Baja Cantina & Grill, Valley Hills Center, 7166 Carmel Valley Road, Carmel Valley; (831) 625-2252. The Baja Cantina offers a serene mountain backdrop, outdoor fireplaces, and frosty margaritas (oh, there's great Mexican food, too) on a large wooden deck.

The Fishwife/Turtle Bay Taqueria, 789 Trinity Avenue, Seaside; (831) 394-2027/899-1010; www.fishwife.com. Although they only have a few outdoor tables, The Fishwife has been known for many years as a place to sit in the sun and enjoy reasonably priced seafood and pasta dishes.

Wild Thyme Delicatessen, 445 Reservation Road, Marina; (831) 884-2414. A few tables and chairs just outside the door offer a picnic opportunity, choosing from their incredible selection of fresh salads, sandwiches, and entrees.

Phil's Fish Market, 7600 Sandholdt Road, Moss Landing; (831) 633-2152; www.philsfishmarket.com. Nestled among the seafood processing plants and marine research buildings in the seaside burg of Moss Landing, this fun, casual restaurant features a covered and heated outdoor patio.

Gutirrez Drive-In, 61 Sherwood Drive, Salinas; (831) 424-8382. Carnitas, Mariscos, Menudo, Ceviche, and mucho more. The most authentic Mexican food on the Central Coast is to be had at this unassuming little place in Salinas. Gutirrez is always packed with locals, so come early and stake out a spot on one of the big, family-style picnic tables outside.

find ample choices on the lunch and dinner menus, including hummus, tabuli, falafel, babaghannouj, Greek salads, and a selection of combination plates. The carnivores among us won't be disappointed either as Petra cooks up savory items such as lamb, beef, and chicken shish kebabs, lamb shanks, couscous, moussaka, roast chicken, dolmas, and gyros. In addition to the gyro, they serve several sandwiches from falafel, chicken, and lamb to the all-American hamburger. If you're dining with friends, The Royal Feast for four is a serious spread that includes five appetizers, Greek salad, and a huge platter piled with rice, chicken, and lamb shish kebabs, and other delights topped with sautéed pine nuts plus dessert and mint tea. Turkish coffee, retsina, Monterey County wines, and a selection of beers are also served. Petra is closed on Sunday.

Taste Cafe & Bistro $$
1199 Forest Avenue, Pacific Grove
(831) 655-0324
www.tastecafebistro.com
Everything in this recently enlarged and remodeled establishment is richly reminiscent of a stylish European bistro, from the menu and service to the ambience and decor. Grilled rabbit, steamed mussels, house-cured salmon carpaccio, and country apple galette are just a few of the items that make their lunch, dinner, and dessert menus shine. The wine list showcases California vintages, including many from Monterey County. Opened in 1990, this family-owned restaurant was purchased by Bill Karaki in 1998. Since then, Bill has expanded the size of the cafe, added live jazz on the weekends, and now has a full bar. Taste Cafe & Bistro is open Tuesday through Sunday.

The Village Corner $$
Dolores Street and Sixth Avenue, Carmel
(831) 624-3588
www.carmelsbest.com
The quaint family atmosphere, reminiscent of a Mediterranean bistro, and a solid reputation for good food has made the Village Corner a favorite for more than 50 years. Dine alfresco by the fireplace on the pleasant outdoor patio. Order chicken, lamb, or your pick of the fresh pasta dishes. Beer and a variety of Monterey County wines are available with your meal. One of the many after-dinner temptations is the incredible chocolate espresso bread pudding. The Village Corner serves breakfast, lunch, and dinner.

FRENCH

Club XIX $$$$
The Lodge at Pebble Beach,
17-Mile Drive, Pebble Beach
(831) 625-8519
www.pebblebeach.com
Assuming that you have the considerable willpower required to take your eyes off the stunning Carmel Bay or 18th green of the Pebble Beach Golf Links, both just outside the windows, the interior and the cuisine are memorable visuals as well. The chef takes a lighter approach to gourmet French cuisine, and each evening two prix fixe meals are offered, one of which is always vegetarian. Elegant appetizers include sautéed Monterey Bay abalone and artichoke hearts with truffle vinaigrette, and hamachi and ahi tuna with shaved fennel and oranges. Stunning entrees such as Rabbit Three Ways with chanterelle mushrooms and caramelized shallots and roasted Sonoma squab with cranberry beans and applewood smoked bacon showcase the chef's mastery of technique. Impeccable, attentive, and gracious service enhances the experience. Club XIX serves dinner only.

French Poodle $$$$
Fifth Avenue and Junipero Street, Carmel
(831) 624-8643
The American Academy of Restaurant Sciences has recognized this elegant dinner house as one of the Top 10 French restaurants in the United States. It serves

classic, light French cuisine. House specialties include crab legs, duck, abalone, lamb, and fresh fish. One of the most requested appetizers is Les Escargot de Bourgogne, six imported French snails prepared with homemade lemon garlic and shallot butter. Popular entrees include grilled sliced breast of duck in port wine sauce; Provimi veal T-bone with fresh cream and morel mushrooms; and fresh Morro Bay abalone (when available). French Poodle's famous French Floating Island, a creamy dessert fit for royalty, is unsurpassed. Wine offerings include port, sauternes, and madeira selections. The French Poodle serves dinner only and is open every day.

Fresh Cream $$$$
99 Pacific Street, Monterey
(831) 375-9798
www.freshcream.com

Since its opening in 1978, Fresh Cream continues to be recognized as one of the Top 100 restaurants in the nation. The stylish interior, dazzling Bay view, and impeccable epicurean reputation make this a distinctive favorite. The culinary presentations combine classic French with California flair in a well-balanced mix of meat, poultry, seafood, and vegetarian entrees. The succulent Canard Croustillant et sa Sauce Cassis—a half duckling roasted crisp, boned, sliced, and served with black current sauce—is trés magnifique.

A selection of well-chosen California and French wines complement the choice foods featured on the menu. The friendly and knowledgeable servers can help you with your decisions. Sac au Chocolat, a chocolate bag filled with a mocha milkshake and topped with a dollop of fresh whipped cream, a true work of art. Fresh Cream serves dinner only.

La Boheme $$$
Dolores Street between Ocean and
Seventh Avenues, Carmel
(831) 624-7500
www.laboheme.com

This inviting Carmel restaurant features casual French country decor, a three-course prix fixe menu (the entree selection changes nightly), and attentive service. Each meal begins with a crisp salad, made from organically grown lettuce and vegetables from the Salinas Valley and served family style. The first course is followed by a special soup prepared with the chef's own stock. Entrees range from filet mignon with a Roquefort-wine sauce to scampi conquistador, served with a compote made of fresh corn, roasted bell peppers, chili pepper, cilantro, and black beans. A vegetarian plate is available nightly. A choice of tempting desserts, such as chocolate mousse or a light lemon tart, round out an exceptional meal. California and French wine selections feature Bordeaux half-bottles and vintages. La Boheme serves dinner only.

Robert's The White House $$$
649 Lighthouse Avenue, Pacific Grove
(831) 375-9626

Located in an elegant, white Victorian that was once a family home, Robert Kincaid's latest culinary venture is The White House in downtown Pacific Grove. There's a palpable sense of intimacy and charm here, from the service and the surroundings to the cuisine and ambience. The White House presents three-course prix fixe dinners every evening (except Monday when they are closed). At just $24 per person, the superb flavors, exquisite presentations, and the surprising number of choices for each course make this a true fine-dining value. While Robert and his staff keep things fresh with frequent changes, typical first-course selections include a gratin of green lip mussels in almond butter, lobster ravioli, and a lovely Atlantic smoked salmon rose. The second-course options are no less impressive with items like a poached artichoke and bay shrimp with chive oil and vinaigrette, a Caesar salad, and tomato basil bisque. And as if that weren't enough, main courses offer entrees such as *cassoulet a la Robert*—confit of duck, fried polenta and garlic sausage over white beans—

sesame-encrusted ahi tuna filet seared medium rare with pineapple rum sauce, and bacon-wrapped filet of beef with *marchand de vin sauce* and Maytag blue cheese. The wine list is ample and reasonably priced. And if there's any room left for dessert, you won't be disappointed.

ITALIAN

Cafe Fina $$
47 Fisherman's Wharf #1, Monterey
(831) 372-5200
www.cafefina.com

Seafood is a specialty at this Italian restaurant. A popular dining spot on the wharf, Cafe Fina is owned by the Mercurios, a third-generation Italian family. Dig your fork into appetizers like deep-fried artichoke hearts or oysters Rockefeller. Don't pass up one of the 8-inch authentic Italian pizzettes baked in a Milanese wood-burning brick oven. Cafe Fina makes its own pasta and covers it with fresh herb sauces. Daily specials include tempting concoctions made with snapper, calamari steak, salmon, swordfish, and other fresh seafood. All fish entrees are served with two fresh vegetables and pasta. Veal, chicken, lamb, and steak are nonseafood entree alternatives. California, French, and Italian wines comprise the wine list. Enjoy an after-dinner drink of Amaro or Grappa from the full bar. Cafe Fina serves lunch and dinner.

Cibo Ristorante Italiano $$$
301 Alvarado Street, Monterey
(831) 649-8151
www.cibo.com

Drop into Cibo (pronounced chee-bo) and you've dropped into one of the area's only restaurant/bars that also serves up nightly live jazz (except Monday). Having undergone an extensive remodel in late 2001, the casually elegant setting showcases photography, paintings, sculpture, and handblown glass by local and Bay Area artists. Owned and operated by Rose and Mario Catalano, mother and son, Cibo specializes in modern adaptations of old family recipes that reflect their Sicilian heritage. Carpaccio, Bresaola, gnocchi, risotto and pasta, beef, veal, chicken, and seafood, all prepared under the supervision of Chef Rose, provide ample choices. New this year are a children's menu, a prix fixe menu, and happy hour with half-price appetizers and $3.00 beer, wine, and well drinks (every day from 5:00 to 7:00 P.M.). This establishment offers an extensive list of Italian and California wines as well as cordials and creative cocktails. Live music is featured every night (except Monday) in a central area where it can be enjoyed by patrons of the bar and restaurant. Cocktail jazz is showcased on Sunday from 7:00 to 10:30 P.M. A lively, danceable mix of jazz, soul, reggae, funk, and Latin music is featured Tuesday through Thursday, 9:30 P.M. to 1:00 A.M., and Friday and Saturday, 10:00 P.M. to 1:30 A.M. Cibo serves dinner only from 5:00 to 10:00 P.M. The bar is open 5:00 P.M. to 2:00 A.M.

Gianni's Pizza $
725 Lighthouse Avenue, Monterey
(831) 649-1500
www.giannispizzamonterey.com

Gianni's, family owned and open since 1974, serves some of the best pizza on the Central Coast. Selections include all the standards plus more than a few surprises like the pizza Alfredo di Ronaldo—a creamy Alfredo sauce topped with mozzarella, Canadian bacon, fresh mushrooms, and a sprinkle of Parmesan and Romano cheeses; pizza di casa with Canadian bacon, sliced tomatoes, olive oil, mozzarella, and ricotta cheeses and topped with a sprinkle of fresh basil; and the pesto di mare, a spinach pesto topped with mozzarella, sliced tomatoes, garlic, shrimp, and olive oil. They also have a selection of

[Facing page] *This historic, charming white Victorian, once a family home, is the namesake of Robert Kincaid's culinary venture—The White House in downtown Pacific Grove.*
MICHAEL CHATFIELD

Doorbell Dining, (831) 373–3333, makes house calls with orders from your favorite restaurants. There is a delivery fee, and not all menu items are available, but it sure beats cooking. Visit www.doorbell dining.com for a list of restaurants, fees, and delivery information.

chicken pizzas, appetizers, pastas, calzones, sandwiches, salads, and a full bar. Gianni's opens at 4:30 P.M. Monday through Thursday and 11:30 A.M. Friday, Saturday, and Sunday. No credit cards.

Pasta Mia Trattoria $$
481 Lighthouse Avenue, Pacific Grove
(831) 375-7709

Try to reserve the table in what was once the restaurant's foyer. Surrounded on three sides with windows and looking out over Pacific Grove's Lighthouse Avenue, it's perfect for two. The food, in a word, is outstanding. The menu features a good selection of antipasti including melazane alla mia, a savory blend of eggplant with tomato sauce, basil, and asiago cheese. Entrees, served with your choice of soup or salad, include ravioli grande (ricotta cheese and chives with tomato meat sauce) and linguini alla Puttanesca (a southern sauce of black olives, capers, tomatoes, anchovies, and spicy red peppers). Don't overlook Nero & Bianco—black and white linguini with scallops, caviar, cream, and chives! House specialties include dishes such as scampi al modo mio, prawns in a champagne cream sauce served over a bed of homemade fettuccine. The homemade desserts are excellent, especially the tiramisu and the chocolate torte. Beer and wine are served. Pasta Mia serves dinner only.

Tutto Mondo Trattoria $$
Dolores Street between Ocean and
Seventh Avenues, Carmel
(831) 624-8977
www.mondos.com

Tutto Mondo, a true old-world Italian trattoria, offers the romance of Italy to loyal patrons and visitors from around the globe. Photos of celebrity diners line the walls. Lovers of Italian food will treasure the cozy atmosphere that is both welcoming and relaxed. Select regional specialties from both northern and southern Italy, such as melone e prosciutto, carpaccio, and salmone affumicato are on the long list of antipasti. The choices in pastas are equally plentiful and feature standouts like the Vongole (fresh clams with white sauce or tomato sauce and a touch of white wine) and La Mafiosa (calamari, prawns, and scallops in spicy tomato sauce). There's a great selection of pizzas and salads as well as the steak lovers' delight, bistecca alla Fiorentina, a 16-ounce T-bone steak, grilled and served with fresh vegetables and polenta. The lunch menu includes many of the same items plus several Italian sandwiches (panini), which are a favorite of this Insider. Italian wines, especially well-known Chiantis, are favored on the wine list, along with a good selection of French and California choices. Lunch and dinner are served at this award-winning Italian restaurant.

SEAFOOD

The Fish Hopper $$
700 Cannery Row, Monterey
(831) 372-8543
www.fishhopper.com

The Fish Hopper's view of the Monterey Bay is one of the best, and you can enjoy it from the oyster bar, dining room, or outside deck. For starters select the Crab Cakes Monterey or the award-winning clam chowder. Signature dishes include Fish Hopper Combo (a deep-fried mix of prawns, cod, and calamari) and The Hopper Mixed Grill (prime top sirloin, baby back ribs, and jumbo prawns). Both dishes are served with garlic mashed potatoes. Seafood prepared a number of ways is also featured, along with pasta, beef, ribs, and chicken. The Fish Hopper has a full bar with a drinks menu featuring its famous Bucket of Fire, a blend of island spirits and tropical juices topped with a flaming sugar cube. Lunch and dinner are served.

The Fishwife $$
789 Trinity Avenue, Seaside
(831) 394-2027
1996 Sunset Drive, Pacific Grove
(831) 375-7107
www.fishwife.com
The Fishwife is known for flavorful, fresh food at affordable prices. The Pacific Grove location is near Asilomar, and the restaurant is an ideal place to have dinner after taking a sunset walk along the beach. California cuisine with a touch of Caribbean influence is reflected in offerings like Prawns Belize and Snapper Lafayette. Feast on fresh chowder, grilled oysters, sautéed calamari, one of several seafood pastas, or a Sea Garden Salad. The famous Key lime pie is the perfect conclusion to a pleasurable meal. Well-chosen, moderately priced, premium California wines are poured by the glass or bottle. Sunday brunch features seafood Benedict and other egg dishes. The mimosas made with fresh-squeezed orange juice are the brunch beverage of choice! The Fishwife is open daily for lunch and dinner.

Flaherty's Oyster Bar and
Seafood Grill $$$
Sixth Avenue between Dolores and San Carlos, Carmel
Oyster Bar (831) 625-0311/Seafood Grill
(831) 625-1500
www.carmelsbest.com/flahertys
If you're hungry for any type of fresh fish or seafood, chart your course for Flaherty's Oyster Bar and Seafood Grill in downtown Carmel. Flaherty's, established more than 20 years ago, is actually two distinct restaurants. Although the lunch and dinner menus of both restaurants now include homemade pastas, meat, and poultry, seafood intentionally dominates.

The lively and brightly colored Oyster Bar features oysters, clams, crabs, and lobster from Carmel's only saltwater tank, along with fresh fish, pastas, sandwiches, and of course, their outstanding crab and clam chowders. The Seafood Grill is a little more on the fine dining side in terms of atmosphere, but the menus are essentially the same. Named one of California's ten best fresh-catch seafood restaurants by the *San Jose Mercury News,* Flaherty's offers fresh regional seafood including Monterey Bay spot prawns and local sand dabs (a real treat), along with a diverse menu of seafood from around the globe and the other options already mentioned. The wine list showcases California wines, many from Monterey County, and a selection of domestic and imported beers are available.

Monterey's Fish House $$
2114 Del Monte Avenue, Monterey
(831) 373-4647
The homelike, jovial atmosphere at Monterey's Fish House will win you over, as will the California/Italian-style cuisine served in generous portions. Begin with the fresh barbecued oysters or sautéed mussels served at the horseshoe bar. You can also opt for the house-made soups and salads. The menu features fresh Sicilian pasta, most prepared with seafood; fish, including snapper, sole, salmon, and swordfish; and meats such as ribeye steak, pork chops, and chicken cooked on an oak barbecue pit. Death by Chocolate cake for dessert needs no further description. The Fish House has a good wine list featuring California wines and champagne, all available by the glass. It serves lunch and dinner.

Passionfish $$
701 Lighthouse Avenue, Pacific Grove
(831) 655-3311
www.passionfish.net
Passionfish is a seafood restaurant with a conscience. Owners Ted (also the chef) and Cindy Walter are actively involved with the Monterey Bay Aquarium in the

Seafood Choices Alliance and The Chef's Collaborative, and they practice what they preach by serving only sustainable seafood. *Fresh* and *inventive* describe the menu here. Ted's innovative nature comes through in items like asparagus fries and incredible sauces that serve as dips and dressings for the seafood as well as poultry, meats, and veggies on the menu. The wine list is exceptional, featuring reasonably priced selections that pair beautifully with the cuisine. Passionfish is open for dinner only every day except Tuesday.

Rappa's Seafood Restaurant $$
End of Fisherman's Wharf #1, Monterey
(831) 372–7562
www.rappas.com

Rappa's, a Monterey landmark, offers sensational views of the Monterey Bay. Its motto of "if it's not fresh, we don't serve it" assures you of the freshest fish possible. Choose (as available) Monterey Bay salmon, sea bass, or Alaskan halibut prepared flame broiled or blackened. House specialties include Rappa's famous cioppino, a flavorful blend of herbs, spices, and tomato with golden crab legs, shrimp, clams, mussels, halibut, calamari, salmon, and bay scallops. Combination platters of fish and shellfish are other popular choices. Pasta selections are also good, especially the crab ravioli prepared with baby shrimp in a light tomato sauce. Enjoy a piece of amaretto devil's food fudge cake with espresso as the finishing touch to a memorable meal. Diners can meet for a predinner drink at Rappa's cocktail lounge. Bayside lunch and dinner are served.

Sardine Factory $$$$
701 Wave Street, Monterey
(831) 373–3775
www.sardinefactory.com

If the exterior and bar look familiar, it's probably because they were both featured in *Play Misty For Me,* the 1971 movie starring and directed by Clint Eastwood. The Sardine Factory, which fostered the resurgence of Cannery Row, has satisfied locals, visitors, and celebrities with its fine food and wine, exquisite desserts, and impeccable service since 1968. A winner of *Wine Spectator*'s Grand Award for Best Wine List in the World every year since 1982, the restaurant houses an impressive collection of 30,000 bottles of wine with more than 1,000 labels. Four distinctive dining rooms highlight the Sardine Factory dining experience. Take the canopy-covered steps to the Cannery Row Room and elevated Grill Room and bar, all adorned with rich wood, soft leather, and walls reflecting the area's history with photographs, paintings, and documents. The Wine Cellar Banquet Room contains a 25-foot-long table and 16th-century antiques. The intimate Captain's Room glows from the light of the fireplace and candlelit tables. In the glass-domed Conservatory a central statue, fully surrounded by lush greenery, sits beneath a crystal chandelier. The menu features appetizers such as "The World Famous" abalone bisque, which was served at the Taste of America for President Reagan's Inaugural. For intermezzo order fresh fruit sorbet elegantly served in a graceful carved-ice swan. House specialties include fresh swordfish with Catalina sun-dried tomato tapenade and seared ahi tuna crusted with black sesame seeds. Sardine Factory desserts are also splendid. We recommend you try the delectable crème brûlée.

TAKEOUT

Bagel Bakery $
452 Alvarado Street, Monterey
(831) 372–5242
1132 Forest Avenue, Pacific Grove
(831) 649–6272
2160 California Avenue, Sand City
(831) 392–1581
539 Carmel Rancho, Carmel
(831) 625–5180

The Bagel Bakery has been providing quality food at reasonable prices since 1976. It offers omelette-on-a-bagel breakfast sandwiches, wraparounds (peaches and cream cheese wrapped in a bagel crust) for breakfast or lunch, and special combination bagel sandwiches. Basic bagels come in a variety of flavors including plain, poppy seed, blueberry, sesame seed, onion, garlic, salt, pumpernickel, whole wheat, and superseed. Top your bagel with plain or flavored cream cheese such as herb, walnut-olive, date-nut, strawberry, garden veggie, and lox spread. Bagel Bakery also sells muffins, cookies, and juices. The Sand City location has drive-through service.

Goodies $
518 Lighthouse Avenue, Pacific Grove
(831) 655-3663
Goodies has uncommonly good deli-type foods including 18 sandwiches and 10 types of salads. Made fresh daily, salad selections might include breast of chicken, Caesar with pasta, red-skin potato, curried rice pilaf, or tuna-stuffed tomato on greens. Goodies also has hot foods such as quiche, pastries, tortas, knishes, veggie burritos, and soup.

International Market and Deli $
580 Lighthouse Avenue, Monterey
(831) 375-9451
This little market and deli serves up excellent Greek and Mediterranean food packaged for takeout, which makes it perfect picnic fare. It can also be enjoyed at one of a few tables in the middle of the market or at the counter that lines the front window. The menu features classics such as gyros, Greek salads, hummus, falafel, dolmas, and a host of other delicacies. This gem is open every day until around 7:00 P.M.

Santa Lucia Market $
484-A Washington Street, Monterey
(831) 333-1111
A European-style deli and market, Santa Lucia Market carries imported German and Italian meats, a variety of European cheeses, and a host of European imported specialty food products. It also stocks organic produce and grocery foods in

In the European tradition, most area restaurants post their menus outside or in the window. A leisurely stroll, particularly in the downtown areas of the Peninsula's cities, along Cannery Row or on Fisherman's Wharf, will yield a generous helping of information on which to base your dining decisions.

addition to coffee, tea, and both imported and domestic wine. Gourmet salads, desserts, and pastries are also sold. Design your own sandwiches choosing from several kinds of bread, spreads, condiments, meats, and cheeses. The market also has sushi, a variety of entrees, and pizza.

Wild Thyme Delicatessen $
445 Reservation Road, Marina
(831) 884-2414
www.wildthymedeli.com
Gourmet and eclectic aptly describe the scrumptious offerings here. Breakfast, lunch, or dinner can be eaten at one of the tables sprinkled outside the deli or, as many prefer, taken to home, office, or park to be enjoyed. The Breakfast Panino (Taylor ham, tomato, and cheddar cheese grilled with egg) is just one of the many delicious starts to your day. For lunch or dinner try the incredible New Orleans Muffuletta (mortadella, cotto salami, Ticino ham, lettuce, and provolone cheese with house-made Muffuletta relish of sun-dried tomatoes, olives, capers, pepperoncini, tomato, and red onion, on a Foccacino roll)—makes this Insider's mouth water just writing about it. They have a dozen different sandwiches, or you can design your own from a selection of breads, meats, cheeses, garnishes, and condiments. The salad selection is international from the Chinese sesame noodle salad and the Cuban black bean rice salad to the Greek salad, Spinach Cobb salad, and Asian chicken salad. A sample of entrees includes meat loaf, grilled salmon, shrimp, crab and crawfish cakes, barbecue

Those who allow themselves to follow the aromas through the unassuming doors of the International Market and Deli in Monterey are rewarded with a memorable selection of authentic Greek and Mediterranean delights. Although takeout is the norm, there are a few tables inside. MICHAEL CHATFIELD

port ribs, tri-tip, roasted chicken, and the list goes on. The menu also features soups, desserts, and daily specials that can be picked up or delivered. Wild Thyme also caters and is open Monday through Saturday, 7:00 A.M. to 7:00 P.M.

WORLD FLAVORS

Blue Moon   **$$$**
654 Cannery Row, Monterey
(831) 375-4155
www.pisto.com
Yet another creation of area restaurateur, chef, and cooking show host John Pisto, Blue Moon features Italian food, some Pacific Rim dishes, and a top-notch sushi bar. Jason, the talented sushi chef, has created an extensive menu that includes the traditional offerings and many of his own innovations. The lunch and dinner

menus sparkle with creativity in entrees like the *edamame* crostini (edamame a/k/a soybeans, pureed with olive oil, garlic, and lemon on grilled ciabata bread); salmon filet sandwich (sesame-crusted with wasabi mayo, avocado, cucumber slaw, and pickled ginger); pizza with pear, walnut, and pesto topped with blue cheese and mozzarella; and cioppino (a hearty seafood stew). We have to mention the impressive selection of live seafood including Monterey Bay prawns, giant lobster, abalone, Dungeness crab, and a variety of oysters. Blue Moon, which replaced Pisto's Paradiso Trattoria in the same location, is open every day. They have a full bar, a *Wine Spectator* award-winning wine list, and desserts that you will dream about long after they're consumed.

Epsilon   **$$**
422 Tyler Street, Monterey
(831) 655-8108

In downtown Monterey, Epsilon has become a favorite of Greek food enthusiasts. Appealing appetizers are the traditional Greek finger foods such as dolmas or gyros. Entrees, served with a tasty Greek salad, offer choices such as perfectly grilled lamb shanks or the crispy and creamy spanakopita. Both are Insider favorites. You will be especially tempted by the baklava for dessert. Epsilon serves lunch and dinner.

Hula's $$
622 Lighthouse Avenue, Monterey
(831) 655-4852

As a restaurant, Hula's is equal parts Asian, seafood, Hawaiian, and absolute fun. The casual beach party atmosphere is enhanced by an entertaining yet professional staff (which includes the owners). The lunch and dinner menus are essentially the same with soups, wraps, bowls, fresh fish prepared a variety of ways, and a lengthy list of creative and tasty appetizers that can be grouped into a meal. The portions are generous, and the sweet potato fries are out of this world, as is pretty much everything on the menu. They now have a full bar complete with a number of unique tropical concoctions, a short but sweet wine list, and a nice selection of beers. Hula's is open for lunch and dinner Tuesday through Saturday, dinner on Sunday, and they're closed Monday.

India's Clay Oven $$
150 Del Monte Avenue, Second Floor, Monterey
(831) 373-2529

Escape to India's Clay Oven for lunch or dinner and sample authentic Indian cuisine. The restaurant, in downtown Monterey across from the DoubleTree complex, serves vegetarian and nonvegetarian foods. Popular starters include pakora (crispy vegetable fritters) and samosa (stuffed vegetables). A particularly savory entree is the tandoori-roasted chicken, lamb, and seafood baked in a clay oven, an Indian tradition for thousands of years. The lunch buffet features 18 different choices; it's all

you can eat of exotic foods from a variety of regions in India.

Max's Grill $$
209 Forest Avenue, Pacific Grove
(831) 375-7997
www.maxgrill.com

Best described as Asian-inspired California cuisine, the menu at Max's Grill includes a little bit of everything, from sushi to steaks. Count on the exquisite flavors, incredible textures, and elegant presentations you might expect from a stylish eatery, without the stylish price. Tokyo-born and French-trained chef Max Muramatsu applies his ample experience (gained at the likes of Maxim's of Paris, Tokyo, and Anton & Michel, Carmel) to this establishment that he opened recently with wife Yuko. Max's Grill is open for dinner Tuesday through Sunday.

Pablo's Mexican Restaurant $
1184 Forest Avenue, Pacific Grove
(831) 646-8888

This casual place serves Mexican food using no animal fats in the preparation. The result is delicious, wholesome food for lunch or dinner. Pablo's serves plentiful portions and offers daily specials along with tried-and-true combination plates. Try one of the house specialties—red snapper tacos, seafood enchiladas, or Snapper Vera Cruz. The chicken and cheese enchiladas are especially tasty, as are the tostadas. Served a la carte, the burrito is a meal in itself. For dessert, try the homemade flan—it's rich, creamy, and very delicious! Pablo's serves a variety of beer and wine.

WORTH THE DRIVE

Cielo at Ventana Inn & Spa $$$$
Highway 1, 28 miles south of Carmel, Big Sur
(831) 667-4242
www.ventanainn.com

Absorb the famed 40-mile panorama of the Big Sur coast while dining on eclectic California cuisine at this internationally

Hula's on Lighthouse Avenue in New Monterey is a favorite of locals for excellent food that won't break the bank, a fun, beach-party atmosphere, and great service. MICHAEL CHATFIELD

known, Mobil 4-star award-winning restaurant. Attention to the little details is what creates perfection. Innovative use of vegetables and herbs from the on-site organic garden is what sets Cielo apart from other restaurants. The menu, a lovely collection of small and large plates, changes with the seasons to capitalize on the use of organically grown vegetables and herbs (many grown in Cielo's gardens) and fresh seafood. Consider the chilled watermelon soup with minted black mission figs; a salad of organic micro greens, morel mushrooms, fava beans, French breakfast radish, and fiddlehead ferns with mushroom-truffle vinaigrette; the sumac-dusted wild Alaskan king salmon with fennel, fava beans, sweet 100 tomatoes, and Pernod foam; and the oak-grilled Colorado lamb loin with roasted vegetable caponata, chickpea fritter, and lamb jus. Freshly baked bread and elegant dessert creations from the on-site bakery are also on the menu. A stellar wine list of California and imported wines concentrates on vintages from the Central Coast. Cielo, which means "heaven" or "sky" in Italian, serves lunch and dinner daily; we recommend Cielo as a divine culinary adventure.

The Covey at Quail Lodge $$$$
8205 Valley Greens Drive, Carmel Valley
(831) 620-8860
www.quaillodge.com

Relax and enjoy a Euro-Californian–inspired dinner overlooking a glistening lake, splashing fountains, lush gardens, and splendid golfing greens. The menu changes daily, but you'll usually find a sumptuous variety of fish such as snapper, sole, salmon, and sea bass. Center-cut veal loin, roast rack of lamb, and New York steak are delectable possibilities for the meat entrees. The wine list includes a full page of half-bottles, highlighted by an award-winning selection of California and Monterey County wines. Desserts fall under the category of unforgettable dining pleasures. The Covey serves dinner only and has a recommended dress code: jackets for men and no jeans, shorts, or athletic attire.

Gutirrez Drive-In $
61 Sherwood Drive, Salinas
(831) 424-8382

The most authentic Mexican food on the central coast is to be had at this unassuming little place in Salinas. The *carnitas* (slow-roasted pork) is quite simply heaven on a plate. A huge serving of savory, succulent pork with rice, beans, salad, and guacamole will set you back less than $6.00 and put leftovers in the fridge for lunch tomorrow. *Mariscos* (seafood) is also a specialty. The *ceviche* is fish, squid, or shrimp with onions, tomatoes, and cilantro, marinated in lime juice and served with crackers. Everything here goes well with one of their selection of Mexican and American beers. Gutirrez is always packed with locals, so come early and stake out a spot at one of the big, family-style picnic tables outside. Open all day, every day.

Nepenthe $$$
Highway 1, 28 miles south of Carmel, Big Sur
(831) 667-2345,
www.nepenthebigsur.com

Family-owned and operated since 1949, Nepenthe maintains a commitment to simple yet delicious food. Spacious decks overlook the Pacific Ocean, the Santa Lucia Mountains, and a 40-mile inspirational view of the Big Sur coastline. Nepenthe's famous Ambrosia burger, made with a special grind of beef, is served on a French roll with Nepenthe sauce and a choice of three salads. Vegetarians can experience the legend, too, by ordering the tofu burger, prepared in the same manner (the secret's in the sauce). Another winner is Lolly's Roast Chicken, stuffed with an aromatic sage dressing and served with cranberry sauce. The homemade desserts are abundant help-

The local restaurant scene is remarkably stable. Sure, you'll find changes here and there, from time to time, but you'll also find an unusually high number of dining establishments that have remained popular for one, two, or many more decades. We think that's a testament to the quality of restaurants we have here on the Monterey Peninsula.

ings of four-layer chocolate cake, apple pie, and triple berry pie, just to name a few. Lunch and dinner are served. Breakfast and lunch are also available at the open-air cafe, Keva, from March to early January (weather permitting).

Phil's Fish Market & Eatery $
7600 Sandholtd Road, Moss Landing
(831) 633-2152
www.philsfishmarket.com

It's unpretentious and informal but that's what makes this Moss Landing restaurant charming and fun. There's indoor and heated outdoor seating. You can't go wrong with any of the fresh seafood selections here! The Sicilian artichokes, stuffed with bread crumbs and whole garlic cloves and poached in white wine and garlic, are tremendous. Pasta lovers will appreciate the huge platter of linguini smothered with olive oil, garlic, olives, capers, mushrooms, white wine, and Dungeness crab. Phil's serves beer and wine. It's open for lunch and dinner daily. Phil's now features live music on Monday and Thursday nights.

Rocky Point Restaurant $$$$
Highway 1, 12 miles south of Carmel
(831) 624-2933
www.rocky-point.com

Location, location, location . . . Rocky Point has it. This landmark restaurant, serving breakfast, lunch, and dinner, is high on top of a bluff overlooking the mighty Pacific Ocean. Floor-to-ceiling glass on the coastal side of the building means that every seat in the house has a magnificent

Walking along the coastal recreation trail, you'll find yourself in a natural setting for a progressive lunch or dinner. Stop on Cannery Row, Fisherman's Wharf, or downtown Monterey. Have an appetizer here, a salad there, and an entree at yet another establishment. It's a great way to "earn" your calories and sample several of our fine eateries.

ocean view. Weather permitting, outdoor seating allows you an even closer ocean-side table. Enjoy a meal while watching for spouting whales, sea lions, otters, pelicans, and shore birds. Lunch features lighter fare including soups, salads, and a selection of south of the border dishes. After sunset you can still enjoy an illuminated view of rocks, cliffs, and ocean. The dinner menu features steaks and fish barbecued over hardwood charcoal and mesquite. Choose from swordfish, salmon, lobster tail, prawns, chicken, pork ribs, lamb chops, or one of several cuts of beef. All dinners include an old-fashioned relish tray, toasted cheddar cheese bread, Boston clam chowder or green salad, and a large baked potato with cheddar cheese butter. For steak-house–style food in an unbeatable locale, stop in at Rocky Point.

Sole Mio Caffé Trattoria $$
3 Del Fino Place, Carmel Valley
(831) 659-9119
www.restauranteur.com/solemio

Prepare yourself for romance at this authentic Southern Italian restaurant tucked away in the village of Carmel Valley. A tiny patio enshrouded by flowering vines creates a garden setting. The addition of umbrella tables and cozy gas heaters make this a year-round option. Adding to the ambience inside are cheery

Mediterranean colors, checkered tablecloths, and Chianti bottles with drippy candles. Antique cooking utensils, straw baskets, and garlic strands accent the Italian decor. The food is no less appealing. A sun-dried tomato sauce and Italian bread are delivered to your table upon arrival. Pasta dishes include mouthwatering crab ravioli in a shrimp-lobster sauce or light gnocchi with a pleasing tomato-basil sauce. For those with a hearty appetite, entrees of seafood, veal, and chicken can be added to a meal of pasta. For dessert try the lemony Torta De La Nona. Sole Mio serves wine only, an excellent selection from Italy and California. It is open for lunch and dinner daily except Monday.

The Whole Enchilada $
Highway 1 and Moss Landing Road, Moss Landing
(831) 633–3038
www.wenchilada.com

For the owners of The Whole Enchilada, a Mexican meal is a melding of regional cuisine with geographic and historical influences. For example, the menu is influenced by old family recipes and the ample supply of fresh seafood from the Monterey Bay. High quality is the hallmark of this restaurant. Everything on the menu is made fresh daily. House specialties include Seafood Sopes, a delicious blend of jumbo prawns and crabmeat topped with refried beans and salsa. The Oaxacan Chicken Mole Tamales are wrapped in banana leaves, which seep a unique flavor into the tamales. Also try the chicken Chile Verde tamales. There is a full-service bar. The view of Moss Landing Harbor and live music and dancing on the weekends make this a great place to unwind. The Whole Enchilada is open for lunch and dinner every day.

WINE COUNTRY

The Monterey County wine industry has experienced explosive growth during the last few decades. Following their success in the wine industry in Napa Valley to the north, the "big players" in California wine turned their attention to the climatologically similar Salinas Valley. Warm summer days are tempered by evening fog from the Monterey Bay, providing for an exceptionally long growing season—perfect conditions for the French varietals currently in vogue among wine consumers.

Soon, the established winemakers were followed by a new breed: young, entrepreneurial, wine-loving mavericks who transformed the county from one that was famous for its lettuce and vegetable crops into a world-class wine region.

Unlike most agricultural products, wine grapes are grown in soil that is often rocky and does not retain moisture well. This allows the winegrower to "stress" the vines by carefully rationing water to obtain the perfect mixture of sugar and acidity that is the hallmark of a premium wine grape.

Wine has been made in Monterey County since the late 1700s, when grapes were planted by Franciscan friars at Mission San Antonio in the southern part of the county. The oldest vines still producing were planted in 1919 on the eastern slope of the Salinas Valley.

Today, there are in excess of 60 wineries in the county and more than 45,000 acres of planted vineyards in seven distinct American Viticultural Areas (AVAs). The most popular varieties produced are chardonnay, cabernet sauvignon, merlot, and pinot noir. Monterey County wines consistently win prestigious awards and are now recognized as among the finest in the world.

Many wineries maintain tasting rooms, offering samples of their vintages and on-site sales. In general, winemakers love to share their passion for wine and the process of making it, and tours are often available. It's best to call and make individual arrangements. The Monterey County Vintners and Growers Association has produced a free Wine Tasting Map and Guide that is available at www.montereywines.org or by calling (831) 375-9400.

AVAs

American Viticultural Area, or AVA, refers to the place of origin of wine grapes. A vineyard's location comprises geography, climate, soil composition, and viticultural practices that combine to create the characteristics unique to that locale. The Monterey County wine-growing region includes seven AVAs, each identified as one-of-a-kind winegrowing districts or appellations. With even a cursory understanding of each Monterey County AVA, the name of the appellation on the wine label provides insight into the wine's special flavor and character.

Monterey AVA—The Monterey AVA, the largest appellation in Monterey County, encompasses a wide range of microclimates varying by proximity to the climatic influence of Monterey Bay. This appellation offers winegrowers one of California's longest, gentlest ripening seasons. More than 50 percent of the Monterey AVA is planted to chardonnay.

Carmel Valley AVA—Although Father Junipero Serra's padres established vineyards here in the 1800s, it wasn't until 1968 that commercial grape growing began with 40 acres of cabernet sauvignon in the Cachagua region of the Carmel Valley. The Valley's 19,200 mountainous acres were granted unique AVA status in 1983. The well-drained, gravelly terraces of the district, along with warm days and cool nights, are well suited to the red varieties of the Bordeaux region of France. More than 70 percent of the area's 300 cultivated acres are planted to cabernet sauvignon, merlot, and cabernet franc.

Arroyo Seco AVA—First planted in 1962, this AVA extends from a steep canyon at its westernmost border, opening to encompass the benches around the Salinas River near the towns of Soledad and Greenfield. Bordeaux grape varieties prosper in the mouth of the canyon, protected from wind and warmed by heat generated by the surrounding cliffs. The valley floor is much cooler, providing ideal conditions for the Burgundian varietals. A unique aspect of this AVA's soil, "Greenfield Potatoes" are small cobblestones that store and release heat and provide excellent drainage.

San Lucas AVA—This area of Monterey County was cattle grazing range for around 150 years until vineyards were first planted here in 1970. With very warm days and cool nights, daily summer temperatures can swing by nearly 50 degrees. This AVA is made up of alluvial fans and terraces with elevations ranging from 500 to 1,200 feet. The soil is a combination of diatomaceous shale and varying types of sandstone.

Santa Lucia Highlands AVA—Approved in 1991 as an AVA, the area's vineyards are planted on the southeast-facing terraces of the Santa Lucia Mountains. Ancient, glacial soils pair with ocean fog and breezes to create an ideal environment for cool climate varietals such as chardonnay, riesling, and pinot noir. Bordeaux and Rhone grape types thrive in the region's warmer, protected canyons.

Chalone AVA—Planted in 1919, the Chalone AVA is home to the oldest producing vines in the county. Chalone sits at 1,800 feet in the Gavilan Mountain Range, near the Pinnacles National Monument. This dramatic locale can see daily temperature shifts from the high 90s to the low 50s. This AVA's unique soils consist of clay and limestone, and it is planted to

300 acres of primarily chardonnay, pinot noir, and pinot blanc.

Hames Valley AVA—The newest AVA in Monterey County, Hames Valley was approved as an AVA in 1994. The grape growing section of the district is sheltered from the strong winds of the Salinas Valley. On average, Hames Valley is much warmer than the majority of the county's northern wine-growing regions, yet the cool air of Monterey Bay still makes its presence felt. The soil composition is primarily shaley loam, and its warmer climate is best suited to growing red wine grapes.

A SAMPLING OF THE TASTING ROOMS IN MONTEREY COUNTY

A Taste of Monterey
700 Cannery Row, Monterey
(831) 646-5446
127 Main Street, Salinas
(831) 751-1980
www.tastemonterey.com
A convenient place to sample wines from many Monterey County producers in one stop. The Cannery Row location offers the bonus of stunning views of the Monterey Bay. This establishment has a large selection of wines for sale, and the gift shop offers wine-related merchandise.

Baywood Cellars
381 Cannery Row, Suite C, Monterey
(831) 645-9035
www.baywood-cellars.com
Located across the street from The Monterey Plaza Hotel, Baywood offers tastings of their award-winning wines, including chardonnay, pinot grigio, and symphony varietals. Baywood also produces a port made from grapes imported from Portugal.

Bernardus Winery
5 West Carmel Valley Road, Carmel Valley
(831) 659-1900
www.bernardus.com
One of the newer stars in the Monterey

County wine constellation, Bernardus has taken its rightful place among the top producers in the area. Known for an exquisite chardonnay, this winery makes wonderful reds as well. There is a $5.00 charge for tasting, and a $10.00 "reserve pour" includes a wine charm. Reservations for groups of eight or more are recommended.

Blackstone Winery
800 South Alta Street, Gonzales
(831) 675-5341
www.blackstonewinery.com
Taste Blackstone Winery's flagship merlot and other vintages at their Monterey County winery and tasting room. Enjoy the rotating art exhibit in the tasting room and bring a picnic to savor on their lovely grounds. Open every day.

Chalone Vineyard
Highway 146 East and Stonewall Canyon Road, Soledad
(831) 678-1717
www.chalonevineyard.com
"Producing some of the world's most hedonistic wines," Chalone Vineyards offers its world-famous chardonnay as well as pinot blanc, chenin blanc, pinot noir, and syrah vintages. Tastings and tours are available 11:30 A.M. to 5:00 P.M. weekends and on weekdays by appointment only.

Chateau Julien Wine Estate
8940 Carmel Valley Road, Carmel Valley
(831) 624-2600
www.chateaujulien.com
Guests are welcome daily at this winery located in Carmel Valley. The beautiful gardens are perfect for a picnic with a bottle of Chateau Julien wine. This winery also presents several special events during the year, including an elegant winemaker's dinner among the barrels of its unique "chai" room.

Chateau Sinnet
13746 Center Street, Carmel Valley
(831) 659-2244
www.chateausinnet.com
Located in Carmel Valley Village, the Chateau Sinnet tasting room pours

chardonnay, pinot noir, cabernet sauvignon, sparkling wines, and fruit-flavored specialties.

Cloninger Cellars
1645 River Road, Salinas
(831) 675-9463
www.usawines.com/cloninger/
The Cloninger tasting room is located in a vineyard planted with chardonnay and pinot noir grapes. Tours of the winery are available upon request.

Galante Vineyards
18181 Cachagua Road, Carmel Valley
(800) 425-2683
www.galantevineyards.com
It's a long drive to Galante but well worth it. The rows of vines here are interspersed with roses, and cattle graze in the distance. Carmel Valley enjoys a warmer climate than that of the Salinas Valley, and red wine grapes such as cabernet sauvignon and merlot flourish here. Tasting by appointment only.

Visit www.montereywines.org or call (831) 375-9400 for a free copy of the Wine Tasting Map and Guide *created by The Monterey County Vintners and Growers Association.*

Georis Winery
4 Pilot Road, Carmel Valley
(831) 659-1050
www.georiswine.com
Situated in an old adobe building surrounded by lush gardens and outdoor tables, Georis' tasting room provides the perfect atmosphere in which to sample the winery's exquisite cabernet and merlot. Owner Walter Georis is also a highly regarded Carmel restaurateur.

Hahn Estates/Smith & Hook Winery
37700 Foothill Road, Soledad
(831) 678-2132
www.hahnestates.com
In a lovely setting overlooking the Salinas

Many winemakers host elegant events such as the winemaker's dinners at Chateau Julien.
CHATEAU JULIEN

Valley, this new facility offers tasting in a fun and informative setting. A gift shop features wine-related merchandise, and the winery has a facility for weddings and special events. A standout here is the Hahn Estates chardonnay, made from grapes grown on the premises of the winery.

Heller Estate
69 West Carmel Valley Road,
Carmel Valley
(831) 659-6220
www.hellerestate.com
Heller Estate's 100-percent certified

organic wines are showcased at a rustic tasting room close to Carmel Valley Village. A sculpture garden featuring the 15-foot "Dances on Your Palate" is adjacent to the building. Heller is world-renowned for both red and white varietals.

Joullian Vineyards
2 Village Drive, Suite A, Carmel Valley
(866) 659-8101
www.joullian.com
A tasteful, attractive Carmel stone building in Carmel Valley Village houses the

Joullian Vineyards tasting room. The room is lined with photos of the vineyards taken by a local photographer. Joullian's chardonnay, sauvignon blanc, zinfandel, and cabernet sauvignon are highly regarded.

Paraiso Vineyards/Cobblestone Vineyard
38060 Paraiso Springs Road, Soledad
(831) 678-0300
www.paraisovineyards.com
An open and airy room that features a panoramic view of the Salinas Valley houses the Paraiso/Cobblestone tasting room. The friendly, knowledgeable staff is happy to guide even first-time tasters through the many varieties produced by these two world-class wineries.

Pavona Wines
1645 River Road, Salinas
(831) 646-1506
www.pavonawines.com
Brand-new, the Pavona tasting room features chardonnay, pinot noir, syrah, and zinfandel. The winery was established in 1995 and has quickly gained rave reviews for its approach to premium winemaking.

Robert Talbott Vineyards
53 West Carmel Valley Road,
Carmel Valley
(831) 659-3500
www.talbottvineyards.com
One of the oldest established and highly respected premium wineries in Monterey County, Robert Talbott is a family operation—several wines are even named after members of the Talbott family. Talbott wines are exceptional, and production is small, with an emphasis on quality rather than on quantity.

San Saba Vineyards
19 East Carmel Valley Road, Carmel Valley
(831) 753-7222
www.sansaba.com
San Saba is a boutique winery that has been producing wine in very limited quantities since 1981. The tasting room, in

Carmel Valley Village, is open Thursday through Sunday in summer, weekends only the rest of the year.

Scheid Vineyards
1972 Hobson Avenue, Greenfield
(831) 386-0316, (888) 478-4946
www.scheidvineyards.com
It's easy to find Scheid. Just look for the huge American flag beside Highway 101 south of Greenfield. Scheid people make tasting fun and are likely to challenge your taste buds with unusual combinations of flavors. There is a demonstration vineyard next to the tasting room, showcasing techniques used in producing Scheid's highly regarded vintages.

Check our Getting Here, Getting Around chapter for information on limousine services—a safe and relaxing way to tour Monterey County wine country and sample the fruit of our vines.

Ventana Vineyards/Meador Estate
2999 Monterey-Salinas Highway #10,
Monterey
(831) 372-7415
www.ventanawines.com
In the charming stone buildings that also house Tarpy's Roadhouse, you'll find the tasting room of Ventana Vineyards/Meador Estate. Complimentary tastings of their chardonnay, sauvignon blanc, dry chenin blanc, Riesling, syrah, merlot, and other varietals let you see for yourself why Ventana Vineyards/Meador Estate is known as "the most award-winning vineyard in America." Bring a picnic lunch and enjoy it on their lovely patio, browse the gift shop, and read about winemaker Doug Meador's many contributions to the growth of Monterey County's wine industry. Open daily 11:00 A.M. to 5:00 P.M.

Suggested Itinerary for a Wine-Tasting Tour

A wonderful way to spend a day is by sampling some of the world-class wines produced in Monterey County. And what better place to do that than at the wineries themselves? Although there are more than two dozen tasting rooms in the county, we have chosen seven for our tour. For those wishing to explore further, a free wine-tasting map is available from the Monterey County Vintners and Growers Association at (831) 375-9400 or at www.montereywines.org.

To begin a wine-tasting tour from the Monterey Peninsula, head east on Highway 68 toward Salinas. The best time to depart is about 10:30 A.M. since most of the wineries open at 11:00 A.M. and you'll need an early start to fit in all seven on this tour by the general closing time of 5:00 P.M. Before reaching Salinas proper, take the off-ramp for River Road (G-17), which follows the Salinas River south along the foothills of the eastern edge of the Santa Lucia Mountains. (Note that at about mile 9, River Road jogs off to the right: Don't follow the highway straight to the town of Chualar.) The first vineyards begin to appear as you approach the start of the wine region near the town of Gonzales.

At mile 15, **Cloninger Cellars,** on your left at 1645 River Road in Salinas, is one of the smallest wineries in Salinas Valley and the first stop on our tasting tour. This 51-acre vineyard has quickly gained a strong reputation for its chardonnay, pinot noir, and cabernet sauvignon. Cloninger has a small, pleasant tasting room with a nice view overlooking the Salinas Valley. Its wines are available at only a few select markets and shops, so your best bet is to purchase directly from the winery. Tasting hours are 11:00 A.M. to 4:00 P.M. Monday through Thursday, 11:00 A.M. to 5:00 P.M. Friday through Sunday. Reach them by calling (831) 675-9463 or visit www.usawines.com/cloninger.

From Cloninger Cellars, continue south on River Road. At approximately mile 17, the road will bend to the east at Gonzales Road, and you have to make a right turn at the elbow in order to continue south on River Road. At approximately mile 24, River Road ends. Take the right fork to Foothill Road and continue onward for another 3 miles. There you will find a signed dirt road, at 37700 Foothill Road in Soledad, that rises into the foothills to **Smith & Hook Winery,** (831) 678-2132, www.hahnestates.com. The dirt road meanders about 1.5 miles uphill to the wine-tasting room and extensive gift shop. Smith & Hook Winery produces from five vineyards and bottles its wine under two labels. The Smith & Hook label features premium cabernet sauvignon, merlot, and viognier wines meant to be laid down in the cellar for a number of years to achieve peak drinkability. Hahn Estates is the name of the label of Smith & Hook wines sold for immediate enjoyment. And for the money, they are some of the nicest wines available from Monterey County. You can enjoy a very pleasant merlot, a light French-style chardonnay, a spicy Cabernet Franc, or a blended Meritage. If you happen to be visiting the Monterey Peninsula in early December, check out the schedule for Smith & Hook's annual wreath-making party. Each year it draws up to 1,000 participants who make their holiday wreaths out of dried grape vines while sampling the splendid wines and enjoying a hearty barbecue. Tasting hours are 11:00 A.M. to 4:00 P.M. daily.

Continue south on Foothill Road about 2 miles to the entrance to **Paraiso Vineyards,** 38060 Paraiso Springs Road, Soledad, (831) 678–0300, www.paraisovineyards.com. This 400-acre estate affords excellent views of the Salinas Valley below and the Pinnacles in the Gabilan Mountains beyond. An outdoor deck with ample seating is an excellent spot to enjoy a picnic lunch along with your bottle of wine. And what a great selection of wine it is. Current releases include chardonnay, syrah, pinot noir, and Riesling. The winemaker also bottles his own Cobblestone Chardonnay, a smooth, smoky wine aged in first-year French oak. Then there are the specialty selections like the pinot blanc reserve, syrah, port souzao, a late-harvest Riesling, and a sweet dessert wine, a late-harvest pinot noir, excellent poured lightly over vanilla ice cream. Tasting hours are noon to 4:00 P.M. Monday through Friday, 11:00 A.M. to 5:00 P.M. Saturday and Sunday.

As you leave Paraiso Springs, cross Foothill Road and continue east on Paraiso Springs Road approximately 1 mile to Arroyo Seco (G-17) and turn right (south). Follow Arroyo Seco for about 4 miles to Thorn Road. Turn left (east) and drive 2.5 miles to El Camino Real. Turn right and drive 1.5 miles to Walnut, turn left 1 mile to U.S. 101 south. Proceed 3 miles south on U.S. 101 to Hobson Avenue and exit west (right) to **Scheid Vineyards** at 1972 Hobson Avenue, Greenfield, (831) 386–0316, (888) 478–4946, www.scheidvineyards.com. There you'll find a converted 1920s-era barn that now serves as a modern tasting room. Scheid Vineyards was founded in 1972 and, with more than 6,000 acres under its ownership or management, is among the country's largest independent producers of premium varietal wine grapes. The wines are actually produced at Storrs Winery in Santa Cruz under the Scheid label. More than 4,500 cases of high-quality chardonnay, white Riesling, merlot, pinot noir, Gewurztraminer, sauvignon blanc, and cabernet sauvignon are bottled each year. The tasting room is open 11:00 A.M. to 5:00 P.M. daily.

From Scheid, it's a long but beautiful journey to our next destination. Carefully cut back across U.S. 101 and continue east on Hobson Avenue to the end at Metz Road. Turn left (north) and follow Metz Road through the beautiful foothills of the Gabilan Mountains for approximately 6 miles until you reach Highway 146, the western entrance to Pinnacles National Monument (see our write-up in the Day Trips chapter). Turning right on Highway 146, you'll wind approximately 6 miles up a narrow canyon until you reach Stonewall Canyon Road. Turn left at the sign and continue about a mile to the tasting room of **Chalone Vineyard,**

Monterey County now produces more than 45,000 acres of grapes, with more than 60 wineries in the county. MARTIN BROWN/MONTEREY COUNTY CONVENTION AND VISITORS BUREAU

(831) 678-1717, www.vineyard.com. Chalone is open for public tasting 11:30 A.M. to 5:00 P.M. every weekend and on weekdays by appointment only, so call ahead Monday through Friday. Chalone features a nice selection of chardonnay (barrel fermented and aged), pinot noir, cabernet sauvignon, chenin blanc, syrah, viognier, and pinot blanc. The reserve pinot noir is deep and intense, and the limited-quantity A-Frame cabernet sauvignon is available exclusively at the tasting room.

For our final destination, proceed back east on Highway 146 to Metz Road and turn right (north). Go approximately 2.5 miles to the town of Soledad and turn left on East Street and then a quick right on Front Street.

Front Street will take you back to U.S. 101, where you will proceed north for about 7 miles to the city of Gonzales. At Gonzales, exit on Alta Street and continue west less than a mile to **Blackstone Winery,** 800 South Alta Street, Gonzales, (831) 675-5341, www.blackstonewinery.com. The expansive wine-tasting room is open daily from 11:00 A.M. to 4:00 P.M. The Blackstone wine portfolio includes merlot, cabernet sauvignon, and chardonnay.

To return to Monterey Peninsula, continue north on Alta Road, which hooks back up with U.S. 101, and proceed north on U.S. 101 to Highway 68 West.

WINE TOUR OPERATORS

There are many options for touring and tasting Monterey County's wineries. Although the area's limousine services are happy to accommodate your personal wine adventure, the following businesses specialize in wine-tasting tours.

Ag Venture Tours
(831) 643–9463
www.agventuretours.com

Half-day and full-day tours visit Salinas Valley and Carmel Valley wineries led by fun, friendly, and knowledgeable guides. Ag Venture can accommodate large groups.

Many area restaurants feature Monterey County wines, some by the glass, so you can enjoy a little wine tasting with your meal.

Monterey Bay Scenic Tours (MBST)
(800) 343–6437
www.mbstours.com

This company will put together a wine tour based on the client's preferences. Want to check out the robust reds of Carmel Valley? Desire to taste the winning whites of the Santa Lucia Highlands? MBST can arrange a tour to satisfy every wine lover's desire.

NIGHTLIFE ⓨ

When we told friends we were working on the Nightlife chapter for this book, a common response was a sarcastic, "It will be a short chapter, won't it?" That'll give you a hint of how some locals perceive nightlife on the mostly quiet Monterey Peninsula.

It's true that compared to many larger urban areas, such as San Francisco and San Jose to the north, the Monterey Peninsula does not have a highly spirited night scene. Part of the reason can be traced back to the roots of Carmel and Pacific Grove, both of which have histories of imposing near-Puritanical restrictions on such lurid activities as drinking alcohol or playing raucous music. Monterey, however, has long been a center of nightly entertainment for, first, the merchants and laborers of the sea and, second, the soldiers stationed at the Presidio of Monterey and Fort Ord. Readers of John Steinbeck's *Cannery Row* are familiar with the types of late-night entertainment that Monterey has historically offered. Today, even with both the canneries and the army base long gone, the Monterey Peninsula nightlife still provides a smattering of activities to please locals and visitors looking for a night on the town.

Since the Peninsula is a tourist destination, you'll find an ample supply of bars and pubs, a number of which are inside the major hotels and leading restaurants that populate the area. For live music and dancing, the choices are more limited. Still, there seems to be a sufficient number of late-night clubs to meet the not-so-high demands of local night owls. In fact, over the last few years, a number of clubs have opened and then suddenly closed their doors due to lack of community support. As the California State University at Monterey Bay continues to grow, locals hope the area will be able to support a couple more live music and dance venues. Notable nighttime choices for the teen crowd are especially lacking, but there are coffeehouses, movie theaters, and other entertainment choices to draw out people of all ages for an enjoyable night.

Note that the legal drinking age in California is 21, and minors are prohibited in most bars and pubs. Also, smoking is prohibited in nearly all indoor public establishments in the state, including bars (see our Close-up in this chapter).

In this chapter we provide a list of some of the most popular Peninsula nightspots, arranged by type of activity and, where numbers warrant, by locale. This list is by no means exhaustive, and the details regarding what venues offer which entertainment on what nights change frequently. We recommend that while in town you check out the local newspapers (*The Monterey County Herald* and *The Pine Cone*) and entertainment weekly (*Coast Weekly*) for a list of the current nighttime activities (see our Media chapter for more about these publications). Have fun, but be safe and careful!

BARS AND PUBS

Listed here is a sampling of Monterey Peninsula bars and pubs, including sports bars and microbreweries. A few places provide live or DJ music on the side, but the more dynamic music and dancing establishments are listed in this chapter under the heading "Clubs."

Monterey

Britannia Arms
444 Alvarado Street, Monterey
(831) 656-9543
www.britanniaarms.com

At Britannia Arms, you'll find a comfortable tavern with plenty of hearty beers (24 drafts, including Guinness) and good English fare like steak and kidney pie or bangers and mash, along with American choices. You'll find live music on Thursday through Saturday, karaoke on Sunday, and a fun trivia contest on Thursday nights. Serious games of darts and dominoes are not for the faint of heart.

Bulldog British Pub
611 Lighthouse Avenue, Monterey
(831) 372-5565
Great Britain comes to Monterey at this small New Monterey neighborhood bar. You'll find plenty of English ales as well as a variety of British menu items such as shepherd's pie or bangers and mash. Try one of the 16 beers on tap, or live dangerously and order "Red Silk Knickers." Darts are the game of choice at the Bulldog. Night owls will appreciate the fact that breakfast is served all hours. The Bulldog British Pub is open nightly until 2:00 A.M., but the kitchen closes weeknights at 11:00 P.M.

Casa Cafe & Bar
700 Munras Avenue, Monterey
(831) 375-2411
In the Casa Munras Garden Hotel, the Casa Cafe & Bar is a rather quiet but popular gathering spot for downtown locals and hotel guests to mix and mingle after work or on weekend evenings. There's a low-key atmosphere that allows for friendly conversation and a relaxing evening. You can enjoy live easy-listening music Friday and Saturday nights until 11:00 P.M.

Characters Sports Bar & Grill
350 Calle Principal, Monterey
(831) 647-4023
Located in the Monterey Marriott Hotel, Characters is a lively downtown sports bar full of sports memorabilia and big-screen TVs to catch a variety of professional and college events. The full bar features a wide selection of beers and ales, and the bar snacks and grill fare are rather good, with complimentary appetizers during weekday happy hours. DJ dance music is provided Friday nights. There is karaoke on Tuesday, Wednesday, Thursday, and Saturday evenings. Characters is open until 2:00 A.M.

Crown & Anchor
150 West Franklin Street, Monterey
(831) 649-6496
www.crownandanchor.net
This downtown establishment has been voted the number-one pub in Monterey. Models of old sailing ships and other nautical artifacts provide an ideal atmosphere. The 20 beers on tap include English ales and Irish stouts, as well as pilsners and microbrews. You'll also find nice single-malt scotches, smooth bourbons, and tasty ports and wines. Plus, there's a full menu of traditional pub fare, wonderful appetizers, and great burgers. Crown & Anchor has a daily happy hour from 4:00 to 6:00 P.M. and is open nightly until 2:00 A.M.

El Palomar of Monterey
724 Abrego Street, Monterey
(831) 372-1032
Margaritas and Mexican beer are the chart toppers at El Palomar, a Mexican seafood restaurant that showcases a full bar with ample seating if you just want to drop in for some nachos and a cold one. The indoor setting is cantina-casual, while the open patio has a cozy fire pit, perfect for cuddling or relaxing on a pleasant evening. Acoustic Latin music adds to the cantina atmosphere on Saturday and Sunday nights. The bar is open until 11:00 P.M. on Friday and Saturday, but closes at 9:30 P.M. Sunday through Thursday.

El Torito
600 Cannery Row, Monterey
(831) 373-0611
This Mexican restaurant chain specializes in margaritas of many flavors. It's a great happy-hour spot for inexpensive food and drink. A big plus is that you're right on the water on Cannery Row with great bayside

views. El Torito is open until midnight on Friday and Saturday and until 11:00 P.M. Sunday through Thursday.

The Fish Hopper
700 Cannery Row, Monterey
(831) 372-8543

For a festive happy hour or early nightcap after a stroll down Cannery Row, consider The Fish Hopper. This popular restaurant has a large bar that offers many tropical specialties to enjoy indoors or on the outside patio. Try the "Volcano" and feel the heat on a cool Monterey evening. Take advantage of the great views during the weekday 4:00 to 7:00 P.M. happy hour, with inexpensive drinks and tasty seafood treats like shrimp cocktail and fresh oysters. The Fish Hopper bar usually closes by 9:00 P.M. on weekdays and 10:00 P.M. on weekends, depending on the level of restaurant activity.

Knuckles Historical Sports Bar
1 Old Golf Course Road, Monterey
(831) 372-1234

At the Hyatt Monterey, Knuckles is the biggest and typically the most active sports bar on the Peninsula. It has 17 TVs, some with satellite hookups, to provide a wealth of sports programming year-round. Local sports fans love the free popcorn and peanuts to enjoy with their choice of 16 beers, plus there's an extensive pub menu. The full bar has ample seating to accommodate big crowds. Two pool tables add to the fun. Knuckles is open until midnight Sunday to Thursday, and until 1:00 A.M. on Friday and Saturday.

LALLApalooza
474 Alvarado Street, Monterey
(831 645-9036

LALLApalooza is a stylish martini bar and restaurant that caters to a young professional crowd that appreciates a well-made libation—including 14 kinds of martinis. Try the Classic, cold and dry, or the house special LALLApalooza martini with a citrus flair. The Big American Menu offers a choice of appetizers, salads, steaks, and pastas. LALLApalooza is open nightly until midnight and occasionally features live acoustic music.

Lighthouse Bar and Grill
281 Lighthouse Avenue, Monterey
(831) 373-4488
www.lighthousebarandgrill281.com

This casual neighborhood bar caters to the gay and lesbian community and welcomes everyone. Pool tables provide friendly diversions, including a Thursday night coed tournament. The Sunday beer bust and evening barbecue is a local favorite. Monday Night Football brings in a lot of people during the season. Lighthouse has a full bar, good grill fare, and a fun and friendly crowd. It's open daily until 2:00 A.M.

London Bridge Pub
Municipal Wharf #2, Monterey
(831) 655-2879

The London Bridge Pub offers more than 60 beers, festive games of darts and cribbage, and a traditional English pub menu—right at the entrance to Wharf #2. There's even a tea room in the back for traditional cream tea. "The Smarty Pants Show," a Monday-night trivia game with lots of fun and prizes, has become a Monterey tradition. Thursday is open-mike night, and Friday and Saturday feature live music. The bar is usually open until 2:00 A.M. nightly, and the kitchen serves food until 11:00 P.M. Friday and Saturday and 10:00 P.M. other nights.

Monterey Jacks Fish House and Sports Bar
711 Cannery Row, Monterey
(831) 655-4947

[Facing page] *Guys' night out? Consider Characters Sports Bar & Grill, located in the Monterey Marriott Hotel in downtown Monterey.* TOM OWENS

This upstairs sports bar and fish house in the heart of Cannery Row is frequented largely by a local crowd, so come prepared to root for the 49ers, Giants, and other San Francisco Bay area teams while dining on some good local seafood. Play Foosball or video games when the pros aren't in action. Monterey Jacks is open nightly until 11:00 P.M.

Montrio
414 Calle Principal, Monterey
(831) 648–8880
www.montrio.com

Montrio restaurant has a great little bar with intimate seating that's perfect for a quiet drink and sweet dessert after the movies or theater. There's also a wonderful wine list with a range of choices by the glass or bottle. Montrio is open until 11:00 P.M. on Friday and Saturday and 10:00 P.M. Sunday through Thursday.

Peter B.'s Brewpub
2 Portola Plaza Monterey
(831) 649–4511

Nestled in the back corner of the Double-Tree Hotel is Monterey's favorite microbrewery. Try one of the eight Carmel Brewery exclusives—the pilsner is highly recommended—while you watch the brewmaster at work. Pizza and other pub fare are served daily until 1:00 A.M., and a happy hour is held weekdays from 5:00 to 6:30 P.M. Pool tables and plenty of sports on TV make for a lively evening.

Sandbar & Grill
Municipal Wharf #2, Monterey
(831) 373–2818

Visitors are often surprised to find a true piano bar right under Municipal Wharf #2 in Monterey. The Sandbar & Grill is a small, cozy restaurant with a great harbor view, full bar, and the soothing sounds of a live pianist Friday and Saturday evenings. It's open until midnight Sunday through Thursday and until 1:00 A.M. Friday and Saturday. There's also a fun happy hour from 4:00 to 6:00 P.M. Mon-

day through Friday. Trivia note for film buffs: A scene from Clint Eastwood's *Play Misty For Me* was shot here when the establishment was known as the Windjammer.

Schooners Bistro on the Bay
400 Cannery Row, Monterey
(831) 372–2628
www.montereyplazahotel.com

Located on the bay side of the Monterey Plaza Hotel. Schooners Bistro on the Bay is an excellent choice for sunset-watching drinks and appetizers while down on Cannery Row. The outdoor patio sits right out over the bay, and on warm evenings you can watch the sky change from blue to purple to pink to red while watching otters and sea lions swim by. If it's too chilly, move indoors to the mahogany-floored restaurant decked in a nautical flair. You'll find a full bar with four beers on tap and a wide selection of wines by the glass. Schooners is open until 11:00 P.M. Sunday through Thursday and until midnight Friday and Saturday.

Tarpy's Roadhouse
2999 Monterey-Salinas Highway, Monterey
(831) 647–1444
www.tarpys.com

Got romance on the mind? Here's a great out-of-the-way restaurant and bar for a quiet after-dinner (or after-movie) drink for two. Tarpy's is in a historic stone house about 2.5 miles east of Highway 1 on the Monterey-Salinas Highway (Highway 68). It has a cozy atmosphere and a great wine list, full bar, and warm fireplace. The bar closes with the restaurant, which means most evenings by 11:00 P.M.

The Wharfside Restaurant and Lounge
60 Fisherman's Wharf, Monterey
(831) 375–3956

Although a number of the Fisherman's Wharf restaurants have full bars with a nice spot for an evening drink, the downstairs bar at the Wharfside is perhaps the

The bar inside Peppers Mexicali Cafe is a popular local hangout for Mexican beers and nachos. The sangria isn't bad either! TOM OWENS

most popular. The atmosphere is upscale, and the appetizers are downright delicious. Weeknight happy hours include free pizza. Live music is provided Friday evenings.

Pacific Grove

Peppers Mexicali Cafe
170 Forest Avenue, Pacific Grove
(831) 373-6892
A very popular local Mexican restaurant and hangout, Peppers serves beer and wine only in its friendly, cantina-style bar. Enjoy the neighborhood ambience with some nachos and one of the many microbrewed or Mexican beers or a tasty wine margarita. Peppers serves more than 20 local wines by the glass and makes a nice fruity sangria. It's open until 9:30 P.M. Sunday, Monday, Wednesday, and Thursday and until 10:30 P.M. Friday and Saturday. Peppers is closed on Tuesday.

Tinnery at the Beach
Ocean View Boulevard and 17th Street, Pacific Grove
(831) 646-1040
www.thetinnery.com
One of the few full bars in previously dry Pacific Grove, the Tinnery provides a relaxing atmosphere to enjoy the evening—with a great bay view. Live music, primarily light jazz and acoustic rock, is provided Wednesday through Saturday nights and during the Wednesday happy hour from 5:00 to 7:00 P.M. Other weeknights, happy hour runs from 4:00 to 6:00 P.M. with a complimentary buffet. The Tinnery is open until midnight Sunday through Thursday and until 1:00 A.M. Friday and Saturday.

Carmel

You aren't going to find too many towns with a quieter nightlife than Carmel. City ordinances prohibit such wild activities as loud music or the dastardly game of pool—which starts with P, which rhymes with T, which stands for trouble in By-the-Sea City. Seriously, though, within Carmel proper you'll find some great places to enjoy a quiet evening, indoors or out, with a refreshing drink, good food, and delightful company. Outside of the city proper, such as at The Barnyard and The Crossroads shopping centers at the mouth of Carmel Valley, things pick up a bit with some lively music.

The Forge in the Forest
Fifth Avenue and Junipero Street, Carmel
(831) 624-2233,
www.forgeintheforest.com
On a starry evening, sipping a hot B-52 drink while snuggled around one of the two fireplaces on the beautifully landscaped outdoor patio at The Forge can be an unforgettable Carmel experience. The indoor bar has its own crackling fire and serves 12 wines by the glass and four beers on draft. The bar at The Forge is open until midnight Sunday through Thursday and until 1:00 A.M. Friday and Saturday.

Highlands Inn's Sunset and Lobos Lounge
Highway 1, Carmel Highlands
(831) 624-3801
www.highlandsinn.com
Even if you're not staying at the Highlands Inn, a visit to the Sunset Lounge is worth the scenic drive south on Highway 1, especially for jazz fans. Plan on a cruise down the Big Sur coast to watch the sunset, then stop by this intimate piano lounge with quality music nightly by local artists. Piano music is presented 6:00 to 9:00 P.M. Thursday and Sunday, and a live jazz trio plays Friday and Saturday evenings from 9:00 P.M. until midnight. Specialty drinks include a tasty Absolut Mandarin Cosmopolitan and flavored martinis. The Sunset Lounge is open until midnight Sunday through Thursday and until 1:00 A.M. Friday and Saturday nights.

Jack London's Bar & Grill
Dolores and Sixth Avenue, Carmel
(831) 624-2336
www.jacklondonsgrill.com
Here's a lively local hangout, a bar and grill that offers casual fare and your favorite drink. The pub features four beers on tap and a full margarita menu. Happy hour with a complimentary buffet is offered Monday through Friday from 4:30 to 6:30 P.M. Jack London's is open nightly until 2:00 A.M., and the kitchen serves until midnight Sunday through Thursday.

Mission Ranch
26270 Dolores Street, Carmel
(831) 625-9040
The Mission Ranch, owned by Clint Eastwood, is a popular nightspot among local singles in the 30-plus crowd. The dining room features a festive piano bar with live music every night. There's mellow dinner music from 6:00 to 9:00 P.M. and a lively open-mike sing-along from 9:00 P.M. until midnight. Food is served until 10:00 P.M.

During the summer, arrive at sunset to stroll the splendid grounds, then sit back and enjoy a friendly fun-filled evening. On Dolores Street back behind the Carmel Mission, the Ranch can be a little hard to find in the dark, but it's definitely worth the effort.

Rio Grill
101 Crossroads Boulevard, Carmel
(831) 625-5436
www.riogrill.com
Here's a popular early evening choice for a drink and appetizers among the young urban professionals and local jet-setters. It's a place to see and be seen and is often frequented by out-of-town celebrities during the Pebble Beach Pro-Am and Concours d'Elegance. Besides all that, there's an extensive wine list and tasty margaritas, including the signature Rio Rita made with premium tequilas. The food is great too. Rio Grill is open until 10:00 P.M. Sunday through Thursday and until 11:00 P.M. on Friday and Saturday.

The piano bar at Mission Ranch in Carmel is a popular nightspot among the 30-something crowd. TOM OWENS

Sade's
Lincoln Street and Ocean Avenue, Carmel
(831) 624-0787

A local hangout since 1926, Sade's (pronounced "Sadie's") is a Carmel landmark. Named after Sade Latham, a Follies Girl, this 20-stool bar has welcomed such famous visitors as Bing Crosby, Bob Hope, Eddie Cantor, and Dean Martin. Today, you can join the locals in a friendly game of dice or darts while enjoying a great Bloody Mary or your own favorite drink. Sade's is open until 2:00 A.M. nightly.

Sherlock Holmes Pub & Restaurant
3772 The Barnyard, Carmel
(831) 625-0340

This isn't really a late-night spot since it closes at 9:00 P.M. most evenings, but it's still a worthwhile mention for fans of the master sleuth. The indoor and outdoor patios, both with fireplaces, are pleasant spots to enjoy one of the 40 beer selections, including Bass and Guinness on tap. If you're hungry, Sherlock Holmes makes good American burgers with decidedly British names, as well as the traditional bangers and mash, fish and chips, and pasties.

Pebble Beach

Peppoli/Lobby Lounge
The Inn at Spanish Bay, Pebble Beach
(831) 647-7500

For an early evening of live piano music Friday and Saturday, visit Peppoli at The Inn at Spanish Bay. Seating is provided until 10:00 P.M. nightly, with a full bar, an award-winning wine list, and great Italian desserts. Meanwhile, the Lobby Lounge outside of Roy's restaurant presents live music Thursday through Sunday from 7:00 to 11:00 P.M. Drinks and munchies are served.

Tap Room Bar & Grill
The Lodge at Pebble Beach,
17-Mile Drive, Pebble Beach
(831) 625-8535

The Tap Room is a favorite of hotel guests and locals who enjoy mingling in the casual, elegant atmosphere of The Lodge. The full bar features dozens of beers, including local microbrews on tap. The munchies menu ranges from oysters on the half-shell to great half-pound burgers. You'll also enjoy the fascinating collection of golf memorabilia, including many celebrity photos from The Crosby. The Tap Room is open nightly until midnight.

Terrace Lounge
The Lodge at Pebble Beach,
17-Mile Drive, Pebble Beach
(831) 624-3811

Enjoy live jazz from 6:30 to 10:30 P.M. Tuesday, 7:00 to 11:00 P.M. Wednesday and Thursday, and 8:00 P.M. until midnight Friday and Saturday. The lounge is open nightly until 1:00 A.M.

Traps
The Inn at Spanish Bay, Pebble Beach
(831) 647-7500

Here's a cozy Spanish Bay setting for a relaxing drink in a comfortable chair before a warm fireplace. There's a full bar with a terrific wine and single-malt selection plus late-night snacks and appetizers. Traps is open nightly until 1:00 A.M.

BILLIARDS

Monterey is definitely the place on the Peninsula for a nightly game of billiards. Although many bars, pubs, and clubs provide a table or two for your enjoyment, the only two billiard halls are your best bet for a serious game of 8-ball.

Blue Fin Cafe and Billiards
685 Cannery Row, Monterey
(831) 375-7000
www.bluefinbilliards.com

One of the busiest nightspots in town, Blue Fin Cafe offers 18 billiards tables, snooker, a shuffleboard court, air hockey, Foosball, and darts. Plus it's open every day until 2:00 A.M. The cafe serves freshly made sandwiches and other light fare all night, and the full bar features 22 ales and lagers on tap and premium single-malt scotches, enjoyable from the bayview patio. You'll find good deals on billiards and food at the 4:00 to 7:00 P.M. Monday through Friday happy hour. Live or DJ music is presented Friday and Saturday nights starting at 9:00 P.M. Tuesday is Swing Night, with free swing dance lessons at 8:00 P.M. Wednesday features DJ dance parties beginning at 8:30 P.M.

Easy Street Billiards
511 Tyler Street, Monterey
(831) 333-0825

Hustlers welcome! This serious pool hall offers 13 tournament tables and some of the best billiards play in town. For refreshments, there's draft and bottled beer. Open seven days a week and all ages are welcome. Call regarding the regularly held competitive tournaments.

CLUBS

Monterey

Of all the sections in this book, the following listing of clubs will probably be the most unreliable. Believe me, it's not because we were distracted or otherwise impaired while doing our research. It's just that these places tend to come and go, disappear and reappear, on a moment's notice. And even those clubs that have staying power tend to change their weekly line-ups and types of music as frequently as we change our mind. With that caveat, here's what was happening on the Peninsula club scene at the time of this writing.

CLOSE-UP

Smoking Ban at Bars and Clubs

As the cry of "Happy New Year" rang out on January 1, 1998, a law went into effect prohibiting smoking in all California bars and clubs that have employees. Only owner-operated establishments that have no employees and bars and casinos on Indian reservations are exempt from the ban. And none of the bars and clubs listed in this chapter now allow smoking. The California law, known as SB 137, follows a 1995 smoking ban for restaurants and most other indoor workplaces. It is aimed at protecting bartenders and other employees from secondhand smoke. Bar owners face a $100 fine for a first offense and up to $7,000 for repeated violations. So, please, no smoking inside these establishments. Some bars and clubs have designated outdoor smoking areas.

Cibo Ristorante Italiano
301 Alvarado Street, Monterey
(831) 649–8151
www.cibo.com

Cibo (pronounced "chee-bow") has become one of the poshest elbow-to-elbow spots among the hip Monterey 30-ish crowd who enjoy tasty Italian food and good live music. Six evenings a week (all but Monday), jazz, rhythm and blues, and reggae draw full crowds that often pack the bar and compact dance floor. The full-size bar is known for its oversize martinis. Cibo is open until 1:00 A.M., and 1:30 A.M. on Friday and Saturday.

Club Octane
321 Alvarado Street, Monterey
(831) 646–9244
www.cluboctane.com

OK, club freaks. This is the closest thing you're going to find to a vibrant, hot, and nasty club scene anywhere on the Peninsula. There are three bars and two separate dance floors, each catering to a target clientele on any given night. Take Friday night, for instance. The front room features top-40 hits while the back room pumps out hip-hop and house music. On Saturday, it's hip-hop and top-40 hits up front

and old school out back. Sunday features house and electronic music. Monday takes on a different twist with burlesque dancers—males grinding up front and the ladies swinging and swaying in the rear. Tuesday is no-cover-charge open-mike night. On Wednesday it's live hip-hop while Thursday pulses with both DJ and live music. There's a cover charge of $5.00 or so most nights, and you have to be 21 or over and pass the dress code to enter.

The Mucky Duck
479 Alvarado Street, Monterey
(831) 655–3031

This British pub and restaurant has slowly transformed into a lively nightspot. In fact, the Mucky Duck recently won a local readers' poll as the area's biggest singles bar. You can dance to DJ-spun tunes on Thursday through Saturday nights around the fire pit out on the back "Beer Gardens" patio. Live music is featured on Sunday, Tuesday, Wednesday, and Friday night. The indoor pub offers 70 beers, including 21 drafts, and dozens of single-malt scotches, plus boisterous games of darts. The Mucky Duck is populated with the local military and college scene and draws a 20-something crowd at night.

Ocean Thunder
214 Lighthouse Avenue, Monterey
(831) 643-9169
www.oceanthunder.com
Over in New Monterey rolls Ocean Thunder. It's a kick-back, get-down, let-it-loose kind of establishment that caters to the rock and blues crowd. You'll find live bands rockin' Friday and Saturday nights. Sundays during the summertime there are early evening barbecues out back on the Ocean Thunder "Backlot Patio," and Monday is typically reserved for sports on the big-screen televisions. There's a pool tournament every Tuesday night, and darts take center stage on Wednesday. Don't be intimidated by the lines of Harleys you might see parked out front. This is a friendly, back-slappin' kind of place that invites head-bobbing fun.

Sly McFly's Refueling Station
700 Cannery Row, Monterey
(831) 649-8050
www.slymcfly.com
Traditionally a favorite bar and restaurant among auto-racing fans with its classic-car decor, Sly McFly's recently remodeled to become one of the hottest new clubs as well. Live music is now offered seven nights a week, smack dab in the center of Cannery Row. There's a 4:00 to 7:00 P.M. happy hour Monday through Friday. Sly's is a good place to meet out-of-towners; it's open nightly until 1:30 A.M.

Viva Monterey
414 Alvarado Street, Monterey
(831) 646-1415
www.vivamonterey.com
Viva Monterey plays live, loud music nightly from 9:00 P.M. to 1:00 A.M. with no cover charge. This small, often packed club also offers three pool tables, including two black light tables where games glow in the dark. On Friday, Saturday, and Monday nights there's live rock music. Tuesday and Wednesday nights feature DJ music, Thursday is Ladies' Night with live music and special drinks. Viva Monterey is open every night until 2:00 A.M.

Carmel

The Jazz & Blues Company
236 Crossroads Boulevard, Carmel
(831) 624-6432
www.thejazzandbluescompany.com
A music store by day, The Jazz & Blues Company at The Crossroads in Carmel converts into an intimate live-music club about 60 nights a year. It's a recital concert atmosphere with a maximum capacity of about 70 people, so reservations are nearly always a must. No food or drinks are served, but you can bring your own beverages. Tickets are in the $20 to $30 range for these great jazz and blues shows by nationally known talents. Shows typically begin at 7:30 P.M. with artists playing two sets. Jazz fans should definitely check out the schedule while in town.

COFFEEHOUSES
Monterey

Morgan's Coffee and Tea
498 Washington Street, Monterey
(831) 373-5601
Morgan's schedules a scattering of local and national musical acts on weekends. Typically shows start around 7:00 to 8:00 P.M. with two sets nightly. Cover charges for name acts usually range from $8.00 to $10.00, while some local acts have no cover. The upcoming schedule is available by calling (831) 642-4949. Oh yeah, Morgan's serves fine coffees, teas, and other goodies

Sly McFly's Refueling Station offers live music every night and weekend afternoons, including performances by local favorites The Blue Tones. TOM OWENS

and offers indoor and sidewalk seating. It's open until 1:00 A.M. Tuesday through Sunday and until 10:00 P.M. on Monday.

Plumes Coffee House
400 Alvarado Street, Monterey
(831) 373-4526

Plumes is a popular late-night hangout for the young downtown Monterey crowd. No entertainment is provided (except from your fellow caffeine freaks), but a good variety of local pastries and decadent desserts is available. Plumes is open until 11:00 P.M. Sunday through Thursday and midnight on Friday and Saturday.

Carmel

Caffé Cardinale Coffee Roasting Company
Ocean Avenue and Dolores Street, Carmel
(831) 626-2095
www.carmelcoffee.com

Caffé Cardinale features 30 coffees roasted right on site and a full espresso bar. You can enjoy your beverage indoors or on the outdoor courtyard. Caffé Cardinale claims to be one of the first environmentally friendly coffee roasters in the western United States. Caffé Cardinale is open until 10:00 P.M. on Friday and Saturday but closes at 6:00 P.M. other nights.

Pacific Grove

Juice & Java
599 Lighthouse Avenue, Pacific Grove
(831) 373-8652

Here's a nice spot in downtown Pacific Grove to enjoy a nighttime coffee, espresso, mocha, tea, smoothie, shake, fresh juice, or other beverage. For a real kick, come on Friday open-mike night, with local legend Rama P. Jama as your host. You're likely to catch local singers, pickers, dancers, or poets baring their souls. Juice & Java is open until 8:00 P.M. Sunday through Thursday and 10:00 P.M. on Friday and Saturday.

Wildberries
212 17th Street, Pacific Grove
(831) 644-9836
If you're looking for a quiet and cozy spot for your nightly java, pick Wildberries. In a small P.G. Victorian, Wildberries serves up a full coffee menu and a complete selection of leaf and herbal teas. Try a Chinese herbal tonic to cure what ails you. A favorite among mellow P.G. locals of all ages, Wildberries is open until 10:00 P.M. Sunday through Thursday and until 11:00 P.M. on Friday and Saturday.

COMEDY CLUBS

Doc Ricketts' Lab
180 East Franklin Street, Monterey
(831) 649-4241
The newest Monterey nightspot, Doc Ricketts' Lab, is still finding its identity. The name conjures images of the old Doc Ricketts' Lab, the late, great basement club on Cannery Row. Currently, the new Doc's is offering stand-up comedy on Friday and Saturday nights, followed by DJs spinning funk and rhythm and blues. There's talk of live music during the summer season, but plans are still in the making. You might want to check the local papers during your visit to see just what Doc's is up to these days.

Planet Gemini
625 Cannery Row, Monterey
(831) 373-1449
www.planetgemini.com
On the third floor overlooking Cannery Row, Planet Gemini is the longtime king of comedy clubs in Monterey. You'll see both local and nationally known comedy acts Thursday through Saturday from 9:00 to 10:30 P.M., with cover charges

typically $6.00 to $8.00. Afterward, Planet Gemini turns into a dance club with live bands or DJs. Sunday is salsa dance night, Wednesday features banda, nortena, and cumbia music, and DJs spin dance tunes Thursday through Saturday. Enjoy the full bar and light fare. Planet Gemini is open until 1:00 A.M. Wednesday through Sunday.

MOVIE HOUSES

Monterey

Galaxy Six Cinemas
280 Del Monte Center, Monterey
(831) 655-4617
Galaxy Six, in the Del Monte Shopping Center, is one of Monterey's modern six-plex cinemas and shows the latest first-run films. Bargain matinees are offered daily for showings before 6:00 P.M. (*Note:* Plans are in the works for building an even larger multiscreen theater at the Del Monte Shopping Center in 2004. Check out the local papers to see if it's a reality.)

Osio Cinemas
350 Alvarado Street, Monterey
(831) 844-8171
Completed in late 1999 in downtown Monterey, Osio Cinemas is the area's newest movie house. With the demise of the fabulous Dream Theater, it's the closest thing going to an art film house in the area. The Osio features six screens showing first-run films, with bargain matinees for shows starting before 6:00 P.M. Assisted listening systems are available for the hard-of-hearing.

State Theatre
417 Alvarado Street, Monterey
(831) 372-4555
The historic State Theatre in Monterey has been renovated to its former glory as Mon-

terey's premier movie house. The large main theater provides a great atmosphere with a classic movie house architecture and house organ. Unfortunately, the balcony has been enclosed to provide a smaller, separate screen upstairs. Management also owns a less opulent theater right across Alvarado Street where a third feature is shown. Definitely go for the main screen at the State Theatre. Bargain matinees are offered daily before 6:00 P.M.

Pacific Grove

Lighthouse Cinema
525 Lighthouse Avenue, Pacific Grove
(831) 372-7300
With four screens, the Lighthouse Cinema is the only movie house in Pacific Grove. It shows first-run films, offering discount prices every Tuesday and for all matinees before 6:00 P.M.

Carmel

Forest Theater
Mountain View Road and Santa Rita Street, Carmel
(831) 626-1681
During the summer months, the Outdoor Forest Theater in Carmel presents "Films in the Forest," a series of classic movies under the stars. Films show most Tuesday and Wednesday evenings as well as a few weekend nights. This is a very popular Carmel tradition, where locals pack their picnic baskets (don't forget the wine), grab some warm blankets, and enjoy a memorable outdoor cinematic experience. Movies usually begin at dusk.

SHOPPING

F rom T-shirts and local souvenirs to one-of-a-kind clothing, art, and jewelry, the shopping selections on the Monterey Peninsula encompass a wide variety of tastes and budgets. We have organized this chapter to help you find the kind of shopping that's right for you. First, we provide some information about the Peninsula's malls, plazas, and outlet centers. Next, we highlight several geographic areas on the Peninsula that have a high concentration of shopping opportunities. Following that, we provide categories of our favorite places to shop for antiques, books, fresh produce, gifts, items for the home, and specialty food items. We've also added a section on thrift shops for those who enjoy finding a great bargain. Many shoppers come to the Monterey Peninsula just for the art galleries. We've included those in our chapter called The Arts and Galleries. And for the kids, we put a special shopping section in our Kidstuff chapter.

For the most part, local merchants welcome credit cards as a form of payment, and the larger shopping malls and outlets accept personal checks with proper identification. For the thrift shops and the farmers markets, we suggest you have sufficient cash available.

MALLS, PLAZAS, AND OUTLETS

American Tin Cannery Premium Outlets
125 Ocean View Boulevard, Pacific Grove
(831) 372-1442
www.premiumoutlets.com
This outlet center is near the aquarium in a historic cannery building. In the middle of the old cannery, you'll find an 80-foot History Wall that heralds Cannery Row's meteoric rise to become the "Sardine Capital of the World."

The multilevel center, California's first factory outlet, has all the big names you have come to expect: Bass, Big Dog, Izod, Reebok, Van Heusen, and Nine West, to name a few of the many stores here.

When you need refreshment, grab a bite at any one of the Cannery's food and beverage establishments. First Awakenings Restaurant is an Insiders' favorite for breakfast, and we also recommend Archie's American Diner for one of the messiest (and most delicious) burgers in town.

The American Tin Cannery is open seven days a week. Free parking is available in a lot directly behind the outlets.

The Barnyard
26400 Carmel Rancho Lane, Carmel
(831) 624-8886
www.thebarnyard.com
The Barnyard is composed of nearly 50 shops and galleries housed in rustic barns and grouped in a quaint villagelike setting. Each barn, surrounded by fragrant and colorful gardens, has its own personality and charm. Women's and men's apparel, books, music, toys, antiques, fine art, home accents, jewelry, gifts, and accessories can all be procured here.

International cuisine and specialty food shops are also plentiful. Cafes and full-service restaurants offer culinary delights from a multitude of different ethnic origins: Swiss, Japanese, Chinese, Italian, and American to name a few. Afterward, enjoy a cup of tea or fresh-roasted gourmet coffee from around the world at the Carmel Valley Roasting Company.

As you walk through the multi-terraced center, relax and admire the gardens. Benches are thoughtfully placed where you can rest for a moment and enjoy the scenery. Join the horticulturist-led garden tour (typically Sunday at noon in front of the Thunderbird Bookshop) or just ramble through the brick walkways on your own. Many outdoor events are planned here throughout the year, taking advantage of the beautiful setting.

To get to The Barnyard from Monterey, take Highway 1 south. One mile past Ocean Avenue, turn left on Carmel Valley Road. Take a right at Carmel Rancho Boulevard, then another right onto Carmel Rancho Lane. You'll see the barns directly ahead. The Barnyard is open seven days a week. There is free parking in several large lots.

Carmel Plaza
Corner of Ocean Avenue and Junipero Street, Carmel
(831) 624-0137
www.carmelplaza.com
Carmel Plaza, an elegant garden courtyard with hanging floral baskets and fountains, houses a unique marketplace with more than 50 stores, one-of-a-kind shops, and restaurants. You'll find world-famous designer names like Saks Fifth Avenue, Ann Taylor, Louis Vuitton, and Georgiou.

There's also a wide variety of merchandise, including fashions, jewelry, shoes, gifts, leather goods, accessories, art, home decor, and gourmet foods.

Any of the restaurants, some with outdoor dining, will satisfy even the most discriminating palate. Whether it's with a light lunch or a larger meal, the food choices at Carmel Plaza will leave you satisfied and ready for more shopping!

Carmel Plaza is open seven days a week. You can park without charge for two hours, with validation, in the parking garage behind the Plaza on Mission Street.

The Crossroads Shopping Village
159 Crossroads Boulevard, Carmel
(831) 625-4106
Shopping at The Crossroads, with its flower-filled streets and brick sidewalks, evokes an image of roaming through an English village. You'll shop to your heart's delight among more than 90 shopping and dining establishments. You'll find men's and women's apparel, shoes, home accents, cards, gifts, collectibles, jewelry, galleries, specialty foods, videos, a pharmacy, a grocery store, a movie theater, and restaurants. Take care of banking, make travel arrangements, get your shoes repaired, drop off your dry cleaning, or mail a package home.

Enjoy brunch, lunch, or dinner with your favorite wine or cocktail at one of several award-winning restaurants and eateries.

The Crossroads lies at the mouth of the Carmel Valley where the Santa Lucia Mountains begin. To get there from Monterey, take Highway 1 south to 1 mile south of Ocean Avenue, and make a left turn at Rio Road. The shopping center is on the corner to your right. There is plenty of free parking on the premises. The Crossroads is open seven days a week.

Del Monte Center
Highway 1 at Munras Avenue, Monterey
(831) 373-2705
www.delmontecenter.com
The Del Monte Center is an open-air mall, with Macy's and Mervyn's department stores and Whole Foods Market serving as the anchor stores. No matter what you're in search of, you'll surely find it here. The center's diverse selection of shops features cards, gifts, bath and body stores, books, electronics, music, records, video, hobby items, household necessities, jewelry, maternity clothing, shoes, sporting goods, and men's, women's, and children's apparel.

Personal services include a dry cleaner, travel agent, hair salon, eye care, and banking.

Enjoy a cup of java at Starbucks, or if you want something more substantial, the many restaurants include Marie Callender's (save room for the pie), Fresh Choice, and El Indio (Mexican food), among others. If you just have to have a burger, Elli's Great American Food will

A pleasant, flower-filled open air mall, Del Monte Center in Monterey is a relaxing place to browse. MICHAEL CHATFIELD

satisfy your craving. For a "healthy" alternative, Whole Foods has a great gourmet deli and take-out foods section.

The shopping center is just off Highway 1. Take the Munras/Soledad Drive exit when traveling southbound; the Munras Avenue exit from the north. Access to the center is afforded by two boulevard entrances. Nearly 3,000 free parking spaces are provided. It's open seven days a week.

SHOPPING AREAS

Carmel

Carmel is renowned internationally for its extraordinary gallery selection and shopping opportunities offering everything from apparel, books, brass, fine original art and photography, furs, jewelry, leather, linens and lingerie, and exceptional gifts. A basic understanding of Carmel is necessary before you begin a spree in its downtown area. Addresses are identified by location (i.e., Ocean between Mission and San Carlos on the southwest side of the street) because there are no street numbers. The main shopping area is two blocks on either side of Ocean Avenue between Junipero and Lincoln Streets. Wear comfortable walking shoes and plan to spend at least a day drifting around, seeking out all the quaint and charming shops located in hidden alleyways and courtyards. Like thousands before you, you're sure to find Carmel to be a shopping paradise.

At the southeast corner of Junipero Street and Ocean Avenue is the **Carmel Plaza** (see our write-up in the previous "Malls, Plazas, and Outlets" section).

Monterey

CANNERY ROW AND FISHERMAN'S WHARF

Stop at the old Monterey Canning Company building, 700 Cannery Row, where you'll find shops selling candy, jewelry, clothing, food, souvenirs, and toys. **Sand Dollar Gifts,** in the cannery building, (831) 372-2885, is the oldest store on Cannery Row. It stocks everything from sweatshirts and T-shirts to unique oceanic products plus every imaginable souvenir and memento.

Across the way at Steinbeck Plaza Two is **Pebble Beach on Cannery Row,** 660 Cannery Row, (831) 373-1500. It is a great place to pick up quality Pebble Beach apparel, golf accessories, gifts, and souvenirs from the world-famous resorts and golf courses. **Robert Lyn Nelson Studios,** 660 Cannery Row, (831) 655-8500, displays the paintings of the world's foremost marine artist, Robert Lyn Nelson.

Across the street at Steinbeck Plaza One is the **Cannery Row General Store,** 685 Cannery Row, (831) 655-7747, a Disney outlet and a one-stop shopping place for picnic supplies, film, and fine cigars.

Directly across the street, in the Monterey Canning Company warehouse, are numerous clothing, jewelry, gift, and specialty shops such as **Three Ladys of Cannery Row,** 711 Cannery Row, (831) 655-5688. Browse through crafts and handmade gifts from local artists and books by renowned Peninsula authors, or choose from exotic teas, incense, and jewelry.

The cluster of shops on Fisherman's Wharf is the hands-down winner for its inexpensive souvenirs and mementos of your visit to Monterey. The smell of fresh-caught seafood will probably arouse your appetite, so relax and enjoy a sourdough bread bowl of clam chowder at one of the Wharf's many seafood restaurants. Try the free samples offered by many of the Wharf's restaurants before making your choice.

DOWNTOWN MONTEREY

The historic heart of Old Monterey is home to an array of shopping possibilities. Along Alvarado and intersecting streets, you will find fine jewelry and watches, clothing, fine art, musical instruments, gifts, photo supplies, flowers, and home furnishings.

Pacific Grove

Pacific Grove's charming, Victorian-studded downtown area boasts ever-expanding retail shopping opportunities. From antiques and gift shops to thrift stores and boutiques to galleries and stores for the home, this shopping area could easily command an afternoon or entire day. Shoppers of the female persuasion will be especially delighted with the selection of boutiques that carry unique fashions, shoes, and accessories.

For top-quality, stylish shoes and bags, don't miss the art-galleryesque **Details** at 510 Lighthouse Avenue, (831) 372-2207. Next door, at the same address, **The Clothing Store,** (831) 649-8866, carries women's clothing and accessories that you won't find in your average department store.

Be sure to pay a visit to **BiBa,** 211 Forest Avenue, (831) 655-2422, where you'll revel in the big-city designer fashions offered at small-town prices. A little farther up the street at 309 Forest Avenue is **Kathleen's,** (831) 655-3666, where women size 12 and up will be thrilled with the range of leisure, casual, and elegant fashions.

Pebble Beach

A must-do on the Monterey Peninsula is a drive along world-famous 17-Mile Drive, and a stop at the Lodge at Pebble Beach affords an opportunity for excellent shopping as well. The high-end shops here feature original gold jewelry designs, fashions

If you love to shop and have the time, make a day of each distinct shopping area. Check out the wares in downtown Pacific Grove, Carmel, or Monterey, or the Del Monte Shopping Center, The Barnyard, or Crossroads Shopping Center. Break to eat at any of the area's many restaurants, cafes, bars, and coffee shops.

for men and women, antiques, and fine art. This being Pebble Beach, of course there are shops specializing in golf, from the Pebble Beach Pro Shop to others selling official Pebble Beach merchandise and golf antiques. You can also visit them on the Web at www.pebblebeach.com.

ANTIQUES

The Peninsula is home to a bonanza of antiques shops and one award-winning antiques mall with more than 150 dealers. We've highlighted our favorites here. Look in the Yellow Pages of the phone book for complete listings. Once you have investigated the Peninsula, head north on Highway 1 to Moss Landing or out U.S. 101 to San Juan Bautista, where you can explore additional opportunities for finding just the right antique treasure.

Ancients
9700 Carmel Valley Road, Carmel
(831) 626-2656
www.ancientscarmel.com
Although most of the treasures here surpass the weight limit of the average airline, those building a home in the area or traveling by land will be delighted. More antiquities than antiques, Ancients features centuries-old European stone fireplaces, fountains, pots, doors, gates, and reclaimed floors and roofs. They also create masterful reproductions using molds made from the original pieces. For anyone who's explored the Forum in Rome, a visit to Ancients is like a walk down memory lane.

Antique Clock Shop
489 Lighthouse Avenue, Pacific Grove
(831) 372-6435
For more than 20 years, this restored 1887 lemon-colored Victorian in downtown Pacific Grove has featured hundreds of antique clocks elegantly displayed with period furniture and antique curios. When you enter the shop, a symphony of time pieces will greet you. The Antique Clock Shop repairs all kinds of clocks, from cuckoos to grandfathers. And yes, they make house calls.

Cannery Row Antique Mall
471 Wave Street, Monterey
(831) 655-0264
www.canneryrowantiquemall.com
In 1995, on the 50th anniversary of John Steinbeck's immortal novel *Cannery Row,* Cannery Row Antique Mall opened its doors. The mall, housed in the original 1927 Carmel Canning Company Warehouse, is the largest antiques and collectibles mall on the central coast. More than 170 dealers now operate out of the two-story, 21,000-square-foot structure. The mall was named the 1996 Antique Mall of the Year by *Professional Antique Mall Magazine.*

The Carmel Canning Company Warehouse is one of only a few authentic and unchanged structures from the Steinbeck era. After the purchase of the mall in 1994, the owners applied for and received Historic Structure status from the city of Monterey, making the mall the first building on the Row so designated. The rustic, tin-clad warehouse still houses the original endless-belt conveyer.

The mall has good lighting, restrooms, a free coffee bar, and indoor and outdoor seating. There is a small parking lot, a rarity on Cannery Row. The staff is friendly, helpful, and knowledgeable.

The Antique Mall houses everything from American folk art and Oriental furniture to baseball cards and Tiffany lamps. It is also known for the extensive assortment of home furnishings—a boon to local decorators. The mall also sells price guides and books on antiques and collectibles.

Fourtané Estate Jewelers
Ocean Avenue and Lincoln, Carmel
(831) 624-4684
www.fourtane.com
Established in downtown Carmel in 1950, Fourtané is today one of the country's leading estate jewelry and vintage watch retail stores. From the 1800s to present day, their pieces span the range from a simple $100 antique ring to an extraordinary, rare 3.64-carat yellow diamond ring by Oscar Heyman. The owners are happy to share their wealth of knowledge and interesting tales of items in their vast collection.

Holman Antique Plaza
542 Lighthouse Avenue, Pacific Grove
(831) 646-0674
www.holmanbuilding.com
The Holman Building, in downtown Pacific Grove, houses a collection of more than 50 antiques dealers. The historic, multistory building contains period furniture, jewelry, fine art, coins, stamps, swords, decorative art, Oriental rugs, glassware, watches, dishes, dolls, china cabinets, carpets, quilts, kitchenware, and a whole lot more. The third floor is strictly for consignment items and has a wealth of high-quality bedroom and living room furniture.

Patrick's Consignment Store
105 Central Avenue, Pacific Grove
(831) 372-3995
Patrick's carries a large inventory of home furnishings and is a collective of 35 antiques dealers. You'll find estate jewelry, rugs, china, crystal, silver, lamps, chandeliers, tables, chairs, and mirrors all in one location.

Trésors
Seventh Street between Dolores and San Carlos, Carmel
(831) 624-1115
www.tresorsantiques.com
In business since 1972 and in Carmel since 1985, Trésors specializes in European and continental antiques and investment-quality furniture, silver, and jewelry. Trésors, "treasures" in French, lives up to its name by featuring rare, authenticated pieces such as an inkwell from the desk of the last king of Naples presented as a gift to his footman; a piano by François Linke, created for Steinway and Sons in 1911 for the last heiress to the Royal Family of Prussia; and many other intriguing items from centuries past.

Trotter's Antiques
301 Forest Avenue, Pacific Grove
(831) 373-3505
Established in 1965, the spacious showroom at Trotter's allows for numerous pieces of commanding 18th- and 19th-century furniture. Also plentiful are glassware, tableware, silver, porcelain, lamps, and Oriental art. You will also see an uncommon collection of antique dolls.

BOOKSTORES

Bookstores—from the tiny shop dealing in hard-to-find and first editions to megachains and children's bookshops—are everywhere on the Peninsula. In terms of resale, there are scores of places to find used books. Don't overlook the thrift shops; most of them carry any number of paperbacks (see our "Thrift Shops" section). Whatever kind of publication you desire, there is a book dealer on the Peninsula ready to assist you. We have listed a few to get you started.

Bay Books and Coffee House
316 Alvarado Street, Monterey
(831) 375-1855
www.montereybaybooks.com
In a former bank building in downtown Monterey, located right across the street from the Conference Center, Bay Books stocks all sorts of books and has an especially nice children's section. Foreign language books and numerous books written about the Monterey Peninsula area are in stock too. You'll discover books about marine life, kayaking,

The historic building that now houses the Holman Antique Plaza in downtown Pacific Grove was once the Monterey Peninsula's only department store. MICHAEL CHATFIELD

and scuba diving. If you're looking for a Monterey Bay Marine Diver's Map, you'll find it here. There is indoor and outdoor seating at a coffee bar that serves fresh-brewed coffee and espresso drinks.

Books & Things
224 Lighthouse Avenue, Monterey
(831) 655-8784

This little shop is a delightful maze of bookshelves chock-full of more than 60,000 used paperbacks and hard-covers from A to Z. One can find serious bargains on everything from romance novels to biographies and how-to books. Browsing this store, just 2 blocks up from Cannery Row, is an enjoyable way to spend a couple of hours. Those in a hurry shouldn't despair because the offerings are divided into various categories and organized in alphabetical order by author.

Bookworks
667 Lighthouse Avenue, Pacific Grove
(831) 372-2242

The consummate neighborhood book-store, Bookworks is known as a haunt for the local literary crowd. Stop in to check out the newest additions to the ever-changing inventory of fiction and non-fiction books. Bookworks also carries a good selection of magazines and newspapers. The display windows are always fun, often showcasing the talents of local school children. An in-store coffee bar features coffees and other beverages as well as scrumptious pastries.

Borders Books Music & Cafe
Edgewater Center, 2080 California
Avenue, Sand City
(831) 899-6643

Borders is the giant of area bookstores. It not only carries an amazing variety of books but also sells cassette tapes, CDs, calendars, newspapers from around the world, and magazines. The cafe and lounge area is a great place to relax. Weekly programs include lectures by authors, art talks, and musical events.

Thunderbird Bookshop and Cafe
3600 The Barnyard, Carmel
(831) 624-1803
www.thunderbirdbooks.com

For more than 30 years the Thunderbird Bookshop and Cafe has been a Carmel landmark. Insiders know this is the place to go for hard-to-find and special-order books. It carries more than 40,000 volumes as well as magazines, greeting cards, and a few games. The atmosphere is casual, and the staff is friendly and helpful. The adjoining solarium cafe is a cozy spot with a fireplace. The cafe has an espresso bar and serves homemade soups, pot pies, sandwiches, and beer and wine. On some evenings the solarium serves as a lecture hall where musical artists and authors give public talks and performances.

FARMERS' MARKETS

Agribusiness is the largest revenue-generating industry in Monterey County. With so many crops grown in the county, we are fortunate to have a bountiful selection of flowers, fruits, and vegetables year-round. Many chefs at local restaurants shop the farmers' markets to purchase produce at peak freshness. The two farmers markets listed here take place in Monterey each week.

Monterey Bay Certified Farmers Market
Monterey Peninsula College,
980 Fremont Street, Monterey
(831) 728-5060
www.montereybayfarmers.org

A smaller affair than the Old Monterey Market Place, this market primarily features the season's best fruits and vegetables. Vendors also sell honey, nuts, bread,

and eggs. You will also find fresh-cut flowers and potted plants. The market is held in the lower parking lot at the college, just off Fremont Street.

Old Monterey Market Place
Alvarado Street, Monterey
(831) 655-2607
www.oldmonterey.org

Alvarado Street is transformed into a market each Tuesday, rain or shine. From 4:00 to 7:00 P.M. buyers and spectators investigate the goods at up to 134 booths. They search for their weekly supply of fresh fruits, vegetables, flowers, fresh-baked bread, seafood, nuts, honey, and eggs. Each booth represents a different farm, and there are many booths with organic foods. Come hungry and have a quick bite at one of the prepared-food vendors. It's a great way to sample the fare of local restaurants. By evening the place resembles a street festival with live entertainment, face-painting, and a bookmobile. In addition to food booths, you'll find vendors offering handmade crafts, jewelry, artwork, ethnic clothing, used books, and ceramics.

GIFT AND SPECIALTY SHOPS

Shopping for gifts and specialty items is effortless with such numerous choices in each Peninsula city. From the beautiful yet functional to the superfluous but irresistible, you'll have no trouble finding the perfect gift for anyone on your list. Here's a list of suggestions just for starters.

Bittner, The Pleasure of Writing
Ocean Avenue and San Carlos Avenue, Carmel
(831) 626-8828
www.bittner.com

Is there a writer on your gift list? Bittner sells only the finest writing instruments and accessories. This shop carries exquisite products from around the world including pens by Aurora, Delta, Fabergé, and Michel Perchin. The collection includes limited-edition pens by the same companies. Personalized writing materials, journals, inks, refills, and writing paper are part of the elegant inventory.

Friends of the Sea Otter Education Retail Center
381 Cannery Row, Monterey
(831) 642-9037
www.seaotters.org

This unique nonprofit center is dedicated to the southern sea otter, an adorable marine animal found in the Monterey Bay. Sea otter gifts, clothing, and collectibles fill the shelves in the retail section; sea otter books and videos are available in the education center adjacent to the store. You can also pick up a free Otter Spotting Guide here. All proceeds from the center directly benefit sea otter research and preservation.

Although the Monterey Bay Aquarium doesn't offer online shopping, you can browse their selection of books and tapes at www.montereybayaquarium. com and call toll-free, (877) 665-2665, to order.

Ladyfingers Jewelry
Dolores Street near Ocean Avenue, Carmel
(831) 624-2327
www.ladyfingersjewelry.com

Is there a better gift than jewelry? Ladyfingers, established in 1977, has become a showcase for the jewelry industry's unique design talent; more than 45 contemporary jewelers are featured. Represented are such renowned artists as Michael Good, whose hypnotic designs have brought him international acclaim. Check out the outrageous rubber and diamond designs by André Ribeiro and the dynamic and colorful stacking rings by designer Goph Albitz.

Monterey Bay Aquarium
886 Cannery Row, Monterey
(831) 648-4800
www.montereybayaquarium.com

One can easily spend an entire day at this marvel of an aquarium, and it's a shame not to save time for their gift shops. Everything from stuffed animals and learning toys to elegant glassware, clothing, and jewelry is centered on a marine life theme. What better way to remember your visit to the Peninsula than with a souvenir that's actually useful and educational, like a video or book on jellies, sea otters, or whales? And if you're a member of the Monterey Bay Aquarium, just present your membership card for a 10 percent discount.

The Phoenix Shop
At Nepenthe, Big Sur
(831) 667-2347
www.nepenthebigsur.com

Visitors to the area as well as those who live here can't resist a drive on Highway 1, along the dramatic Big Sur coast. An Ambrosia burger at Nepenthe, which sits near the edge of a cliff overlooking the rocky coast, is an added incentive for the trip and an absolute indulgence for the taste buds. The Phoenix Shop is for the other senses. Unique jewelry crafted by area artists, unusual musical instruments from around the world, incense, body lotions, books, clothing, toys, glassware, stationery, and wind chimes just begin to catalog the inventory here. It's a one-of-a-kind shopping experience.

HOME AND GARDEN

The Peninsula is overflowing with places to find items for the home or garden. From homey, handcrafted items to ultra-chic accessories, the possibilities are endless when it comes to finding just the right thing to decorate your home or spruce up your garden.

Brinton's
546 Carmel Rancho Lane, Carmel
(831) 624-8541
www.brintons.com
Brinton's is one of those refreshingly different hardware/housewares stores. Their line of merchandise includes garden supplies, outdoor furniture, and an abundance of functional items for the kitchen and bath.

Clementine's Kitchen
465 Canyon Del Rey Boulevard,
Del Rey Oaks
(831) 392-1494
www.clementineskitchen.com
Clementine's Kitchen has everything for the kitchen and a few things for the rest of the home, including gourmet salsas, jellies and preserves, glassware, ceramics, professional cookware, and kitchen accessories—plus cooking classes from a Le Cordon Bleu–trained chef (and store owner). He and his staff are also available in the shop daily, ready with plenty of free, friendly, and extremely helpful advice.

Grove Homescapes
472 Lighthouse Avenue, Pacific Grove
(831) 656-0864
The old Grove Laundry building has been transformed into a historic treasure. Restoration began in 1994 when new owners purchased the 1927 building. They created a design showroom with a lush garden and Victorian gazebo. Inside, a sweeping staircase draws your eye to the commanding displays of artwork and home furnishings.

Parsley Sage & Thyme
149 Crossroads Boulevard, Carmel
(831) 620-0515
www.pareleysagethyme.com
In the Crossroads Shopping Center, this business is a gold mine of kitchenware and hard-to-find gourmet cookery from about 160 companies throughout the world. For your convenience, the store will ship all of its products via UPS.

The Woodenickel
529 Central Avenue, Pacific Grove
(831) 646-8050
www.woodenickel.com
This precious shop brims with nostalgic gifts and home accessories. Vintage furniture is parceled into cheerful, matched-color vignettes. The store is packed with tea pots, cups and saucers, linens, ribbons, potpourri, things for the garden, and other items to accent every room.

THRIFT SHOPS

Shopping the thrifts is an economical way of getting just about anything at a fraction of the original price. Thrift shops here tend to have high-quality merchandise in near-new condition. We have described some of our favorite places to shop for bargains in designer clothing, housewares, furniture, books, and a host of other items.

American Cancer Society
Discovery Shop
198 Country Club Gate, Pacific Grove
(831) 372-0866
Savvy employees have made this one of the higher-end thrifts around, but good bargains still abound on women's and men's clothing, jewelry, books, and sometimes small pieces of furniture.

Church Mouse Thrift Shop
204 17th Street, Pacific Grove
(831) 375-0838
Though small, this shop has a variety of interesting games, books, children's toys, clothing, shoes, glassware, kitchen items, bedding, and the occasional sewing and knitting accoutrements. You'll often find a good selection of table linens and suitcases, too.

Goodwill Industries
571 Lighthouse Avenue, Monterey
(831) 649-6056
729 Broadway Avenue, Seaside
(831) 394-1212
www.goodwill.org

CLOSE-UP

Shopping the Monterey Peninsula Online

Opportunities abound for online shopping, which means you can take a little of the Peninsula home with you without having to carry it. Many local specialty stores offer shopping sprees of the cyber kind. Check our listings in this chapter for Web site addresses. Or when you're out and about, ask your favorite merchants if they offer on-line shopping. Some of our local retailers offer "club"-type services where, for a set price, you receive a different wine, food item, or coffee each month.

Some of our favorite online shopping opportunities include:

A Taste of Monterey
www.tastemonterey.com

Bittner, The Pleasure of Writing
www.bittner.com

Cannery Row Antique Mall
www.canneryrowantiquemall.com

Carmel Valley Coffee Roasting Company
www.carmel-coffee.com

Carmel Art Association
www.carmelart.org

Clementine's Kitchen
www.clementineskitchen.com

Friends of the Sea Otter
www.seaotters.org

Monterey Museum of Art
www.montereyart.org

Monterey Pasta Company
www.montereypasta.com

The Pebble Beach Company
www.pebblebeach.com

Thunderbird Bookshop and Café
www.thunderbirdbooks.com

Clothing is the outstanding bargain at this well-known thrift store chain. In addition to clothing for the entire family, they have shoes, purses, and accessories, as well as some furniture. Don't forget to rummage through the selection of books and housewares.

Yellow Brick Road Benefit Shop
26388 Carmel Rancho Lane, Carmel
(831) 626-8480
An outreach program of the Carmel Presbyterian Church, the Yellow Brick Road Benefit Shop carries clothing, collectibles, household items, and books. It's a charming little shop, tucked into the Carmel Rancho Shopping Center, with friendly volunteer staff.

SPECIALTY FOOD MARKETS

Artichokes, garlic, carrots, lettuce, and a host of other vegetables are grown in nearby Salinas Valley. The Monterey Peninsula area has long acted as a retail outlet for these foods and products made from them. Monterey County now has more than 40,000 acres of vineyards, making it one of the largest fine wine regions in the United States (see our new chapter, Wine Country, for more details). In this section we emphasize a few stores that carry a cornucopia of local wines, regional and international gourmet products, and health foods.

A Taste Of Monterey
700 Cannery Row, Monterey
(831) 646-5446
www.tastemonterey.com

This visually spectacular center, in a renovated, circa 1918 sardine cannery, houses the largest selection of Monterey County appellation wines on the Peninsula. The showroom boasts a panoramic ocean view, gourmet gift shop, winery maps, and tour information. County-grown wine and produce samplings are held daily at this one-stop Monterey County wine-tasting room. Slide into a window seat overlooking the Monterey Bay and linger over a glass of wine while nibbling delectable tidbits of local produce and appetizers. When you're finished, browse through the interesting and educational exhibits about Monterey County. A second location is next to the National Steinbeck Center in downtown Salinas.

The Bountiful Basket
153 Crossroads Boulevard, Carmel
(831) 625-4457

Retain the flavor of the Monterey Bay Peninsula long after your return home. This specialty shop stocks the pick of the crop in locally produced gourmet foods—flavored vinegar and oil, salsa, garlic, salad dressings, marinades, sardines, coffee, and tea. Shipping and local delivery are available.

The Cheese Shop
Carmel Plaza
(831) 625-2272

Just stepping into The Cheese Shop and inhaling deeply will probably raise your cholesterol 10 points. But what a way to go! Before you are arrayed hundreds of cheeses from the four corners of the earth, many available to sample. If you can think of it, it's either here or the friendly staff can find it. This shop also houses one of the finest selections of wines on the Monterey Peninsula. Picnic baskets, wine and kitchen accessories, and—of course—crackers are also available.

Cornucopia Community Market
26135 Carmel Rancho Boulevard, Carmel
(831) 625-1454

For those seeking wholesome foods, the Cornucopia is an excellent choice. Organic produce, fresh pasta, salad, sauces, sandwiches, soups, and nourishing entrees are all to be found here. Don't leave without some freshly baked bread, gourmet cheese, and wine from local suppliers.

Culinary Center of Monterey
625 Cannery Row, Monterey
(831) 333-2133
www.culinarycenterofmonterey.com

Located in a renovated cannery building, the Culinary Center of Monterey offers a full range of cooking classes taught by professional chefs in two "dream" kitchens. Gourmet take-out foods and an in-house bakery are here, as well as a prime selection of the world's finest cheeses. Join friends on the outdoor patio and enjoy a premium beer, wine, and the appetizer bar while taking in the expansive view of Monterey Bay. A class schedule is available online.

International Market & Deli
580 Lighthouse Avenue, Monterey
(831) 375-9451

Stepping into the International Market is an experience similar to a trip abroad! You'll hear shoppers conversing in Russian, Italian, or French. Middle Eastern, Greek, and Mediterranean foods comprise much of the inventory. Scan the take-out menu, and order up some Middle Eastern dishes prepared lightly (with less olive oil). There are a few tables if you prefer to dine here. Sample some freshly made hummus, dolmas, vegetarian soup, caviar, or basmati rice. Of course, the market has bottled wines and unusual imported beers to round out your meal.

Nielsen Brothers Market & Wine Shop
Corner of Seventh Avenue and San Carlos Street, Carmel
(831) 624-9463

This market can accommodate all of your grocery needs and has a deli with fresh-roasted meats, an array of international cheeses, and a wide assortment of spirits. The wine shop, Carmel's only wine-tasting room, has one of the Central Coast's most extensive selections of California and European wines. Locals regularly depend on employees to help them select just the right wine for a special meal or celebration.

Pezzini Farms Produce
102 Crossroads Boulevard, Carmel
(831) 626-2734

Artichoke lovers congregate at Pezzini Farms to snatch up artichokes harvested earlier that day in Castroville. Other ready-to-eat items found here include a wide selection of gourmet salad dressings, salsas, and a host of specialty products such as artichoke pesto, which is absolutely wonderful. A fresh and colorful portion of the gorgeous produce comes daily from Pezzini's own farm.

Trader Joe's
1170 Forest Avenue, Pacific Grove
(831) 656-0180
www.traderjoes.com

If you haven't already discovered Trader Joe's, you're in for a real treat. It carries a sizable variety of gourmet items such as ready-to-heat and ready-to-eat foods and frozen entrees, pasta, pesto, oil, vinegar, baked goods, cheese, cookies, wine, champagne, and spirits—all at reasonable prices. The selection changes frequently, but you will always find a bonanza of quality foods and beverages.

Whole Foods Market
800 Del Monte Center, Monterey
(831) 333-1660
www.wholefoods.com

Choose from a veritable feast of organic produce, bulk foods, health products, ready-to-eat gourmet deli items, sandwiches, juices, healthy snacks, delicious soups, and fresh-baked bread delivered daily from local bakeries.

ATTRACTIONS

Without question, the primary attraction of the Monterey Peninsula is . . . the Monterey Peninsula. This dramatic meeting of land and sea, complete with shorelines of majestic stands of native Monterey pine and Monterey cypress, has been attracting tourists for more than a century. Still, there are many attractions other than nature-made that are a must-see to make your appreciation of the Peninsula complete. Here is the cream of the crop, sure to please everyone from serious California history and architecture buffs to Walter Mitty-esque deep-sea divers and race car drivers who can live out their high-sea and high-speed fantasies.

Monterey

Cannery Row
200 to 900 Cannery Row, Monterey
(831) 649–6690

"Cannery row in Monterey in California is a poem, a stink, a grating noise, a quality of light, a tone, a habit, a nostalgia, a dream." Those words open John Steinbeck's famous short novel, *Cannery Row*, and still hold true now. Today the stench or grating noise might come from a diesel tourist bus rather than a sardine cannery, but you can still discover the poem, the quality of light, the nostalgia, and the dream lurking behind and between today's Cannery Row attractions. The truth be told, the Cannery Row memorialized by Steinbeck was largely a thing of the past by the time his instant hit was written in January 1945. Steinbeck wrote the masterpiece from New York City, recalling a period in Monterey 10 to 15 years earlier when, as a struggling writer, he hung out with "Mack and the boys" and his biologist buddy Edward F. "Doc" Ricketts. Fortunately for

us all, there are a sufficient number of local Steinbeck devotees on the Peninsula and enough Steinbeck pilgrims from all corners of the globe to keep alive what little remains of the Cannery Row entrenched in the mind of anyone who has read the novel. (*Tortilla Flat* was the first of Steinbeck's Monterey trilogy, while *Sweet Thursday* completed Steinbeck's Cannery Row tale of Doc Ricketts and this most colorful cast of characters.)

We'll begin our trip down Cannery Row, whose original name was Ocean View Boulevard, at the northern end where it intersects with David Avenue at the Monterey-Pacific Grove border. It's where you'll find the kingpin of today's Row, the **Monterey Bay Aquarium** (see separate listing). The world-renowned aquarium sits at 886 Cannery Row on the site of the former cannery of Hovden Food Products and incorporates some of the cannery's structure and equipment into its displays.

Heading south, notice the bright yellow building at 851 Cannery Row called **Kalisa's La Ida Cafe,** (831) 644–9316. That's the very same La Ida Cafe Steinbeck recounts as one of the Row's infamous houses of ill repute. Steinbeck aficionados shouldn't miss the chance to stop in for a bite, a hot cup of joe, or a beer milkshake. If you get the chance, say hello to owner Kalisa Moore, the reigning "Queen of Cannery Row" who has operated this fine establishment since 1957.

Next door to La Ida Cafe at 835 Cannery Row is the **Wing Chong Market.** Built in 1918, this grocery and dry goods store was run by Chinese businessman Won Yee. Steinbeck combined the names of the market and the man to create "Lee Chong," the first character to appear in chapter one of *Cannery Row*. It is here

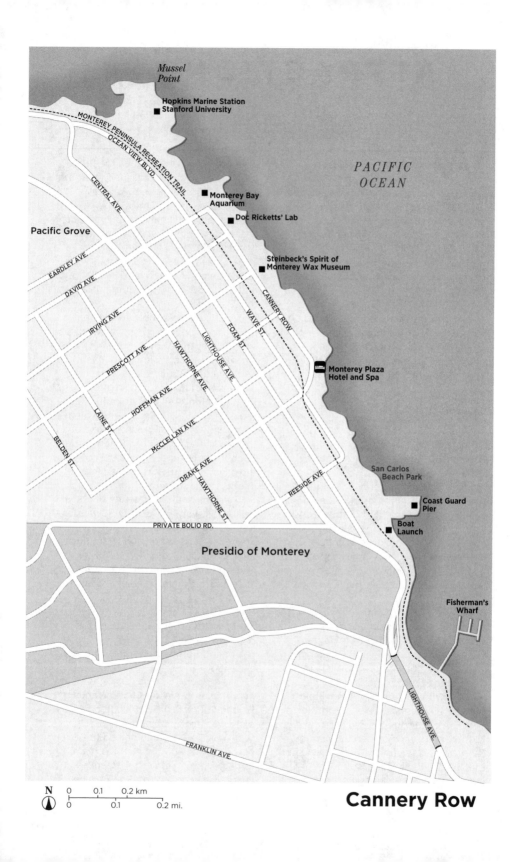

Cannery Row

that Lee Chong stood behind the cigar counter, protecting the Old Tennis Shoes and other not-so-fine whiskeys from the thirsty boys of the Row. Today, you can purchase T-shirts and souvenirs at Wing Chong Market, but, alas, nary a pint nor a quart. The building includes a small John Steinbeck museum as well, featuring newspaper clippings about the author as well as a few older editions of his books.

A stone's throw down the Row on the Bay side of the street is an unassuming wooden building with a simple staircase leading up to an even simpler door. It's **Doc Ricketts' Pacific Biological Laboratories,** or "Western Biological Laboratory" as Steinbeck named it. Here, at 800 Cannery Row, Ed Ricketts prepared the marine animals he collected in the Bay for shipment to schools, universities, and medical facilities. And it is here that Steinbeck spent countless hours in the company of his friend and the inspiration for his great work. Today, Doc's Lab is owned by a local "private men's club," whose social activities, it is rumored, would be heartily approved by Mack and the boys.

Across the street from Pacific Biological Laboratories, you'll find a small plaza and walkway called **Bruce Ariss Way,** named after one of Monterey's best-known artists and cartoonists. There, in addition to an Ariss mural of Cannery Row, stand three small one-room cabins, once homes to cannery workers. Peek inside and you'll see the typical home setting of young Spanish, Japanese, and Filipino workers. While Italians were indeed a predominant part of Monterey's fishing industry, this exhibit points out the valuable contributions of the many ethnic groups who came to stake their claim on the silver harvest of the Bay. This area of Cannery Row is also very near the original sites of the Palace Flophouse, where Mack and the boys resided, and madam Flora Wood's **Lone Star Cafe,** better known to Steinbeck readers as the "Bear Flag Restaurant."

Farther south down both sides of the Row you'll find vacant lots where aban-doned cannery buildings once stood before a series of destructive fires from the 1950s to the 1980s burned them to the ground. These ghostly spaces, slotted for a new hotel, are now hidden from view by a series of aging murals depicting historic scenes from the heyday of Cannery Row. Featured artists include local cartoonists Eldon Dedini, Jay Campbell, and Hank Ketcham of *Dennis the Menace* fame.

Down the street at Prescott Avenue stands the epicenter of today's version of Cannery Row. On the north side of the intersection is the former Monterey Canning Company, consisting of two separate structures on opposite sides of the Row connected by an overhead walkway or "crossover." The cannery, built in 1918, is on the Bay side of the Row. It retains its landmark ornate facade, which was a marked contrast to most of the boxy commercial buildings sharing the street. Today, this building is known by its address, **700 Cannery Row,** home to a lively potpourri of more than 40 shops, galleries, eateries, and attractions. The centerpiece of 700 Cannery Row is **Steinbeck's Spirit of Monterey Wax Museum,** a veritable tourist landmark (see the separate listing in this chapter).

Wine connoisseurs will also appreciate 700 Cannery Row for a tasting room and visitor center aptly named **A Taste of Monterey** (www.tastemonterey.com). Featured here are selections from more than 40 Monterey County wineries, locally grown gourmet plates and appetizers, a large gift shop, educational displays, and even a small theater showing films on winery operations. And to top it all off, you enjoy it all from a comfortable third-story perch with a fabulous panoramic view of Monterey Bay and the scenic shoreline of Cannery Row. Wine tasting at A Taste of Monterey is reasonably priced at $5.00 for six tastes. And the charge is rebated with the purchase of any bottle of wine. A Taste of Monterey is open daily from 11:00 A.M. to 6:00 P.M. The phone number is (831) 646-5446 or (888) 646-5446.

The crossovers on Cannery Row now transport tourists rather than tins of sardines from one side of the street to the other. TOM OWENS

Bargetto Winery, (831) 373-4053, also has its own tasting room on the second level of 700 Cannery Row.

On the inland side of the street, 711 Cannery Row was originally the warehouse of the Monterey Canning Company. Tins of sardines were transferred from the cannery by conveyor belt through the crossover to the warehouse for storage and eventual shipment. Today, the warehouse is home to gift stores, candy and ice cream shops, and restaurants.

Next door to the Monterey Canning Company building, Steinbeck Plaza provides an open view to the Bay at McAbee Beach. This historic site was home to Monterey's last Chinese fishing village after a 1906 fire at China Point (just north of the Monterey Bay Aquarium in Pacific Grove) forced the village to relocate here. Today **McAbee Beach** is the site of a pleasant outdoor plaza featuring beach access and a bronze bust honoring John Steinbeck. On nice days, the Bay off McAbee Beach is a favorite spot for kayakers to paddle around lush kelp forests.

The **Steinbeck Plaza** shops are situated south of the plaza on both sides of Cannery Row. Here, you'll find some of the trendier specialty shops and galleries on the Row, including **Pebble Beach On Cannery Row,** 660 Cannery Row, (831) 373-1500, and **Ghirardelli Chocolate,** 660 Cannery Row, (831) 373-0997.

Now hidden from Cannery Row behind the inland side of the Plaza shops is the **Edgewater Packing Company.** Facing the Monterey Peninsula Recreation Trail, this 1940s packinghouse for fishmeal and fertilizer is now home to a colorful carousel and 21st-century video games. It's a favorite among youngsters of all ages (see our Kidstuff chapter for more about this attraction). Directly in front of the Edgewater Packing Company sit two antique railway cars. The green railcar is home to the **Cannery Row Foundation,** (831) 372-8512, a nonprofit group dedicated to preserving the heritage of the Row. Inside, you'll find pamphlets, books, and maps recalling the area's storied past.

There's also an ATM if you're running a little low on cash. Docents provide guidance, directions, and occasional walking tours. The railcar is open noon to 4:00 P.M. on weekends only.

Farther south down Cannery Row are more pleasant restaurants and shops as well as the charming waterfront **Spindrift Inn** (see our Hotels and Motels chapter). Check out the "dragon roof" architecture at 653 Cannery Row. Formerly the Marina Apartments, this 1929 building exemplifies the Chinese influence on Cannery Row.

Just past Hoffman Avenue, the Row opens up into an undeveloped area that continues to be a hotbed of local debate. Plans for future development are meeting stiff resistance from preservationists who call for a stop to the remodeling and further "touristization" of the Row.

As Cannery Row nears Drake Avenue, it veers inland. On the inland side are two green cottages, which served as the stables and servants quarters for the large Haldorn Estate, built in 1901 on the site now occupied by the stately **Monterey Plaza Hotel** (see our Hotels and Motels chapter). These cottages later served as the movie set for *Clash by Night,* a 1951 film starring Barbara Stanwyck and, in her first co-starring role (as a fish cutter), Marilyn Monroe. A few hundred feet farther, where the recreation trail crosses Drake Avenue, is the site where Doc Ricketts lost his life in an automobile collision with the Del Monte Express. (The recreation trail was built over the path of the railroad tracks that served Monterey and Pacific Grove.) A bust of Ricketts now marks the spot.

Cannery Row turns left here at Drake Avenue and continues south along the entrance to the Monterey Plaza Hotel. More shops and the **Baywood Cellars** wine-tasting room, 381 Cannery Row, (831) 645–9035, line the Row across from the hotel. Wine tasting is available seven days a week from 11:00 A.M. to 9:00 P.M.

Look overhead a little farther down at 299 Cannery Row, and you'll see the Aeneas Sardine Packing Company

crossover. Along with the crossover of the Monterey Canning Company, it's one of only two of the original 16 crossovers to survive.

Just after the **Monterey Bay Inn** (see our Hotels and Motels chapter), Cannery Row opens up into the **San Carlos Beach Park** (see our In and Around the Water chapter). Dedicated as an access point to the Monterey Bay Marine Sanctuary, the park is a favorite among scuba divers, kayakers, and picnickers. It provides a sweeping view of Cannery Row, the Monterey Harbor breakwater, and Fisherman's Wharf. Cannery Row ends at the entrance to the breakwater and Coast Guard pier.

Additional shops and restaurants occupy the 2 blocks above the length of Cannery Row on Wave and Foam Streets: **The Sardine Factory,** 701 Wave Street, **The Whaling Station Inn,** 763 Wave Street, and the **Cannery Row Antique Mall,** 471 Wave Street (see our Shopping chapter).

As tourism grew, parking became a problem near popular Cannery Row. But it's a problem no more. A large multistory parking garage with more than 1,000 spaces is now situated on the full block between Foam and Wave Streets and Prescott and Hoffman Avenues. Limited on-street metered parking is available on Cannery Row itself. A quarter buys you 20 minutes, and most meters have a four-hour maximum. Also on the Row, south of Hoffman Avenue, is a parking lot with extra-large spaces for campers and RVs.

Fisherman's Wharf
99 Pacific Street, Monterey
(831) 373-0600
www.montereywharf.com
Since the time when 19th-century trading schooners arrived in Monterey Bay to unload their precious cargoes after their harrowing trip around Cape Horn, Monterey's Fisherman's Wharf has been a welcome site to Peninsula visitors. Built in 1846 as Monterey's earliest pier of stone, the wharf has gone through more metamorphoses than Monarch butterflies.

Old Fisherman's Wharf bustles with fish markets, seafood restaurants, bay cruises, and a variety of gift shops. © JEFFREY GREENBERG/MONTEREY COUNTY CONVENTION AND VISITORS BUREAU

However, it remains a monument to the fishing industry and an important economic center for the city of Monterey. Only eight years after its erection, Fisherman's Wharf became the core of a booming whaling industry. Vessels docked wharfside with their gigantic cargoes in tow as workers gathered for the arduous task of carving up these majestic behemoths. By the early 20th century, with the whale population decimated, the tiny sardine displaced the enormous mammal as the catch of the day on the wharf. Following the boom and bust of the Cannery Row sardine era, commercial fishers turned to salmon, rock cod, albacore, mackerel, and squid for their livelihood. Today, you'll find more tourists than fishermen on the wharf, as most of the commercial fishing fleet has moved over to the neighboring Municipal Wharf, just a sea lion's bark north in Monterey, or miles up the coast to Moss Landing.

From dawn 'til evening, Fisherman's Wharf bustles with activity. Gift shops selling everything from T-shirts to seashells, along with ice cream parlors, candy stores (sample the saltwater taffy at **Carousel Fine Candies**), and other attractions tempt you as you enter the wharf. But it is still the traditional fish markets, fresh seafood restaurants, and boating activities farther out on the pier that make Fisherman's Wharf so special. You'll find a wide selection of sit-down eateries of all price ranges serving full menus for lunch and dinner. Insiders' favorites include Rappa's Seafood Restaurant for a good view and good food, Abalonnetti Seafood Trattoria with calamari and pizza to die for, and Old Fisherman's Grotto with its famous clam chowder served in a sourdough bread bowl (see our Restaurants chapter for more suggestions). Many wharf restaurants advertise early-bird dinners for the budget conscious, so consider an early evening meal. Or, if you're just looking for a quick snack, try the outdoor vendors' smoked salmon, marinated octopus, fried squid (calamari), steamed mussels, and other seafood delights as you window-shop and stroll in the ocean air. Fisherman's Wharf is the departure point for whale-watching expeditions, Bay cruises, glass-bottom boat harbor cruises, sailing excursions, and fishing charters (see our In and Around the Water chapter for details). It is also home to The New Wharf Theatre and its American Musical Theater Festival (see The Arts and Galleries chapter).

Laguna Seca Recreation Area
Monterey-Salinas Highway (Highway 68), Monterey
(831) 648-5100, (800) 327-SECA
www.laguna-seca.com

Laguna Seca Recreation Area, approximately 7 miles inland from Monterey proper, is a center for a composite of activities, most of which revolve around a love of automobiles. There's the famous **Mazda Laguna Seca Raceway,** home of world-class motor sports competitions, including superbikes, Indy cars, and antique classics. In 2003, for example, Laguna Seca hosted the Grand Prix of Monterey, the Honda International Superbike Classic, the 30th Annual Rolex Monterey Historic Automobile Races, the Monterey Sports Car Championships (American LeMans Series), and the Road and Track U.S. Sports Car Invitational. This is serious racing featuring the best motor sports stars from around the world.

Then there's the **Laguna Seca Campground** (see the County Parks section of our Parks and Recreation chapter). Motor sports enthusiasts bring their recreation vehicles, campers, trailers, tents, or just their sleeping bags and camp out in well-paved and well-maintained campsites amid scrub oak and chaparral. Some of the 100-plus sites overlook the raceway, while others have more serene views of rolling hills. The campground is also open when there are no racing activities under way. While it can't rival Big Sur camping, it does provide a reasonably priced spot to pull in your road-home away from home and put down your temporary

stakes. And you're only 15 minutes inland on Highway 68 from the waters of Monterey Bay.

For those brave souls who'd rather drive Laguna Seca than simply observe it, have we got a treat for you! The Skip Barber Racing School (www.skipbarber.com) sets up shop at Laguna Seca year-round to provide a variety of driving and racing classes. There are half-day and three-day classes for beginners, as well as one- and two-day courses for more experienced drivers. Call (800) 221-1131.

Maritime Museum of Monterey
5 Custom House Plaza, Monterey
(831) 372-2608
www.montereyhistory.org

What started as the private nautical collection of former Carmel mayor and seaman Allen Knight has grown into a remarkably complete history of the seafaring heritage of Monterey Bay. Salty dogs and landlubbers alike will enjoy the impressive collection of maritime artifacts spanning four centuries of men and women on the sea. Housed in the 18,000-square-foot Stanton Center, the museum is a project of the Monterey History and Art Association. Upon entry, you will embark on a high-sea adventure that takes you all the way back to the time of Spanish conquistadors. Expansive exhibit areas spread out over two stories overlooking Monterey Bay allow you to retrace the routes of Spanish sea captain Juan Rodriguez Cabrillo as he mapped out the California coast in the 16th century. Use your imagination to travel with Father Junipero Serra as he establishes Monterey's first mission settlement. Experience the drama of Commodore John Drake Sloat raising the U.S. flag over Monterey, laying claim to the expansive California territory. View the impressive U.S. Pacific Fleet as it pulls into Monterey Bay in the early 20th century. And experience the triumphs and tragedies of the Portuguese whalers, the Chinese squid fishers, the Japanese abalone divers, and the Italian sardine fishermen as they sweat and toil to make Monterey a thriving seaport.

The Maritime Museum brims with artifacts, ship models, paintings, and photographs depicting these historic eras. Rare, finely handcrafted chronometers and sextants, original ships' logs, military weapons, and the everyday tools of the hearty seagoing sailors are all on display. The guardian over the entire museum is the original two-story-high Fresnel lens of Point Sur Lighthouse. This 10,000-pound beacon, designed in 1822 in France, was installed in 1889 to stand watch for ships navigating around treacherous Big Sur Point. For nearly 100 years, this cut-glass beauty warned mariners of the dangerous rocky shore that continues to claim ships that venture too close. Its 1,000 prisms and precision magnifying glass sent out a powerful beam that could be seen more than 20 miles offshore.

Two of the more recent additions to the museum are an expanded World War II exhibit and interactive video stations. The video stations allow you to select topics of interest, such as the story of the USS *Macon* dirigible, which crashed off the Big Sur coast, and then listen to newsreel accounts or interviews with witnesses.

Don't forget to sound the foghorn before completing your visit to the Maritime Museum. And kids who complete the museum's unique treasure hunt are in for a special treat! The Ship's Store features a good selection of books, prints, postcards, toys, games, jewelry, and decorative items for your shipshape home. Ask about education programs including ship model workshops, children's activities, and a 4,000-volume library open 10:00 A.M. to 4:00 P.M. Monday through Friday. You'll find the Maritime Museum of Monterey in the historic Custom House Plaza, a short stroll from the entrance to Fisherman's Wharf. Follow signs to Fisherman's Wharf and parking. It's open from 10:00 A.M. to 5:00 P.M. Tuesday through Sunday except Thanksgiving and Christmas. Admission is $5.00 for adults, $2.50 for senior citizens and active military, $2.50 for youth (ages 13 to 18) and free for children ages 12 and younger. Memberships are available.

Monterey Bay Aquarium
886 Cannery Row, Monterey
(831) 648–4800
www.mbayaq.org

As you gaze out over Monterey Bay, you can't help but wonder what goes on underneath the rolling waves, within the dense kelp forests, and among the rocky crags of the shoreline. Well wonder no more—and you don't even have to don a wet suit. The Monterey Bay Aquarium brings the Bay to Cannery Row in a breathtaking exhibit of life beneath the sea. Opened in 1984, the world-acclaimed, non-profit, and self-supporting facility is now home to more than 300,000 creatures of the deep and not so deep, representing close to 550 species. The vast majority of residents are native to Monterey Bay. The aquarium is neatly laid out over two and three stories of more than 100 exhibits, fed by a system that pumps 2,000 gallons of raw seawater into the tanks each minute.

You'll visit the feathery inhabitants of coastal wetlands as well as the crawly creatures of deep granite reefs. A towering 28-foot-tall kelp forest sways hypnotically with the man-made tide of a 335,000-gallon tank as schools of silvery fish reflect the natural sunlight. Playful sea otters hold court before fascinated observers. Outdoor tide pools teem with life. And we haven't even gotten to the really good stuff yet!

A crown jewel of the aquarium is the Outer Bay exhibit. The only word to describe it is otherworldly. If you haven't visited the aquarium since this wing opened in 1996, a return trip is a must. The million-gallon tank is home to strange open-ocean beings normally found in waters 60 miles outside the mouth of Monterey Bay. From what is purported to be the largest window in the world (54 feet long, 15 feet tall, and 13 inches thick), you'll view giant ocean sunfish, green sea turtles, soupfin and hammerhead sharks, barracuda, and schools of large yellowfin and bluefin tuna. Nearby tanks of jellies look for all the world like visitors from outer space rather than the outer bay.

Bubble windows allow aquarium visitors to get up close and personal with sea life.
MONTEREY BAY AQUARIUM/MONTEREY COUNTY CONVENTION AND VISITORS BUREAU

Kids of all ages enjoy the many opportunities available to get up close and personal with some slithery and slimy friends of the sea. Pet bat rays as they glide past in a wide shallow pool. Don't worry: Their stingers have been clipped. Hold sea stars and their tide pool buddies at the touch pools. Splash Zone is a family-oriented exhibit featuring black-footed penguins, moray eels, tropical sharks, and real-life versions of some of the kids' favorite characters from Disney's *Finding Nemo.* At *Live from Monterey,* a live video broadcast presented up to four days a week, you'll get a backseat view in a research submarine as scientists study unusual sea life in the Monterey Bay canyons. An extensive gift and bookstore provides special mementos of your visit and gifts for friends and family back home. The aquarium's Portola Cafe has a help-yourself cafeteria and a full-service restaurant and oyster bar with great ocean views.

Plan on spending at least three hours at the aquarium. Insiders suggest arriving when the aquarium opens at 10:00 A.M., visiting for a couple hours before the big afternoon crowds arrive, and getting your hand stamped for an optional return visit in the early evening. Spend the afternoon with a lunch along the beaches. Explore the real tide pools (but don't wash off your stamp!) that are only minutes down the Monterey Peninsula Recreation Trail that runs alongside the aquarium and down the shoreline in Pacific Grove. Just remember to pack out your trash, and don't disturb the protected wildlife of the Monterey Bay Marine Sanctuary.

If you've never seen an anchovy without the pizza, the Monterey Bay Aquarium is a must-see. It's open from 10:00 A.M. to 6:00 P.M. daily except Christmas. On holidays and summer months (Memorial Day to Labor Day), the aquarium opens at 9:30 A.M. Admission rates are $17.95 for adults 18 and older; $15.95 for seniors 65 or older and students (ages 13 through 17 or with a college I.D.); and $8.95 for children ages three to 12 and the disabled. Children two and younger are admitted free. Memberships and group rates are available, and an extensive volunteer program allows locals to serve as guides.

Monterey Path of History
5 Custom House Plaza, Monterey
(831) 649-7118
www.oldmonterey.org

Encompassing nearly 40 historic structures from 19th-century California, the 2.8-mile Monterey Path of History meanders throughout the entire downtown area of Old Monterey. Feel free to head out on your personal adventure with your Path of History map in hand (available at any of the visitor centers throughout town). Pick and choose from the many adobes and other storied structures along the route. Some historic buildings are now private residences that can be viewed from the exterior only. But many others open their doors to the public for interior and garden visits. If you prefer, you can take a 90-minute guided walking tour of the path, visiting selected sites. This option provides expert commentary from a local guide and includes interior and garden visits to up to four historic locations that otherwise require an admission fee equal to the cost of the whole tour.

The cost of the guided tour is $5.00 for adults, $3.00 for youths, and $2.00 for children. The guided tours begin daily at 10:00 A.M., 3:00 P.M., and 4:00 P.M. at The Monterey State Historic Park Visitor Center located in the Stanton Center, also home of the Maritime Museum of Monterey (see previous listing). The earlier starting times provide opportunities to tour the interiors of most of the historic sites. Whether you take the guided tour or walk the Path of History on your own, we suggest you begin by viewing the free 14-minute film presented every 20 minutes at the theater in the visitor center. It provides a vivid introduction to the historic sites on the

path as well as insights into some of Monterey's most interesting personalities.

In this write-up we suggest a tour for adventurers who wish to see the highlights of the path on their own. These 14 buildings include the 11 structures that make up the Monterey State Historic Park as well as Colton Hall, the home of California's first constitutional convention, and the Royal Presidio Chapel, the oldest building standing in Monterey. This is a great introductory trip, but be sure to check out all of the structures listed on the Path of History map to see whether others may be of personal interest.

Note: Round markers (the new ones are yellow with the crest of Monterey; the old ones are bronze) in the sidewalks will help guide you along the Path of History route. In front of each historic site you'll find an illustrated tile, set in the sidewalk, and descriptive signs.

So slip on your good walking shoes and let's begin. Prepare for a good two to three hours, depending on how long you stay at each site. The walk itself, at a leisurely pace, takes about 90 minutes. From the Stanton Center near Fisherman's Wharf, take a quick stroll east across the Custom House Plaza to the **Pacific House and Garden.** It's the large white two-story building with dark green trim directly in front of the Stanton Center entrance. This 1847 adobe was first occupied by the U.S. Quartermaster for offices and military supplies and later became a boisterous public tavern. The walled corral behind the house is said to have been an entertainment arena for Sunday bull and bear fights, a popular spectator "sport" of the mid-19th century. Today, the Pacific House is home to two museums. The Pacific House Museum celebrates Monterey's period as capital of Spanish and Mexican California. The Monterey Museum of the American Indian is packed with Native American artifacts—and a real "growling" grizzly bear. The museums are open daily from 10:00 A.M. to 5:00 P.M.

From the front of Pacific House, follow the markers in the sidewalk north across the Plaza toward Fisherman's Wharf. Here, you'll reach **The Custom House,** the oldest public building on the Pacific Coast. Built in 1827, the Custom House presided over Mexico's only legal port of entry into the "Alta California" coast, inspecting cargoes and collecting custom duties and taxes. Later, the Custom House was the site where Commodore John Drake Sloat raised the U.S. flag on July 7, 1846, claiming more than 600,000 square miles of territory for the U.S. government. Today, you'll see a reproduction of the Custom House in action. It is filled with replicas of the types of 19th-century supplies that would likely come into port as well as the hides and tallow the Montereyans used in trade for those goods. Don't leave without your passport stamp. The Custom House is open daily from 10:00 A.M. to 5:00 P.M. and is free of charge.

From the Custom House, follow the markers east down Decatur Street. Cross Oliver Street and enter into Heritage Harbor, a retail and business center. Follow the markers about another 100 feet to a fountain. To your left, you'll discover the **First Brick House and Garden.** This is the first structure in California built by the kiln-fired brick construction method, rather than from the traditional adobe. The modest home was constructed in 1847 by the Dickinson family, original members of the Donner party who, fortunately for them, parted company with the Donners before the fateful crossing of the Sierras. Inside, you'll find displays highlighting some of the home's previous occupants. The First Brick House is open daily from 10:00 A.M. to 5:00 P.M.

Upon exiting, turn left (east) and continue just a few more steps to the **Whaling Station and Garden.** Built in 1847 as a replica of an ancestral Scottish cottage, the two-story adobe with balcony and garden was acquired in 1855 by the Old Monterey Whaling Company to house offices and employee quarters. Note the city's only remaining whalebone sidewalk in front of the building. (The Junior League of Monterey County now maintains this beautifully restored building as well as the neighboring First Brick House.)

The Path of History takes you through the garden gate at the Whaling Station. Continue through this tranquil garden (open daily from 10:00 A.M. to 5:00 P.M.) and exit in the rear, through Heritage Harbor and to Scott Street. Cross Scott Street at the corner of Pacific Street and then turn left down Scott to the chalk-rock and adobe **Casa Del Oro.** Famous Monterey businessmen David Jacks and Joseph Boston ran this 19th-century general store and gold depository. Built in 1845, Casa Del Oro is once again open for business as the Boston Store (open 11:00 A.M. to 3:00 P.M. Thursday through Sunday), a pleasant gift shop run by the nonprofit Historic Garden League. The league also runs the Picket Fence garden shop on the other side of the adjacent Casa Del Oro garden.

To continue on our path, retrace your steps back up Scott Street to Pacific Street. Cross to the southeast corner of Scott and Pacific Streets, where you'll find **California's First Theatre.** Built in 1844 by Jack Swan as a saloon and boarding house for sailors, this wooden frame and adobe structure became a venue for live theatre when the New York Volunteers, a group of local soldiers, began staging productions in 1848. The tavern and theater are still operating today, with live 19th-century melodramas and comedies held weekly since 1937 by the Troupers of the Gold Coast (see The Arts and Galleries chapter for more details on performances). The First Theatre is open for touring from 1:00 to 5:00 P.M. Thursday through Saturday.

As you exit California's First Theatre, turn right (south) and walk one block to 336 Pacific Street. Walk through the front garden gate and witness the exceptionally well-preserved **Casa Soberanes.** This thick-walled beauty is a classic example of

The Custom House, the oldest public building on the Pacific Coast, gives you a taste of 19th-century trade among early Montereyans. SHARON FONG/MONTEREY COUNTY CONVENTION AND VISITORS BUREAU

the Monterey Colonial adobe. Built in 1842 by the commandant of the Monterey Presidio and occupied by the Soberanes family in 1860, it features interconnecting rooms filled with splendid furniture and artwork, a magnificent balcony, and beautiful, well-kept gardens. Tours of the interior are available at 1:00 and 4:00 P.M.

Note: This is the first of four structures on the Path of History that have scheduled tours and charge admission, the others being the Larkin House, the Cooper Molera Adobe, and the Stevenson House. If you take the guided tour from the Stanton Center, your price of admission to each is covered. If you are on your own, one admission ticket purchased at the Stanton Center or at any of the four sites will get you into all four historic structures. As with the tour, the cost of admission is $5.00 for adults, $3.00 for youths, and $2.00 for children.

Upon exiting Casa Soberanes, continue

south on Pacific Street. Pass the Merritt House, former home of Josiah Merritt, the first judge of Monterey County, and continue three blocks to **Colton Hall.** (The sidewalk markers disappear on this section of Pacific Street, as the Path of History detours slightly uphill to take in a few other sites we're not visiting here.)

The first United States public building in California, Colton Hall was the site of the convention that drafted California's first constitution. Named after Walter Colton, the first Chief Magistrate of Monterey after the American occupation of California, Colton Hall was completed in 1849. Notice that it sports a definite New England style that contrasted markedly with the California adobes. It was erected, in Colton's words, "out of the slender proceeds of town lots, the labor of convicts, taxes on liquor shops, and fines on gamblers." Climb the exterior stairs to the second-story museum of this most historic California structure, and you'll enter a scene similar to that created by the 48 delegates as they debated the issues leading to California's constitution in October of 1849. Books, parchments, and fountain pens lie about the well-worn oak tables, as if the delegates had just left the room for a recess. Toward the rear of the museum are mementos of Colton Hall School, which began holding classes here in 1873. The museum is free of charge and open daily from 10:00 A.M. to noon and 1:00 to 5:00 P.M. For an entertaining side trip, follow the walkway that goes behind Colton Hall to find the **Old Monterey Jail.** This small six-cell jailhouse of granite was constructed in 1854 and served as a jail for more than 100 years—without a single reported escape. There was, however, a reported jail storming, where some 19th-century townspeople apprehended a jailed murderer and hanged him from the jail rafters! The cells are set up to re-create the quarters of incarcerated scoundrels from different eras of Monterey's colorful past—including a John Steinbeck character from *Tortilla Flat.*

Walk out to the front of Colton Hall and take the left-hand path through the tranquil garden setting of **Friendly Plaza,** a brick courtyard built in the 1930s with WPA funds. Be sure to read the unusual inscription on the monument to the city of Monterey. Then cross Pacific Street at the adjacent corner (Jefferson and Pacific Streets), and you'll be facing the rear of the **Larkin House.** Walk down Jefferson Street one block to the entrance on Calle Principal. Built by Thomas Larkin, U.S. consul to Alta California, this 1834 two-story adobe is the first example of the architectural style that has become known as "Monterey Colonial" or simply the "Monterey style." The Larkin House is now home to a fabulous collection of period furnishings and antiques from around the world. Don't miss the walled garden to experience a little piece of heaven circa 19th-century Monterey. Admission is required for the interior tours at 11:00 A.M. and 2:00 and 3:00 P.M.

As you exit Larkin House, turn right (south) down Calle Principal and walk past the quarters of William Tecumseh Sherman, the House of Four Winds, and the Monterey Museum of Art to the end of the block. Here, you'll find **Casa Gutierrez,** one of the few remaining examples of the simpler Mexican-style adobe. Built in 1841 by Joaquin Gutierrez, the nephew of Mexico's acting governor of California in the 1830s, this modest adobe is the home of the Thomas Kinkade Museum and Cultural Center (see listing in The Arts and Galleries chapter).

From Casa Gutierrez, cross Calle Principal at Madison Street and make the first left on Polk Street. Cross to the opposite side of Polk at the Gabriel de la Torre Adobe and continue north on Polk one block to Munras Avenue. You'll discover the **Cooper-Molera Adobe,** perhaps the most active spot on this Path of History and the largest complex of the Monterey State Historic Park. In fact, if you only have time to visit one of Monterey's historic adobes, this wouldn't be a bad choice. The Cooper-Molera Adobe was built in 1830 by John Rogers Cooper, a New England sea captain, as a gift for his bride. Over the years, the Cooper family added barns, servants quarters, and other structures to complete the two-and-a-half-acre complex you see today. Frances Molera, Captain Cooper's granddaughter, willed the entire grounds to the National Trust for Historic Preservation, which leases it to the State of California. The Cooper-Molera Adobe grounds are open free of charge every day from 10:00 A.M. to 5:00 P.M. from June through August, and 10:00 A.M. to 4:00 P.M. September through May. Guided tours of the interior are available at 10:00 A.M., noon, and 3:00 P.M. for the fee mentioned earlier in this entry. You're sure to enjoy the interior period garden, where chickens and other barnyard animals roam. There are also an exhibit room, barn, carriage display, and other sites of interest to see. Visit the Cooper Store, which features wooden toys, pottery, and other goods reminiscent of days gone by. Try to take advantage of the special history and art programs that are held throughout the year for both adults and children. The Cooper-Molera Courtyard is also the starting point for historic garden tours of Old Monterey on selected days (currently Saturday and Tuesday at 1:00 P.M.) from May through September. Adults are asked to pay a modest donation.

To proceed to our next stop, turn right (south) from the entrance of the Cooper Store and head down Munras Avenue past the Simoneau Plaza Transit Station. Cross Munras at the crosswalk, then continue across Tyler, following the brass markers. Follow a large sign pointing to a path that enters the rear garden of **Stevenson House.** (If the garden gate is closed, continue down Munras one block, take a left on Webster Avenue and another left on Houston Street to the front entrance.) Built in 1840, this historic hotel is said to have been the residence of author Robert Louis Stevenson during the fall of 1879. (There is debate whether Stevenson actually lived here or was just a frequent visitor, but who are we to quibble?) The story goes that Stevenson came to Monterey in search of his true love, Fanny Osbourne. Here, Stevenson resided in what was then known as the French Hotel as he courted his future bride. Today, you'll find period furnishings as well as perhaps the world's greatest collection of manuscripts, first-edition books, photos, and other personal belongings of the Scottish-born writer. Admission is required for the interior tours at 10:00 A.M. and 2:00 and 4:00 P.M., as mentioned earlier in this entry.

Our final destination is, fittingly, the oldest building in existence in Monterey and its last remaining structure of 18th-century Spanish origin. Exiting the front of Stevenson House, turn right (south) on Houston Street. At the first corner, turn left on Webster Street and make a right on Abrego Street, heading past Casa Pacheco. Make another left across Abrego at Church Street. Continue down Church Street a long block past San Carlos School to the **Royal Presidio Chapel.** Built in 1770 as part of California's second Franciscan mission (San Carlos de Borromeo de Monterey), the original chapel was destroyed by fire in 1789. The chapel that stands today was rebuilt in 1794 and is the oldest church in continuous service in California as well as the smallest cathedral in the United States. Note the exquisite "Virgin of Guadalupe" that adorns the facade. The Royal Presidio Chapel is open daily from 8:30 A.M. to 6:00 P.M. free of charge.

To return to our starting point, the Custom House Plaza, backtrack your route to the Stevenson House. Continue north on Houston Street to Pearl Street. Turn left (east) on Pearl and go one block to Tyler Street. Turn right (north) and go one block to Bonifacio Place. Turn left and go one block to Alvarado Street. Cross Alvarado and turn right (north) on Alvarado, following Monterey's main street through downtown until it ends at Del Monte Avenue. Cross Del Monte and continue north across Portola Plaza and along the shops outside the DoubleTree Hotel. Keep walking another few yards and you're there. After your long walk, you're probably ready for an ice cream cone, beverage, or full meal out on Fisherman's Wharf. Enjoy!

Steinbeck's Spirit of Monterey Wax Museum
700 Cannery Row, Monterey
(831) 375-3770
www.wax-museum.com
Sure, it's pure kitsch compared to computer-age standards of lifelike robotics and 3-D visual displays found at today's mega-amusement parks. But

there's something pleasantly nostalgic about a genuine wax museum of sculptured figures that take you through a 20-minute Cliff Notes version of the history of Monterey. It's all here: Spanish explorers, early Native Americans, Father Serra and the missions, Robert Louis Stevenson, and John Steinbeck himself narrating stories of his Cannery Row characters. Some of the figurines are so lifelike, you'll swear you see them breathing. Steinbeck's Spirit of Monterey Wax Museum is open daily from 10:30 A.M. to 8:00 P.M. The price of entry is $5.95 for adults, $4.95 for seniors and students, and $3.95 for children ages six to 18. Children five and younger get in free.

Pacific Grove

Monarch Grove Sanctuary
Ridge Road, Pacific Grove
(831) 375-0982
www.pgmuseum.org

In 1990 the citizens of Pacific Grove enthusiastically cast their votes on a bond measure authorizing the city to spend more than $1.2 million on a rather nondescript 2.4-acre lot of spindly pine, cypress, and eucalyptus trees. As a real estate investment, the purchase certainly didn't make much sense. But for a city that proudly calls itself "Butterfly Town USA," it made all the sense in the world.

Taxpayer money was voluntarily spent to purchase this small private lot facing imminent development so it could be preserved and restored as a permanent butterfly sanctuary. Since the purchase, hundreds of volunteers organized by three citizen groups, the Monarch Habitat Restoration Committee, Friends of the Monarch, and the Pacific Grove Eco-Corps, have devoted countless hours maintaining the grounds. They've also planted hundreds of seedlings of trees and flowering plants that future generations of monarch butterflies will call home.

The Monarch Grove Sanctuary serves as an overwintering site for monarch butterflies from October through February. In fact, it is one of two primary sites within the city that provides the microclimate that monarchs need to withstand the cold and wind of winter. The other site is a grove of pine trees at George Washington Park, which also has benefited from the restoration efforts of the citizen groups.

If your visit takes you to the Monterey Peninsula during the fall and winter months, take time to visit one of the monarch habitats. Follow the clearly marked trails to the designated sites. Look up into the trees about 20 to 30 feet above the ground. On chilly, foggy, or cloudy days, you may not immediately notice the butterflies. In cold weather, they cluster with their wings closed, looking much like bunches of triangular brown leaves. Keep looking and you'll eventually spot them. When the weather warms above 55 degrees, the monarchs come to life, opening their wings and exposing the bright orange tops we're all familiar with. Should the sun warm them further, they will flutter and fly about in a showy display. Recent estimates place the winter Monarch population at more than 15,000, though the numbers can vary dramatically from year to year.

Where did they all come from? The monarchs fly into Pacific Grove from as far north as Canada and Alaska and as far east as the Rocky Mountains. Their long journeys take up to eight months.

How the butterflies find their way back to Pacific Grove year after year is very much a mystery. Actually, the butterflies you see today are likely the great-great-great-grandchildren of the monarchs who overwintered here the previous year. Those butterflies flew east or north to lay their eggs and die. The next three to four generations fly even farther north and east, living abbreviated life-spans of just a few weeks before laying their eggs. This year's monarch emerged from a chrysalis that hung at the farthest northern and eastern regions of the migration and made the entire return trip, flying up to 2,000 miles and reaching altitudes of 10,000 feet.

Scientists theorize that the monarchs rely on magnetic fields, the position of the sun, or pure genetic instincts to find their way home to Pacific Grove. Regardless, they do return to be celebrated by the citizens of Pacific Grove, who hold a festive Butterfly Parade on the second Saturday every October (see our Annual Events chapter).

Remember that the butterfly habitats are very fragile and require great care. Please stay on the trails to minimize impact on the sanctuaries. Don't disturb the clusters and watch out for butterflies on the ground. As the sign at the Monarch Grove Sanctuary says, "Leave only footprints and take away only memories."

The two butterfly habitats are open every day sunrise to sunset. The Monarch Grove Sanctuary is on Ridge Road adjacent to the Butterfly Trees Lodge. Ridge Road is off Lighthouse Avenue, directly across from The Wilkie's Motel. George Washington Park is at the corner of Alder Street and Pine Avenue. There is no admission charge at either site. While driving to the habitats, be alert to the "Butterfly Crossing" signs!

Pacific Grove Historic Walking Tour
Forest and Central Avenues,
Pacific Grove
(831) 373-3304

While not as elaborate as the Monterey Path of History (see separate listing in our Monterey section), the Pacific Grove Historic Walking Tour is of special interest to lovers of Victorian and Queen Anne architecture. You can pick up a map of the tour at the Pacific Grove Chamber of Commerce or the Pacific Grove Museum of Natural History, both of which are at the corner of Forest and Central Avenues. The walking-tour map includes 18 points of interest, beginning with the Museum of Natural History (see separate listing). Highlights include St. Mary's By-The-Sea (a Gothic-style church with two Tiffany windows), Seven Gables, Gosby House, and Chautauqua Hall. Other than a few private residences, most of the buildings on the walking tour are open to the public during daylight hours.

Pacific Grove Museum of Natural History
165 Forest Avenue, Pacific Grove
(831) 648-5716
www.pgmuseum.org

Recognized nationwide as one of the finest museums of its size, the Pacific Grove Museum of Natural History is a must-see for those intrigued by the fauna and flora of the Monterey Peninsula. Sandy the Whale, local artist Larry Foster's life-size sculpture of a California gray whale, greets you at the bottom of the entrance steps. Climb aboard, kids: Sandy is friendly and nearly indestructible, and she may be the most photographed gray whale in the world!

Once inside this adobe-style museum, erected in 1932, you'll see intriguing zoological specimens of many local birds, mammals, reptiles, and insects that roam throughout Peninsula beaches, forests, and streets. Unique marine creatures are on display, too, including an eerie-looking big skate. The museum's collection of more than 400 birds is especially impressive, as is the extensive multimedia exhibit honoring the local monarch butterfly—delivered in three different languages! You'll also find artifacts from local Native Americans, such as the Costanoan, Salinan, and Esselen tribes.

An interesting exhibit of geology and mineralogy includes a working Geiger-Muller counter, an enclosed booth of fluorescent minerals, marine fossils, and impressive relief maps of Monterey County and the deep canyons of Monterey Bay, completed in 1936. A Children's Touch Gallery includes hands-on specimens and artifacts and live subtidal sea animals from the Monterey Bay. Outside, the museum grows a garden of native Monterey County plants and trees.

In springtime, be sure to catch the annual wildflower show, usually the third weekend in April. Check the museum's schedule for selected Smithsonian Institution traveling exhibitions as well. Mementos of your visit can be purchased at the well-stocked gift shop. The Pacific Grove Museum of Natural History is open Tuesday through Sunday from 10:00 A.M. to 5:00 P.M. Admission is free, though a donation is greatly appreciated. It's closed New Year's Day, Thanksgiving, Christmas Eve, and Christmas Day.

Point Pinos Lighthouse
Asilomar Boulevard at Lighthouse
Avenue, Pacific Grove
(831) 648–5716, ext. 13
www.pgmuseum.org
The oldest continuously operating lighthouse on the West Coast of the United States, Point Pinos Lighthouse has been marking the entrance to Monterey Bay for seafarers since 1855. And what you see is what you get: The building, the lenses, and the prisms are all original equipment. The light is a third-order Fresnel manufactured in France in 1853. A whale-oil lantern was its first power source, followed by lard oil, and later kerosene. An electrical light was

finally installed in 1915. Today, a 1,000-watt bulb produces a 50,000-candlepower beam that, on a clear night, can be spotted up to 15 miles offshore.

Visitors will find the procession of Point Pinos lightkeepers as interesting as the lighthouse itself. The original lightkeeper, Charles Layton, was killed in 1856 as a member of a sheriff's posse chasing notorious Mexican outlaw Anastacio Garcia. He was succeeded by his widow, Charlotte, who served until she married her assistant in 1860. Lightkeeper Alan Luce was once host to Robert Louis Stevenson, who wrote of his pleasant visit in 1879. The most famous Point Pinos lightkeeper of all, however, was Emily Fish, known as the "Socialite Keeper." Mrs. Fish used the lighthouse to entertain many guests and kept the building well decorated and meticulously clean. Today's visitors get a glimpse of the lighthouse under Fish's 1893 to 1914 reign, as the lighthouse is decorated much as she kept it.

Point Pinos Lighthouse is the oldest continuously operating lighthouse on the West Coast.
MONTEREY COUNTY CONVENTION AND VISITORS BUREAU

The Point Pinos Lighthouse shines on daily from the northernmost point of the Monterey Peninsula, sharing its scenic site with the Pacific Grove Municipal Golf Course. Parking is behind the course's 10th green, off Asilomar Avenue between Lighthouse Avenue and Ocean View Boulevard. The lighthouse is open to the public from 1:00 to 4:00 P.M. Thursday through Monday. Requested donation is $2.00 for adults and $1.00 for children. Volunteer docents are on hand to provide historical background.

Carmel

Carmel Mission Basilica
3080 Rio Road, Carmel
(831) 624-3600
www.carmelmission.org

The Basilica of Mission San Carlos Borromeo del Rio Carmelo, or Carmel Mission, is home to some of the most significant religious artifacts in all of California. Padre (Father) Junipero Serra, founder of the California missions, is buried here, and many of his personal belongings are on display. Padre Serra arrived in Monterey Bay by sea in 1770, having established the first California mission in San Diego the previous year. He chose this idyllic site in Carmel over the original Monterey site of San Carlos de Borromeo de Monterey because of its rich soil and proximity to the bountiful Carmel River. Serra took up permanent residence in the mission in 1771. At first, it was a simple wooden structure. But before long, the Spaniards enlisted the Native Americans who had converted to Catholicism to construct the more substantial adobe buildings. The mission soon became an important center of commerce, serving as a safe enclave for early Spanish settlers who sought rest, company, and supplies on their long arduous journeys up and down Alta California.

From Carmel, Padre Serra presided over the founding of nine of the eventual 21 missions in California. He passed away in 1784 at the age of 71. During his final days, Serra requested burial at Carmel Mission, beside his longtime friend Padre Juan Crespi, who had died two years prior.

Following Padre Serra's death, Padre Lasuen led Carmel Mission and, in 1793, undertook Serra's plans for building the present stone church. Built from native sandstone from the Santa Lucia Mountains in Big Sur and plastered with lime made from burnt seashells gathered along the coast, the church at Carmel Mission Basilica was completed in 1797. The turn of the 19th century marked the height of prosperity for Carmel Mission. The population of Native Americans was nearing 1,000, and the mission adobes continued to expand. But within the next 20 to 30 years, the mission began to fall into decay. By 1823 the population was less than 400. By 1836 Padre Jose Real officially moved the church to Monterey, taking most of the mission's ornaments and other effects with him. Services at Carmel Mission eventually ceased, and by 1880 the grounds were in ruin, pillaged of anything of value that had been left behind. Father Casanova's installation of a new roof on the old mission in 1884 was the first important step in its eventual restoration. The 1920s saw further restoration efforts and the erection of a memorial to Serra and the other padres buried on the site. Then in 1931 Monsignor Philip Scher, pastor of San Carlos in Monterey, appointed Harry Downie as curator in charge of mission restoration. It was Downie who directed the painstaking rebuilding of the mission to its former grandeur.

Today, visitors can get a taste of mission life as it was in the late 18th and early 19th centuries. A mission museum displays a remarkable collection of artifacts dating back to Padre Serra's time.

[Facing page] *Carmel Mission is one of 21 California missions built by the Franciscans.*
MONTEREY COUNTY CONVENTION AND VISITORS BUREAU

The California Missions

San Carlos Borromeo de Carmelo, or **Carmel Mission** (see the listing in this chapter), was the second of the 21 Franciscan missions built in California by the Spanish. Founded between 1769 and 1823, the missions were part of an attempt by Spanish King Charles III to secure the land north of Mexico before either the Russians, advancing south from the Bering Sea, or the English, moving west from what is now the United States and Canada, could lay claim to it.

As father of the mission system, Padre Junipero Serra oversaw the founding of the first nine missions, including Carmel Mission where he is buried. Today, the missions that stretch from San Diego in the south to Sonoma in the north are in varying states of restoration.

Counting Carmel Mission, 10 of the missions are located between San Luis Obispo and San Francisco along U.S. 101. This route largely follows El Camino Real, the original "King's Road" that connected the missions. There are nine other missions within a few hours of the Monterey Peninsula you might want to visit. We've organized them from south to north.

San Luis Obispo de Tolosa, the fifth mission, was established in 1772. It is noted as being the first mission to use in large scale the red-clay roof tiles now associated with California's Spanish architectural style. The padres in San Luis Obispo found that the tile roofs held up much better to flaming arrows from disgruntled local tribes than the thatched tule roofs that had been used previously. Today, despite some rather horrendous remodeling over the years, there is a pleasant Mission Plaza and a quality museum and gift store to visit. Mission San Luis Obispo is at the corner of Monterey and Chorro Streets, approximately two hours and 40 minutes (145 miles) south of Monterey. Call (805) 543-6850 for tour information.

San Miguel Arcangel, the 16th mission, was built in 1797 approximately 8 miles north of Paso Robles. The church interior is considered one of the best examples of mission art, featuring colorful and ornate work of Native Americans under the direction of renowned artist Estevan Munras. Of special note is the "Eye of God" tilework behind the altar. The mission is approximately two hours and 10 minutes (110 miles) south of Monterey. Call (805) 467-3256 for tour information.

San Antonio de Padua, the third mission, was constructed in 1771 about 6 miles west of the town of Jolon. It retains one of the most idyllic settings of the missions, especially during the height of the spring wildflower season. Some of the grounds still occupied by Franciscan monks are off-limits to the public, but the mission has a nice museum that is well worth the visit. Off U.S. 101 on the small, winding County Highway G-14, San Antonio de Padua is approximately two hours (85 miles) south of Monterey. Call (831) 385-4478 for tour information.

Nuestra Señora de la Soledad, the 13th mission, was built in 1791, 3 miles northwest of today's town of Soledad. One of the most desolate and least popular of the missions during the 19th century, it is also one of the last to go through restoration. Still, a small museum that chronicles the history of triumphs and misfortunes makes Soledad Mission an interesting attraction. The mission is on Fort Romie Road, approximately one hour (45 miles) south of Monterey. Call (831) 678-2586 for tour information.

San Juan Bautista, the 15th mission, was founded in 1797 and has been in continual use as a parish church ever since. This, the largest mission church, is part of a tranquil State Historic Park that includes a hotel, stable, and two adobe houses. A museum includes fascinating musical instruments and transcripts, reflecting the mission's peaceful past. Located alongside the very visible San Andreas Fault line, San Juan Bautista is 35 minutes (30 miles) north of Monterey on Highway 156. Call (831) 623-4881 for tour information.

Santa Cruz, the 12th mission, has suffered a series of disasters since it was built in 1791. Plundered by vagabonds, rocked by earthquakes, and undermined by a tidal wave, the original mission was finally leveled in 1857. Today a small-scale replica of the original church, with a modest museum is all that remains at the site at Emmett and High Streets in Santa Cruz. The mission is approximately 45 minutes up Highway 1 (40 miles) north of Monterey. Call (831) 279-3732 for tour information.

Santa Clara de Asís, the eighth mission, was founded in 1777 and boasted the greatest number of Native American baptisms, more than 8,500. The church that stands today is actu-ally a replica built in 1929. It is faithful to the original 1825 church, including three-dimensional concrete renderings of painter Agustin Davila's original designs. On the campus of the University of Santa Clara, the mission is approximately one hour and 20 minutes (75 miles) north of Monterey off of U.S. 101. For tour information, call (408) 554-4023.

San Jose, the 14th mission, was constructed in 1797. One of the most prosperous of the missions, it featured a large military presence to combat local hostile tribes. Today there is little left of the mission but a small museum housing a few artifacts. In the city of Fremont, San Jose Mission is approximately one hour and 40 minutes (85 miles) north of Monterey at Highway 238 and Washington Boulevard. Call (510) 657-1797 for tour information.

San Francisco de Asís, the sixth mission, was built in 1776. Commonly referred to today as Mission Dolores, it was founded by Juan Bautista de Anza, who led 240 settlers on an amazing journey from Sonora Mexico to Monterey and eventually San Francisco to claim this strategic Bay for Spain. The present church was completed in 1791 and has changed little since then, still featuring original Native American-designed chevrons on the ceiling beams. The mission was never very prosperous due to the cold, foggy weather, which contributed to illness and epidemics. Located at 16th and Dolores Streets in San Francisco, the mission is a little more than two hours (120 miles) north of Monterey. For tour information, call (415) 292-1770.

A little-known Carmel attraction is the colorful mural of Point Pinos and Carmel found on the side of Bruno's Market at Junipero Street and Sixth Avenue. Check it out!

The spartan cell where Serra lived is recreated in detail. You'll also see his ornate "cloth of gold" vestments of Chinese silk, his personal Bible, and redwood remnants of his original coffin. The museum also houses California's first library as well as a collection of tools, equipment, and appliances used by the Spaniards and Native Americans in day-to-day life at the mission. In the rear of the museum is the Junipero Serra sarcophagus, designed and created in 1924 by renowned California artist Jo Mora. At the head of the sarcophagus is a spectacular wooden cross, also a Mora design. It is a common misconception that Serra is buried beneath the sarcophagus. Actually, he is buried within the church, which is located just outside the right rear exit of the museum.

As you enter the church, notice the tower and the mission bells that date from the late 18th and early 19th centuries. The bells are still rung by hand, as they were back in 1770. Inside, the church faithfully reflects its original design, even though it was rebuilt almost totally from the ground up in the 1930s. Notice, to the left, the side chapel of Our Lady of Bethlehem with its intricately brocaded and jeweled statue. The front altar, of mid-20th-century design, contains many of the mission's original statues. Serra's grave is located under the floor on the left side of the altar, along with the graves of two fellow padres.

The outer grounds of the Carmel Mission are equally fascinating. Of particular interest is the cemetery to the right of the church as you face its entrance. A large cross is erected in memory of the more than 3,000 Native Americans buried in the mission grounds. To the left of the church is the main mission courtyard, a photographer's delight with the stately mission bell tower and the bright flowering bougainvillea. One final spot of interest is a small second museum near the cemetery. Here you can learn all about the exacting restoration project of Harry Downie.

To find the Carmel Mission from the Monterey Peninsula, take Highway 1 south to the mouth of Carmel Valley. Turn right at Rio Road and proceed approximately a half-mile. Off-street parking is available in front of and behind the mission. The Carmel Mission museum and gift shop are open from 9:30 A.M. to 5:30 P.M., Monday through Saturday and 10:30 A.M. to 5:30 P.M. on Sunday. A donation is requested—$2.00 for adults and $1.00 for children five to 18.

Tor House
**26304 Ocean View Avenue, Carmel
(831) 624-1813 (Monday through
Thursday), (831) 624-1840 (Friday and
Saturday)
www.torhouse.org**
Lovers of Robinson Jeffers's poetry are in for a special treat when they visit the mystical Tor House, home to Jeffers and his wife, Una, from the time it was originally completed in 1919 until Jeffers's death in 1962. Here on Point Carmel, overlooking the Pacific Ocean, Carmel Bay, and Point Lobos, Jeffers spent his mornings penning some of his most treasured poems. Then in the afternoon, he would put aside his pen and work on his masterpiece of stone and lumber, Tor House. He spent exhausting hours carrying or rolling large granite rocks up from the shoreline to his beloved homesite set atop a large outcropping of stone, or "tor."

The original Tor House was designed and built largely by famous California architect and builder M. J. Murphy. Jeffers worked alongside Murphy and soon learned how "to make stone love stone." Later, Jeffers himself built the mystical

Hawk Tower that became a special retreat for Jeffers, his wife, and their twin sons.

Today, docent-led one-hour tours take you through the main living quarters of Tor House, a quaint, unpretentious cottage of low ceilings, dark wood, and rugged stonework. See and feel where Robinson and Una lived their idyllic, somewhat spartan life during the day and often entertained world-famous poets, painters, photographers, and other luminaries of the art world in the evening. Indeed, visitors were welcome only after 4:00 P.M., as the sign Una posted on the garden gate clearly pointed out.

You'll visit the original west wing of Tor House, including the homey living room, small kitchen, and high-ceilinged dining room Jeffers later added on to entertain the growing pilgrimage of guests who came to Carmel to discover his poetic world. A memorable moment for Jeffers fans is time spent in the guest room that includes the bed by the window where Jeffers correctly prophesied he would die.

Throughout the house and lush outdoor gardens, docents point out special stones, shards of ancient pottery, and other artifacts from around the globe that were gifts from Jeffers's world-famous friends. They were brought to Jeffers specifically to be built into Tor House. You'll find pieces of history, such as the Great Wall of China, Pompeii, and the Pyramid of Cheops, in the walls, garden paths, and stone planters.

The tour highlight, of course, is ascending Hawk Tower, the three-story, 40-foot stone spire Jeffers built as a monument to his love for Una. Four years of devotion and sweat went into this labor of love, and the results are nothing short of enchanting. From the below-ground "dungeon" to the observation deck with its spectacular ocean view, Hawk Tower is a joy to explore. The hidden winding staircase up to Una's sanctuary is a tight fit, but a delightful adventure for all but the most claustrophobic.

Tor House is open to the public Friday and Saturday only. (Jeffers's daughter-in-law still lives in the newer east wing of the home, so please respect her privacy.) Docent-led tours are given on the hour beginning at 10:00 A.M., with the last tour conducted at 3:00 P.M. Tours are limited to six people and are by appointment only. The cost is $7.00 for adults, $4.00 for full-time college students, and $2.00 for high school and middle school students. Children must be age 12 or older to visit. Be sure to wear comfortable walking or hiking shoes for the climb up Hawk Tower.

The best way to find Tor House is to take Ocean Avenue south through downtown Carmel to Scenic Drive and turn left. From Scenic Drive, turn left on Bay View Avenue and then make a right turn onto Ocean View Avenue. Tor House will be on the right-hand side of Ocean View before you reach Stewart Way. Limited off-street parking is available.

Pebble Beach

17-Mile Drive
Pebble Beach
(831) 625–8530, (800) 654–9300
www.pebblebeach.com/17miledrive.html

Since the 1880s, guests at the elegant Hotel Del Monte in Monterey, now part of the Naval Postgraduate School, were given the opportunity to enjoy the natural wonders of the Monterey Peninsula via horse-drawn carriage and later automobile. The tour, called the "Circle of Enchantment," wound through Pacific Grove and into the dense Del Monte Forest, made up largely of native Monterey pines and Monterey cypress. The hotel tours often included extravagant picnics on the pebbled beaches of the Pacific Ocean and Carmel Bay. The scenic round-trip excursion along the winding gravel road was about 17 miles in length.

Today, you can enjoy a similar scenic route through the 5,000-acre forest by the sea that comprises the area known as

Pebble Beach. This breathtaking route is simply called 17-Mile Drive, even though the round-trip loop measures about 12 miles. Five guarded gates provide entrance into Pebble Beach, which is not an incorporated city but a private community owned largely by the Pebble Beach Company. An entrance fee of $8.00 per vehicle is charged for admittance. (The fee is reimbursed to guests staying at any of the resorts within the gates.) Admittance includes a map that points out the major highlights of the tour.

You can begin your tour at any of the five gates. Signs and the red and yellow stripes painted on the pavement guide your way along the drive. Your best choice of gates depends on your starting point. From Carmel, you can enter the Carmel gate near the south end of Ocean Avenue. From Highway 1, use the Highway 1 Gate at the top of Carmel Hill. From Highway 68, there's the Samuel F. B. Morse Gate near the Pacific Grove City line. And from Pacific Grove or Monterey, you can choose the Pacific Grove Gate off Sunset Drive near Asilomar State Beach or the Country Club Gate at Congress Avenue and Forest Lodge Road.

We'll start our tour at the Pacific Grove Gate, which provides the closest access to the beach route from the Monterey side of the Peninsula. Upon entering the gate at 17-Mile Drive and Sunset Drive, you'll immediately pass **The Inn and Links at Spanish Bay.** Named 1996's No. 1 Mainland Resort in the *Condé Nast Traveler* Readers Choice Awards, this luxury resort features 270 guest rooms and an authentic Scottish linksland golf course designed by Robert Trent Jones. Visitors can enjoy a casual lunch with a great view at Roy's at Pebble Beach in the main inn (see our Hotels and Motels and Restaurants chapters).

Past the Inn at Spanish Bay, turn right, following the signs to the 17-Mile Drive Beach route. You'll wind to the coast at **Spanish Bay** itself, where explorer Juan Portolá camped in 1769 while trying to locate the entrance to Monterey harbor. A

parking lot and picnic area are available.

Just a few minutes farther down the Drive, a rare ocean phenomenon occurs off the coast at **Point Joe.** "The Restless Sea," as it is called, is a convergence of two ocean currents that cause the sea to boil and bubble even on the calmest of days. Waves, white caps, and spray will often be evident here while the sea in both directions can be glassy calm. As poet Robinson Jeffers wrote, "Point Joe has teeth and has torn ships; it has fierce and solitary beauty." Indeed, there is a long history of shipwrecks here, as seamen unfamiliar with the area often mistook Point Joe for Point Pinos, which marks the entrance into Monterey Bay. In case you're curious, Point Joe was named after a Chinese fisherman who for many years lived here in a small lean-to shack, tending goats and selling trinkets to tourists.

On the inland side of 17-Mile Drive is the ocean course of the **Monterey Peninsula Country Club.** Out on the course you'll see an outcropping of stone called China Rock, also named in honor of the Chinese who settled here and formed an active fishing village. Farther down the coast, you'll spot **Bird Rock** and **Seal Rock.** These offshore nursery and breeding grounds are home to black cormorants, sea gulls, and other shoreline birds as well as herds of sea lions, leopard seals, and harbor seals. During the heyday of the sardine industry, many of the birds that nested here flew out from these rocks to meet fishing boats and returned in great numbers at sunset. The Seal Rock picnic area along the coast provides a great vantage point for observing the marine life. Directly inland from this spot is the **Bird Rock Hunt Course.** Home to world-class equestrian events, this course was used prior to World War II for 11th Calvary riding and saber practice.

Continuing onward, we pass **Spyglass Hill Golf Course.** A turn up Spyglass Hill Road takes you along the course to **The Grill,** a pleasant lunch spot right off the ninth green. Returning to the coast, we come next to **Fanshell Beach** and its gleaming white sands. The beach gets its name from the shells of immature giant rock scallops that appear when the tides and seasons are just right. *Note:* During the spring, temporary fencing may block beach access and obscure the view. This is necessary to protect the harbor seals that return to this spot each year to bear and raise their young.

As the Drive begins to wind up around **Cypress Point,** we enter one of the most beautiful spots of the entire Peninsula. Large ancient Monterey cypress create a beautiful canopy above a rugged stretch of coast. Sunny or foggy, the effect can be spectacular. Take advantage of the Cypress Point Lookout to stretch your legs and take in this spectacular view. As you wind around Cypress Point and the private Cypress Point Golf Course, the forest grows thicker and darker. You've entered **Crocker Grove,** a natural preserve encompassing 13 acres of some of the largest and oldest Monterey cypress in **Del Monte Forest.** This is one of only two naturally growing stands of *Cupressus macrocarpa* in the world. The other is south of Carmel Bay at Point Lobos State Preserve. A picnic area provides a great setting for lunch.

Farther along this magnificent coast, you'll observe some of the most splendid of the villas and estates of Pebble Beach. And it is here that you'll find Pebble Beach's most famous landmark, the **Lone Cypress.** This ancient tree clings stubbornly to a granite headland above the rugged shoreline, defiantly surviving the seemingly inhospitable environment of rock, wind, and salty sea spray. Its spirit and beauty have made it an inspiration for photographers and painters worldwide.

Another famous tree resides a bit farther down the coast just before Pescadero Point. It's the **Ghost Tree,** so named for its bleached-white trunk and gnarly, twisted limbs. It is near here, too, that the legendary ghost of Maria del Carmen Garcia Barreto Madariaga, who once

owned all of Rancho El Pescadero (now Pebble Beach), is said to wander through the fog-shrouded forest late at night.

Past **Pescadero Point,** 17-Mile Drive turns north, winding above Stillwater Cove. Just ahead is the world-famous **Lodge at Pebble Beach.** Since 1919, The Lodge at Pebble Beach has offered luxurious accommodations and challenging golf to visitors from around the globe (see our Hotels and Motels and Golf chapters). But even if you're not staying at The Lodge or playing a round at Pebble Beach Golf Links, it's still worth a visit. You can enjoy the manicured grounds, the fine shops, and a choice of dining options, from casual to elegant. **The Gallery,** a popular golfers bar and grill, is perfect for an informal breakfast or lunch overlooking the putting greens and first tee at Pebble. In the evening, **The Tap Room** provides a warm and friendly pub filled with golf memorabilia from past Pebble Beach tournaments. The **Stillwater Bar and Grill** is noted for its fresh seafood, Friday night clambakes, and Sunday brunches, while **Club XIX** offers award-winning French cuisine (see our Restaurants chapter). Another option is the **Pebble Beach Market,** which offers gourmet picnic fare, coffees, and pastries for the road as well as fine wines and cheeses for a romantic evening.

In the mood for some major pampering? The **Spa at Pebble Beach** offers massage, therapeutic baths, body wraps, and facials. Be sure to make your reservations at least two weeks in advance by calling (831) 649-7615.

Stillwater Cove Beach behind The Lodge makes for an excellent stroll when the weather is pleasant. This protected cove is a favorite safe harbor for sailors and was the site of a Chinese fishing village from the 1860s until 1912. Access to the beach is provided through the Beach & Tennis Club, but advanced visitor parking reservations are needed. You can call (831) 625-8507 up to two weeks in advance to reserve your spot.

The 17-Mile Drive continues along the Pebble Beach Golf Links and among homes of the rich and famous. Soon you will come across a turnoff to the Carmel Gate entrance of Pebble Beach, and you'll have a decision to make. You can exit here and enjoy the rest of the day or evening in Carmel. Or you can continue on the 17-Mile Drive loop, which will lead you back to the Pacific Grove Gate.

This trip from Pacific Grove to Carmel along the coast has included most of the major sites the Drive is known for. The return trip travels up away from the coast through the Del Monte Forest. It features some beautiful vistas from Shepard's Knoll and Huckleberry Hill as well as a peek at Poppy Hills Golf Course.

KIDSTUFF 👥

ids love the Monterey Peninsula. Whether it's combing the beaches for seashells and driftwood, searching the tide pools for creepy crawly creatures, or getting up close and personal with a California gray whale, children will have amazing tales to tell all the friends back home. In this chapter, we deviate from our usual geographic headings so you and the kids can more easily find your favorite types of fun-filled activities available on the Monterey Peninsula. Some of the attractions, restaurants, and shops mentioned here will be covered in greater length in other chapters of this book, so check elsewhere for added details. Here, we'll focus solely on their kidstuff possibilities. Pull out your pen, pencil, or crayon and get ready to circle the activities of choice for the kids of all ages in your family.

AQUARIUM

Monterey Bay Aquarium
866 Cannery Row, Monterey
(831) 648-4800
www.mbayaq.org
The Monterey Bay Aquarium amazes young and old alike. Kids will be especially pleased to find that it includes exhibits specifically designed for them. Among these exhibits, the hands-down favorite is the Touch Pool filled with prickly, slimy, bumpy, lumpy moving creatures of the sea. Here, wide-eyed kids pick up and examine sea stars, abalone, chitons, and other strange but gentle ocean inhabitants. Right next door to the Touch Pool is a supercool pool for the young daredevil in the family—the Bat Ray Pool. Go ahead, kids: Lean over the ledge, dip your hand into the shallow pool, and pet the slithery rays as they glide by. We dare ya!

"Flippers, Flukes, and Fun" is a lively children's exhibit in the Outer Bay Wing. Designed for youngsters aged four to

seven, it's an interactive exhibit where kids and parents can learn about the similarities and differences between people and marine mammals. You'll discover what marine mammals eat, how they care for their young, how they swim and navigate through the oceans, and how they communicate. Kids also enjoy exploring with the microscopes, telescopes, and viewer-guided underwater video cameras throughout the aquarium exhibits. Splash Zone, the aquarium's premier kid-space, features more than 50 species specially selected for their kid appeal. Among them, you'll find penguins, eels, sharks, and the real-life version of characters from Disney's *Finding Nemo*. There are hands-on displays, videos, and other educational exhibits, so Mom and Dad will probably learn just as much as Junior and Sissy. See our Attractions chapter for information on hours and prices.

The Monterey Bay Aquarium Web site at www.mbayaq.org/lc/ includes a fun, interactive kid's corner that is both entertaining and educational. ℹ️

ARCADE

Edgewater Packing Company
640 Wave Street, Monterey
(831) 649-1899
On your trip to Cannery Row, save an hour or so for family fun at the Edgewater Packing Company. Located along the Monterey Peninsula Recreation Trail at Prescott Avenue, this former cannery warehouse provides old-fashioned amusements right alongside the latest in video games. A delightful carousel is the hallmark of the arcade. Its bright colors,

Kids love anchovies without the pizza at the Monterey Bay Aquarium. ROB LEWINE/MONTEREY COUNTY CONVENTION AND VISITORS BUREAU

whirling lights, and spirited music are inviting to parents as well as the kids. So don't be shy, take a whirl! Other amusements include the Old Time Photo Emporium, where you can pose for a sepia-tone family photo in one of many Wild West settings.

If kids are suffering from video-game withdrawal, they'll love the wide selection of popular arcade games. In addition to the usual shoot-em-ups, you'll find virtual snow skiing, Indy car driving, motorcycle racing, and baseball batting cages that test your virtual athletic skills. Lower-tech pinball machines, air hockey, and basketball shoot-outs will delight the arcade traditionalist. Edgewater Packing Company opens at 10:30 A.M. daily. It stays open until 11:00 P.M. Sunday through Thursday and until 1:00 A.M. Friday and Saturday.

BEACHES

The Monterey Peninsula is awash with beaches, so your options are aplenty. For kids who enjoy the traditional beach-blanket outing, complete with sand pail, lunch, and wading in the surf, try the sandy Monterey State Beach just east of the Municipal Wharf in Monterey. Other good choices are Carmel Beach at the end of Ocean Avenue in Carmel and Lovers Point Beach in Pacific Grove. If Rover and Spot are coming along, check out Moss Beach at Spanish Bay just south of Asilomar between Pacific Grove and Pebble Beach. While this spot is canine friendly, doggie-do cleanup is a must, so please use plastic bags or other scooping devices. Free plastic bags and trash cans are located at the trailhead at the beginning of the boardwalk, just across Sunset Drive from the Asilomar Conference Center. Smaller sandy coves amid rocks and tide pools are located all along Ocean View Avenue, from just south of the Monterey Bay Aquarium to Sunset Drive in Pacific Grove. A similar terrain continues along the coast through Pebble Beach. Walking trails and wooden boardwalks make beach access easy.

Two important words of caution to pass on to kids:

First, Monterey Peninsula beaches can be extremely dangerous, with riptide currents, large waves, slippery rocks, and cold, cold water. Going into the water is highly discouraged except for the most experienced swimmers, and only along the sandy, rock-free beaches mentioned above. Children should never be left unattended wading at the water's edge or climbing on the shoreline rocks, no matter how safe it may seem. Sea conditions change rapidly, and the big wave can be next in line. Typically, the safest, most protected spot for swimming or wading is Lovers Point Beach in Pacific Grove. But even there, caution is a must!

Second, kids should be instructed that the Monterey Bay is a National Marine Sanctuary. Never disturb wildlife and don't try to personally aid baby seals or other creatures that may appear abandoned or injured. Check beach ordinances before removing shells, driftwood, or other natural objects. And, please, let's all leave the shoreline as clean or cleaner than we found it.

For more about our beaches, see our In and Around the Water chapter.

BIKING

Young bike riders enjoy the long expanse of the Monterey Peninsula Recreational Trail, which stretches from Lovers Point in Pacific Grove all the way to the northern border of Monterey and beyond. Kids can pedal to their hearts' delight as long as commonsense safety rules are followed. In California, bicycle helmets are mandatory for all minors 17 and younger, and the helmet law is strictly enforced. Also, the recreational trail is shared by cyclists, in-line skaters, skateboarders, joggers, and walkers, many of whom are more intent on observing the local scenery than paying attention to where they are going. Bike defensively, and stay on the right side of the path. Be especially careful

where the trail crosses streets since the local scenery can distract drivers, too.

While bicycling is permitted on most city streets, caution is advised. Again, drivers unfamiliar with the area may be so intent on trying to follow a map, find their hotel room, or enjoy the spectacular scenery that they fail to look out for cyclists. Obey the laws, avoid busy thoroughfares, and use appropriate hand signals. Also wear bright clothing or reflectors to make yourself as visible as possible, especially after sunset. Kids and parents can rent bikes at shops along the recreation trail.

Adventures by the Sea
299 Cannery Row, Monterey
201 Alvarado Mall, Monterey
The Beach at Lovers Point, Pacific Grove
(831) 372-1807
www.adventuresbythesea.com
Mountain and hybrid bikes are available starting at $6.00 per hour, $18.00 for four hours, and $24.00 per day. Overnight rentals are $30.00. Locks and helmets are provided, and bike tours are available. You can also rent trailers for the toddlers. Adventures by the Sea offers some free pickup and delivery, so call for details.

Wheel Fun Rentals @ Bay Bikes Rentals & Tours
585 Cannery Row, Monterey
(831) 646-9090
99 Pacific Street/Fisherman's Wharf, Monterey
(831) 655-8687
www.baybikes.com
Bay Bikes, located in front of the Edgewater Packing Company above Cannery Row and at the Heritage Harbor near Fisherman's Wharf, offers bike rentals for $10.00 for the first two hours and $4.00 per additional hour. You can rent for a full day for $24.00 and not have to return the bike until the following day. Child trailers and baby seats are available. Bay Bikes also rents the four-wheel surreys you'll see all along the recreation trail. For $18.00 to $28.00 per hour, the whole family can pedal together! Guided bicycling tours are also offered.

Rental bikes and four-wheel surreys are popular forms of family transportation along the Recreation Trail that stretches from Fisherman's Wharf through Cannery Row and along the shoreline to Pacific Grove's Lovers Point. TOM OWENS

BOATING

A high-sea adventure may be just the ticket for your hearty buccaneers. Motorboats and sailboats provide Monterey Bay tours of various lengths from Fisherman's Wharf (see our In and Around the Water chapter for details). Here are a couple of low-key boating options kids will enjoy.

A B Seas Kayaks
32 Cannery Row #5, Monterey
(831) 647-0191, (866) 824-2337
www.montereykayak.com
For the more adventurous kids, how about paddling a kayak out on Monterey Bay? A B Seas Kayaks offers a guided tour for novice kayakers, which consists of a two- to three-hour excursion along the shoreline of Monterey Bay. Plus, if you and the kids haven't gotten your fill, you can continue kayaking for the rest of the day, all for $50 per person. If you are experienced kayakers, forego the tour and venture out on your own for $30 per person. These

are stable, sit-on-top kayaks, and you are equipped with paddles, seat back, wet suit, dry bag, and instruction. On calm days, the Bay waters are very gentle, but you should probably avoid taking younger kids out for the first time if the swells are high or strong winds are kicking up the white caps. You'll find A B Seas Kayaks at the entrance to the Coast Guard pier.

Baywatch Cruises
90 Fisherman's Wharf, Monterey
(831) 372-2203, (800) 200-2203
www.montereybaywatch.com
If you or your little ones aren't quite ready for the open sea, consider a 45-minute bay excursion on the Baywatch Cruises, which depart from Fisherman's Wharf. It's a relaxing way to enjoy the waters and get an upclose look at sea lions, otters, starfish, crabs, and other harbor inhabitants. The cost is $14.95 for adults and $7.95 for children 10 and younger. During the peak summer season, boats leave daily between 10:00 A.M. and 6:00 P.M.

El Estero Boating
Lake El Estero, Monterey
(831) 375-1484

For leisurely freshwater boating, there's the popular El Estero Boating on Del Monte Boulevard at the corner of Camino El Estero. This company rents paddle boats, kayaks, and canoes. The whole family can paddle or pedal around the gentle city lake, enjoying the many waterfowl and the tranquil park setting. Boats rent for $8.00 per half-hour or $13.00 per hour. Paddle boats seat up to four people; canoes and kayaks seat two. Be sure to enjoy an ice cream, soda, popcorn, or hot dog from the snack bar. El Estero Boating is open seven days a week from 10:00 A.M. until dusk, weather permitting.

BOWLING

Monterey Lanes
2161 North Fremont Street, Monterey
(831) 373-1553

If bowling is your kid's cup of tea, visit Monterey Lanes. The lanes are open seven days a week, starting at 9:00 A.M. Saturday morning junior leagues are available from 9:15 to 11:00 A.M. for children ages six through 12. Call for rates and details regarding public lane availability. Ask about the popular glow-in-the-dark "Galactic Bowling" on Friday nights and the Saturday night "Rock and Bowl" program for teens.

CAMPS

Children who spend a substantial part of their summers on the Peninsula, whether as residents or visitors, might relish the thought of a fun-filled summer-camp experience. There is a range of options, from simple summer day camps to complete live-in academic and training programs. Check out the choices below as well as city recreation programs, which offer additional summer-camp options.

Camp Carmel
Location varies, Carmel
(831) 625-3321

Camp Carmel offers one- and two-week day-camp sessions from late June through early August for children ages three to 12. "Cub Camp," a combination of planned recreation and free play for preschoolers, features games, songs, stories, skits, crafts, water play, and small-animal care. Camp Cubs can attend all full days, all half-days, or any combination that fits your schedule. Camp Carmel for the older kids features full days of sporting activities such as archery, tennis, soccer, softball, Frisbee golf, basketball, and swimming as well as dance, art, nature study, hiking, trail marking, and film making. Campers select their activities of interest and are grouped according to age to heighten enjoyment and social interaction. Camp Carmel is held at the Carmel High School or the Carmel Middle School campus. One-week sessions cost $150; two-week sessions are $260.

Carmel Valley Tennis Camp
20805 Cachagua Road, Carmel Valley
(831) 659-2615
www.carmelvalleytenniscamp.com

Tennis, anyone? Carmel Valley Tennis Ranch was recently selected as one of the top junior tennis camps in the country by *Tennis* magazine. It's located more than 20 miles out Carmel Valley Road in rural Cachagua, but that only adds to the adventure. Husband-and-wife owners Steve Proulx and Susan Reeder, both noted coaches and players in their own right, hold one- and two-week sessions from June through August for kids ages 10 to 17. It's a well-planned program of tennis instruction and competition, but the fun doesn't end there. It's a real camp, with campfires, cookouts, arts and crafts, swimming, hot-tubbing, table tennis, Foosball, volleyball, hiking, dancing, karaoke, and even movies. The cost is $875 for one-week sessions; $1,750 for two weeks.

Robert Louis Stevenson Camp
3152 Forest Lake Road, Pebble Beach
(831) 626-5315
www.rlstevenson.org

Holy Willy Wonka! In neighboring Seaside, you can take a free chocolate factory tour that includes samples. The Chocolate Factory is at 1291 Fremont Boulevard. Call (831) 899-7963.

Robert Louis Stevenson Camp, within the Del Monte Forest in Pebble Beach, is open to boys and girls ages 10 to 15. The five-week sessions, which begin the last week of June and continue through mid-July, are offered on both a day-camp and resident-camp basis. Resident campers live in school dormitories under full-time supervision with hot meals served in a large dining hall. Morning workshops include academic programs in math, English, and biology as well as art classes in ceramics, drama, music, and photography. Afternoons are reserved for sporting activities such as swimming, biking, archery, fencing, tennis, and golf. Sailing is offered on the school's sailboats in nearby Stillwater Cove. Each weekend, resident campers go on overnight hiking trips in the local Los Padres National Forest. Tuition for day students is $2,200; for resident students it's $3,900.

Santa Catalina Summer Camp
1500 Mark Thomas Drive, Monterey
(831) 655-9386
www.santacatalina.org
This residential and day camp at the 35-acre Santa Catalina School campus is for girls from age eight to 14. Both five-week and 2½-week sessions are offered, typically beginning in late June. College-age women counselors live in the dormitories with resident students to organize evening and weekend activities in and around the Monterey Peninsula. The wide variety of activities to choose from include musical theater, drama, jazz dance, tap, ballet, art, painting and sketching, ceramics, crafts, fashion design, creative writing, photography, computers, marine biology, cooking, sewing, swimming, tennis, riding, golf, and team sports. Students can choose six of these activi-

ties as part of the school's General Program or specialize in musical theater, horseback riding, marine biology, or tennis. Tuition for the two-week camp is $2,100 for resident camp and $1,150 for day camp. For the five-week session, it's $3,800 for residents and $2,300 for day camp. There are additional fees for riding and golf programs. Day camp hours are 9:00 A.M. to 4:30 P.M.

GOLF

As strange as it may seem in this golf mecca, there are no miniature golf courses on the Monterey Peninsula. However, there is a golden opportunity to take your budding Tiger Woods for a memorable outing at Pebble Beach.

Peter Hay Golf Course
17-Mile Drive at Stevenson Drive,
Pebble Beach
(831) 625-8518, (800) 654-9300
www.pebblebeach.com
Adjacent to the world-famous Pebble Beach Golf Links, Peter Hay Golf Course was designed by former Pebble Beach professional Peter Hay. It's a nine-hole, par 3, 819-yard course that provides a fun and affordable round of golf for players of all ages. Best of all, children younger than 12 play for free when accompanied by a parent. Golfers 13 to 17 pay a very reasonable $5.00, while those 18 and up pay $20.00. Each foursome must include at least one adult. Call for reservations. For residents of the Monterey Peninsula, the AT&T Pebble Beach Junior Golf Association provides free lessons and other programs for kids age seven to 17. Call (831) 625-1555 for details.

HORSEBACK RIDING

Pebble Beach Equestrian Center
Portola Road at Alva Lane,
Pebble Beach
(831) 624-2756
www.ridepebblebeach.com

Pebble Beach Equestrian Center presents a wide range of options for both novice and experienced horseback riders. Pony rides will thrill kids as young as three, while children seven to 12 can enjoy escorted walking trail rides along some of the 34 miles of winding paths through Del Monte Forest. Those 12 and older can partake in the hour-plus beach ride, which takes travelers through the forests, across the sand dunes, and down to the water's edge on an expanse of sandy beach. Group and private lessons are also available for both English and Western riding. The Pebble Beach Equestrian Center is about a half-mile from The Lodge at Pebble Beach. Rides range from $20 (pony) to $47 per person. Group lessons start at $25 per hour, and private lessons start at $47 per hour. Summer and holiday camp programs are also available for kids ages seven to 14, at $260 for a four-day session.

KITE FLYING

Kite flying is a popular beach activity, and the Peninsula features some fantastic shops with just the right kite or windsock for you. Favorite kite-flying areas for participants and spectators are the sands just north of the Monterey Beach Hotel in Monterey and Carmel Beach at the foot of Ocean Avenue in Carmel. But any long stretch of sand and sky will do. So what are you waiting for? Go fly a kite!

Windborne Fun
125 Ocean View Boulevard, Pacific Grove
(831) 375-0851, (877) 272-5483
www.windbornefun.com
Windborne Fun brings the latest in kites, banners, spinners, and windsocks to The American Tin Cannery near Cannery Row, with a nice selection for young beginners. All kites are unconditionally guaranteed, and Windborne has a liberal return, trade-up, and refund policy. Expert repairs are also provided.

LIBRARIES

For a little quiet time, visit any of the local public libraries, which are understandably proud of their children's programs.

City of Monterey Public Library
625 Pacific Street, Monterey
(831) 646-3932
www.monterey.org/library
The Monterey Public Library Storytime for Kids program includes Baby and Me Rhymetime for babies up to age two and toddlers ages two to five the second Friday of each month at 10:30 A.M. Storytime for children age two and three is held Tuesday mornings at 10:15 A.M. Preschool Storytime is held Tuesday morning at 11:00 A.M. for kids ages three to five. Pajama Storytime for kids age three and up is offered the last Tuesday of each month at 7:00 P.M. Special seasonal storytime programs are also scheduled. Call (831) 646-3934 for details on all children's programs.

Pacific Grove Public Library
550 Central Avenue, Pacific Grove
(831) 648-5760
www.pacificgrove.lib.ca.us
Pacific Grove Public Library has a storytime program for kids of various ages. Baby Time presents stories, songs, and other play activities for children age two and younger on Thursday at 10:30 A.M. Preschool Storytime for two- to four-year-olds is held Wednesday at 10:30 A.M. After-school Storytime for four- to eight-year-olds takes place Wednesday at 3:30 P.M. Junior Friends of the Library is a club for fourth and fifth graders who meet Tuesday at 3:30 P.M., September through April, for crafts, field trips, and other activities. Children's Librarian Lisa Maddalena will be happy to provide information on all children's library programs.

Harrison Memorial
Public Library, Park Branch
Sixth Avenue and Mission Street, Carmel
(831) 624-4664
www.hm-lib.org

Harrison Memorial Public Library's special Park Branch caters to kids. Storytime programs include Lap-Sit Storytime for babies and toddlers on Friday at 10:30 A.M., Preschool Storytime on Tuesday and Wednesday at 10:30 A.M., and Pajama Storytime on Tuesday at 6:45 P.M. The library also features six computers specifically for kids, with more than a dozen different educational computer games and programs. Children's librarian Susan Jones says she loves to have kids and parents from outside the Peninsula drop by to visit.

MUSEUMS

It used to be that museums and active kids didn't necessarily mix. But these days, more and more museums are featuring exhibits specifically for the younger set. In fact, Monterey has one special museum designed exclusively for children younger than 10. For other museums, see our Attractions and The Arts and Galleries chapters.

Monterey County Youth (MY) Museum
601 Wave Street, Suite 100, Monterey
(831) 649-6444
www.mymuseum.org
Monterey County Youth Museum, or "MY Museum" for short, is on the third level of the Cannery Row Parking Garage. MY Museum is a 2,700-square-foot, highly interactive place where young kids and parents can explore, create, and share in a fun-filled learning environment. Educating and entertaining, the museum's exhibits of exciting sights and sounds are designed to stimulate curiosity and learning among the younger set. Kids will discover The Row, a hands-on, interactive replica of Cannery Row. Using their imaginations, they can cook a pizza, drive a fire truck, or build a house. They can heal animals at the Pet Vet and learn about good health at Body Works, a pretend medical office. Then there is My Theater, where puppet shows and costume plays bring out the real ham in all kids. At Creation Station, kids explore all forms of art, including a giant loom to create their own weavings. Best of all they

can proudly take their creations home with them! There is also a birthday room that can be reserved for up to 12 kiddies. You bring the cake, juice, snacks, and presents, and MY Museum provides the party favors and loads of fun things to do. MY Museum is open from 10:00 A.M. to 5:00 P.M. every day except Sunday, when it opens at noon, and Wednesday, when it's closed. Admission for each child and adult is $5.50, and wee ones younger than two play for free.

Maritime Museum of Monterey
5 Custom House Plaza, Monterey
(831) 372-2608
www.montereyhistory.org
The Maritime Museum of Monterey has designed a treasure hunt that keeps the young ones entertained while mom and dad enjoy the historic artifacts. Complete the treasure hunt, and ring the big ship bell (see our complete listing in the Attractions chapter).

Pacific Grove Museum of Natural History
165 Forest Avenue, Pacific Grove
(831) 648-5716
www.pgmuseum.org
This award-winning natural history museum maintains special hands-on exhibits for kids. Plus, there's the ever-popular Sandy the Whale, an outdoor life-size sculpture that just loves to be climbed upon. Call for details on additional children's programs (see our Attractions chapter for more information).

PLAYGROUNDS

In addition to the many splendid beaches and parks on and around the Monterey Peninsula, there are some great playgrounds for kids to enjoy. Also see our Parks and Recreation chapter.

Caledonia Park
Caledonia Street and Central Avenue, Pacific Grove
(831) 648-3130
www.pacificgroverecreation.com

The old steam engine is one of the most popular attractions at Dennis the Menace Playground, a great place for the kids to burn energy during your visit to Monterey. TOM OWENS

There are small Peninsula playgrounds for kids that, while not on the grand scale of Dennis the Menace Playground, provide pleasant spots for fun and exercise. Among the favorites of Pacific Grove youngsters is Caledonia Park, bounded by U-shaped Caledonia Street and Central Avenue, directly behind the Pacific Grove Post Office. You'll find the usual slides and swings, plus a submarine-shaped jungle gym, baseball field, and basketball court. (*Note:* The south end of Pacific Grove's George Washington Park, which also includes a Butterfly Tree Grove, has swings, slides, and other equipment along Sinex Avenue.)

Dennis the Menace Playground
Pearl Street at Lake El Estero, Monterey
(831) 646–3860
The biggest and most famous Peninsula playground for kids is Dennis the Menace Playground, located in downtown Monterey adjacent to Lake El Estero. Acclaimed for its unique design, the park opened in 1956 amidst much fanfare. Cartoonist Hank

Ketcham, creator of Dennis the Menace, and local sculptor Arch Gardner dreamed up some of the wildest playground equipment ever seen. Salt air and years of rugged use proved too much for some of the original equipment. Fortunately, the park was renovated in 1988 and once again provides a great place for kids to burn energy. Featured attractions include a real train steam engine, a swinging rope bridge, a roller slide, and a hedge maze. A snack bar is right outside the playground entrance in the parking lot on Pearl Street, between Camino Aguajito and Camino El Estero. Dennis the Menace Playground is open daily from 10:00 A.M. until dusk, but closed on all nonholiday Mondays November through May.

Forest Hills Park
Scenic Road and Camino del Monte, Carmel
(831) 624–3543
In Carmel, Forest Hills Park features a pleasant forest setting. You'll find horse-

shoe and shuffleboard facilities as well as an enjoyable playground area. (As an alternative, Mission Trails Park off Rio Road near the Carmel Mission is a good spot for an adventurous hike.)

RESTAURANTS

As in most upscale resort areas, there are restaurants where kids are warmly welcomed, and there are restaurants where, at best, they are tolerated. It's always advisable to check with the restaurant when kid-friendliness is in question, especially at the higher-end establishments that cater to the formally dressed or specialize in quiet romantic evenings. That being said, there are plenty of restaurants where kids can feel free to let loose and have a grand old time.

Monterey

Abalonetti Seafood Trattoria
57 Fisherman's Wharf, Monterey
(831) 373-1851
www.restauranteur.com/abalonetti
Abalonetti is a great spot to introduce the young ones to calamari. (Wait till after the meal to tell them they just ate squid!) You'll also find great brick-oven-baked pepperoni pizza, fish and chips, burgers, and spaghetti.

Bagel Bakery
452 Alvarado Street, Monterey
(831) 372-5242
539 Carmel Rancho Shopping Center, Carmel
(831) 625-5180
1132 Forest Avenue, Pacific Grove
(831) 649-6272
Young bagel lovers will relish the many choices at the Bagel Bakery, a local icon for breakfast or lunch. Fresh boiled and baked bagels come with a choice of toppings. Even kids who don't like the usual bagel with cream cheese will enjoy the pizza bagel or a toasted cinnamon-raisin bagel with honey-butter.

Bubba Gump Shrimp Company Restaurant and Market
720 Cannery Row, Monterey
(831) 373-1884
www.bubbagump.com
On Cannery Row, Bubba Gump Shrimp is the choice of young *Forrest Gump* fans. They can have their picture taken on the famous bench with a box of chocolates and then go inside for a kid-size portion of shrimp. Burgers, pizza, and corn dogs are also on the menu for oceanview lunch and dinner.

Chef Lee's Mandarin House
2031 North Fremont Boulevard, Monterey
(831) 375-9551
For good Chinese food for lunch and dinner in a family environment, try Chef Lee's in Monterey. Chef Lee's is on Fremont Boulevard just east of Highway 1.

El Torito Mexican Restaurant
600 Cannery Row, Monterey
(831) 373-0611
www.eltorito.com
If Mexican food is a family favorite, try El Torito on Cannery Row. Tacos, tostados, burritos, chicken fingers, and other selections all come in children's portions, with or without rice and beans. El Torito has one of the best ocean views in town.

Forge in the Forest Restaurant
Fifth and Junipero Avenues, Carmel
(831) 624-2233
www.forgeintheforest.com
This is an ideal choice for sharing the true Carmel experience with the kids. The heated patio with outdoor fireplaces makes for a great place to unwind on a pleasant Peninsula night. An inexpensive children's menu is featured, as is a doggie menu for Fido.

Gianni's Pizza
725 Lighthouse Avenue, Monterey
(831) 649-1500
www.giannispizzamonterey.com
Pizza-loving kids won't complain at Gianni's Pizza in New Monterey. They have

hand-tossed dough and good fresh toppings and will make any combination the kids want. This noisy, action-packed pizzeria is great for lunch or dinner with large family groups. It's a perfect spot for picking up a pizza to take back to the motel room, too.

Jamba Juice
398 Alvarado Street, Monterey
(831) 655-9696
www.jambajuice.com
If the kids are into fresh juices and smoothies, Jamba Juice is just the ticket. It features a wide choice of fruit smoothies, fresh squeezed juices, and hearty soups. They're great energy boosts for walks around town and strolls down the beach.

Rappa's Seafood Restaurant
101 Fisherman's Wharf, Monterey
(831) 372-7562
www.rappas.com
Located at the end of the wharf, Rappa's welcomes children of all ages. The children's menu features hamburgers, fish and chips, shrimp and chips, and spaghetti. An outdoor observation deck and great harbor views of boats, sea lions, and sea gulls provide entertainment for lunch or dinner.

Pacific Grove

First Awakenings
125 Ocean View Boulevard, Pacific Grove
(831) 372-1125
For a hearty breakfast before your trip down Cannery Row, stop by First Awakenings in the American Tin Cannery. You'll find eggs fixed any way the kids like them as well as pancakes, waffles, hot cocoa, juices, cereals, and other morning favorites. Outdoor seating is available.

Shnarley's Bronx Pizza
650 Lighthouse Avenue, Pacific Grove
(831) 375-2002
688 Cannery Row, Monterey
(831) 373-8463
www.shnarleys.com

Here's a local pizzeria with a New York flair. Mom and dad will enjoy a fine selection of beers and wines as well. Buyers beware: The large pizza is truly LARGE. Check out the sizes before ordering, and then be prepared to sink your teeth into a really great pizza pie.

The Fishwife
1996 Sunset Drive, Pacific Grove
(831) 375-7107
www.fishwife.com
The Fishwife caters to kids for lunch and dinner, featuring a large fish tank, crayons to color the paper table cloths, and good fish and chips with incredible air fries. After dessert, take the kids on a family stroll down nearby Asilomar State Beach.

Tinnery at the Beach
Lovers Point Park, 631 Ocean View
Boulevard, Pacific Grove
(831) 646-1040
www.thetinnery.com
A great view of the Bay from Lovers Point in Pacific Grove is the perfect setting for a quality breakfast, lunch, dinner, or in-between at a reasonable price. Special children's breakfasts are good deals.

Toasties Café
702 Lighthouse Avenue, Pacific Grove
(831) 373-7543
In downtown Pacific Grove, Toasties Café is a local favorite for a delicious home-style breakfast. Kids like the pancakes and the hot chocolate stacked with whipped cream, and mom and dad will enjoy the peaceful Pacific Grove ambience. Lunch and dinner are also served.

Carmel

Em Le's Old Carmel Restaurant
Dolores Street and Fifth Avenue, Carmel
(831) 625-6780
A great Carmel breakfast or lunch spot is Em Le's, with its award-winning French toast and vintage soda fountain. The cozy setting and fireplace make for great memories.

Plaza Cafe and Grill
Carmel Plaza on Ocean Avenue, Carmel
(831) 624-4433
Try a late breakfast of pancakes or waffles at the Plaza Cafe and Grill. The heated patio is nice for a family lunch or dinner as well.

SKATING AND SKATEBOARDING

Over the past few years, in-line skating has been a very popular activity on the Monterey Peninsula Recreation Trail. However, because the cost of purchasing skates has dropped considerably, the demand for renting skates has diminished. In fact, there are no longer vendors offering skate rentals anywhere on the Peninsula. Still, if you pack your own gear, there is great skating available. In addition to the Recreation Trail, there is an excellent skate park at El Estero Park, where skateboards are also welcome.

Del Monte Gardens
2020 Del Monte Avenue, Monterey
(831) 375-3202
Del Monte Gardens is the traditional roller-skating rink in Monterey. Both roller skates and in-line skates are allowed on the indoor oval rink. The doors open to the public Thursday through Monday. Matinees are 2:00 to 4:00 P.M. on Saturday ($5.00), Sunday ($5.00), and Monday ($4.00). The rest of the schedule looks like this: Thursday night from 7:00 to 9:00 P.M. is $4.00. Friday evening has sessions from 6:30 to 8:30 P.M. or from 8:00 to 10:00 P.M. for $5.00 each or $7.00 combined. Saturday sessions include a 3:30 to 5:30 P.M. afternoon skate ($4.00) and evening sessions at 5:00 to 7:00 P.M. ($4.00), 6:30 to 8:30 P.M. ($5.00), and 8:00 to 10:00 P.M. ($5.00), with double sessions costing an extra $2.00. Skate Sunday evening from 7:00 to 9:00 P.M. for $4.00. Roller skates rent for $1.00, in-line skates for $3.00. You can use your own skates if they pass rink inspection. Roller hockey games are

held through local leagues, and Saturday lessons are provided for $18 a month.

Monterey Bay SK8 Station
1855 East Avenue, Sand City
(831) 899-7587
Monterey Bay SK8 Station is the Peninsula's premier indoor skate park. Off California Street near Costco in Sand City (just north of Monterey along Del Monte Boulevard), SK8 Station features a vert ramp, corner bowl, quarterpipes, spine ramp, and more. (Don't worry, Mom and Dad, your kids will know what that means.) It's open Monday through Thursday from 3:30 to 8:00 P.M., Friday from 3:30 to 10:00 P.M., Saturday noon to 10:00 P.M., and Sunday noon to 8:00 P.M. The price of entry is $12. in-line skates and skateboards are always welcome; bikes allowed on Monday evening.

SHOPPING

The Monterey Peninsula is world famous as a shopper's paradise. That holds true for kids as well as for adults. Check out our Shopping chapter for a wider selection, but here's a quick rundown of places kids like.

Monterey

Del Monte Center
Highway 1 at Munras Avenue, Monterey
(831) 373-2705
www.delmontecenter.com
In Monterey, the Del Monte Center has an array of clothing, toy, and gift shops for the kiddies. Major chains as well as local shops make up the more than 100 stores, restaurants, and services. Favorite shops for kids include Gap Kids, Gymboree, Thinker Toys, Games & Things, and KB Toys.

Fuzzybops Toys
700 Cannery Row, Monterey
(831) 643-2342
Fuzzybops. Funny name, funny store. It's a great place to pick up a little treat for the

kids after a well-behaved day of touring Cannery Row. There are lots of humor and joke toys, kites, die-cast toys, lunch boxes, and many types of collectibles, including Hello Kitty and other Sanrio toys.

Pacific Grove

Chatter Baux Children's Shoppe
157 Fountain Avenue, Pacific Grove
(831) 647-8701
Chatter Baux Children's Shoppe carries new and used clothing, toys, books, and accessories for the wee ones through high schoolers. You can find great deals on reconditioned high chairs, car seats, play-pens, and other kid equipment. A choice of European strollers, too.

Kid's Closet
229 Grand Avenue, Pacific Grove
(831) 647-1250
Forget to pack the kid's sweater, raincoat, blanket or other badly needed item, but not interested in paying top dollar for brand-new? Try the Kid's Closet in Pacific Grove. There you will find hardly used children's clothing, furniture, toys, quilts, and blankets, as well as new toys and collectibles.

Learning Depot
168 Central Avenue, Pacific Grove
(831) 372-8697
Learning Depot in Pacific Grove specializes in educational toys and supplies. This is a good choice for preschool-age children who enjoy imaginative puzzles and games.

Tessuti Zoo
171 Forest Avenue, Pacific Grove
(831) 648-1725
This colorful, one-of-a-kind shop features wild handmade dolls, animals, and other-worldly creatures along with tin windup toys, great kids' books, crazy clocks, and cute clothing. While the kids check out the creatures, mom can discover the wearable art of the Playful Spirit clothing line. You'll find Tessuti Zoo across the street from Peppers Mexicali Cafe.

Carmel

Bib 'N Tucker
Ocean Avenue and Dolores Street, Carmel
(831) 624-2185
Bib 'N Tucker is the place for the baby set in Carmel. You'll find a nice selection of clothing and toys for infants as well as for young children through preschool age.

Nana's for Remarkable Kids
26366 Carmel Rancho Lane, Carmel
(831) 625-6262
For American and French-made children's clothing, check out Nana's for Remarkable Kids. You'll discover a unique collection for girls age infant to 14 and boys age infant to seven years. Handmade rockers, blankets, and other gift items are a browser's delight.

Sandcastles by the Sea
3722 The Barnyard, Carmel
(831) 626-8361
Sandcastles by the Sea in The Barnyard features an amazing display of wooden toys. You'll also find a good selection of beach toys, games, and crafts and a charming collection of dress-up clothes.

Thinker Toys
Seventh Avenue and San Carlos Street, Carmel
(831) 624-0441
www.thinkertoys.com
Thinker Toys is the largest toy store on the Peninsula and has tons of new brand-name merchandise. Train sets are a store specialty, and you'll enjoy the great dis-play. There's now a second area location at the Del Monte Shopping Center in Mon-terey, (831) 643-0534.

SWIMMING

We can't emphasize enough the unpre-dictable nature of the ocean around the Monterey Peninsula. Ocean swimming is best left to experienced adults and only on the sandy beaches, away from the rocky shores. For kids, stick to the hotel or motel pools or visit the Monterey Sports Center.

Monterey Sports Center
301 Franklin Street, Monterey
(831) 646-3700
www.monterey.org/sportscenter
Located across Del Monte Avenue from Fisherman's Wharf, The Monterey Sports Center features two indoor pools that can accommodate kids of all ages. The main pool is kept at a comfortable 82 degrees. Older kids will love the 112-foot corkscrew water slide that twists and turns you on a wild ride from high above the pool, then dumps you unceremoniously into the warm water. The second smaller pool at the Sports Center is a cozy 20 feet by 75 feet yards and ranges in depth from 1 to 5 feet. A ramp makes the pool accessible to the disabled, and the water is kept at a bath-like 90 degrees. The Monterey Sports Center is open Monday through Friday from 5:30 A.M. to 9:30 P.M., Saturday from 8:00 A.M. to 5:00 P.M., and Sunday from 9:00 A.M. to 5:00 P.M. Admission for out-of-town visitors is $2.50 for children age five and younger, $3.75 for youths six to 17, $6.00 for adults 18 to 54, and $4.50 for seniors 55 and older. Monterey residents receive $1.00 off these rates. Showers, lockers, towel service, and babysitting are available. Call for recreational swimming hours.

THEATER

There is a strong contingent of local theater groups on the Monterey Peninsula that produce shows by and for children. Check out the local papers to see which theater and dance productions might suit your little one's tastes. Here are a few to keep an eye on. For other cultural entertainment options, see The Arts and Galleries chapter.

California's First Theatre
336 Pacific Street, Monterey
(831) 375-4916

The old-time comedies and melodramas at California's First Theatre in Monterey are kid favorites. Hear them laugh out loud, boo the villains, and cheer the heroes. You'll enjoy the ambiance of the state's first theater, built in 1844.

Children's Experimental Theater
Indoor Forest Theatre, Santa Rita Street
and Mountain View Avenue, Carmel
(831) 624-1531
www.cetstaff.org
Since 1960, this group has presented opportunities for local kids grades kindergarten through five to perform on stage. Inquire into special programs and children's theater productions. There is a Spring Play Festival, a Traveling Troupe Program, and four- and one-week theater programs in the summer and fall.

The Forest Theater Guild
Indoor Forest Theatre, Santa Rita Street
and Mountain View Avenue, Carmel
(831) 626-1681
www.foresttheaterguild.org
Bring the kids and a picnic and enjoy theater under the stars. With this Carmel tradition, you can experience live theater and films outdoors during the summer months. A big bonfire helps fight off the evening chill.

WHALE WATCHING

"I saw a whale! I saw a whale!" Those shrieks of joy are repeated by children from around the world, in many languages, upon return from a whale-watching expedition in Monterey Bay. Peak California gray whale-watching season is from December through March, with one- to two-hour excursions leaving hourly off Monterey's Fisherman's Wharf. Prices average $18 for adults and $12 for children, but call for current rates and schedules. From June to September, the boats head out into deeper waters in search of humpback, blue, and minke whales, as well as orcas and dolphins. These excursions typically last three hours and cost approximately $25 for adults and $15 for kids. Remember: Boat trips on the Bay can be cold, windy, and wet. Bring multiple layers of clothing, waterproof gear, and motion-sickness relief (see also our In and Around the Water chapter).

Chris' Fishing Trips & Whale Watching
48 Fisherman's Wharf #1, Monterey
(831) 375-5951
www.chrissfishing.com
Chris' offers whale-watching boats every hour from 9:00 A.M. until dusk from December through April. Six-hour summer charter cruises in search of sea mammals are also available for large groups.

Monterey Bay Whale Watch
84 Fisherman's Wharf #1, Monterey
(831) 375-4658
www.gowhales.com
Monterey Bay Whale Watch, located at Sam's Fishing Fleet, offers year-round excursions. They claim to be the only whale-watching group on the wharf with marine biologists present on all cruises. Most boats leave at 9:00 or 10:00 A.M. or 1:30 or 2:00 P.M.

Monterey Whale Watching
96 Fisherman's Wharf #1, Monterey
(831) 372-2203, (800) 200-2203
www.montereywhalewatching.com
December through March, 1/2- to two-hour cruises go out to sea to follow the migration of the California gray whales. From June through September, three- and four-hour cruises head for deep waters in search of blue whales, orcas, humpbacks, minkes, and dolphins.

Randy's Fishing and Whale Watching Trips
66 Fisherman's Wharf #1, Monterey
(831) 372-7440, (800) 251-7440
www.randysfishingtrips.com
With whale-watching trips from mid-December through March, Randy's Fishing Trips feature fully narrated two-hour excursions. Boats leave every two hours on weekdays and every hour on weekends from 9:30 A.M. until 3:30 P.M.

YOUTH CENTERS

City youth centers, recreation departments, and other community activities for kids abound on the Peninsula. While many programs are limited to city residents, some centers have summertime programs open to visitors. The best way to discover the scope of activities available is to request a written activity guide from the organizations.

Carmel Youth Center
Torres Street and Fourth Avenue, Carmel
(831) 624-3285
Founded by Bing Crosby nearly 50 years ago, Carmel Youth Center is geared toward teens ages 12 to 19. Activities include sports, live music, pool tables, and games. Visitors are welcome.

Monterey Youth Center
777 Pearl Street, Monterey
(831) 646-3873
Next to Dennis the Menace Playground, the Monterey Youth Center Teen Room provides games and activities for ages 13 to 18. Call for visitor programs.

Pacific Grove Youth Center
302 16th Street, Pacific Grove
(831) 648-3134
This modern facility provides a wealth of activities for teens in grades six through 12 who reside within the Pacific Grove Unified School District boundaries. Table tennis, pool, dances, karaoke, and movies are just some of the activities. Call for visitor programs.

ANNUAL EVENTS

The scenic beauty and rich cultural history of the Monterey Peninsula are continually celebrated in a multitude of yearly events and festivals. Several of our events are held outdoors and focus on our natural resources. The annual Whale Festival is a celebration honoring gray whales' migration from Alaska to Baja, California, and back. Other aquatic-related events, such as the Sardine Festival, gather locals and visitors to enjoy the bounty of the Monterey Bay. Pebble Beach and Mazda Raceway Laguna Seca entice car buffs with several international auto shows and races, while history enthusiasts will enjoy the many opportunities to participate in events of historical significance. In this chapter you will discover the hometown celebrations of Pacific Grove, events that bring people together in a spirit of cooperation and good old-fashioned fun. Pacific Grove's Good Old Days, where local police officers compete in a motorcycle race, and the Butterfly Parade, when school children dress up as butterflies and walk through town welcoming back the monarchs that spend the winter here, are town favorites.

Monterey has been known for its festivals since the early days of Spanish settlement, when fiestas were a common occurrence. Alvarado Street, in the historic district of Old Monterey, is perfect for holding street festivals. Numerous times during the year the entire street is blocked off for celebrations. Among them is the Sidewalk Fine Arts Festival, when Alvarado Street becomes a huge gallery. This event is like a sidewalk sale for various painters, photographers, and other artists.

Carmel events tend to focus around food and the arts. The annual Masters of Food and Wine Festival at the Highlands Inn draws an international crowd each February. The Carmel Bach Festival, held in July and August, is also world-renowned and has been well attended for more than 60 years. Each year the Carmel Music Society hosts a series of concerts featuring internationally acclaimed pianists, vocalists, violinists, and ensembles who perform classical compositions.

Pebble Beach has its share of events, too, with the Concours d'Elegance classic car show, the widely acclaimed AT&T Pro-Am golf tournament, and horse-jumping events at the Pebble Beach Equestrian Center. The AT&T is one of the largest events on the Peninsula, bringing in thousands of out-of-towners who love golf and hobnobbing with pro golfers and celebrities like local resident Clint Eastwood.

Events are listed in the month in which they are held. The events we've listed occur annually, but in all cases it is best to confirm the dates, times, and fees by calling the phone number indicated or visiting the Web site.

JANUARY

AT&T Pebble Beach National Pro-Am
Various golf courses, Pebble Beach
(800) 541-9091
www.attpbgolf.com
The AT&T golf tournament is a 72-hole PGA Tour Championship Tournament hosted by Spyglass Hill, Pebble Beach, and Poppy Hill golf courses. Professionals compete for a $4 million purse and are paired with amateurs in two-man teams competing for a $100,000 purse. Foursomes rotate to each of the three courses on Thursday through Saturday. The famous cut is made Saturday night, and the 25 low Pro-Am teams play the Pebble Beach Golf Links on Sunday for the championship. If there is a playoff, sudden

Actor Bill Murray is a favorite celebrity player at the annual AT&T Pebble Beach National Pro-Am Golf Tournament. © KELLI ULDALL

death starts on the 18th hole. Celebrities who have played in past tournaments include Clint Eastwood, Huey Lewis, Andy Garcia, Ray Romano, Donald Trump, Neil Young, and Alice Cooper, to name only a few. The weeklong event usually occurs at the end of January. For tickets there are basically three options: daily tickets, a season badge, or a grandstand badge. Daily tickets cost around $40 for practice Monday to Wednesday and $40 per day for tournament rounds. The season badge and the grandstand badge cost $95 to $150 and get you in for all seven days, but the grandstand badge includes seating. The AT&T brings thousands of golf enthusiasts to the Monterey Peninsula over the week of the tournament.

Monterey Swingfest
Hyatt Regency, 1 Old Golf Course Road, Monterey
(805) 937-1574
www.centralcoastswingdance.com
This annual event held in mid-January offers swing dance workshops with past and present world and national champions, a swing dance contest, and more than 40 hours of open dancing. West Coast swing dancing is emphasized with a concentration on rhythm and blues music. Advance tickets are $95. Call for specific event registration and schedule.

Rio Resolution Run
Crossroads Shopping Center, Highway 1 at Rio Road, Carmel
(831) 644-2427
www.riogrillsresolutionrun.com
This annual 6.8-mile run and 3-mile family fun run/walk, a benefit for the Suicide Prevention Center, is always held on the first day of the new year. The cross-country course is mapped out to travel from the Crossroads Shopping Center into Carmel, ending at the Carmel Mission. Here's your chance to start the new year off right by getting plenty of exercise and helping out a local charity at the same time. Entry fee for participants is $25 for adults, $17 for ages 12 and younger.

Whalefest
Fisherman's Wharf
(831) 784-6464
This family event celebrates the annual migration of the California gray whales. Whale-watching trips, special exhibits, and museum tours educate, enlighten, and entertain.

FEBRUARY

Day of Romance in Old Monterey
Various historical locations, Monterey
(831) 647-6204
www.monterey.org/historicmonterey
Held in mid-February, this event is an opportunity to see musicians, dancers, and a living history pageant featuring actors in period clothing telling romantic stories of Old Monterey in the actual homes where the stories took place. Food is available. This is a very popular event, so get your tickets early! Ticket price is approximately $15; tickets are available at Bay Books and the Cooper Museum Store.

The Great Taste of Pacific Grove
Various locations
(831) 642-4943
A benefit for Pacific Grove schools, The Great Taste affords a chance to sample the cuisine and wines of P.G.'s finest restaurants.

The Masters of Food and Wine
Highlands Inn, Highway 1, Carmel
(800) 401-1009
www.mfandw.com
This annual weeklong celebration features an international gathering of chefs and master winemakers at the Highlands Inn. Winery tours and tastings, cooking demonstrations, a wild mushroom hunt, and fabulous gourmet lunches and dinners highlight the event. Event prices range from $125 to $350 and typically include the Opening Night Extravaganza and lunchtime demos by world-famous chefs. Reservations are highly recommended.

Steinbeck's Birthday Weekend
National Steinbeck Center, Salinas
(831) 796-3833
www.steinbeck.org

The last weekend in February is set aside to honor the life and times of the internationally acclaimed author John Steinbeck. Celebrate Steinbeck's birthday with tours, speakers, luncheon at the Steinbeck House, and a visit to the National Steinbeck Center interactive museum. Many events are free to the public; others include admission charges which vary according to the individual event. Call for specific information.

Wine Passport Weekend
Various locations
(831) 375-9400
www.montereywine.org

Participants pick up a personalized passport and commemorative wine glass and set off to discover the wines of Monterey County. Each tasting room stamps the passport, and when eight stamps are accumulated, it can be turned in for chances at prizes. This event takes place around Valentine's Day.

MARCH

Carmel Kite Festival
Carmel Beach at the foot of Eighth Avenue, Carmel
(831) 626-1255

Nothing says spring is on the way like kites! This event offers judging in both homemade and commercial kite categories, and prizes are awarded in several age groups. But competition or not, the real joy is in simply flying a kite on the beach.

Cutting Day
Friendly Plaza, corner of Pacific and Jefferson Streets next to Colton Hall, Monterey
(831) 646-3860
www.monterey.org

This is an excellent opportunity to exchange cuttings and plants. All Monterey Peninsula gardening buffs are invited to this popular event to exchange softwood cutting materials, seedling plants, bulbs, potted plants, and so on. The Parks Division has free seedling trees available for the public. Participants are encouraged to bring cuttings and plants for the exchanges. This event is free and takes place on a Saturday in March. For exact date and time, contact the Parks Division.

Dixieland Monterey
Various locations around the Peninsula
(831) 443-5260
www.dixieland-monterey.com

This annual event consists of a weekend of traditional Dixieland jazz. National and international bands appear in various cabaret locations and at the Monterey Convention Center. Previous headliners have included The Bob Crosby Bob Cats, Generic Swing Orchestra, Night Blooming Jazz Men, and the Frisco Jazz Band. The event also features youth bands, jam sessions, a parade, and parties. Dixieland Monterey usually takes place the first week of March. Admission prices are $30 to $70 depending on days of attendance and seating preference.

APRIL

Annual Adobe Tour
Historic Adobes, Monterey
(831) 372-2608

The Annual Adobe Tour features the gardens of Monterey's many historic adobes and includes garden-related activities for both adults and children. Living history programs and performances are also on the schedule. The Sensory Garden area is a showstopper with floral displays by local merchants and growers. Antique gardening tools are on display at the Doud House. Children's gardening workshops are held at the Stevenson House, Cooper-Molera Adobe, and the Monterey Museum of Art. The Historic Fashion Gallery presents a 1920s Garden Party, and a Famous Author Book Signing is held at the Mayo Hayes O'Donnell Library. The event is held at the end of April. Call for exact dates and ticket prices.

Annual Easter Egg Hunt
Frank Sollecito Ballpark,
777 Pearl Street, Monterey
(831) 646-3866
www.monterey.org
Children love this special event, held for preschoolers through third graders. More than 5,000 eggs and 100 golden prize eggs are hidden in four age-designated hunt areas. Parents are asked to bring a basket for their kids to collect the Easter eggs. The free event takes place the Saturday before Easter Sunday.

Annual Wildflower Show
Pacific Grove Museum of Natural History,
Forest and Central Avenues, Pacific Grove
(831) 648-3116
www.pgmuseum.org
The museum hosts its annual display of more than 600 varieties of wildflowers, many at the height of their blooming cycle. The flowers are either potted or in vases and are displayed in the museum. Visitors may wander through the exhibit and admire specimens. The event takes place in mid-April. There is no admission fee.

Big Sur International Marathon
Highway 1, Carmel
(831) 625-6226
www.bsim.org
The Big Sur International Marathon is known as the "World's Most Beautiful Marathon." Entrants run along the gorgeous California coastline from Big Sur to Carmel, cheered on by extra-enthusiastic volunteers and classical musicians at choice locations. A 5K run/walk and the marathon are held concurrently. A carbo-loading party is held the evening before the race. Held at the end of April, the race has an entry fee of $98 for runners and $55 for walkers. There is no charge for spectators.

Breakfast with Bunny and Eggstravaganza
Devendorf Park, Ocean Avenue between
Junipero and Mission Streets, Carmel
(831) 626-1255
www.carmelcalifornia.com
Bring the entire family to the park for a $3.00 pancake breakfast. Then join Mr. Bunny in a personal appearance at Eggland, where face-painting, cookie decorating, carnival games, and other fun activities are held to celebrate Easter. The event takes place on Easter weekend. Entrance to Eggland costs about $5.00.

Good Old Days Celebration
Lighthouse Avenue, Pacific Grove
(800) 656-6650
www.pacificgrove.org
P.G.'s annual celebration of the late 1800s includes a parade, more than 200 exhibitors at an arts and crafts fair/street bazaar, an antique fashion show, and a police officers' motorcycle competition and drill team. There are also pie-eating contests, a quilt show, live entertainment, a golf tournament, and more. The event takes place early April.

Monterey Bay Spring Faire
Custom House Plaza, Monterey
(831) 622-0100
www.pacrep.org
One hundred West Coast artists and craftspeople sell original, handmade creations, including jewelry (beadwork and precious metals), wearable art (clothing and hats), wooden toys, birdhouses, pottery, and metalwork sculptures.

Monterey Wine Festival
Monterey Conference Center,
1 Portola Plaza, Monterey
(800) 656-4282
www.montereywine.com
America's original wine festival brings together more than 150 California vintners presenting more than 800 different wines. The Scholarship Wine Auction features private reserves, artist series, and oversize, decorative, and unique bottles of wine. Events include winery tours, wine-

maker dinners, workshops/seminars, cooking demos, gourmet tastings, entertainment, and the festive finale brunch. The four-day Wine Festival takes place in mid-April each year. The events are held at various locations with tickets starting around $30.

Old Monterey Seafood and Music Festival
Custom House Plaza and Alvarado Street, Monterey
(831) 655-8070

This event celebrates seafood, including shrimp, abalone, squid, and more. There are crafts, music, and food all wrapped into one street festival staged in historic downtown Monterey. There is continuous musical entertainment featuring local musicians on two outdoor stages. The free event takes place during mid-April.

Sea Otter Classic
Laguna Seca Recreation Area, 1021 Monterey-Salinas Highway, Monterey
(650) 367-7797
www.seaotterclassic.com

The Sea Otter Classic, the premier cycling festival in the United States, has been deemed "the hippest cross-platform happening in two-wheeled racing." This sports festival also features mountain bike races, roller hockey, and in-line skating events. Sports enthusiasts will enjoy the nonstop action, food courts, and vendors at this three-day event. Admission charge is under $10 per person.

Spring Horse Show
Pebble Beach Equestrian Center, Alva Road and Portola Lane, Pebble Beach
(831) 624-2756
www.ridepebblebeach.com

This annual equestrian competition is held in early April. You'll see horse-jumping events and finely groomed horses. There are pony rides for the kids, food tents, and vendors selling items appealing to horse lovers. There is no admission fee.

Spring Trade Fair and Expo
Monterey Conference Center, 1 Portola Plaza, Monterey
(831) 648-5356
www.mpcc.com

The Monterey Peninsula Chamber of Commerce sponsors this annual event featuring chamber members touting their goods and services. The expo is an excellent opportunity to acquaint yourself with local businesses, pick up some useful giveaways, taste the gourmet spreads of various restaurants, and enter contests for free prizes. The Expo, held at the end of April, has a nominal admission fee.

MAY

Carmel Art Festival
Various locations
(831) 626-1766
www.carmelartfestival.org

Carmel was originally an artists' colony, and the arts are very much alive here. Held over a four-day weekend, the Carmel Art Festival includes gallery events, lectures, children's workshops and competitions, artist's receptions, and demonstrations at many of the city's fine art-galleries. An outdoor sculpture show at Devendorf Park features bronze, glass, stone, marble, and acrylic sculpture. The festival is presented by the Carmel Gallery Alliance, and proceeds benefit area youth art programs.

Castroville Artichoke Festival
Various locations in Castroville
(831) 633-2465
www.artichoke-festival.org

Held the third weekend of May, the famous and fun Artichoke Festival features a parade, 10K run, classic car show, and, of course, artichokes prepared in every conceivable manner. A Marilyn Monroe look-alike contest celebrates the fact that the actress was named Artichoke Queen in the 1950s.

CLOSE-UP

Carmel Art Festival

A highlight of the Carmel Art Festival is the Plein air competition. From the French for "open air," Plein air is the term used to describe paintings executed outdoors, as opposed to in a studio. More broadly, according to *The Encyclopedia Britannica,* it is "the achievement of an intense impression of the open air in a landscape painting."

A select group of 75 accomplished painters meet each morning at Carmel City Hall to have a canvas dated and stamped. Dispersing to chosen locations limited to the Monterey Peninsula, artists then have until 8:00 P.M. to complete and deliver up to two framed paintings for inclusion in competition for $20,000 in cash prizes.

Part of the fun for enthusiasts is poking around the Peninsula to find artists working on their entries and observing a highly accomplished painter at work. Kind of like an artist treasure hunt.

Sponsored by various Carmel art galleries, the festival is intended as a celebration of Carmel's rich artistic tradition. Proceeds benefit youth art education programs, in particular, a program of the Cultural Council for Monterey County that provides funding to place professional artists in classrooms.

More than 60 local gallery sponsors host receptions and artist demonstrations throughout the festival, with represented artists making themselves available to collector and student alike. It's a rare opportunity to observe working artists involved in the creative process.

At the heart of the festival are its youth programs. Artworks are solicited from local schools for a Youth Art Show, and all art chosen for display is professionally framed so that families can take the works home with them after the show.

A complete schedule of events for the Carmel Art Festival is available by calling (831) 642-2503 or by visiting the festival's Web site at www.carmelart festival.org.

The Human Race
Monterey Bay Recreational Trail
(800) 408-9191
www.yesillhelp.org
An 8.5 and 10K run/walk that allows participants to designate pledged funds to the charity of their choice. The course starts at Lovers Point and follows the Recreation Trail to Custom House Plaza and back. The early morning Pacesetter's Breakfast starts the day off right, and T-shirts are given to participants. The event usually occurs mid-May. Participants can collect pledges or pay a $35 entry fee.

Marina Festival of the Winds
Various locations in Marina
(887) 973-2233
www.marinafestival.com
Kites, hot-air balloons, hang gliding, and paragliding races—if it uses the wind, it's at the Festival of the Winds. Also included

are competitions, live music, international foods, and much more.

Monster Truck Jam
Salinas Sports Complex
(831) 775-3105
www.ushra.com

Every year, more than 1.5 million fans in the United States experience the phenomenon known as Monster Trucks. The third Sunday of May sees the likes of Bigfoot, Gravedigger, Gunslinger, Eradicator, and Blue Thunder invade the Salinas Sports Complex. Admission charge.

National Chamber Music Competition
Sunset Center, San Carlos Street between Eighth and Ninth Avenues, Carmel
(831) 625-2212

The Chamber Music Society of the Monterey Peninsula hosts this prestigious annual student competition at the Sunset Center in Carmel. Ten groups of students playing piano and stringed instruments compete for scholarships. The age limit for entrants is 26. A winners' concert is held the following Sunday. The free event takes place the first week of May.

Red, White & a Little Blues. Some Rock and Latin too!
Alvarado Street, Monterey
(831) 655-8070
www.oldmonterey.org

Continuous live entertainment on several stages, arts, crafts, and eclectic food booths are the highlights of this always-popular street fair. A showcase for local musicians and performers, this festival is a great way to sample the music scene.

JUNE

Grand Prix of Monterey
Mazda Raceway at Laguna Seca
(800) 327-7322
www.laguna-seca.com

Fans of open-wheel auto racing from around the world converge at Laguna Seca to watch drivers like Mario Andretti, Christian Fittipaldi, and Jimmy Vasser battle for top honors. Also featured are the Shell 300, the CART FedEx Championship Series, and the Shelby Cobra Challenge Senior Racing Series. Various admission packages and camping are available.

Monterey Bay Blues Festival
Monterey Fairgrounds, 2004 Fairgrounds Road, Monterey
(831) 394-2652
www.montereyblues.com

The annual Monterey Bay Blues Festival is dedicated to preserving blues as an American art form. Three separate shows are held on three stages. Two shows, each featuring numerous acts, are held each day. Past lineups have included artists such as Etta James, Frankie Lee, and Clarence Carter. More than 30 veteran blues artists and several newcomers are showcased in this weekend event held at the end of June. There are also food, merchandise, and exhibit booths on the grounds. Ticket prices are from $15 to $70 (for a two-day pass).

Monterey Bay TheatreFest
Custom House Plaza, Monterey
(831) 622-0100
www.pacrep.org

The TheatreFest features live music on stage, a Human Chess Game, and fairy tale classics in the open air. The Pacific Repertory Theatre players produce the plays and the Human Chess Game, which has a yearly theme. Bleacher seating is set up near a stage at the Plaza. Pacific Repertory players march onto the Custom House Plaza and carry out full-scale chess game war on the chess board stage. The TheatreFest is held at the end of June, and performances are free to the public.

Spirit West Coast
Laguna Seca Recreation Area
(831) 443-5399
www.spiritwestcoast.org

More than 60,000 people attend this three-day Christian music festival, the only one of its kind in the western U.S. The nonprofit event features concerts by more than 50 of the top performers in Christian music on six stages as well as speakers, camping, sports, and recreation.

JULY

California Rodeo Salinas
Salinas Sports Complex, 1034 North Main, Salinas
(831) 775-3100
www.carodeo.com
See world champion cowboys compete at the biggest Rodeo in California. While PRCA cowboys compete in the main arena, trick riders, clowns, and horse races take place on the track. Put on your boots and hat, eat your fill of barbecue from the many food vendors, listen to some cowboy poetry, and have a true Western experience. The annual Rodeo is usually scheduled the second or third weekend in July. Admission fees start around $10.

Carmel Bach Festival
Various locations on the Peninsula
(831) 624-2046
www.bachfestival.org
This internationally known event has featured world-class baroque music for more than 60 years. The season presents concerts, recitals, master classes, open rehearsals, and a children's concert. Recitals, about an hour and a half long, are held prior to each performance. There are two or three evening concerts held each week. Each concert is repeated several times over the three-week period, allowing a greater number of people to attend the concerts. The Bach Festival begins in mid-July. Prices vary according to the event. Attending the recitals is the least expensive way to go. Call or visit the Web site for a schedule and information.

Carmel Shakespeare Festival
Various theaters, Carmel
(831) 622-0100
www.pacrep.org

The Forest, Golden Bough, and Circle theaters host this annual event with professional and community actors in a selection of works from Shakespeare. The season includes a total of four productions. On the weekends, two plays run simultaneously on separate stages for the first half of the season, followed by the second pair. The event is held late July through mid-October. Call or visit the Web site for venues and ticket information.

Equestrian Classic
Pebble Beach Equestrian Center, corner of Alva Road and Portola Lane, Pebble Beach
(831) 624-2756
www.ridepebblebeach.com
More than 500 ponies and thoroughbreds compete in equestrian events, including hunter and jumper events, at the Equestrian Classic. Children's classes are held, and the $30,000 Grand Prix Jumping contest is a big draw. Many people like to attend the jumper events because it is more colorful and bold. The Children's Fun Fair features a petting zoo, and there are also food booths. The event takes place over a two-week period at the end of July. Horses that qualify will compete in the Grand Prix Jumping event for prize money. Admission is free except for the entrance fee at the Pebble Beach gate.

Feast of Lanterns
Various locations, Pacific Grove
(831) 373-7625
Feast of Lanterns, an annual Pacific Grove community celebration, includes street dancing, a pet parade, a pageant at Lovers Point Beach, and fireworks. The weeklong event takes place during the last week of July. There is no admission charge.

Fourth of July
Locations throughout Monterey Bay
(831) 646-3996
www.monterey.org

A morning parade on Alvarado Street in downtown Monterey includes bands, community groups, and floats kicking off the July Fourth celebration. In the evening, fireworks synchronized with patriotic music are presented over the Monterey Bay. Good locations to see the free fireworks show are Monterey State Beach and Fisherman's Wharf.

Garlic Festival
Christmas Hill Park, Miller Avenue, and Santa Theresa Boulevard, Gilroy
(831) 842-1625
www.gilroygarlicfestival.com

Gilroy, the Garlic Capital of the World, loves to celebrate garlic, the beloved "stinking rose." Numerous food booths feature garlic dishes from a variety of ethnic backgrounds. Celebrity chefs are on hand to demonstrate the preparation of various dishes made with garlic. You'll want to sample delicacies such as garlic ice cream (seriously, it's delicious) and gator tail and ostrich cooked with garlic. Vendors sell fine arts and crafts and other items such as garlic braids and wreaths. There is continuous musical entertainment, including rock, country, reggae, and jazz. Admission for this popular annual event, held the last full weekend of July, is $10.00 for adults, $5.00 for seniors and children six through 12.

Moss Landing Antique Street Fair
Off Highway 1, Moss Landing
(831) 633-4501

More than 100 vendors showcase their antiques and collectibles and sell everything imaginable at this shoppers' heaven. You'll find Victorian furniture, vintage linens, toys, glassware, tableware, books, and other paper products. The quantity and variety of antiques is staggering. We suggest that serious shoppers wear sunglasses, layers of clothing (it can get hot around midday when the morning fog burns off), and comfortable shoes. The event usually takes place the last Sunday of July. A nominal admission fee includes parking.

Obon Festival
Buddhist Temple, 1155 Noche Buena, Seaside
(831) 394-0119

The Monterey Peninsula Buddhist Temple hosts this annual event that celebrates an international Buddhist tradition. The local festivities feature bonsai dwarfed-tree exhibits, delicious Asian foods (such as teriyaki and tempura), tea ceremonies, crafts, and spectacular Obon Dance performances. This lively bazaar is held in early July.

United States World Superbike Championship
Mazda Raceway Laguna Seca
1021 Monterey-Salinas Highway, Monterey
(800) 327-7322
www.laguna-seca.com

This international motorcycle event brings champion riders from more than 10 countries to this Monterey County track for the eight-race series. The race times vary for categories, including motorcycles like Supersport, Pro Thunder, Big Twins, Triumphs, and Harley-Davidsons. The only World Superbike event in North America usually occurs mid-July. Tickets are $10 to $45 per day, depending on seating preference.

AUGUST

BlackHawk Collection Exposition Sale
Classic Cars
Peter Hay Golf Course, Pebble Beach
(510) 736-3444
www.blackhawkcollection.com

More than 75 rare, vintage, classic, and one-of-a-kind automobiles are displayed and offered for individual sale at the Peter Hay Golf Course on 17-Mile Drive near The Lodge at Pebble Beach. The event is held mid-August each year as part of the Concours d'Elegance. There is no admission fee to view the automobiles, but you must pay the $8.00 gate fee to enter Pebble Beach.

Carmel Bach Festival
Various locations on the Peninsula
(831) 624-2046
www.bachfestival.org
The Bach Festival, held over a three-week period beginning in mid-July, has events featuring world-class concerts, recitals, master classes, open rehearsals, and a children's concert. See our July entry for more details.

Carmel Shakespeare Festival
Various theaters, Carmel
(831) 622-0100
www.pacrep.org
Several local theaters host this annual event with professional and community actors starring in works by Shakespeare. The event starts in the end of July and is held through mid-October. See our July entry for more information.

Concorso Italiano
Black Horse Golf Course, Seaside
(425) 688-1903
www.concorso.com
Attendees from around the world come to view an impressive display of more than 400 classic Italian and other automobiles and motorcycles on the fairways of Black Horse Golf Course. Individual auto makes, such as Porsche, BMW, Viper, and Lamborghini, are set up in separate areas. The annual event, held in conjunction with the Concours d'Elegance, occurs in mid-August each year. Ticket prices are $60, which includes a parking pass.

Concours d'Elegance
The Lodge at Pebble Beach
(831) 659-0663
www.pebblebeachconcours.net
For more than 50 years this internationally recognized premier showcase of more than 100 classic automobiles has graced the lawn at The Lodge. With the breathtaking 18th green and the rugged coastline as the backdrop, this is an automobile extravaganza one will never forget. Pre- and postwar marquees feature an exclusive selection of classic autos. In addition to the cars, many people come to see the stars. Celebrities such as comedian Jay Leno and clothing designer Ralph Lauren have both entered cars in past events. Proceeds from the event, held in mid-August, benefit local organizations including United Way of Monterey County. Tickets cost $100 and include the program and shuttle service.

Jewish Food Festival
Congregation Beth Israel,
5716 Carmel Valley Road, Carmel Valley
(831) 624-2015
This festival features a crafts fair, Jewish food, dance, music, and entertainment, and a village market with costumed vendors. Nosh on traditional Jewish fare like kugel and latkes. There are also wandering storytellers, pushcart peddlers, strolling musicians, Israeli dance lessons, synagogue tours, and more. Admission is free.

Monterey County Fair
Monterey County Fairgrounds,
2004 Fairgrounds Road, Monterey
(831) 372-5863
www.montereycountyfair.com
Who doesn't love the fair? The Monterey County Fair is an exciting blend of carnival rides, craft and food booths, produce and flower displays, art and photography, livestock, contests, demonstrations, 4-H club exhibits, and lively entertainment. The event is held at the end of August each year. Admission is $8.00 for adults, $7.00 for seniors, $4.00 for children ages six to 12, and free for children younger than five.

Monterey Sports Car Auction
Monterey Conference Center,
1 Portola Plaza, Monterey
(310) 246-9880
Another world-famous auto event, the two-day auction is held in conjunction with the Concours d'Elegance. A preview of the vintage sports cars and

Carmel's historic Golden Bough Theater is home to the Pacific Repertory Theatre. PacRep stages the Carmel Shakespeare Festival each year from July through October in addition to a full season of live theatre. MICHAEL CHATFIELD

classic automobiles, including Corvettes, Porsches, Formula 1 race cars, Cobras, and MGs, takes place in the Custom House Plaza prior to the sale. The event is held mid-August each year. Tickets are $50 for two and includes a catalog.

Rolex Monterey Historic Automobile Races
Mazda Raceway Laguna Seca
1021 Monterey-Salinas Highway, Monterey
(800) 327-7322
www.laguna-seca.com
The "Historics" are yet another opportunity to see vintage cars during the "classic car weekend" festivities. Watch Mustangs, Cobras, Corvettes, and other rare autos race around the Laguna Seca Raceway. Races are for seven groups, from pre-1928 sport and racing cars through 1981 cham-

pionship cars. Tickets range from $45 to $90 depending on seating preference.

Scottish Games and Celtic Festival
Toro County Park
Monterey-Salinas Highway, Salinas
(831) 647-6311
www.montereyscotgames.com
This is a giant three-day event, held in early August, with bagpipe bands, dancing, athletic events, competitions, clans, kilts, blarney, and killarney. A Caber parade takes place, in which brawny lads wearing kilts toss around an object that looks like a telephone pole. Other competitions include shot put and a hammer throw. All the judges for the competitive events are themselves teachers of the sports. About 150 dancers from as far away as Canada compete individually in Highland step dances. Items such as kilts, sweaters, and handmade crafts are for sale by vendors.

Ticket prices in recent years were $11 to $50 depending upon days of attendance and seating preference.

Steinbeck Festival
Various locations in Salinas
(831) 775-4720
www.steinbeck.org
Four full days of activity with speakers, presenters, films, and tours highlight the annual festival honoring John Steinbeck. A bus tour features historic ranches, views, scenes, and readings from Steinbeck's novels and short stories that take place in the Salinas Valley. You'll also visit the site where Steinbeck was laid to rest. A walking tour of historic Salinas points out the new Steinbeck Center and restored buildings in Old Town Salinas. You may also tour the Steinbeck Archives for a look at the 30,000 items in the vault. The events, which usually take place in early August, have various ticket prices. A festival passport is available for $75. Call for reservations and information.

Winemaker's Celebration
Custom House Plaza, Monterey
(831) 375-9400
www.montereywinecountry.org
The Winemaker's Celebration features more than 40 Monterey County winemakers and local restaurants presenting wine tasting, food sampling, and wine-education events at the end of August each year. Jugglers, musicians, barrel-building demos, viticulture displays, and entertainment make this an exciting and informative event. Tickets are $30 in advance, $35 the day of event. The price includes a souvenir glass and wine-tasting tickets. Children enter for free.

SEPTEMBER

Big Sur Ride
(831) 373-1839
www.cypressgroup.org
The Big Sur Ride is a spectacular two-day, 170-mile bicycle ride that includes 11,100 feet of climbing. The ride begins and finishes in Carmel Valley Village. The route runs along the rugged Big Sur coastline, through the beautiful Salinas Valley, and into the dramatic rolling hills of Carmel Valley.

Carmel Mission Fiesta
Carmel Mission, Rio Road, Carmel
(831) 626-9272
The free annual Carmel Mission Fiesta includes mariachis, as well as more than 55 vendors selling food and crafts. Mexican, Irish, and country-and-western–style dancing take place. Foods served include barbecue chicken, tri-tip sandwiches, and tacos. Handmade crafts for sale include paintings, clothing, and holiday ornaments. The fiesta is always held the last Sunday in September.

Carmel Shakespeare Festival
Various theaters, Carmel
(831) 622-0100
www.pacrep.org
Several local theaters host this annual event with professional and community actors starring in works by Shakespeare. The event starts in the end of July and is held through mid-October. See our July entry for more information.

Cherries Jubilee
Laguna Seca Recreation Area, 1021
Monterey-Salinas Highway, Monterey
(831) 759-1836
Cherries Jubilee is a car show and festival featuring parties, dancing, food booths, and vendors selling everything from T-shirts and jewelry to handcrafted items. Beautifully restored street rods from 1972 and earlier cruise Alvarado Street in downtown Monterey on Thursday, the first day of the event, followed by an After the Cruise party. Official Cherries Jubilee memorabilia, such as hats, T-shirts, and buttons are for sale at the events. On Saturday night there are dances held at various locations in downtown Monterey.

At the Mazda Raceway Laguna Seca Midway, food vendors tempt race fans with delicious dishes. Pride of Monterey is an upscale food area in a relaxed, smartly decorated environment. Chefs at open-style cooking stations prepare culinary delights such as stir-fry, seafood or artichoke pasta, steamed artichokes, carne asada or chile verde burritos, and clam chowder. Dale's Diner is a food concession tent with an entrance resembling a '50s-style diner. Favorite diner foods like hamburgers, hot dogs, chili dogs, burritos, and salads are served in this casual setting.

This annual event takes place at the end of September and benefits the Salinas Valley Memorial Hospital Foundation. Expect to pay about $8.00 for teens and adults, $2.00 for children ages six to 12, and nothing for children younger than six.

Festa Italia/Santa Rosalia Festival
Custom House Plaza, Monterey
(831) 655-8070
www.sonsofitalymonterey.org

Nearing its seventh decade, this annual Italian celebration includes a parade, the National Bocce Ball Tournament with 60 teams (with a $3,000 prize), and food booths. There is continuous musical entertainment on stage with favorite Italian songs sung in English and Italian. The adventurous will want to enter the "O Sole Mio" singing contest; the prize is usually a salami. You'll find around 50 arts and crafts booths, most with handmade items such as jewelry, pottery, and the like. The free festival takes place on a weekend in mid-September.

Great Sand Castle Contest
Carmel Beach at the end of Ocean Avenue, Carmel
(831) 626-1255

This annual event begins early in the morning, and judging takes place in the early afternoon. Each entrant has designated boundaries for her or his creation. Each year there is a theme; the castles must represent the theme in some way, but the interpretation is entirely up to the artists. Bribing of judges, especially with food and drink, is absolutely permitted (no cash, though). Begging is also an effective means of winning. Award-winning entrants receive

trophies made by the City of Carmel Recreation Department and the Monterey Bay Chapter of American Institute of Architects, who cosponsor the event. The date of the event, never announced until just before it occurs, is usually at the end of September. There is no registration or entrance fee required.

Monterey Jazz Festival
Monterey County Fairgrounds,
2004 Fairgrounds Road, Monterey
(831) 373-3366
www.montereyjazzfestival.org

The Monterey Jazz Festival, an annual tradition for more than 40 years, is the oldest continually held jazz festival in the world. Artists and attendees from around the country come to celebrate jazz. Each year fans are entertained by famous and up-and-coming artists such as Sonny Rollins, David Sanborn, Diana Krall, Wynton Marsalis, Dave Holland, Herbie Hancock, Taj Mahal, Thomas Chapin, Jim Hall, Charlie Haden, Ivan Lins, and many others. High school all-star bands from around the country are also featured. Continuous entertainment takes place on three stages at this heavily attended three-day festival. Food, drink, and merchandise vendors are also on the grounds. Prices for one-day grounds passes and season tickets can be found on the Web site or by calling.

Monterey Sports Car Championships/ American Le Mans Series
Mazda Raceway Laguna Seca
(800) 327-7322
www.laguna-seca.com

Patterned after the famous 24 Hours of Le Mans, the American Le Mans Series gives fans a taste of the French event. Spectators get a chance to see the cars in the paddock area and to get autographs from their favorite drivers.

TomatoFest
Quail Lodge Resort, Carmel
www.tomatofest.com

Tired of the tasteless, hard-as-a-ketchup-bottle varieties found in grocery stores, the founders of TomatoFest began to raise

If you're on a budget, a great way to enjoy the Monterey Jazz and Monterey Bay Blues Festivals (both held at the Monterey County Fairgrounds) is to purchase grounds admission tickets. Blues tickets are $20 for Friday, $25 for Saturday or Sunday. The Jazz Festival offers Friday tickets for $25, Saturday or Sunday for $35, or all three for $80. You can't get in the main arena with these tickets, but it's not unusual for main stage artists to "sit in" with bands on the grounds stages.

"heirloom" tomatoes, hybrids lost to time through commercial agriculture's search for the perfect fruit. Over time, what began as a group of friends sharing recipes and a good time has evolved into a charity event that has donated more than $130,000 to local causes. More than 300 tomato varieties are showcased in recipes by 50 of California's finest chefs. A Best of the Fest Tomato Salsa Contest, wine and olive oil tasting, live music, and dancing are also part of this joyous celebration. Very popular with locals and visitors, this event always sells out. Tickets and more information are available on the Web site.

OCTOBER

Butterfly Parade
Lighthouse Avenue, Pacific Grove
(831) 373-3304
www.pgmonarchs.org/fomb.html
Each year from October to mid-February thousands of monarch butterflies spend the winter in Pacific Grove. It's not unusual to see hundreds of butterflies flying from flower to flower on a sunny day. To pay tribute to this phenomenon, Pacific Grove children make their own costumes and parade down Lighthouse Avenue. The parade is held in early October. This free annual event is followed by a street bazaar in downtown Pacific Grove. Also as homage to the butterflies, the town of Pacific Grove commissioned the sculpture by the late Christopher

Bell that's in front of the post office. The sculpture has a small boy and girl dressed in monarch costumes.

California Constitution Day Reenactment
Colton Hall, Monterey
(831) 646-5640
www.monterey.org
Be transported back to 1849 as actors in period costume re-create the scene of the debates and signing of California's first constitution, which led to statehood. Reservations are required for this free event.

California International Airshow
Salinas Airport, 30 Mortensen Avenue, Salinas
(831) 754-1983
www.salinasairshow.com
One of the premier aviation events on the West Coast is usually held mid-October. Pyrotechnics (including the Wall of Fire), air acts, and ground acts by military and civilian teams are the highlights of this annual event. Previous performers include the Blue Angels, the Thunderbirds, and the Canadian Snowbirds. General admission tickets are $12.00 for adults and $9.00 for children ages six through 12. Under six free.

Carmel Performing Arts Festival
Various locations in Carmel
(831) 624-7675
www.carmelfest.org
The annual Carmel Performing Arts Festival is a three-week community cultural event that highlights regional and distinguished guest performing artists. Beginning in mid-October and continuing until early November, theater, dance, and music performances for all ages occur in intimate venues in and around Carmel. Call or visit the Web site for admission prices.

Carmel Shakespeare Festival
Various theaters, Carmel
(831) 622-0100
www.pacrep.org
Several local theaters host this annual event with professional and community actors starring in works by Shakespeare. The event

starts at the end of July and is held through mid-October. See our July entry for more information.

Historic Home Tour
Various locations in Pacific Grove
(831) 373-3304

Cosponsored by the Pacific Grove Chamber of Commerce, the Pacific Grove Art Center, and the Heritage Society, this tour takes you inside many of the town's immaculately restored Victorian homes and businesses. The number of houses varies from year to year, depending upon the residents and innkeepers who wish to participate. A committee selects participants based on the home's historic value and the quality of restoration done on the property. Docents dressed in period costume conduct the tours and give information about each home or inn. The event occurs in early to mid-October each year. Tickets are $12.

Old Monterey Historic Festival & Faire
Custom House Plaza, Monterey
(831) 655-8070

The Old Monterey Historic Festival & Faire is a celebration of arts, crafts, and food that takes place at the end of Alvarado Street at the Old Custom House Plaza. It's held on a weekend in early to mid-October. You'll find handmade items such as pottery, jewelry, wood products, metal work, and wearable art in the form of clothing and hats. Musical entertainment is also provided at this free event.

Old Monterey Seafood and Music Festival
Downtown Monterey
(831) 655-8070
www.oldmonterey.org

Alvarado Street is closed to traffic for this two-day, family-friendly celebration of music, art, and seafood. The best of the area's musical talent is showcased on several stages, and food booths and interesting arts and crafts are offered for sale. The festival is presented by the Old Monterey Business Association during Columbus Day weekend. Free admission.

NOVEMBER

Christmas Tree Lighting Ceremony
Steinbeck Plaza on Cannery Row, Monterey
(831) 649-6690

The holidays officially begin on Cannery Row with caroling by what remains of the old canneries, the arrival of Santa, and the lighting of the Christmas tree, a huge Douglas fir. It all happens at the end of November.

Dia de Los Muertos Procession
Main Street, Salinas
(831) 775-4737

In Mexico, Dia de Los Muertos—"Day of the Dead"—on November 1 is a joyous, if somewhat macabre, celebration honoring the memory of one's deceased friends and family. In downtown Salinas, it is celebrated with a procession and dancing on downtown Main Street, ending at the National Steinbeck Center.

Great Wine Escape Weekend
Various locations
(831) 375-9400
www.montereywines.org

This event features more than 25 wineries at 15 locations, with narrated bus tours or self-guided tours. Other events throughout the weekend include The Great Wine Escape Golf Tournament; The Monterey Wine Auction & Gala; Winemaker Dinners by world-renowned chefs; a Wine Symposium featuring a panel of Monterey County vintners; an evening jazz concert; and The Great Wine Escape Finale with more than 30 Monterey County wineries pouring their world-class wines. Ticket prices vary by event and are available on the Web site.

Monterey Bay Holiday Gift Faire
Custom House Plaza, Monterey
(831) 622-0100

Each year the Custom House Plaza becomes a shopping destination for those seeking the handmade wares of artists and craftspeople. You'll discover jewelry made from beads and precious metals, pottery, wooden toys, wearable art, weather vanes, and birdhouses. The artists themselves sell their goods. The free event takes place in late November, right around the time you're looking for the perfect holiday gifts.

Robert Louis Stevenson's Un-Birthday Week, Stevenson House, 530 Houston Street, Monterey (831) 649-6204

The Stevenson House honors the famous author and poet with tours and un-birthday cake. The event, hosted for schoolchildren, has costumed docents and an actor playing Robert Louis Stevenson. It celebrates Stevenson's gift of his birthday to a young friend who was born on Christmas Day. Stevenson thought that no one should have to share his or her birthday with Christ. The free annual event is sponsored by the California Parks Department and the Old Monterey Preservation Society. It's held mid-November each year. There is also a gala reception open house, which costs $25.

Thanksgiving Community Dinner Monterey County Fairgrounds, 2004 Fairgrounds Road, Monterey (831) 372-5863

For more than 20 years, the Kiwanis of Monterey and volunteers have been putting together this very special community dinner for anyone who doesn't want to spend the holiday alone. Clothing and toiletry items are available for those in need, and the event continues to grow in popularity and numbers each year. All the food and supplies are donated by various people in the community. There is no charge for the event, which always takes place on Thanksgiving Day.

DECEMBER

Carmel Lights Up the Season Devendorf Park, Ocean Avenue between Junipero and Mission Streets, Carmel (831) 624-0137

The official Carmel Christmas tree, situated at the intersection of Ocean Avenue and Junipero Street, is lighted during the first week of December. An open house follows at Carmel Plaza. The event is free.

Christmas at the Inns Various locations in Pacific Grove (831) 373-3304

Seven of Pacific Grove's bed-and-breakfast inns dress up in Victorian holiday splendor for this self-guided tour. Docents in period costumes, live entertainment, and refreshments add to the ambience of this festive event, held on a Tuesday in early December. Tickets are $10 and can also be used to receive a discount at several Pacific Grove restaurants and shops.

Christmas in the Adobes Various locations in Monterey (831) 647-6226

Candlelight walking tours and visits to 20 beautifully decorated Monterey adobes are hosted by the Old Monterey Preservation Society and Monterey State Historic Parks. The annual event takes place mid-December. Tickets are $12.00 for adults (18 and older), $2.00 for kids (ages six to 17), and free for children younger than six.

Christmas Community Dinner Monterey County Fairgrounds, 2004 Fairgrounds Road, Monterey (831) 372-5863

The Christmas Community Dinner is a celebratory meal for those in need of giving or receiving. Volunteers are always welcome to participate at this long-standing event. The free dinner, open to all, is always held on Christmas Day. The dinner is sponsored by businesses and individuals in the community.

First Night Monterey Various locations in Monterey (831) 373-4778 www.firstnightmonterey.org

The Alta California Dance Company—California State Parks volunteers—perform in 1840s period costume at the Custom House during Christmas in the Adobes in Old Monterey.
MARGIE GILLASPY, CALIFORNIA STATE PARKS

Celebrate the start of the New Year at this alcohol-free, family-oriented event. An outstanding lineup of local artists and musicians furnishes music, entertainment, dancing, food, arts and crafts, and hands-on projects for all ages. Join the "Auld Lang Syne" gathering at 11:30 P.M. in Custom House Plaza to ring in the New Year. The under-$10 fee includes shuttle service from Monterey Peninsula College, 980 Fremont Boulevard in Monterey.

Hospice Foundation Trees of Life
Monterey Conference Center, Monterey
National Steinbeck Center, Salinas
(831) 333-9023
www.hffcc.org
Each light on this tree represents a donation in memory of a loved one. Music and refreshments are also part of the ceremony. The free event takes place at the beginning of December.

La Posada
Monterey Conference Center, 2 Portola Plaza, Monterey
(831) 646-3866
www.monterey.org
A candlelight procession, mariachi bands, piñatas, and food are the focus of this free annual event, held on a Friday in early December. Participants are asked to bring a candle to join in the awe-inspiring candlelight procession as it meanders through the adobes in Old Town Monterey. The event is a reenactment of Christmas night, with costumed actors posing as Joseph and Mary. Participants sing carols during the procession. It terminates at the conference center, where a piñata party is held and refreshments are served.

Monterey Cowboy Poetry and Music Festival
Monterey Conference Center
(800) 722-9652
www.montereycowboy.com

The largest event of its kind in Northern California, this festival draws the finest practitioners of the uniquely American art form that is cowboy poetry. The festival also features cowboy troubadours and artisans showcasing Western crafts. Admission charge.

Monterey Tree Lighting Ceremony
Colton Hall Museum, 351 Pacific Avenue, Monterey
(831) 646-3866
www.monterey.org
Choral groups and bands perform while the 35-foot fir Christmas tree on the front lawn at Colton Hall is lighted. Participants are asked to light a candle in the ceremony. Apple cider and refreshments are served afterwards. The free event takes place the first week of December.

Pacific Grove Tree Lighting Ceremony
Jewell Park, Central Avenue between Grand and Forest Avenues, Pacific Grove
(831) 373-3304
Pacific Grove opens the holiday season with a tree lighting, live entertainment by school bands, caroling, and a visit from Santa. The evening also heralds the

Pacific Grove Hometown Holidays with a window-decorating contest among the downtown merchants. The free event takes place at the beginning of December.

Streets of Bethlehem
First Baptist Church,
1130 San Vincente Street, Salinas
(831) 422-9872
www.1stbaptist.net/streets
A cast of 200 volunteers reenacts the sights and sounds of Bethlehem at the time of the birth of Jesus. Period costumes, live animals, and beautiful sets enliven the scene. A production of the First Baptist Church in Salinas, Streets of Bethlehem has been presented every December since 1992.

Wine and Wreaths Open House
Joullian Winery, Carmel Valley
(831) 659-2800
www.joullian.com
This is a unique event at which attendees are invited to craft a holiday wreath using cuttings from Joullian's vines. Of course, excellent wines are available for tasting, and it's a wonderful spot for a picnic in the warm Carmel Valley sun.

THE ARTS AND GALLERIES

The arts have long held a special place in the hearts of Monterey Peninsula residents. From the Bohemian artists of Carmel to the jazz lovers of Monterey, locals embrace culture with great vigor. Why the fascination with the arts? It could be the spectacular natural scenery in this area that draws artists and stirs the passion for things beautiful. Maybe it was the influx of writers, painters, and musicians who migrated here from San Francisco following the great 1906 earthquake and fire. Perhaps it's because many creative talents who can choose to live virtually anywhere choose to live here. In truth, it's a combination of these three reasons and more. Regardless of the reasons, arts and culture continue to thrive in this bountiful community.

In this chapter we'll take a look at the various art forms prevalent on the Peninsula, with a special focus on the area's famous art galleries. As one of the oldest art colonies in the country, Carmel remains the cultural center of Peninsula life. And in Carmel, the Sunset Cultural Center between San Carlos and Mission streets at Ninth Avenue is the cultural heart of the village. It's home to the newly renovated and vastly improved Sunset Center Theatre, where you'll see symphonies, dance, drama, and other artistic performances. Also inside the center are smaller workshops and studios that give rise to tomorrow's top performers.

We'll now take a quick look at some of the local institutions and organizations that make up the art and culture scene on the Monterey Peninsula. Also be sure to check out our Annual Events chapter, which lists many of the most popular yearly cultural events in the area. While in town, check out the *Go!* section of the Thursday *Monterey County Herald* and the recent issue of *Coast Weekly* for the listings of current art and culture activities (see our Media chapter for more information about these publications).

VISUAL ARTS

Galleries

Painters and photographers play a very important part in the history of the Monterey Peninsula. Since the towns of Carmel, Monterey, and Pacific Grove sprang up, artists have been drawn to and inspired by the area's rugged beauty. Carmel, in particular, is an artist's haven. Its history is filled with the Bohemian influences of artists such as Robinson Jeffers, Edward Weston, Henry Miller, and Armin Hansen. That influence lives on today, as new generations of painters, photographers, and other artists continue to rise on the scene and make a name for themselves worldwide.

In this section, we have provided a sampling of the art galleries you can enjoy on the Peninsula. Most are in Carmel, but we mention a few in Monterey, Pacific Grove, and Pebble Beach as well. Our goal is not to try to provide a list of the "best" galleries. Because tastes in art vary so widely, that designation would be too subjective and presumptuous. Instead, we have attempted to provide a good mix of galleries and artistic styles that will appeal to a variety of tastes. The Carmel galleries have done a fine job of organizing themselves and providing walking tour maps, which are available in many of the galleries. Our suggestion is to pick up these maps while in town and enjoy breakfast or lunch while planning your own art walk route through the village based on your personal interests and tastes. Fortunately, most of the Carmel galleries are within a few square blocks. Your best bet is to focus on San Carlos and Dolores Streets between Fifth and Seventh Avenues. Also, Sixth Avenue between Lincoln and Mission Streets has some of the most wonderfully unique galleries. If you have the time, don't hesitate to venture beyond these limits to discover your own personal favorites.

MONTEREY

California Views
469 Pacific Street, Monterey
(831) 373-3811
www.caviews.com
Discover a visual treasure of Monterey Peninsula history at California Views, a fascinating photographic gallery of 19th- and 20th-century Monterey Peninsula images. In downtown Monterey, this is an internationally known collection of historic photos archived by Pat Hathaway. He has catalogued more than 80,000 images from 1870 to the present and can provide off-the-shelf or custom-made prints. Also for sale are negatives, stereo views, postcards, and photo albums. California Views is open Tuesday through Saturday.

Thomas Kinkade Museum and Cultural Center
590 Calle Principal, Monterey
(831) 655-1477
www.kinkademuseum.org
Following in the tradition of 19th-century American Luminists, Thomas Kinkade has developed a worldwide reputation as a "Painter of Light." Now fans can enjoy learning the history of Thomas Kinkade and enjoy an array of his original works at the Thomas Kinkade Museum and Cultural Center, located in the historic Casa Gutierrez Adobe in old-town Monterey. Both the permanent collection and temporary exhibits are sure to please Kinkade aficionados.

Admission is free, and the renovated adobe adds to your viewing pleasure.

PACIFIC GROVE

Lisa Coscino Gallery
216 Grand Avenue, Pacific Grove
(831) 646-1939
Lisa Coscino Gallery, now in a new Pacific Grove location, features the works of emerging and established artists from coast to coast. The gallery's exhibitions change regularly, and you'll find many fine works from local artists. Exhibitors have included Alfredo de Batuc, Bobbi Bennett, Carlos Bueno, Justin de Leon, Jose Lozano, Patricia Prescott, Joan Towers, and Sergio Vasquez. The gallery also features classic furniture of the 20th century by Mies Van der Rohe, Le Corbusier, and Noguchi, among others.

Hauk Fine Arts
206 Fountain Avenue, Pacific Grove
(831) 373-6007, (800) 393-HAUK
www.artnet.com/hauk.html
Hauk Fine Arts specializes in California art from the 19th and 20th centuries. Early painters include Armin Hansen, whose dramatic seascapes express the power of nature. Contemporary painters include Carmel artist and author Belle Yang, whose depictions of Chinese life through whimsical paintings and books are a joy. Other contemporary artists include Jay Hannah, William Saroyan, Kate Carew, and Judith Deim. Hauk Fine Arts is open Wednesday through Saturday.

Pacific Grove Art Center
568 Lighthouse Avenue, Pacific Grove
(831) 375-2208
www.pgartcenter.org
In the heart of downtown P.G., the Pacific Grove Art Center has been a gathering spot for Butterfly Town's local artists since 1969. About a dozen artists maintain their studios in the center, and most are glad to let you peek in at their works. Exhibitions of works by famous and not so famous local artists are held in the

center's David Henry Gill Gallery, Elmarie Dyke Gallery, Boyer Gallery, and Photography Gallery. The Pacific Grove Art Center is closed Monday and Tuesday.

Tessuti Zoo
171 Forest Avenue, Pacific Grove
(831) 648-1725

"Tessuti" is Italian for fabrics, and that is precisely what you'll find at Pacific Grove's Tessuti Zoo. Coproprietor Emily Owens, the artist formerly known as Emily Ann Originals, uses fabric as her canvas and palette, and scissors, thread, and needle as her brush to create wild and wonderful artwork for the home. Her line of fantasy creatures and dolls attracts children and adults alike, while her wall hangings and quilts are magic. Tessuti Zoo partner Mary Troup has developed a loyal clientele for her fashionable wearable art clothing. She is equally talented in creating hand-painted furniture, paintings, collages, and other designer decor. You'll find this intensely colorful gallery on Forest Avenue below Lighthouse Avenue, right across the street from the popular Peppers Mexicali Cafe. Tessuti Zoo is open Monday through Saturday.

CARMEL

Atelier
Dolores Street and Fifth Avenue, Carmel
(831) 625-3168
www.ateliercarmel.com

The 17th- through 20th-century artwork available at Atelier is nothing short of museum quality. Ray Ramsey has gathered a breathtaking collection of European masters that includes Renoir, Degas, Picasso, Pissaro, Monet, Cézanne, and Gauguin. Early California artists include George Innes, Franz Bischoff, and Armin Hansen. This is history, folks, a can't-miss adventure worthy of your time and attention. The Atelier galleries are a bit back off the street on Del Dono Court at Dolores and Fifth, so look carefully. It's well worth it.

Bleich Gallery
Dolores Street and Ocean Avenue, Carmel
(831) 624-9447
www.bleich4art.com

Set your eye on a George Bleich seascape, and you sense his deep understanding of the subject (he was a seaman since the age of 15). Gaze at his impressionist gardens, and you feel his kinship with Monet, Gauguin, and Renoir. Bleich Gallery, established in 1969, features an array of works from this noted Carmel artist, including paintings from Monet's gardens in Giverny and Provence and landscapes and seascapes from the Monterey Peninsula. His paintings hang in homes and museums worldwide, including the White House. Bleich has a unique approach to commissioned paintings and other works. He allows family members to apply a portion of the underpainting and thus become closer to the art. Limited-edition prints and drawings are also available. Drop in on a Saturday, and there's a good chance you'll meet the artist himself, sharing stories and possibly strumming his own compositions on guitar. Bleich Gallery is open daily.

Lilliana Braico Gallery
Sixth Avenue and Dolores Street, Carmel
(831) 624-2512
www.lillianabraicogallery.com

Lilliana Braico has been making a name for herself locally and internationally since she first moved to Carmel in the 1960s. Her brightly colored oil and acrylic florals, Mediterranean seascapes, portraits, and abstracts have a light yet playful quality that reflect her experiences living on the Isle of Capri and in Paris and London. Her festive studio is up a narrow path off Sixth Avenue near Dolores Street. Prints and calendars of her work are also available.

Chapman Gallery
Seventh Avenue and San Carlos Street, Carmel
(831) 626-1766
www.chapmangallery.com

Tessuti Zoo is a wacky place! Enjoy the soft sculpture creatures and dolls, hand-painted furniture, wall hangings, wind-up tin toys, and so much more. TOM OWENS

At a time when a few Carmel galleries are starting to look a bit too trendy for the old village, it's nice to experience one that gives a feel of Bohemian Carmel. Dean and Joanna Chapman have captured that feel in this historic spot on Seventh Avenue between San Carlos and Mission Streets. The Chapman Gallery's emphasis is on regional California artists, with many from the Monterey Peninsula. Featured are S.C. Yuan, Reed Farrington, Gail Hodin Reeves, and cartoonist Hank Ketcham (of *Dennis the Menace* fame). The gallery, which also includes an interesting used-book store, is closed Mondays.

The Digital Giraffe
Dolores Street and Eighth Avenue, Carmel
(831) 624–1833
www.giraffe.com

There's a whole different wave of art in Carmel. The Digital Giraffe, a.k.a. Corrine Whitaker, brings digital painting to the quaint village of Carmel. Whitaker is known worldwide as a groundbreaker in her field. Since 1981, she has shown her computer-generated works in more than 70 solo exhibitions and has taken part in excess of 200 group exhibitions. Her most famous series, "Jane and Dick Revisited," was exhibited in India at the Centre for Photography as an Art Form as the first ever digital fine art exhibit in the country. She has also been commissioned to produce work for the Kennedy Space Center and the American Embassy in Minsk, Belarus. The works are output as digital dye prints on paper, canvas, Plexiglas, glass, and other surfaces. Her newest ventures are in digitally designed sculptures. It's worth the trip down Dolores Street between Seventh and Eighth Avenues to see this unique and friendly gallery. And it's worth a visit to the Digital Giraffe Web site for art commentary, news, and more.

Nancy Dodds Gallery
Hampton Court, Seventh Avenue and San Carlos Street, Carmel
(831) 624-0346
www.nancydoddsgallery.com
Nancy Dodds is a contemporary art gallery that features works of California artists in a variety of media. You'll find innovative watercolors, oils on paper, lithographs, monotypes, and etchings from artists such as Bruce Botts, David Smith-Harrison, Chris Newhard, Leslie Toms, Randall Sexton, Carolyn Lord, Gail Packer, and Anita Toney. Drop in and meet Nancy and Topper, her cocker spaniel. Nancy Dodds Gallery is closed on Tuesday except by appointment.

Galerie Plein Aire
Dolores Street and Sixth Avenue, Carmel
(831) 625-5686
www.galeriepleinaire.com
They are called "The Informalists," this group of local Carmel artists who operate Galerie Plein Aire and create colorful landscapes of the place they live in and love. Meet Johnny Apodaca, Mark Farina, Barry John Raybould, Jeff Daniel Smith, Richmond P. Woodson, Gerard Martin, and gallery founder Cyndra Bradford. They work and play at Galerie Plein Aire so you are indeed likely to meet one or more of them, and perhaps Jake the dog, when you walk inside the gallery's bright blue door. The gallery is located behind Highland Sculpture, so don't miss it. The Informalists are open every day but Tuesday.

Gallerie Amsterdam
Dolores Street and Sixth Avenue, Carmel
(831) 624-4355
www.amsterdamfineart.com
If European art of the 18th, 19th, and 20th centuries holds a special place in your heart, visit Gallerie Amsterdam. This elegant gallery is one of the largest in Carmel and displays the works of more than 70 artists. Featured are Hungarian ultrarealist Vida Gabor, impressionist Anatoli Belakoni,

Netherlands plein air artist Jacobus Abels, Russian-born painter Alexander Volkov, and Vietnamese sculptor Tuan. Whether your pleasure is still life, plein air, landscapes, seascapes, portraits, or figuratives, Gallerie Amsterdam provides a relaxing stroll through European and other art.

Gallery Twenty-One
Dolores Street and Ocean Avenue, Carmel
(831) 626-2700
www.gallery21.com
Gallery Twenty-One is home to the paintings, serigraphs, and sculptures of the late modern artist and Carmel resident Eyvind Earle. Once referred to as "the artist of the 21st century," Earle painted introspective and mysterious landscapes from a deep inner world that convey drama and wonder in the balance of darkness and light. Lovers of modern art will not want to miss this exceptional gallery north of Ocean Avenue on Dolores Street. Available are books of Earle's graphic art, Christmas card art, and his words and poetry.

Highlands Sculpture Gallery
Dolores Street and Fifth Avenue, Carmel
(831) 624-0535
www.highlands-gallery.com
Hands on! There aren't many galleries where the staff greets you with an encouragement to place your fingers on the art. But that's the case at Highlands Sculpture Gallery, a 100 percent contemporary sculpture gallery that claims to the "oldest modern art gallery in Carmel." The pieces themselves are remarkable, with beryllium and bronze sounding sculptures that ring like bells when stroked, and bronze, metal, stone, ceramic, glass, and wood sculptures for indoors and out. Artists include amazing Bulgarian sculptor Ana Daltchev as well as Ken Matsumoto, Carolyn Cole, Winni Brueggemann, Norma Lewis, Eileen Hill, and Robert Holmes. You'll surely enjoy the brightly colored mobiles of Lauront Davidson and the equally vibrant fused-

Galerie Plein Aire on Dolores Street is home to "The Informalists," a group of local Carmel artists who create colorful landscapes. TOM OWENS

glass hangings of Yolanda Adra. So take the time to look, touch, and feel at Highlands Sculpture Gallery.

It's Cactus
Court of the Fountains, Mission Street and Ocean Avenue, Carmel
(831) 626-4213
www.itscactus.com

If folk art rather than fine art is your cup of tea, don't miss It's Cactus on Mission Street between Ocean and Seventh Avenues. Owner Casey Eastman collects folk art from around the world and puts together an eclectic display of carvings, weavings, paintings, and other forms of indigenous folk art. You'll find a definite Central and South American theme at It's Cactus, but pieces from Asia, Africa, and other environs (including the good old U.S.A.) are also present. If you've been looking for a Bolivian chumpas to add to your sweater collection, a "Day of the Dead" skull or skeleton, or a folk art nativ-

ity scene for the holidays, this is definitely the place to be. It's Cactus is open daily.

Kinkade Family Galleries
Ocean Avenue and Dolores Street, Carmel
(831) 626-6700
The Tuck Box, Dolores Street and Ocean Avenue, Carmel
(831) 655-5520
www.thomaskinkade.com

One of the most commercially astute and successful artists of the day, Thomas Kinkade is known appropriately as the "Painter of Light." Working with advanced techniques developed by a group of 19th-century American painters known as Luminists, Kinkade produces paintings that seemingly emit light from his landscapes, cityscapes, and country cottages. His Ocean Avenue gallery down Del Ling Lane between Lincoln and Dolores Streets is the best for first-timers, while the gift gallery in the Tuck Box Tea Room on

Dolores Street features smaller Kinkade collectibles.

Richard MacDonald Galleries
San Carlos Street and Sixth Avenue, Carmel
(831) 624-8200, (800) 972-5528
www.richardmacdonald.com

Perhaps you saw Richard MacDonald's *The Flair,* a 24-foot bronze monument of a gymnast that was part of the 1996 Summer Olympics in Atlanta. Or maybe you visited the monument at Pebble Beach commemorating the 100th U.S. Open Championship in 2000. If so, then you have a hint of the true artistry that MacDonald sculpts from clay and casts in bronze. If you enjoy the beauty and emotion of the human form, enter here. MacDonald's depictions of dance, mime, mythology, and simple childhood moments have a delicate, whimsical charm. Other figurative forms, like *The Flair,* express power and strength. You'll also find MacDonald's dramatic drawings, lithographs, and serigraphs. Richard MacDonald Galleries now has a second location at The Shops at the Lodge in Pebble Beach.

New Masters Gallery
Dolores Street and Ocean Avenue, Carmel
(831) 625-1511
www.newmastersgallery.com

For more than 25 years, New Masters Gallery has been bringing fine paintings and sculpture to Carmel. Today this large Dolores Street gallery between Ocean and Seventh Avenues houses an extensive collection representing international artists such as DeWitt Whistler Jayne, Mou-Sien Tseng, Tinyan, Stephen Stavast, Gerald Brommer, Alexsander Titouets, Pino Daeni, Kurt Ard, Ovanes Berberian, and Yi-Fu Zhao. Fans of marquetry inlaid woodwork will marvel at the works of Jean-Charles Spindler. Also featured is Carmel favorite Will Bullas, a local watercolorist who specializes in whimsical depictions of geese

and barnyard critters. In fact, New Masters Gallery owners Bill and Jennifer Hill also run the Will Bullas Fun Art Gallery on San Carlos Street between Ocean and Seventh Avenues. With paintings, books, stuffed animals, clothing, and greeting cards all reflecting the Will Bullas touch, this new gallery is sure to be a favorite of children of all ages.

Pitzer's of Carmel
Dolores Street and Sixth Avenue, Carmel
(831) 625-2288
www.pitzersart.com

Representing more than 60 artists, Pitzer's is a large, bright gallery that offers traditional paintings, sculptures, and limited edition prints, from realism to impressionism. You'll immediately notice that sculpture is a Pitzer's specialty. The gallery displays an array of bronze works both large and small, for indoors and the garden. Among the paintings, the bold beachscapes of William Berra are sure to catch your eye. Nelson Boren's western themes, local landscapes by Brian Blood, and James Kramer's watercolors are other favorites.

Rodrigue Studio
Sixth Avenue and Lincoln Street, Carmel
(831) 626-4444
www.georgerodrigue.com

Everywhere you look, you see those haunting yellow eyes of that soulful Blue Dog. There's Blue Dog with Elvis, Blue Dog with crocodile, and Blue Dog as vampire. If you aren't familiar with Louisiana Cajun artist George Rodrigue and his more than 500 bold and bright "Naïve Surrealism" Blue Dog paintings, you owe it to yourself to get acquainted at Rodrigue Studio (formerly Galerie Blue Dog) on Sixth Avenue between Dolores and Lincoln Streets. First created in 1984, Blue Dog is based on the mythical "loup garou," a French-Cajun ghost dog, and Tiffany, Rodrigue's own pooch who had passed away a few years prior to the notoriety. Since then, Rodrigue, already an internationally acclaimed painter, has taken Blue Dog on a fanciful journey, with the moon-eyed rascal showing up in some of the most unusual places, with some of the most unusual characters. Don't miss this one. The gallery is open daily.

Loran Speck Gallery
Sixth Avenue and Dolores Street, Carmel
(831) 624–3707
www.loranspeck.com

Is still life your cup of tea, or your bowl of cherries? Then California native Loran Speck is your man when visiting the galleries of Carmel. You'll find a wide selection of original paintings reminiscent of the Dutch Masters, as well as limited-edition Giclee prints, photoprints, and signed posters from this prolific local artist. Speck has been showing his original oils, watercolor contés, charcoals, and etchings in Carmel for more than 25 years. He also makes exquisite frames and mirrors, most gilded in 22-carat gold leaf or metal leaf and handcarved in his own studio. Loran Speck Gallery is open daily.

Richard Thomas Galleries
Dolores Street, at Fifth and Sixth Avenues, Carmel
(831) 625–5636, (800) 243–7600
www.richardthomasgalleries.com

One of the most spacious galleries in Carmel with two locations on the same block of Dolores, the Richard Thomas Gallery has an impressive collection of American and international art covering a wide range of styles, with an emphasis on contemporary realism. From the Romantic Renaissance of mixed media artist Csaba Markus to the emotional acrylic portraits of Michael Wilkinson to the peaceful landscapes of Henry Peeters, visitors are bound to find a favorite among this large and impressive collection. Other featured artists include Alexandra Nechita and Alexander Volkov.

Weston Gallery
Sixth Avenue and Dolores Street, Carmel
(831) 624–4453
www.westongallery.com

The Monterey Peninsula and Big Sur coastline have been home to some of the greatest 19th- and 20th-century photographers in the world. Ansel Adams, Edward Weston, and their contemporaries found the rugged coastline and mountains a stunning subject for their art. Weston Gallery on Sixth Avenue between Dolores and Lincoln Streets is a virtual museum of this area's photographic art history. Works by the masters Adams and Weston as well as the following generation of Weston photographers, Cole and Brett, grace the walls. Yousuf Karsh's portraits of celebrities from Albert Einstein to Brigitte Bardot to Winston Churchill are especially fascinating. Photographs of other contemporary artists such as Michael Kenna and Jeffrey Becom of Maya Color fame are featured. Portfolios, books, posters, and great greeting cards are available for purchase.

Zantman Art Galleries
Sixth Avenue and Mission Street, Carmel
(831) 624–8314
www.zantmangalleries.com

No listing of Carmel galleries is complete without a mention of Zantman Art Galleries. Established in 1959, Zantman has grown to be one of largest and most popular galleries in the village. It continues to display high-quality paintings and sculptures as it celebrates its 40th year. Current featured artists include sculptor Dennis Smith as well as painters Ted Goerschner, Marilyn Simandle, Richard Murray, Lucio Sollazzi, Gilles Archambault, Dorothy Fitzgerald, Wilson Chu, Frank Ashley, and George Hamilton.

PEBBLE BEACH

Ansel Adams Gallery
The Inn at Spanish Bay, Pebble Beach
(831) 375-7215, (888) 361-7622
www.anseladams.com
The Ansel Adams Gallery offers a large collection of works by the noted nature photographer. The black-and-white images of Yosemite, Big Sur, and other California natural treasures are stunning in their dramatic beauty. The gallery represents other fine art photography as well as Native American crafts and jewelry, books, and other gift items.

Museums

Small in number but large in stature and charm, the art museums on the Peninsula include two museums operated by the city of Monterey.

Monterey Museum of Art Pacific Street
559 Pacific Street, Monterey
(831) 372-5477
www.montereyart.org
Once called "the best small-town museum in the United States," the Monterey Museum of Art Pacific Street offers a great collection of California art, photography, Asian art, and international folk art. Featured artists include painters Armin Hansen and William Ritschel and photographers Edward Weston and Ansel Adams. The museum's education department hosts a variety of classes and workshops. Admission to the museum is $5.00 for nonmembers. The Monterey Museum of Art Pacific Street is closed Monday and Tuesday.

Monterey Museum of Art La Mirada
720 Via Mirada, Monterey
(831) 372-3689
www.montereyart.org
At the Monterey Museum of Art La Mirada, the setting of the museum and grounds, across Fremont Street from Lake El Estero, is as spectacular as the art itself. Originally an elegant adobe home, it still features exquisite furnishings and spectacular gardens of roses and rhododendrons. The Dart Wing of the museum houses four contemporary galleries featuring a fine permanent collection, including folk and Asian art, and changing exhibitions. The Monterey Museum of Art La Mirada is closed Monday and Tuesday. Admission is $5.00 for nonmembers.

PERFORMING ARTS
Dance

World-renowned dancers of all genres periodically grace the stages of the Peninsula for special engagements, with Carmel's Sunset Center Theater the most likely venue for top-name stars. The bulk of the dance activity on the Peninsula, however, centers on local groups—both adult and children, professional and amateur—who study the art and provide entertaining performances for appreciative audiences. Call the Sunset Center Theatre, (831) 624-3996, or check the local entertainment calendars for the schedule of upcoming headliners. On the local dance scene, for both performances and instruction, check out these fine studios.

Carmel Ballet Academy
Mission Street and Eighth Avenue, Carmel
(831) 624-3729
www.carmelballetacademy.com
Since 1954 the Carmel Ballet Academy has been providing instruction and performances for generations of Peninsula families. The Academy provides instruction in ballet, jazz, tap, pointe, modern, hip-hop, drama, voice, and musical comedy for children as young as age three as well as adults. Dance and theater camps are held each winter, spring, summer, and

fall, and Carmel Ballet Academy performs an annual showcase each June.

Dance Kids Inc.
Mission Street and Eighth Avenue, Carmel
(831) 626–2980

Featuring ballet and other forms of dance, Dance Kids Inc. provides instruction for children as young as four years of age as well as for adults. In conjunction with the Carmel Ballet Academy it performs regular annual events, including a spring musical, a summer performing arts camp, and a winter presentation of *The Nutcracker.*

Monterey Peninsula Dance Inc.
71 Soledad Drive, Monterey
(831) 648–8725

This is the place in Monterey to learn a wide variety of dance steps, including ballroom, nightclub, country and western, waltz, fox trot, tango, rumba, cha cha, swing, samba, salsa, and disco. Youths, singles, and couples are welcome. Lessons are provided Monday through Friday, with a dance party held every Friday and Saturday night. Monterey Peninsula Dance Inc. is a member of the Imperial Society of Teachers of Dance.

Peninsula Ballet Center
568 Lighthouse Avenue, Pacific Grove
(831) 372–0388
www.balletfantastique.org

Kira Ivanovsky, formerly of Ballet Russe, and Milou Ivanovsky codirect the Peninsula Ballet Center out of the Pacific Grove Art Center in downtown Pacific Grove. Classes are offered for beginners through to professionals, from children age five to adults. The Center is home of Ballet Fantastique, a nonprofit dance company of professional, semiprofessional, and student dancers. Founded in 1974, it performs a repertoire of classical, ethnic, and interpretive dance, including *The Nutcracker,* spring gala performances, and summer ballet festivals.

LITERARY ARTS

As home to Robinson Jeffers, Robert Louis Stevenson, and other well-known writers, the Monterey Peninsula remains an active literary community. Poetry is in the limelight these days, but songwriters and spoken-word artists also share their craft at local coffeehouses, bookstores, and other small venues.

The best-known literary event in the area is Carmel's Poetry on the Beach, held on Carmel Beach at sunset on the last Saturday of every month, weather permitting. Take Scenic Drive to the beach at 13th Avenue and look for the bonfire. Feel free to bring along a poem or story as well as a blanket, a potluck dish to share, a bottle of wine, and some firewood.

Other spots to hear or share the spoken word include the following.

Borders Books Music & Cafe
2080 California Avenue, Sand City
(831) 899–6643
www.bordersstores.com

Borders bookstore and cafe presents poetry and literary readings, as well as musical and other events, most evenings. Call for the current schedule of events or drop by and pick up a free monthly calendar.

Juice and Java
599 Lighthouse Avenue, Pacific Grove
(831) 373–8652

Friday is open-mike night at Juice and Java in Pacific Grove. Poets, authors, and songwriters should sign up at 7:00 P.M. for the 7:30 P.M. presentation.

Sally Griffin Senior Center
700 Jewell Avenue, Pacific Grove
(831) 373–5602
www.sallygriffenseniorcenter.org

Seniors share their wit and wisdom at open poetry readings at the Sally Griffin Senior Center, home to Meals on Wheels in Pacific Grove. Open poetry readings are held the fourth Thursday of each month at 3:00 P.M.

Thunderbird Bookshop and Cafe
3600 The Barnyard, Carmel
(831) 624-1803
www.thunderbirdbooks.com
Readings, lectures, writing workshops, and book signings are almost a nightly event at this, the largest independent and family-owned bookstore and cafe on the Peninsula. Call for information or pick up a monthly calendar of events.

MUSIC

The Monterey Peninsula has long been noted for its exceptional music festivals, including the Monterey Jazz Festival (September), the Carmel Bach Festival (July and August), and the Monterey Bay Blues Festival (June). These events are included in our Annual Events chapter. In addition, the Peninsula offers a nice blend of professional and amateur music groups that provide performances across the Peninsula.

Carmel Music Society
Sunset Center Theatre, San Carlos Street and Ninth Avenue, Carmel
(831) 625-9938
www.carmelmusic.org
Each year, the Carmel Music Society presents a world-class series featuring top-flight artists from October through May. Internationally known pianists, vocalists, violinists, and ensembles perform classical compositions in concerts and competitions. Season tickets and individual performance tickets, when available, can be purchased.

Monterey Symphony
Sunset Center Theatre,
San Carlos Street and Ninth Avenue,
Carmel
(831) 624-8511
www.montereysymphony.org
Since its first performance in Carmel in 1947, Monterey Symphony has been providing a fully professional orchestra for locals and visitors alike. The symphony performs a series of seven concerts from October through May, performing at the Sunset Center Sunday afternoon at 3:00 P.M. and Monday night at 8:00 P.M. Tuesday night concerts are held at the Sherwood Hall in Salinas, 940 North Main Street. Kate Tamarkin is the symphony's 10th—and first woman—conductor. Single tickets may be purchased by phone.

Mozart Society of California
(831) 625-3637
The Mozart Society of California hosts a series of five concerts featuring the compositions of this brilliant Austrian composer. The concerts are held October through May at the Sunset Center Theatre in Carmel, at San Carlos Street and Ninth Avenue. The Mozart Society is an affiliate of the International Mozart Foundation in Salzburg, with members receiving season concert tickets, admission to lecture demonstrations, and other foundation benefits.

Youth Music Monterey
2911 Garden Road, Suite C-175, Monterey
(831) 375-1992
www.youthmusicmonterey.org
Youth Music Monterey offers performance opportunities through its Youth and Honors Orchestras, which hold formal and collaborative concerts with the Monterey County Symphony and the Santa Cruz County Youth Symphony. In addition, the South County Strings Program offers entry-level students in the Salinas Valley to train and perform on the violin, viola, and cello. Youth Music Monterey presents an annual playathon each December at Del Monte Center, collecting pledges from the community. Participating students audition for placement in an orchestra and participate in a fall weekend residential retreat.

THEATER

As with dance, the Monterey Peninsula theater scene is primarily made up of fairly modest productions by local, mainly amateur, performers. But that doesn't mean you are not likely to find high-quality dramas, comedies, and musicals by very talented actors, singers, and dancers. Many of the local theater groups have long-running traditions and pride themselves in bringing quality theater to the Peninsula. Check out the following theater groups for their schedule of performances.

Bruce Ariss Memorial Wharf Theater
Fisherman's Wharf, Monterey
(831) 372-1373
Not many visitors to Monterey are aware there is a theater right on Fisherman's Wharf. The Bruce Ariss Memorial Wharf Theater presents four shows a year, primarily musicals, with each show running anywhere from five to 10 weeks. This is primarily amateur theater that holds open auditions for each show. It's a great place for newcomers to break into the local theater scene.

California's First Theatre
Pacific Street and Scott Street, Monterey
(831) 375-4916
The oldest theater in the state of California still holds authentic melodramas and comedies from the 19th century. The Troupers of the Gold Coast (California's oldest continually performing theatrical company) stage performances each Friday and Saturday night from September through June and each Thursday through Saturday night from July through Labor Day Weekend. The curtain goes up at 8:00 P.M. You'll have a ball cheering the heroes and heroines and hissing the villains. *Note:* At press time, California's First Theatre was closed for renovation. Be sure to call the number above before making plans to attend.

CSUMB World Theater
100 Campus Center, Building 28, Seaside
(831) 582-4580
worldtheater.csumb.edu
The World Theater at California State University Monterey Bay is the most technologically sophisticated theater in the area. It was renovated from a historic 900-seat movie theater built more than 50 years ago for the soldiers stationed at the U.S. Army's Fort Ord. In the late 1990s the building was radically remodeled as a multiuse theater and opened in 1999 with a seating capacity of 450. It is used for theater, music, dance, and other functions sponsored by the university.

The Forest Theater Guild
Mountain View and Santa Rita Streets, Carmel
(831) 626-1681
www.foresttheaterguild.org
Chartered in 1949, the Forest Theater Guild provides community theater and films in Carmel's historic Outdoor Forest Theater. The Guild welcomes participation by all interested parties and is dedicated to providing quality theater at affordable prices. The Forest Theater Guild productions, which include classics, comedies, and musicals, are held outdoors during summer nights. Locals often show up well before the performance starts with a picnic dinner, wine, hot coffee, and plenty of warm coats and blankets. It's a local tradition and one any Insider shouldn't miss.

Magic Circle Center
8 El Camino Road, Carmel Valley
(831) 659-1108
www.magiccirclecenter.com
This small theater company debuted in 1994 and has been pleasing local audiences with its contemporary and thought-provoking plays ever since. A children's theater group has been recently added, and musical events are now also held at the Magic Circle Center's Carmel Valley Village location.

Monterey Peninsula College Theatre Company
980 Fremont Street, Monterey
(831) 646-4213
www.mpc.edu

MPC, the Peninsula's community college, has a solid reputation for its drama department and fine theater presentations. Drama, comedy, and musicals are presented in its 350-seat main house and 50-seat studio, and in the Carl Cherry Center for the Arts in Carmel. The works of O. Henry, Neil Simon, Arthur Miller, Cole Porter, and Shakespeare have recently graced the stage.

Pacific Repertory Theatre
Golden Bough Playhouse, Circle Theater, Monte Verde Street and Ninth Avenue, Carmel
(831) 622-0100
www.pacrep.org
Founded in 1982, Pacific Repertory Theatre presents its annual Great Play Series of productions and participates in community outreach programs such as the free Monterey Bay TheatreFest, a summer weekend series at Monterey's Custom Plaza. Pacific Repertory Theatre also holds The Carmel Shakespeare Festival, with performances held from August through October at Carmel's Outdoor Forest Theater. In 1994 the group purchased the historic Golden Bough Playhouse in Carmel and has renovated it into a fine two-venue theater. Performances are held in the 305-seat Golden Bough and the 99-seat Circle Theatre year-round.

Staff Players Repertory Company
Mountain View and Santa Rita Streets, Carmel
(831) 624-1531
www.cetstaffplayers.org
Founded in 1969, Staff Players Repertory Company is the oldest continually producing theater company in Carmel. It produces both ancient and modern theater classics. The repertory company is a major supporter of the Children's Experimental Theatre, a local training program for kids ages six through 18. The Staff Players and the Children's Experimental Theatre perform at the Indoor Forest Theatre, Santa Rita and Mountain View Streets, in Carmel.

Unicorn Theatre
320 Hoffman Avenue, Monterey
(831) 649-0259
www.unicorntheatreinc.org
One of the most active theaters on the Peninsula, the Unicorn Theatre presents a wide range of performances for all ages. Children delight in the afternoon presentations, while adults can enjoy contemporary plays and the classics evenings at 8:00 P.M. (7:00 P.M. Sunday). Then there are the late-night performances that often feature the unusual, the sensual, or the macabre.

SUPPORT ORGANIZATIONS

The arts are widely supported by Peninsula residents, who volunteer their time and provide financial assistance to promote the many creative endeavors they enjoy. The artists, gallery owners, and others within their own community also volunteer much time and effort to promote their avocations. Below are a few of the local organizations that help keep the arts alive on the Peninsula.

Carmel Art Association
Dolores Street and Fifth Avenue, Carmel
(831) 624-6176
www.carmelart.org
Started in 1927 by a group of local artists, the Carmel Art Association is still an active and vibrant force in the community. Members have included such dignitaries as Armin Hansen, William Ritschel, Arthur Hill Gilbert, Paul Dougherty, Francis McComas, and John O'Shea. Made up of several gallery rooms exhibiting the works of some of the more than 120 artist members, the Carmel Art Association deserves a spot on your gallery tours. Exhibits change monthly, and lectures, demonstrations, and openings are often open to the public. Call for details about special programs.

Carmel Gallery Alliance
(831) 642-2503
www.carmelartfestival.com
A standing committee of the Carmel Business Association, this alliance of Carmel art galleries works to showcase the art of member galleries and to perpetuate the city's long-standing tradition as a fine arts village. Each spring the nonprofit organization hosts the Carmel Art Festival. The Carmel Gallery Alliance also publishes a great gallery guide, *Art In Carmel*, that profiles its members.

Center for Photographic Art
Sunset Center, San Carlos Street and Ninth Avenue, Carmel
(831) 625-5181
www.photoctr.mbaynet.com
As a California nonprofit public benefit corporation, the Center for Photographic Art encourages an awareness and appreciation of photography as a fine art form. Supported by memberships, grants, and gifts, the center provides an ongoing program of exhibitions (six to eight annually) and workshops featuring the works of both established and new photographers. The center is closed on Monday.

Cultural Council for Monterey County
(831) 622-9060
www.culturalmonterey.org
Founded in 1982, the Cultural Council for Monterey County promotes and financially supports education, appreciation, and excellence in the arts. As the county's partner with the California Arts Council, CCMC is a networking organization for the many cultural entities of Monterey County.

Monterey Jazz Festival
2000 Fairgrounds Road, Monterey
(831) 373-3366
www.montereyjazzfestival.org
There's more to the Monterey Jazz Festival than the world-famous Monterey Jazz Festival event held each September. It is a major supporter of music education throughout Monterey County and the state of California. Over the years it has raised more than $2 million for music education through scholarships, the California High School Jazz Competition (held each April and free of charge to attend), and the Jazz Education Fund. This unique fund pays for music instruments, sheet music, and clinician training for Monterey County Middle and High School jazz bands. The festival also funds a tour of Japan by the California High School All Star Jazz Band.

PARKS AND RECREATION

The natural beauty of the Monterey Bay, our pine forests, clean air, and nearly perfect weather provide the ideal setting for all types of recreation. Walking, biking, in-line skating, camping, and hiking top the list of favorite activities for both locals and visitors.

The number of parks in our area is impressive. We've listed a few of the city, county, state, and regional parks to get you started, but don't hesitate to stop at any one of our open spaces to enjoy gorgeous views of the Bay, the rocky coastline, or our magnificent forests.

In most cases, turnout areas are available at scenic spots for parking. Always use these areas rather than park illegally. Parking laws are strictly enforced, and the fines can be hefty.

Some useful recreation-oriented phone numbers are highlighted in the Close-up in this chapter. These numbers are invaluable to those who have specific questions or want more information.

Several recreational opportunities are covered in depth in other chapters of this book. See our In and Around the Water chapter for diving, fishing, beaches, and all other water-related activities. The Peninsula's many golf courses, some of which are world-famous, are written up in our Golf chapter. You'll find bicycle and surrey rentals in the chapter called Getting Here, Getting Around.

CITY PARKS

Monterey

www.monterey.org

El Estero Park Complex
Camino El Estero, Monterey
(831) 646-3866

The complex is a 45-acre park in the center of Monterey. It incorporates Lake El Estero, a popular place for fishing, paddleboating, picnicking on the lawn, and feeding ducks. You can circle around the entire lake, a pleasant moderate walk, by following the designated path. El Estero Park is the site of an imaginative play area, Dennis the Menace children's playground, designed with the help of Hank Ketcham, creator of the popular comic strip. There is also a youth center, a multiuse field with a lighted baseball diamond, a skate park, a dance studio, and a boating concession with pedal-powered paddle boats. The park has areas for group barbecue picnics, a 17-station fitness course, and restrooms. There is no entrance fee for admission, but you need to call ahead to reserve the group areas. With the exception of the ball field, park hours are from dawn to dusk daily.

Fisherman's Shoreline Park
Cannery Row, Monterey
(831) 646-3866

This five-acre coastline park borders the recreation trail and has a grassy lawn and seating areas with Bay views. The park is between Fisherman's Wharf and the Coast Guard pier. There is no entrance fee. The park is open every day from dawn to dusk.

Hilltop Park and Hilltop Park Center
Jessie Street and David Avenue, Monterey
(831) 646-3975

This 2.8-acre neighborhood park has a grassy area, a picnic area with barbecues, play equipment, a tennis court, a basketball court, baseball backstop, and a multipurpose facility. There is no entrance fee, and the park is open from dawn to dusk every day.

San Carlos Beach Park
Cannery Row, Monterey
(831) 646-3866

This 2.87-acre coastline park at the foot of Reeside Avenue has a landscaped grassy lawn, paved walkways, beach access, outdoor showers for divers, and restrooms. Seating areas provide close-up views of Monterey Bay. In-line or roller skates and skateboards are not allowed. There is no entrance fee, and the park is open every day during daylight hours.

Veterans Memorial Park
Jefferson Street and Skyline Drive, Monterey
(831) 646-3865

This 50-acre city park offers 40 sites for RV and group camping, hiking trails, picnic areas, restrooms, and playing fields. Camping sites are around $15 per night. The sites have no hookups and are available on a first-come, first-served basis. Group picnic areas can be reserved in advance. The park also provides access to the Huckleberry Hill Nature Preserve, an 81-acre park with numerous, well-established hiking trails that offer wonderful bay views.

Pacific Grove

www.pacificgroverecreation.org

Berwick Park
Ocean View Boulevard, Pacific Grove
(831) 648-3130

This one-acre park between Ninth Street and Carmel Avenue on the coastal side of Ocean Avenue Boulevard offers a well-manicured lawn, the perfect spot to enjoy superb views of Monterey Bay and the surrounding coastline. This park is a popular place for outdoor weddings. There is no entrance fee, but use permits begin at around $25, depending on the size of the group. The park is open every day from dawn to dusk.

Caledonia Park
Caledonia Street, Pacific Grove
(831) 648-3130

This open space, located on the corner of Central and Caledonia Streets, contains a children's play area, baseball field, basketball court, climbing equipment, and picnic tables. There is no entrance fee, but group use permit fees start at $25. The park is open every day during daylight hours.

George Washington Park
Sinex Street, Pacific Grove
(831) 648-3130

This six-block, forested park, the largest in Pacific Grove, is at the corner of Sinex and Alder Streets. Most of the park is left in a natural state on unimproved forest land that provides a habitat for wildlife. Monarch butterflies reside here from October to March. The park has a full-size baseball field, picnic tables, barbecue grills, a play area, and restrooms. There is no entrance fee; however, a use permit is required for large groups (the minimum group fee is $25). The park is open every day during daylight hours.

Jewell Park
Central Avenue, Pacific Grove
(831) 648-3130

Jewell Park, located at the corner of Central and Forest Avenues, is next to the library and across from the natural history museum. A nice lawn area makes it an ideal place to bring young children. The park has a small meeting room with a kitchen and a gazebo that is sheltered by trees. A fee and a use permit are required for the gazebo. The "Little House" meeting room has a rental fee, and a use permit is required. Use permits start at $25 depending upon the size of the group. There is no entrance fee, but you must apply in person at the Pacific Grove Recreation Department (515 Junipero Street) to reserve either the gazebo or the meeting room. The park is open every day from dawn to dusk.

Lovers Point Park
Ocean View Boulevard, Pacific Grove
(831) 648-3130

This beautiful oceanside, landscaped park

is at the foot of 17th Street. The park's amenities include a large green lawn area, a sand volleyball court, a toddler's swimming pool, two small sandy beaches, rocky outcrops, a concrete pier structure, a snack bar, and restrooms. The park is a popular place for family gatherings, picnics, fishing, sunning, swimming, watersports, diving, and surfing. There is no entrance fee, but you must obtain a permit for weddings or large group gatherings. Use fees vary according to group size; the minimum fee is $25. Daylight hours are observed, and the park is open every day.

Monarch Butterfly Sanctuary
Grove Acre, Pacific Grove
(831) 373-7047
This park, between Short Street and Lighthouse Avenue, was purchased by the city of Pacific Grove in 1992. It is protected as an open space and butterfly habitat and is one of the original winter locations for the beautiful monarch butterfly. Docent-led tours are available by appointment. The park has no entrance fee and is open daily from dawn to dusk (see our Attractions chapter for more detailed information).

Carmel

www.carmelcityhall.com

Mission Trail Park
Rio Road, Carmel
(831) 624-3543
Park visitors can follow in the footsteps of Father Junipero Serra and the Indians on the same trail they used when traveling from the mission to Monterey. Three main trails form a walking loop around the park. The terrain, with a stream in the winter months and a few hills, is a fairly easy walk. Benches are set up along the way where one can sit and admire the variety of trees such as willow, oak, pine, and eucalyptus. In spring California poppies, lupine, honeysuckle, and other colorful flowers are in full bloom.

Within the park is the Rowntree Arboretum, a native garden worth exploring. Lester Rowntree started a career as an independent naturalist at the age of 53. She (yes, she) delighted in harvesting seeds from native plants and began planting them in this garden setting. The plants in the arboretum are at their peak of beauty in spring. To reach the arboretum, take the Doolittle trail. The park entrance is on Rio Road across from the mission. There is no fee, and the park is open every day during daylight hours.

COUNTY PARKS

www.co.monterey.ca/parks

Jacks Peak County Park
25020 Jacks Peak Park Road, Monterey
(831) 484-1108
Located off Highway 68, this 525-acre mountain-top park is a natural reserve offering more than 10 miles of hiking and equestrian trails through cathedral-like pine and oak forests to breathtaking ridge-top vistas of the Monterey Peninsula. The Skyline Self-Guided Nature Trail has vistas of Carmel and Point Lobos. The park has restrooms, picnic areas, barbecues, and a group site that can accommodate up to 50 people. A paved road goes almost to the top of Jacks Peak. At 1,068 feet, the peak is the highest point on the Monterey Peninsula. There is a nominal fee for cars entering the park. Free parking is also available just outside the gates with an easy walk to the trailheads. Park hours are from 10:30 A.M. to 6:30 P.M. daily.

Laguna Seca Recreation Area
1025 Monterey-Salinas Highway, Monterey
(831) 484-1108
This county recreation area has more than 180 campsites for RVs or tents. There are hiking trails, bike trails, picnic areas, restrooms, and areas to watch wildlife. Laguna Seca is the home of the Mazda Raceway Laguna Seca, which hosts frequent automotive and motorcycle races. There is

also an outdoor amphitheater for music concerts and a rifle/pistol shooting range. For information about the shooting range, call (831) 757-6317.

Toro Park
501 Monterey-Salinas Highway, Salinas
(831) 647-7799

Off the Monterey-Salinas Highway just 13 miles east of Monterey, Toro Park is a pastoral setting with more than 20 miles of well-maintained hiking trails. It's an expansive site with 4,756 acres of rolling grassland, wooded canyons, and hills rising to 2,000 feet. From March to May the area is filled with wildflowers. The park has playgrounds, softball fields, a volleyball court, horseshoe pits, and restrooms. Several picnic areas suitable for large groups have barbecue pits, tables, electrical outlets, and water. To reserve the group area, call (888) 588-2267. A map can be obtained at the entrance to the park and should be used when hiking. Bring your own drinking water when hiking, as there are no safe sources of water. Parking is free, but there is a small entrance fee to the park. The park is open every day from 8:00 A.M. to 7:00 P.M.

MONTEREY PENINSULA REGIONAL PARK DISTRICT

www.mprpd.org

Frog Pond Wetland Preserve
Canyon Del Rey Road, Del Rey Oaks
(831) 659-4488

This 16.88-acre nature reserve is off Canyon Del Rey across from the Via Verde intersection. A seasonal freshwater marsh, acquired by the Monterey Peninsula Regional Park District in 1977, provides a habitat for the rare Pacific tree frog and is also a wetland habitat, perfect for birdwatching. A short trail passes through willow, oak, and redwood trees as it circles the property. Free parking is available across from the entrance to the park at City Hall, where you can pick up a brochure. Numbered posts in the reserve correspond with descriptions found in the brochure. There is no entrance fee, and the park is open every day from dawn to dusk.

Garland Ranch Regional Park
700 West Carmel Valley Road,
Carmel Valley
(831) 659-4488

Miles of hiking and equestrian trails are the focal point of this 4,462-acre park that rises from the Carmel River to the slopes of the Santa Lucia Mountains. Viewing wildlife, hiking, horseback riding, walking, and nature study are among the popular activities at Garland Park. The park has picnic areas and restrooms. You can call ahead to arrange ranger-guided walks and lectures. Information on the species of birds, mammals, and plants found in the park is available at the visitor center located at the entrance of the park. The park is open every day from early morning to sunset. There is no entrance fee.

Laguna Grande Community Park
Canyon Del Rey Boulevard, Seaside
(831) 899-6236

This 34-acre park is at the corner of Canyon Del Rey Road and Del Monte Avenue. The park, surrounding a freshwater marsh and lake, borders the cities of Seaside and Monterey. It features two picnic areas, bicycling and pedestrian paths, and two children's playgrounds. On Sunday in the summer months, free jazz concerts are held on the hillside area. A picturesque Russian Orthodox Church sits between the two picnic areas. The park has no entrance fee and is open every day during daylight hours.

STATE PARKS

www.parks.ca.gov

Asilomar State Beach
800 Asilomar Avenue, Pacific Grove
(831) 372-4076

This beach park is at the border of Pacific Grove and Pebble Beach overlooking the ocean. The name Asilomar means "refuge by the sea" and was chosen by the YWCA, which founded the retreat in 1913. It's a beautiful park with fishing, surfing, wildlife viewing, food service, lodging, picnic areas, exhibits and programs, and hiking trails that provide wheelchair access. There are several historical buildings, sand dunes, the Pacific shoreline, and a Monterey pine forest filled with wildlife. Park rangers are available to lead cultural and natural history walks, but you must call ahead to schedule.

The Asilomar Conference Grounds offer a full-service facility of year-round meeting rooms, overnight lodging, dining, and a park store. Adjacent to the conference grounds is the dune boardwalk, which meanders through a restored sand-dune area. The boardwalk follows a self-guided nature walk where visitors can learn more about this unique ecosystem.

If you feel inclined to take a walk on the beach, there are several choice spots. A long strip of unbroken beach, which meets a rocky shoreline sheltering several sandy coves, is perfect for exploring. You'll often see harbor seals, California sea lions, and sea otters swimming offshore. There is no entrance fee. The beach is open every day from dawn to dusk.

Garrapata State Park
Highway 1, Carmel
(831) 624-4909

This 2,879-acre park with 4 miles of coastline is about 10 miles south of Carmel. Parking is available in one of several highway turnouts near Soberanes Point. The undeveloped park has no entrance signs or exclusive parking areas. Hiking trails are diverse and include trails to ocean beaches, a steep ascent to a hilltop with amazing views of Pacific horizons, and trails through cacti and dense redwood groves.

Monterey State Historical Park
Visitor Center in the Stanton Center, Monterey
(831) 649-7118

The starting place for guided tours of the park is the visitor center, where a free history film is shown every 20 minutes or so. Pick up a brochure for the walking tour, which guides you to Monterey's adobes, historic sites, and unique gardens. The visitor center is open daily. Guided tours are available for a nominal fee (see the Monterey Path of History write-up in our Attractions chapter for more information).

The day-use pass for California State Parks is good that same day for entrance to other California State Parks with the same or lower day-use fee. Visit www.parks.ca.gov for a list of parks and fees.

Point Lobos State Reserve
Highway 1, Carmel
(831) 624-4909

Some of the Peninsula's most dramatic, scenic, and memorable ocean panoramas are located at Point Lobos. This 1,200-acre reserve, located 3 miles south of Carmel, features 7 miles of hiking on 14 intersecting trails that meander through pine forests and spectacular coastal scenery. The reserve is a popular spot for scuba diving (by reservation only) and viewing wildlife, such as sea otters, harbor seals, sea lions, pelicans, and gulls. Picnic areas and restrooms are available. The reserve offers guided tours, exhibits, and programs. The entrance fee is under $10 and provides same-day entrance to other area state parks. The reserve is open every day from 9:00 A.M. to 7:00 P.M. (5:00 P.M. during the winter months).

NATIONAL PARKS

Los Padres National Forest
Forest Headquarters
6755 Hollister Avenue, Suite 150, Goleta
(805) 968-6640
www.fs.fed.us/r5/lospadres

The Monterey Ranger District of the Los

Asilomar State Beach in Pacific Grove affords a leisurely walk along the dune boardwalk and is one of the Peninsula's most treasured sunset viewing spots. MICHAEL CHATFIELD

Padres National Forest, the rugged northern part of the Santa Lucia Mountains, extends south from Carmel Valley to the northern part of San Luis Obispo County near San Simeon. On the east its boundary is the Salinas Valley and to the west, the Pacific Ocean.

At its highest point, 5,000 feet, a coastal ridge plunges dramatically to the rocky shore below. The mountains are rugged with narrow coastal canyons, picturesque cliffs, and waterfalls. The upper ridges of the mountains are mostly covered with brush and can be accessed only where trails have been cut through the undergrowth. Hiking in the park is advisable only for the experienced hiker, due to the rigorous wilderness conditions.

Those who do visit will notice a wide range of plant life. Flowers found in the woods tend to be less noticeable, while the fields showcase golden California poppies, deep pink owl's clover, Johnny jump-ups, shooting stars, blue hound's tongue, and Douglas' iris. Redwood canyons harbor a wide variety of ferns and shade-loving plants such as woodwardia, maidenhair, and five-finger ferns. You will also see wood sorrel, huckleberry, and wood rose.

Redwoods, tanbark oak, red and white alder, big-leaf maple, and several varieties of willow are scattered throughout the low areas. Higher up, you'll find coast live oak, black oak, interior live oak, and pines such as Coulter, ponderosa, and sugar. Chaparral, an impenetrable brush, is found throughout the forest, forming fragrant flowering shrubs that bloom throughout the year.

An abundance of wildlife allows hikers and campers to observe a full spectrum of birds and animals. Predators such as mountain lion, coyote, and bobcat present little problem to hikers. Raccoons, known as camp bandits, can be a problem for campers who leave their food supplies out in the open. Wild pigs are sometimes seen, but unless they're wounded or cornered, they mostly avoid humans. The most familiar birds in the forest are hawks, eagles, turkey vultures, and a wide variety of owls. The Ventana Wilderness Sanctuary programs include the California Condor Recovery Program and the monitoring of bald eagle territories.

The Monterey Ranger District encompasses more than 300,000 acres. More than 200,000 acres make up the Ventana Wilderness, and more than 14,000 acres comprise the Silver Peak Wilderness. Hikers must check with the Forest Service, (831) 385-5434, for prevailing conditions such as weather, fire, landslides, and vegetation growths when planning hikes or camping trips.

For those interested, the Ventana Chapter of the Sierra Club has published the Trail Guide to Los Padres National Forest for the Monterey Ranger District; the book offers guidelines and information to both the Ventana and Silver Peak Wilderness areas. The book is available at the Sierra Club Office and Bookstore, located in Carmel on the south side of Ocean Avenue between San Carlos and Dolores Streets, on the second floor. Bookstore hours are 12:30 to 4:30 P.M., Monday to Saturday. Put on your hiking boots and make the ascent! For more information call (831) 624-8032.

A campfire permit is required (at no charge). An Adventure Pass is required to gain entrance to the park. The passes can be purchased by mail from Los Padres National Forest, 6755 Hollister Avenue, Suite 150, Goleta, CA 93117. Passes can also be purchased at the following locations:

Big 5
1300 Del Monte Shopping Center, Monterey
(831) 375-8800

Big 5
1000 Northridge Shopping Center, Salinas
(831) 449-6768

Big Sur Multi-Agency Facility
Big Sur Station #1, Big Sur
(831) 667-2315

Forest Service Monterey Ranger District
406 South Milred, King City
(831) 385-5434

Lynn's Liquors
601 Broadway, King City
(831) 385-6715

Zen Mountain Center
39171 Tassajara Road, Carmel Valley
(831) 659-9961

Adventure Passes are $5.00 per visit or $30.00 for an annual pass.

RECREATION CENTERS

Monterey Sports Center
301 Franklin Street, Monterey
(831) 646-3700
www.monterey.org/sportscenter
The Monterey Sports Center, a beautiful, modern, and incredibly well-equipped facility operated by the City of Monterey, is located at the corner of Washington and Franklin Streets in downtown Monterey. The Sports Center is the largest, most comprehensive family fitness facility on the Monterey Peninsula. It features two heated indoor pools (one with a 112-foot water slide), two group exercise studios, weight training and cardio fitness centers, a three-court gym, therapeutic/assessment center, men's and women's locker rooms with showers, sun deck, and the Sports Café and Pro Shop. They offer personal training, towel service, and Kids Zone, an on-site babysitting service for children ages six months to eight years. The Sports Center is open every day and can be rented for birthday parties, corporate

meetings, or other special events. Current day use fees are $5.00 for Monterey residents and $6.00 for nonresidents. Call or visit the Web site for more information.

Patullo Swim Center
1148 Wheeler Street, Seaside
(831) 899-6272
bbs.ci.seaside.ca.us/patulloswim

To reach the swim center, follow Fremont Street north to Kimball Street. Turn right on Kimball then left on Wheeler, and you'll see the swim center on the right. The center offers adult lap swims, water aerobics, senior swims, and recreation swims as well as adult and youth lessons. The center is open daily from early morning until late in the evening. Prices range from $2.50 (nonresidents) for lap swims to $37.50 for a 25-visit swim card. Fees for residents are lower. Some recreational and senior swims are free. Schedules vary so call or visit the Web site for current information.

BASEBALL/SOFTBALL

Cages
414 Adams Street, Monterey
(831) 375-1800
www.cagesindoorbatting.com

Cages, located in downtown Monterey across from the Sports Center, is the only indoor batting center on the Central Coast that uses state-of-the-art pitching

If you're age 62 or older, you can purchase a Golden Age Passport for $10. The Passport provides free admission— for a lifetime!—to National Parks, National Wildlife Refuges, and Forest Service and Bureau of Land Management sites that charge entrance fees. Passports are available at all Forest Service Offices. A Golden Eagle Passport, $65 for one year from date of purchase, is available for those under age 62.

and retrieval equipment. Each cage allows the batter to choose the type of ball and the height and speed of the pitch. Batters as young as age five are welcome. In addition to batting, you'll find video games, pool tables, and air hockey as well as homemade pizza and beverages. Parties and special events can be arranged. They sell a large selection of bats, shoes, gloves, and other equipment for baseball, softball, and T-ball. They have summer and winter hours, and the fees vary by activity, so it's best to call or visit the Web site for the most current information. Multiuse passes are also available.

Frank E. Sollecito Jr. Ballpark
Camino El Estero, Monterey
(831) 646-3969
www.monterey.org

Although a multiuse field, the ballpark has a standard baseball diamond with night lighting, bleachers, and restrooms. The field is used for adult and kid leagues so call ahead for availability. Picnic kits are available from the Monterey Recreation Department, 546 Dutra Street. A kit contains recreational equipment including baseballs, bats, etc. Rental costs vary. For reservations, call (831) 646-3969.

Jack's Ballpark
Franklin Street at Figueroa Street, Monterey
(831) 646-3969
www.monterey.org

This 3.7-acre multiuse municipal sports park is at Franklin and Figueroa Streets in downtown Monterey. It has a ball field with night lighting and bleachers, a play area with a sand pit and climbing structures, and restrooms. The field is used for adult and kid leagues; call the ballpark for specific scheduling. Picnic kits, including baseball, bats, and other related equipment, are available from the Monterey Recreation Department, 546 Dutra Street. The kits rent for $25 for Monterey residents, $33 for all others, and can be reserved by calling (831) 646-3969.

Pacific Grove Municipal Ballpark
17-Mile Drive, Pacific Grove
(831) 648-3130
www.93950.com

The ballpark is located at the corner of 17-Mile Drive and Pico Street. The park is used for adult softball/soccer/slow-pitch leagues, pony baseball/softball, and high school softball. Permits are required for use of the ballpark and may be obtained at the Pacific Grove Recreation Department, 515 Junipero Avenue. Permit prices depend on the number of people attending the event. For a fee of around $20, you can rent a kit containing recreational equipment including baseballs, bats, bases, etc. Reservations are necessary, so call the Pacific Grove Recreation Department at the number above to schedule a field or to reserve a kit.

BASKETBALL

Public courts are available throughout the Peninsula. For more information see the listings for Caledonia, Hilltop, and Veterans Memorial parks in the "City Parks" section of this chapter. Picnic kits, available from the Monterey Recreation Department, 546 Dutra Street, contain recreational equipment including basketballs. The kit rental fees are $25 for Monterey residents and $33 for nonresidents. Reserve a kit by calling (831) 646-3969.

Picnic kits are also available from the Pacific Grove Recreation Department at 515 Junipero Avenue, (831) 648-5730. A $20 fee covers the rental cost of a kit containing recreational equipment including basketballs.

BOWLING

Monterey Lanes
2161 North Fremont Street, Monterey
(831) 373-1553

The bowling alley has 24 lanes. Open daily. Call for hours. Leagues play evenings Monday through Friday so the facility is not open to the public during that time.

Check out www.reserveamerica.com for online campsite reservations at state parks including Julia Pfeiffer Burns State Park and Pfeiffer Big Sur State Park. Both are a short, scenic drive from the Monterey Peninsula.

CAMPING

In addition to the Laguna Seca Recreation Area (see our listing in the County Parks section of this chapter), there are two state parks and one National Forest near the Peninsula where camping is permitted. Reservations for campsites are always necessary in California, especially during the spring and summer months. (A few campgrounds are available only on a first-come, first-served basis.)

Julia Pfeiffer Burns State Park
Highway 1, Big Sur
(831) 667-2315
www.parks.ca.gov

This state park is 37 miles south of Carmel and encompasses nearly 4,000 acres stretching from the Pacific coastline to the 5,682-foot Junipero Serra Peak, the highest point in the Santa Lucia range. An environmental camp has a hike-in distance of ¼ mile. No drinking water is available. Two cypress-shaded campsites accommodate up to eight people. You must register at the Pfeiffer Big Sur Station. Dramatic coastal vistas and the only major coastal California waterfall, McWay Falls, which tumbles into the Pacific Ocean, are two highlights of this camp area. No dogs are allowed at the environmental camp.

Los Padres National Forest
406 Mildred Avenue, King City
(831) 385-5434

The Monterey Ranger District of the Los Padres National Forest, the rugged northern part of the Santa Lucia Mountains, extends south from Carmel Valley to the northern part of San Luis Obispo County near San Simeon. On the east its boundary is the Salinas Valley and to the west, the Pacific Ocean.

Most of the developed campgrounds on the Monterey Ranger District are open year-round. Family units are all on a first-come, first-served basis. Each campsite has a table and stove, and the camp-ground has restrooms and potable water. Although designed for tent camping, some of the units can accommodate recreational vehicles (self-contained) up to 30 feet long. There are no hookups or electricity. Camping within the camp-ground is limited to a maximum of eight people and two vehicles per group. See our "National Parks" section in this chap-ter for reservation information. There are nine developed campgrounds in the Los Padres National Forest, three of which are fairly close to the Monterey Peninsula.

Botchers Gap is 8 miles east of High-way 1 on Palo Colorado Road. The intersec-tion of Highway 1 and Palo Colorado Road is approximately 15 miles north of Big Sur and 11 miles south of Carmel. The camp-ground, at an elevation of 2,100 feet, is sit-uated among oaks and madrone, featuring an excellent view of the Ventana Double Cones in the Santa Lucia Mountains. There is trailhead parking for the Ventana Wilder-ness. The campground has 11 units with no water. The fee is around $10 per day.

China Camp and White Oaks Camp-grounds are along the unsurfaced Jamesburg-Tassajara Road. Access is by Cachagua Road off Carmel Valley Road, approximately 23 miles from the junction of Carmel Valley Road and Highway 1. China Camp is a departure point for the Ventana Wilderness. The road is not rec-ommended for trailers during winter. China Camp sits at an elevation of 4,500 feet and has only six units. White Oaks is at 4,000 feet and has seven units. Neither camp-ground has potable water at this time.

Pfeiffer Big Sur State Park
Highway 1, Big Sur
(831) 667-2315
This 218-site campground, 31 miles from Carmel, is open year-round. Established in 1933, the park offers hikes through red-wood canyons as well as glorious views of the Big Sur coastline. Amenities include restrooms, hot showers, laundry facilities, and a camp store. The park is open to trail-ers (maximum length of 27 feet) and motor homes (maximum length of 32 feet). Rates range from $12 to $26 depending on time of year, site size, and location.

CLIMBING

Sanctuary Rock Gym
1855-A East Avenue, Sand City
(831) 899-2595
www.rockgym.com
For a different kind of workout, visit Mon-terey County's first rock-climbing gym. The gym contains more than 6,000 square feet of molded, sculpted terrain with extensive bouldering that provides a challenge and also includes a padded floor to protect against injury. Classes and lessons are offered. Monthly and annual memberships as well as day-use passes and a variety of punch-card options are also available. A full rental package con-taining shoes, a harness, and a chalk bag rents for under $10. Call or visit the Web site for hours and costs.

CYCLING, RUNNING, WALKING

Don Dahvee Greenbelt
Munras Avenue, Monterey
This greenbelt is a 35.8-acre recreation area that lies adjacent to Munras Avenue in Monterey between El Dorado Street and Del Monte Shopping Center. There are miles of trails to explore and tables for picnic lunches. The park is open daily from dawn to dusk, and there's no entrance fee.

Monterey Peninsula Recreation Trail
The Recreation Trail is an 18-mile ocean-front linear park system that expands from Pacific Grove to Castroville. The trail, laid

Walking, cycling, in-line skating, and running along the Monterey Peninsula Recreation Trail combines exercise with a serious view. MICHAEL CHATFIELD

out along the water's edge, is a popular place to bike, walk, and in-line skate. It passes Lovers Point, the Aquarium, Cannery Row, and Fisherman's Wharf. The trail is always open and is free to the public.

HIKING

Don Dahvee Greenbelt
Munras Avenue, Monterey
This 35.8-acre recreation area lies adjacent to Munras Avenue, between El Dorado Street and Del Monte Shopping Center. Hike miles of trails. Picnic tables are available. The park is free and open daily from dusk to dawn.

Garland Ranch Regional Park
700 West Carmel Valley Road, Carmel Valley
(831) 659-4488

Varied hiking trails are the focal point of this 4,462-acre park, which rises from the Carmel River to the slopes of the Santa Lucia Range. Amenities include picnic areas and restrooms. Call ahead to arrange ranger-guided walks or ask for information at the visitor center, which is at the park's entrance. Garland Park has no entrance fee and is open every day from 8:30 A.M. to sunset.

Point Lobos State Park
Highway 1, Carmel
(831) 624-4909
www.parks.ca.gov
Point Lobos, a 1,200-acre reserve 3 miles south of Rio Road on Highway 1, Carmel, is a spectacular area to hike. It has 7 miles of hiking on 14 intersecting trails that meander through pine forests and spectacular coastal scenery. A map of the specific trails is given to you when you pay the entrance

fee to the park. The entrance fee is under $10 and provides same-day entrance to other area state parks. The reserve is open daily from 9:00 A.M. to 7:00 P.M. It closes at 5:00 P.M. during winter months.

Toro Park
501 Monterey-Salinas Highway, Salinas
(831) 647-7799
Toro Park, just off the Monterey-Salinas Highway 13 miles east of Monterey, includes more than 20 miles of well-maintained hiking trails. There's something for everyone here—trails vary in level of challenge, terrain, and views. A map is provided at the entrance to the park and should be used when hiking. Don't forget to bring your own drinking water as there are no safe sources of water out on the trails. The park is open every day from 8:00 A.M. to 7:00 P.M. See the Toro Park listing under "County Parks" in this chapter for more information on other features of this Monterey County gem.

HORSEBACK RIDING

Molera Horseback Tours
Andrew Molera State Park
(800) 942-5486
www.molerahorsebacktours.com
Located 22 miles south of Carmel on Highway 1, Andrew Molera State Park includes 4,800 varied acres that feature secluded beaches, flower-filled meadows, pristine streams and magnificent redwood groves. Certified guides share intriguing stories of Big Sur's history, native plants, and indigenous animals. A variety of rides are available, and all include the beach. Reservations are suggested, but walk-ins are welcome based on availability. Riders must be at least six years old and less than 250 pounds. Call or visit the Web site for information on hours, rides, and prices.

Monterey Bay Equestrian Center
19805 Pesante Road, Salinas
(831) 663-5712
www.montereybayequestrian.com

Parks and Recreation Departments

Carmel Recreation Department
San Carlos between Eighth and Ninth, Carmel, (831) 626-1255

City of Monterey Recreation and Community Services Department
546 Dutra Street, Monterey
(831) 646-3866

Monterey Parks Division Office
23 Ryan Ranch Road, Monterey
(831) 646-3860

Monterey County Parks Department
P.O. Box 5249, Salinas
(831) 755-4899 (reservations),
(888) 588-2267 (toll free)

Pacific Grove Recreation Department
515 Junipero Avenue, Pacific Grove
(831) 648-3130

Seaside Recreation Department
896 Hilby Street, Seaside
(831) 899-6800

State Parks & Recreation Department
District Office, 2211 Garden Road, Monterey, (831) 649-2836

Monterey Bay Equestrian Center offers individually tailored rides along the Monterey Bay, through wooded hills, and other settings, all by advance reservations only—at least 24 hours. They bring the horses to the trail for groups as small as two; single riders are matched with existing rides. They also offer horseback riding lessons, ponies for private parties, and horse-drawn carriages for weddings and other special occasions. Call for reservations or visit the Web site for photos and more information.

Pebble Beach Equestrian Center
Portola Road and Alva Lane,
Pebble Beach
(831) 624-2756
www.ridepebblebeach.com
The experienced instructors at the Pebble Beach Equestrian Center welcome all levels of riders for trail rides in the forest or on the beach. They work with individuals and private groups. Trail rides can be arranged for picnics or special events. Guided trail rides are offered four times daily. Call or visit the Web site for times and cost. Reservations are necessary.

PUBLIC SWIMMING POOLS

See Recreation Centers.

SKATING

Del Monte Skating Arena
2020 Del Monte Avenue, Monterey
(831) 375-3202
This traditional public roller rink is popular Thursday through Sunday for the in-line skate and roller skate crowd. Monday through Wednesday is booked for private groups. Call for exact hours, skate rental fees, and skating fee.

Monterey Bay SK8 Station
1855 East Avenue, Sand City
(831) 899-7587
www.skateboardparks.com
Skateboarding at the SK8, a 5,500-square-

foot indoor in-line skate and skateboard park, features a death box, 10½-foot vert ramp, corner bowl, fun box, quarterpipes, spine ramp, and wall rides to challenge your skills. The SK8 Station is open daily. Lessons and equipment rentals are available. Call or visit the Web site for hours and costs.

SKYDIVING

Skydive Monterey Bay
721 Neeson Road, Marina
(831) 384-3483
www.skydivemontereybay.com
Just 10 minutes away from Monterey, Skydive Monterey Bay offers tandem, accelerated freefall, and static-line training programs. All training programs meet the requirements necessary for membership in the U.S. Parachute Association. Groups are welcome. Family and friends can observe your landing at the airport's drop zone. Rates for a tandem jump begin at $199. Video or still photography is available to commemorate the occasion. Reservations are recommended on weekends and necessary on weekdays. The facility is open daily, weather permitting.

TENNIS COURTS

Monterey Tennis Center
401 Pearl Street, Monterey
(831) 646-3881
www.montereytenniscenter.com
The center, at the corner of Pearl and Adams Streets, has six lighted courts and a pro shop. An extensive lesson program, directed by certified and experienced members of the U.S. Professional Tennis Association, is offered for all ages and abilities. A "Buddies List" has the names of people who are looking for a match. The Monterey Tennis Center is open daily. Call or visit the Web site for lesson fees, court use fees, and hours.

Morris Dill Tennis Courts
515 Junipero Avenue, Pacific Grove
(831) 648-5729
www.pacificgroverecreation.org
Racquet stringing is available at the fully

stocked pro shop here. A comprehensive program of lessons and leagues is offered to include any age and level. Racquet and ball-machine rentals are available. There is a nominal fee per person per hour for court use. Reservations are accepted for court times. Open daily from 9:00 A.M. until dusk.

VOLLEYBALL

Del Monte Beach
Del Monte Avenue, Monterey
(831) 646-3866
www.monterey.org

Del Monte Beach, adjacent to Tide Avenue and Surf Way in Monterey, has one sand volleyball court. Picnic kits, available from the Monterey Recreation Department, 546 Dutra Street, contain recreational equipment including volleyballs and nets. There is a rental fee, reduced for Monterey residents. Reservations are necessary. The beach is open during daylight hours.

Lovers Point Park
Ocean View Boulevard, Pacific Grove
(831) 648-3130
www.pacificgroverecreation.com

This beautifully landscaped, oceanside park is at the foot of 17th Street. The park has one sand volleyball court, a snack bar, and restrooms. Picnic kits containing volleyballs and nets are available from the Pacific Grove Recreation Department, 515

Get some serious exercise with a view on the 1.2-mile exercise trail around Lake El Estero near downtown Monterey. There are 18 exercise stations, grouped in three clusters. Each station provides a type of exercise: warm-up, muscle stretching, muscle strengthening, cardiovascular conditioning, and cooldown, combined with walking, jogging, or running in between stations. An information board is located at each cluster.

Junipero Avenue, for a $20 rental fee. There is no entrance fee, but you must call ahead to reserve the court. The park is open every day from dawn to dusk.

Monterey Bay Waterfront Park/Window on the Bay
Del Monte Avenue, Monterey
(831) 646-3866

This 4.1-acre park is adjacent to the beach and has five sand volleyball courts. Picnic kits, available from the Monterey Recreation Department at 546 Dutra Street, contain recreational equipment including volleyballs and nets. The kits rent for around $25 for Monterey residents and $33 for nonresidents. Reservations are necessary. The park is open every day during daylight hours.

YOGA

Spa on the Plaza
201 Alvarado Street, Monterey
(831) 647-9000

This full-service spa across from the Double-Tree Hotel in historic downtown Monterey includes a yoga center. Iyengar, Ashtanga, and Shivananda yoga are available in group sessions scheduled Monday through Thursday. Drop-ins are welcome, a discount is provided when four sessions are purchased, and special couple sessions are available. Visit the Web site or call for details.

Yoga Center of Carmel
San Carlos Street, Carmel
(831) 624-4949
www.yogacentercarmel.org

The Yoga Center, founded in 1989, is at the corner of 10th and San Carlos Streets, in the Sunset Center. They offer a variety of classes and workshops for beginners on up. Drop-in class fees start at $15, multiple-class passes are available at a discount, and monthly and annual unlimited use passes are available. Call or visit the Web site to double-check class schedules.

IN AND AROUND THE WATER

The mesmerizing waters of Monterey Bay have provided inspiration and sustenance for many individuals beginning with the first Native American inhabitants of the area. The incredible power and beauty of the Pacific Ocean in our section of California are key factors in the decision to visit or live here. From commercial and recreational fishing and tour boat operations to restaurants, real estate, art, and photography, the lives of local residents are very much linked to this body of water. As one of the richest, most diverse marine environments in the world, the varied physical aspects of the Bay—its rocky coasts, sandy beaches, and deep marine canyons—create many different habitats for a vast array of plant, animal, and marine life. In 1992, Monterey Bay became a National Marine Sanctuary.

In this chapter we explore the various beaches and the activities made possible by our proximity to the magnificent Monterey Bay. Boating, fishing, surfing, diving, and the ever-popular walk along the water's edge are a few of the recreational possibilities available in and around the water.

BEACHES

Visitors captivated by the sights of scenic coastal vistas often are unaware of the potential hazards contained in the deceptively tame waters. Although there is the temptation to think of Monterey Bay as protected waters, it is always advisable to use caution when boating, swimming, surfing, wading, or walking along the beach or rocky headlands. Because of the expanse of the Bay and its submarine canyons, every precaution taken in the open ocean should apply to the Bay. Dangerous undertows and riptides exist at nearly every beach, so extreme caution and strict attention to posted regulations are necessary. Walking out on rocky outcrops during low tide should be done, if at all, with utmost care and awareness of the incoming tides.

Tides in the Monterey Bay have a variance of 7½ feet. This means the tides will vary around 3½ feet above or below the shoreline base. A range of about 8½ feet can occur on days of maximum tides. The water level throughout the harbor is almost always a minimum of 8 to 10 feet. For your own safety, check the tide tables each day in the local newspaper or pick up a tide book, available wherever fishing tackle is sold.

Asilomar State Beach
End of Highway 68, Pacific Grove
(831) 372–4076
www.parks.ca.gov

Asilomar has a long sandy stretch of beach perfect for walks and watching sunsets. It's also a great surfing beach. Located at the border of Pacific Grove and Pebble Beach, Asilomar has steady, offshore breezes, making it ideal for kite flying. There are several choice spots for walking on the beach. At one spot, a long strip of unbroken beach meets a rocky shoreline, sheltering several sandy coves perfect for wading in tide pools. Another alternative is to follow the wooden boardwalk as it weaves along the rocky shoreline and through extensive restored dune areas, where you'll see native plants in their natural environment. You'll often see and hear harbor seals, California sea lions, and sea otters swimming offshore. There is no entrance fee, and the beach is open every day from dawn to dusk.

Carmel Beach
West end of Ocean Avenue, Carmel
(831) 624-3543
www.carmelcityhall.com

Carmel Beach is quite possibly one of the most beautiful beaches in the world and certainly one of California's most famous. As you stand at the main entrance to the beach, at the end of Ocean Avenue, you can see the spectacular Pebble Beach Golf courses on your right. On your left, the view is just as amazing, with the picturesque Point Lobos State Reserve visible. The beach is surrounded by bluffs and has white sand, native cypress trees, and spectacular scenery. It is excellent for long walks, surfing, sunning, and picnics. To be on this beach and watch the sun sink into the Pacific at sunset, especially on a clear day, is an experience you won't soon forget.

Carmel River State Beach
Carmelo Road, Carmel
(831) 649-2836
www.parks.ca.gov

To get to this beach (1 mile south of Ocean Avenue), head south on Highway 1. Turn right on Rio Road, then left on Carmelo Road and into the parking lot. The beach has hiking trails, areas for viewing wildlife, a lagoon, and restrooms. Stewart's Cove, tucked into the northern tip of the ocean basin, is frequently uncrowded. It's a good place to view the ocean, especially on stormy days when the waves crash into the boulders along the shore. Climbing on the rocks, swimming, and wading are prohibited due to unpredictable wave patterns and a lethal undertow. Dogs are permitted if they are kept on a leash. The beach has no entrance fee and is open every day from 7:00 A.M. until 10:00 P.M. The parking lot closes at sunset.

China Cove and Gibson Beach
Point Lobos State Reserve,
Highway 1, Carmel
(831) 624-4909
www.pt-lobos.parks.state.ca.us

Four miles south of Ocean Avenue, these pristine, photogenic beaches are at the southern end of the Point Lobos State Reserve. China Cove, accessible from a steep stairway along the cliff, is a tiny beach with white sand leading into emerald-green water. Otters and other marine life can be seen from this fascinating hideaway. China Cove once inspired Robert Louis Stevenson, who used the setting in his popular book *Treasure Island*. If the tide is out, explore the small cave at the water's edge.

After ascending the steps, take the path along the top of the cliff to a second staircase, which descends to Gibson Beach. Down below, gigantic rocks are found in interesting formations along the narrow beach. Solitude, save for the seabirds circling overhead, is one of the highlights of this small beach.

The entrance fee to the reserve is under $10 and covers same-day access to other area state parks. The reserve is open every day.

Lovers Point Beach
Ocean View Boulevard, Pacific Grove
(831) 648-5730
www.pacificgrove.com

This beautiful beach and landscaped park is at the foot of 17th Street, below the Old Bath House Restaurant. There are two small sandy beaches, rocky outcrops, and a concrete pier structure. The park's amenities include a large green lawn area, a sand volleyball court, a toddlers' swimming pool, a snack bar, and restrooms. The protected cove at Lovers Point makes it a popular place for family gatherings, picnics, fishing, sunning, swimming, scuba diving, and surfing. It's open every day during daylight hours, and it is free to the public.

Monastery Beach
Highway 1, Carmel
(831) 624-4909
www.parks.ca.gov

Monastery Beach, about 1.5 miles south of Ocean Avenue across from the Carmelite Monastery, is a great spot for scuba

Surfers, divers, swimmers, and sun lovers flock to Lovers Point Cove in Pacific Grove.
MICHAEL CHATFIELD

diving, but only for the very experienced. A sharp drop-off and a dangerous under-tow make the beach unsafe for swimming or wading. The "sand" is actually coarse-grained rocks that can be very hard on bare feet. Be sure to wear suitable shoes for walking. The beach has no entrance fee and is open every day from 7:00 A.M. to 10:00 P.M.

Monterey State Beach
Canyon Del Rey Road, Monterey and Seaside
(831) 649-2836
www.parks.ca.gov
Shared by the cities of Monterey and Sea-side, Monterey State Beach is actually three separate beaches about a mile apart. It stretches along Del Monte Avenue from the Monterey Municipal Wharf up the coast to Seaside. An easy access to the beach is found at the west end of Canyon Del Rey Road. At the southern end, the beach has lots of rocks, rounded smooth by the surf. Dune restoration is currently under way at the northern end of the beach. Hiking trails provide wheelchair access. Other activi-ties include bike trails, fishing, scuba div-ing, kayaking, swimming, volleyball, and kite flying. There is no entrance fee to the beach. It's open from dawn to sunset.

Point Lobos State Reserve maintains a small but interesting museum showcasing the whaling industry on the Monterey Peninsula. Commercial whaling at Point Lobos ended around 1900. Call (831) 624-4909 or access ptlobos.parks.state. ca.us.

San Carlos Beach
Cannery Row, Monterey
(831) 646-3866
www.monterey.org
An almost three-acre park with a grassy area lines the beachfront at San Carlos. Seating areas provide a chance to stop and enjoy the view. Access to the beach is easy, and there are safe currents due to the protection of Breakwater Cove. Restrooms and picnic tables are available. There is no entrance fee, and the park is open during daylight hours.

Estuary

Elkhorn Slough National
Estuarine Research Reserve
1700 Elkhorn Road, Moss Landing
(831) 728-2822
www.elkhornslough.org
The Elkhorn Slough Reserve is about 20 miles north of Monterey, northeast of Moss Landing and 2 miles north of Dolan Road, and is one of the few undeveloped coastal wetland areas in California. The estuary area has 5 miles of walking trails. The reserve is a nursery area for many fish, sharks, and rays and is home to more than 200 species of birds. Docent-led tours are available on weekends. The reserve is open Wednesday through Sunday from 9:00 A.M. to 5:00 P.M. There is a nominal admission fee for adults and children 16 and older.

Lake

Lake El Estero
Del Monte Avenue, Monterey
(831) 646-3866
www.monterey.org
Lake El Estero is in the Lake El Estero Park Complex at the corner of Del Monte Avenue and Camino El Estero. Fishing is allowed in designated areas, mainly the two piers on Pearl Street. The lake is stocked with rainbow trout, Sacramento perch, Sacramento blackfish, Sacramento hitch, carp, tule perch, and yellow bullhead. Anyone 16 years and older is required to have a fishing license (see our "Fishing" section in this chapter for more on licenses).

BOATING

Regulations and Equipment

Recreational vessels are required to carry specified safety equipment, the amount and type of which varies according to type of propulsion, construction, number of people aboard, and the area and time of use. All Coast Guard-approved equipment must be kept in good, serviceable condition, readily accessible, and must be the proper type and/or size. For equipment purposes, sailboats, canoes, rowboats, and inflatable rafts equipped with motors are considered motorboats.

Sailboats and manually propelled vessels must carry personal flotation devices (PFDs), navigation lights, sound signaling devices, and visual distress signals. Motorboats less than 16 feet in length must carry personal flotation devices, a fire extinguisher, a backfire flame arrestor, muffling system, ventilation system, sound signaling devices, visual distress signals, and navigation lights. Required equipment for motorboats more than 16 feet in length varies. For more information contact the Department of Boating and Waterways, 1629 South Street, Sacramento, California, (916) 445-6281.

State law requires that all children age six or younger wear a Type I, II, or III life jacket while on board a moving vessel that is 26 feet or less in length. The only exceptions are on a sailboat if the child is restrained by a harness tethered to the sailboat or in an enclosed cabin.

The number and type of U.S. Coast Guard-approved PFDs required on a vessel depends on the length of the craft and the number of persons on board. All boats, canoes, and kayaks of any length must carry at least one personal flotation device for each person on board.

All boats 16 feet or longer, except canoes and kayaks of any length, must carry one wearable PFD (Type I, II, III) of the appropriate size for each person on board and one throwable (Type IV) device in each boat.

PFD Types I, II, and III must be readily accessible, meaning they may not be kept inside a plastic bag or protective covering. They must be easy to reach and stowed with the straps untied. All throwable PFDs (Type IV) must be immediately available. The law requires them to be kept in an open area where persons aboard can reach them quickly in an emergency.

It is recommended that vessels in semiprotected waters carry the following additional equipment: anchor and cable; bailing device; boat hook; a bucket; compass; depth-sounding device; emergency drinking water; fenders; first-aid kit with manual; flashlight and spare batteries; heaving line; local charts; a mirror for signaling; mooring lines; an extra supply of motor oil and grease; spare set of oars; spare parts; radio direction finder; radio/telephone; additional ring buoys; shear pins if used; current tables; tide tables; and tools.

Registering Your Boat

California law requires current registration of most vessels, including moored vessels whether used or not. All vessels must be registered and numbered with the exception of sailboards, boats that are manually propelled, sailboats of 8 feet or less propelled solely by sail, or vessels having valid registration in the state of principal use and not remaining in California for more than 90 consecutive days.

Applications to register a vessel can be made at the Department of Motor Vehicles (DMV), 1180 Canyon Del Rey Road, Monterey, (831) 649-2935. The DMV will issue a Certificate of Number, a Certificate of Ownership, and a set of registration stickers. The stickers must be displayed on each side of the forward half of the vessel so that enforcement officers do not have to board the boat to determine if the vessel is currently registered.

Transient boaters should report to the harbor office at the head of Wharf #2 for berth assignments. The harbormaster can be contacted on VHF channel 5 or 16. Quarantine, customs, and immigration services are handled by representatives from San Francisco, (831) 373-1155.

Navigation

Monterey Bay, located between Point Pinos and Point Santa Cruz, is a 20-mile-wide open roadstead practically free of dangers. The shores are low with sand beaches backed by dunes or low sand bluffs. A 10-fathom curve lies at an average distance of .7 of a mile offshore. The Submarine Monterey Canyon (with a depth of more than 50 fathoms) heads near the middle of the Bay about a half-mile from the beach near Moss Landing.

Point Pinos, on the south side of Monterey Bay, is low and round with visible rocks extending offshore for less than .3 of a mile. The point is bare for about .2 of a mile back from the beach; beyond is covered with pines. The light at the Point Pinos Lighthouse (36° 38.0' N, 121° 56.0' W), 89 feet above the water, is shown from a 43-foot white tower on a dwelling near the north end of the point. A radio beacon is at the light, and a fog signal is 450 yards northwest.

The breakwater at the head of the harbor is about 1,700 feet long, affording protection in northwesterly weather. The outer end of the breakwater is marked with a light and a fog signal. You will hear the barking sea lions when approaching the breakwater.

The Monterey Harbor (36° 37'N, 121° 53'W), 3 miles southeast of Point Pinos, is a compact resort harbor with some commercial activity and fishing. Depths of more than 20 feet are available in the outer harbor and the entrance and 6 to 10 feet in the small-boat basin. There are many sportfishing landings, and the small-craft basin provides good shelter for about 500 boats. Prominent features include the Presidio Monument on the brow of a barren hill and a radio tower .6 of a mile north of the monument. The speed limit in the harbor is three knots.

Municipal Wharf #2 (East Municipal Wharf) is 1,600 feet long and 86 feet wide at the outer end. Depths alongside the outer east and west sides are 24 feet. Freight and supplies are trucked directly onto the wharf. A 2-ton hoist is available. Municipal Wharf #1, also called Fisherman's Wharf, 300 yards west, is lined with restaurants and shops. A crane hoist lifts boats, up to 8 tons, for ordinary repairs.

For safe navigation, the U.S. Department of Transportation and the U.S. Coast Guard mark all waters by the lateral system of buoyage. California's waterway-marking system employs buoys and signs with distinctive standard shapes to show regulatory or advisory information. These markers are white with black letters and orange borders. They signify speed zones, restricted areas, danger areas, or general information. Hanging on to a beacon or tying up to any navigation buoy (except mooring buoys) is prohibited.

Red buoys, always even numbered, are kept to the starboard (right) side when proceeding from the open sea into port. Likewise, green buoys, always odd numbered, are kept to the port (left) side. Conversely, when proceeding toward the sea or leaving port, red buoys are kept to the port side and green buoys to the starboard side.

Port-hand buoys are painted green with fixed or flashing green lights. Starboard-hand buoys are painted red, with fixed or flashing red lights. Safe-water buoys, also called midchannel or fairway buoys, and approach buoys are painted with red and white vertical stripes and have flashing lights. Preferred channel, or junction, buoys are painted with red and green horizontal bands and have flashing lights. Special markers (traffic separation, anchorage areas, dredging, fishnet areas, etc.) are painted yellow and have a fixed or flashing light (if lighted).

Public Boat Ramps and Marinas

Monterey Marina
Commercial Wharf #2, Monterey
(831) 646-3950
www.monterey.org

Monterey Marina, open year-round, is between Fisherman's Wharf and Wharf #2. There are two concrete public ramps with two lanes each, an anchorage and buoying area, and more than 400 slips with dockside electricity. The wharf at the marina also has restrooms and benches. Fishing licenses, rod rentals, bait and tackle, marine supplies, boat maintenance, boat and motor rentals, motor parts, and repairs can all be obtained at the marina.

Breakwater Cove Marina
32 Cannery Row, Monterey
(831) 373-7857
www.montereybayboatworks.com

This modern, well-maintained facility is open daily from 8:00 A.M. to 5:00 P.M. There are 75 slips complete with power, water, and telephone hookups. Guest berthing is available for vessels of up to 120 feet. Restrooms, hot showers, laundry facilities, and mail and fax services are also available. The fuel dock has both gasoline and diesel oil. Monterey Bay Boatworks at the marina provides expert repair in wood, metal, fibreglass, or cement. Paint jobs and engine repairs are additional services offered. A 70-ton travel lift or strapless-keel lift system, a launching ramp, and marine supplies are available. You'll find a convenience store and a picnic area as well. Breakwater Cove Marina monitors VHF channels 16 and 67.

Marine Supply Stores

The Compass Boating and Fishing Supplies
Commercial Wharf #2, Monterey
(831) 647-9222

This convenient store at the foot of the harbor carries boating supplies and equipment including hardware, spare parts, engines, pump hoses, rope, and cordage. It also carries everything you'll need for fishing.

Quarter Deck Marine Supply
32 Cannery Row, Monterey
(831) 375-6754
www.montereybayboatworks.com

At Breakwater Cove, this full-service marine chandlery serves both the pleasure and commercial boating community. It provides complete painting, electrical, plumbing, and rigging systems. If it's not on the shelf, they can usually have it by noon the next day.

Boat Sales, Repairs, and Fuel

Gateway Outboard Service
490 Orange Avenue, Sand City
(831) 394-0126

Established in 1969, Gateway sells marine hardware, parts, and accessories. It is an authorized dealer for Johnson, OMC, and MerCruiser. Electronics can be special ordered and usually arrive within two days. Gateway also offers outboard sales and service for Yamaha, Mercury, Honda, and Mariner motors.

Monterey Bay Boatworks
32 Cannery Row, Monterey
(831) 375-6921
www.montereybayboatworks.com

This facility at Breakwater Cove offers full-service haul outs and boat repair. It offers restoration and repairs for both motor and sailing vessels weighing up to 70 tons. A special keel lift is available for wood vessels. Services include sandblasting, spray painting, fiberglass repair, welding, and fabrication. A clean concrete yard has power, water, and compressed air in all work areas.

Monterey Mariner In Board-Out Board
Coast Guard Pier, 32 Cannery Row, Monterey
(831) 655-3207

Specializing in small and large diesel engines, this company offers sales and service of Mariner, MerCruiser, and Volvo Penta powered inboard/outboard engines.

In Case of Emergency on the Water

Recognized distress signals include a continuously sounding fog horn, a gun fired at one-minute intervals, Mayday by radio, radiotelegraph alarm, or a radiotelephone alarm. You could also hold your arms out and wave them up and down if you are within sight of another vessel.

One danger signal to remember is the sound of five or more short blasts sounded in rapid succession. This indicates a risk of collision or the intent of the other vessel is not understood. A short blast is one second in length.

The nonemergency phone number for the U.S. Coast Guard is (831) 647-7300.

FISHING

Recreational fishing is a popular activity on Monterey Bay. You have the choice of spearfishing, hook-and-line fishing from wharves and the shore, or chartering a boat and fishing offshore. Bottom-fishing is very popular because it is a relatively simple method of angling, and a variety of fish will take bait on or near the bottom.

For those who would rather fish by ocean trolling, group charters are available from Fisherman's Wharf, so you can try your luck reeling in salmon, rockfish, mackerel, perch, or lingcod. Fishing hours on the Monterey Bay are from one hour before sunrise to one hour after sunset.

Licenses

Anyone older than 16 years of age must have a fishing license to fish from the shore or offshore from a boat. Fishing from a California ocean pier, such as Municipal Wharf #2, is excepted; pier fishing in California does not require a license.

You can get an annual or single-day fishing license from the following stores. Call the store or visit www.dfg.ca.gov for license fees. Licenses can also be purchased online.

Big 5 Sporting Goods
1300 Del Monte Shopping Center,
Monterey
(831) 375-8800

The Compass Boating and Fishing
Supply
Monterey Marina
(831) 647-9222

Department of Fish and Game
20 Lower Ragsdale Road, Suite 100,
Monterey
(831) 649-2870

Kmart
1590 Canyon Del Rey Road,
Monterey
(831) 394-6523

Longs Drugs
686 Lighthouse Avenue, Monterey
(831) 655-5404
2170 North Fremont Street, Monterey
(831) 373-6134
6 Crossroads Mall, Carmel
(831) 624-0915

Sportfishing Regulations

In general, one person can take up to 20 finfish in any combination of species, with not more than 10 of any one species. When fishing offshore, and filleting your catch, please note that unless otherwise indicated in the regulations book, each fillet must have a 1-inch square patch of skin remaining. For detailed information about sportfishing regulations, the publication "California Sport Fishing Regulations" is provided when you purchase your fishing license. You can also request one in advance by writing the California Department of Fish and Game, 1416 Ninth Street, Sacramento, CA 95814, by visiting www.dfg.ca.gov, or by calling (916) 653-7664.

Guides and Charters

Chris' Fishing Trips
48 Fisherman's Wharf #1, Monterey
(831) 375-5951
www.chrissfishing.com
Chris' has four large craft used for daily fishing trips: the 70-foot *New Holiday,* 58-foot *Check Mate,* 56-foot Tornado, and 55-foot *Holiday.* These diesel-powered, government-inspected vessels are equipped with fish finders, ship-to-shore radios, radar, and comfortable deck lounges. Chris' rents rods, offers fish cleaning, sells one-day fishing licenses, and provides free bait and ice. Individual ticket prices range from $30 to $100 depending on the specific tour (cod, salmon, and albacore fishing trips are featured). Group charters for up to 20 people are offered; call or visit the Web site for exact rates and reservation information.

Randy's Fishing and Whale Watching
Trips
66 Fisherman's Wharf #1, Monterey
(831) 372-7440, (800) 251-7440
www.randysfishingtrips.com
Randy's three fully insured and Coast

Guard-approved boats are available for fishing trips and private charters. Rates for a deep-sea cod fishing trip on a 65-foot boat for an adult are $35 weekdays or weekends. Children age 16 and younger pay $20. Daily salmon fishing trips cost $45. Group charters for cod-fishing trips for up to 17 people start at $525. Salmon-fishing trips for up to 13 people start at $630. Randy's rents fishing rods and tackle and offers fish cleaning. It also sells fishing licenses, bait, sack lunches, and ice.

Sam's Sportfishing
Fisherman's Wharf #1, Monterey
(831) 372-0577

Sam's offers deep-sea fishing trips aboard three Coast Guard-certified and -approved boats. It has fishing rods for rent, tackle, fish bags, bait, fishing licenses, and free ice. Fish cleaning is also available. Sam's can accommodate any size group up to 50 people. All-day, deep-sea cod-fishing trips on the Star of Monterey are $28 for adults on weekdays and $32 on weekends. Children age 12 and younger pay $15 on week-days and $20 on weekends. Salmon and albacore fishing trips are also available in season. Sam's welcomes beginning anglers.

Outfitters and Bait and Tackle Shops

Big 5 Sporting Goods
1300 Del Monte Center, Monterey
(831) 375-8800

This national chain carries a variety of tackle, lures, fishing licenses, and related fishing equipment and supplies.

The Compass Boating and Fishing Supply
Commercial Wharf #2, Monterey
(831) 647-9222

The Compass is a one-stop shop for all your fishing needs. It sells fishing licenses, lures, and bait (anchovies and squid) and rents poles and tackle.

That green glow in the bay in springtime isn't an alien invasion. The lights are used by commercial squid fishermen to attract mollusks to the surface, where they are captured in nets.

Gone Fishin'
1675 Contra Costa Street, Sand City
(831) 899-1111

An unlikely location—upstairs from an auto repair shop in landlocked Sand City—is home to one of the best fishing supply stores on the Monterey Peninsula. Rods and reels for fresh and saltwater fishing from top manufacturers are available along with lures, tackle, and accessories. And Gone Fishin' is a great place to swap stories about "the one that got away."

SAILING

Charters

Chardonnay II Bay Cruises
790 Mariner Park Way, Dock FF, Santa Cruz
(831) 423-1213
www.chardonnay.com

The *Chardonnay II* is a beautiful 70-foot sailing yacht available for cruises or pri-vate charter. Accommodating up to 49 passengers, the boat sails out of the Santa Cruz Yacht Harbor. There are many regularly scheduled theme cruises to choose from including whale-watching, astrology, winetasting, brewmaster, and more. Reservations can be made by phone or online.

Monterey Bay Sailing and Diving
Fisherman's Wharf, Monterey
(831) 372-7245
www.montereysailing.com

This company offers many ways to experi-ence the thrill of cruising the Monterey Bay under sail. Dinner cruises, sunset sails, wildlife excursions, photo expeditions, and even wedding ceremonies are offered on a 30-foot Cornada sailboat. The adventurous will enjoy the Extreme Sail, and corporate team building races and private company parties are also offered.

Sailing Courses

Monterey Bay Sailing and Diving
Fisherman's Wharf, Monterey
(831) 372-7245
www.montereysailing.com

In addition to charter operations, Monterey Bay Sailing and Diving operates a sailing school. Students learn to handle sailboats and earn American Sailing Association certifications that enable graduates to charter boats for self-sailing cruises. All levels of proficiency are accommodated, from raw beginner to old salt.

Monterey Peninsula Yacht Club
Municipal Wharf #2, Monterey
(831) 372-9686
www.mpyc.com

This yacht club offers a junior sailing program during the summer months. It also has sailing leagues throughout the year for high school students.

Whale-Watching and Harbor Tours

Chris' Whale Watching
48 Fisherman's Wharf #1, Monterey
(831) 375-5951
www.chrisswhalewhalewatching.com

Chris' offers daily whale-watching cruises from December to April. Two-hour narrated trips, Monterey Marine Sanctuary tours, and private group charters are available. Call ahead for reservations and rates.

Glass Bottom Boat Tours
90 Fisherman's Wharf #1, Monterey
(831) 372-7150

This company offers calm-water cruises in a fully enclosed glass-bottom boat around Monterey Harbor. Cruises depart frequently throughout the day from Fisherman's Wharf. Observe sea lions, seals, fish, otters, and other marine life in their natural habitat. The fully narrated, 25-minute tours are under $7.00 for adults and under $5.00 for children younger than 12. Individual, group, or private parties are welcome. They also offer whale-watching, marine mammal, and Bay tours. Call for availability, reservations, and rates.

Monterey Amphibious Tours
601 Wave Street, Suite 200, Monterey
(831) 373-0770

It's both a boat and a bus! The rather odd-looking, custom-made Hydra Terra embarks from Cannery Row on a fascinating 45-minute tour highlighted by a cruise around the calm waters of the Monterey Harbor. A colorful narration gives visitors a taste of what life was like during the heyday of Cannery Row when Doc Ricketts and John Steinbeck roamed the streets.

Monterey Bay Whale Watch
84 Fisherman's Wharf #1, Monterey
(831) 375-4658
www.gowhales.com

These whale-watching trips depart from Sam's Sportsfishing on Fisherman's Wharf. During the four-hour trips, you'll observe a variety of marine mammals and seabirds, while you're accompanied by a marine biologist who narrates and answers questions during the excursion. Common sightings include both humpback and blue whales; Pacific white-sided, Risso's, bottle-nosed, and common dolphins; and harbor and Dall's porpoise. Trips are offered year-round. Call or visit the Web site for fares and departure times.

Monterey Whale Watching
96 Fisherman's Wharf #1, Monterey
(831) 372-2203, (800) 200-2203
www.montereywhalewatching.com

Climb aboard and enjoy a two-hour whale-watching cruise during the migration of California gray whales. There are seven departures daily, December through April. Tours cost under $20 for adults, less for children age 12 and younger. Enjoy a three- to four-hour cruise during the summer (June through September) in the search for blue whales, orcas, humpbacks, minkes, dolphins, marine birds, and more. Three cruises depart daily. Rates are higher during the summer. Call for exact rates and departure times.

Randy's Fishing and Whale Watching Trips
66 Fisherman's Wharf #1, Monterey
(831) 372-7440, (800) 251-7440
www.randysfishingtrips.com
The fully narrated two-hour cruise provides a chance to see the magnificent California gray whale. Six daily departures on weekends (four on weekdays) are available from December through March. Four-hour and all-day group charters are also available. Call for rates and availability.

Sanctuary Cruises
"A" Dock, Moss Landing Harbor
(831) 643-0128
www.sanctuarycruises.com
Operating out of Moss Landing Harbor, Sanctuary Cruises is owned and operated by dedicated whale and ocean preservationists. The *Princess of Whales,* a comfortable, 149-passenger power catamaran departs Tuesday through Sunday for four- to five-hour cruises year-round. She has a full galley with freshly prepared hot foods and beverages. The *Sanctuary* is a more intimate boat, carrying 39 passengers. Detailed narratives and marine mammal orientations are presented on each trip, with an emphasis on conservation and preservation. Bookings can be made online or by phone.

Sea Life Tours/*Baywatch* Cruises
90 Fisherman's Wharf #1, Monterey
(831) 372-2203
www.baywatchcruises.com
Sea-life tours of the Monterey Bay Marine Sanctuary and seasonal (December

through March) whale-watching cruises are narrated by marine biologists on the distinctive yellow-and-red *Baywatch.* In the high season, there are up to eight departures per day. Reservations can be made online or by phone.

DIVING AND SNORKELING

The Monterey Bay is a world-renowned diving spot. Giant kelp forests, sea otters, sea lions, and an abundance of other marine life make the Monterey Bay a fascinating place for diving. If an emergency arises, the region's only hyperbaric chamber is on the Peninsula.

Dive Sites

Divers can swim out from several beaches along the shoreline or launch from a dive boat in the Bay. One of the best spots for beginners (or for those taking their first dive in the Monterey Bay) is the breakwater at **San Carlos Beach,** adjacent to the Coast Guard Pier in Monterey. The beach's mild currents allow for easy entry and exit. Diving here you'll see huge boulders; a variety of fish, anemones, starfish; and maybe an otter or sea lion.

Lovers Point Beach in Pacific Grove is another popular spot with easy beach access and lots of parking.

Divers of all levels will find Point Lobos one of the best diving spots. **Whaler's Cove** and **Bluefish Cove** provide plenty of chances to view sea otters and sea lions. Only a limited number of divers are allowed into the reserve each day. To make reservations, call (831) 624-8413 or visit www.pointlobos.com.

Carmel's **Monastery Beach** is one of the region's most popular dive sites. It is a good place to hook up with a dive buddy. However, the deep water, a steep drop-off, and severe undertow make this an area limited to the very experienced diver (see our "Beaches" section in this chapter).

Scuba divers from all over the world come to Monterey for world-class diving in the kelp forests of Monterey Bay. MICHAEL CHATFIELD

Dive Centers

Aquarius Dive Shop
2040 Del Monte Avenue, Monterey
(831) 375-1933
32 Cannery Row, Monterey
(831) 375-6605
www.aquariusdivers.com
Open since 1970, Aquarius is one of the locals' favorites. The shop is an authorized dealer for Scubapro, USD, and Body Glove merchandise. A full scuba kit, which includes all gear and one air tank, rents for around $60. Rental gear for snorkeling is $35.

Bamboo Reef
614 Lighthouse Avenue, Monterey
(831) 372-1685
Bamboo Reef is diving-equipment headquarters for sales, rentals, service, and instruction. It has the West Coast's largest compressor,

so there's no waiting in line for air refills. It also offers scuba tours and a certified diving school. All gear is available for rental individually, or a full scuba kit, including one tank of air, rents for about $65 per day. Snorkeling gear costs about $30 per day.

Monterey Bay Dive Center
225 Cannery Row, Monterey
(800) 607-2822
598 Foam Street, Monterey
(831) 655-1818
www.mbdc.to
The Dive Center has a retail shop at the Cannery Row location and a training facility on Foam Street. It provides equipment rentals including a full scuba kit ($69 per day) and a full snorkeling kit ($39 per day). It also offers instruction with 16 different classes. It can handle equipment repairs too.

The Dive Center offers guided underwater tours for up to four divers, night dives, and guided snorkeling tours. Tours can be scheduled any day of the week, and a 24-hour advance notice is appreciated. Call or visit the Web site for costs.

Dive Boats

Monterey Express
Operates from the City of Monterey Marina
(888) 422-2999
www.montereyexpress.com
Rates vary depending on the number of divers and length of dive. Call or visit the Web site for booking information.

The Silver Prince
(831) 656-0454
www.mbdc.to/boattrip
The Silver Prince is a roomy 40-foot dive boat that has recently undergone an extensive remodel.

SURFING

The most popular surfing spots in the Monterey area are **Asilomar** and **Lovers Point,** both in Pacific Grove. Both beaches have easy access to the water and plenty of parking. **Carmel Beach** gets its fair share of surfers, too, but parking is limited, especially during the summer months. See the listings for these beaches at the beginning of this chapter. The following retail shop provides all the necessary equipment for riding the perfect wave.

Sunshine Freestyle Surf and Sport
443 Lighthouse Avenue, Monterey
(831) 375-5015
Surfboards, swimwear, and wet suits are all in stock at Sunshine Freestyle. Service and rentals of surfing gear are offered as well.

SWIMMING

The water temperature is typically a chilly 55 degrees in the Monterey Bay. If you're willing to experience the invigoratingly cold waters, the best swimming beaches are in the protected cove at **Lovers Point** and along the shoreline of **Monterey State Beach.** See the listings for these beaches at the beginning of this chapter. Wet suits are highly recommended! See the diving and surfing listings for wet-suit sales and rentals.

KAYAKING

If an upclose and personal view of marine life along the coastline sounds like your kind of adventure, you'll rate kayaking on the Monterey Bay as one of the area's most enjoyable attractions. The rugged coastline and chance meetings with aquatic birds, whales, sea lions, sea otters, and other inhabitants of the kelp beds provide a unique opportunity for exploration.

Adventures by the Sea
299 Cannery Row, Monterey
(831) 372-1807
201 Alvarado Mall, Monterey
(831) 648-7253
Lovers Point Beach, Pacific Grove
(831) 373-1807
www.adventuresbythesea.com
Explore the wonders of Monterey Bay in ocean kayaks. Kayak tours include all the necessary gear, paddling instruction, and a marine wildlife orientation. The docent-led two- to three-hour tours are $50, with an option to use the equipment after the tour is finished. All-day kayak rentals including gear and instruction are $30.

Monterey Bay Kayaks
693 Del Monte Avenue, Monterey
(800) 649-5357
2390 Highway 1, Moss Landing
(800) 649-5357
www.montereybaykayaks.com
Natural history tours with professional naturalists and marine biologists are recommended for novices. The interpretive tours provide an introduction to the various ecosystems of the Monterey Bay. Tours last three-and-a-half hours and are

available (by reservation) on weekdays and weekends for $55.

Personal classes are offered to develop your skills in paddling techniques, boat control, rescues, surf zone, etc. Basic Skills 1 and 2 classes are offered in closed-deck single kayaks. Each class is around $95.

Rental of open kayaks for good swimmers requires no paddling experience. Closed-deck kayak rental requires the basic skills two-day sea kayaking class (or equivalent). The rate per person for open kayaks, including all gear and a wet suit, is around $30. The fiberglass boat (closed-deck kayak) rate is about $35 per person.

Monterey Bay Kayaks is one of the area's largest outfitters in sea kayaking. It carries more than 50 different kayak models, a wide range of accessories, clothing, and hardware. The facility includes an on-the-beach location, plenty of parking, changing rooms, and outside hot showers.

Paddleboating and Canoeing

El Estero Boating
Lake El Estero, Monterey
(831) 375-1484
Paddle around Lake El Estero aboard a paddleboat, kayak, or canoe. El Estero Boating rents boats for $8.00 per half hour, or $13 per hour. You'll see ducks, coots, sea gulls, and a variety of other seabirds as you tour the lake by boat.

Motorized Personal Watercraft

A motorized personal watercraft is defined as any motorized vessel less than 15 feet in length that can exceed 17 miles per hour and can hold up to two people. The term includes, but is not limited to, JetSkis, wet bikes, surf jets, miniature speed boats, air boats, and hovercraft.

To help protect the sensitive marine life and its habitats of the Monterey Bay Marine Sanctuary (the entire Monterey Bay), it is unlawful to operate motorized personal watercraft outside the access route and the designated zone. Launching is permitted only at the Monterey Harbor, and you must proceed directly to the operating zone. Look for signs posted at the harbor launch explaining where you can go and the bright yellow buoys and navigation aids marking the area.

As a personal watercraft rider, you are also considered a boater (these craft are defined as Class A inboard boats by the U.S. Coast Guard) and are required to follow most boating regulations.

Speeding can be dangerous to marine life and people. Avoid areas concentrated with wildlife, such as large gatherings of seabirds resting on the water or groups of marine animals. Minimize disturbance by riding slowly near sensitive habitats such as kelp forests.

PROTECTING THE BAY
Pollution

California state law prohibits dumping garbage into navigable waters or loading garbage on a vessel with intent of dumping it. It is illegal to dump plastic, paper, rags, glass, food, metal, crockery, lining, or packing materials that float into the Bay.

Plastic in particular is a hazard to marine life. Birds, fish, and even sea lions will die when a six-pack holder gets stuck around their necks and bodies. Some animals will eat plastic, which makes them feel full, causing them to slowly starve to death. Plastic debris in the water can cause life-threatening situations for boaters by fouling propellers and clogging engine-intake systems. This can result in disabled vessels and expensive repairs.

Plastic pollution has become an international issue. So prevalent, in fact, that the International Treaty to Prevent Pollution from Ships was created to address the plastic-pollution problem. The treaty prohibits the dumping of plastic into the water. All boats longer than 26 feet must display, in a prominent place where the crew and passengers can read it, an informational placard on the subject of these prohibitions. The placards can be purchased at marine supply dealers or can be requested free of charge from the Department of Boating and Waterways, 1629 S Street, Sacramento, CA 95814, or online at www.ca.gov.

As a boater you can become a part of the solution to marine pollution by helping to keep our bay and its beaches clean. Develop a simple vessel trash plan by separating plastics and storing trash on board. Dispose of it in Dumpsters at port, recycling whenever possible. You can further help by always using care when fueling, changing oil, or repairing your boat.

Residents of Monterey County take pride in their Bay. Since the mid-1980s, an annual coastal cleanup has taken place around the Monterey Bay. This data collection effort supports legislation protecting our ocean and dunes. The event is sponsored by numerous local businesses, and all necessary materials are provided to volunteers.

Environmental Service Organizations

Friends of the Sea Otter
2150 Garden Road, Monterey
(831) 373-2747
www.seaotters.org

This organization is dedicated to the rare and threatened southern sea otter as well as sea otters throughout the north Pacific range and all sea otter habitats. It provides educational materials and gives presentations to schools and community groups.

Monterey Bay National Marine Sanctuary
299 Foam Street, Monterey
(831) 647-4201
www.bonita.mbnms.nos.noaa.gov

Part of a system of 13 National Marine Sanctuaries governed by the National Oceanic and Atmospheric Administration, the Monterey Bay Sanctuary was established in 1992 and stretches from Marin in the north to Cambria in the south.

Strict environmental regulations assure that this section of coastline is protected. For example, oil exploration and drilling are banned within the sanctuary boundaries.

Save Our Shores
2222 East Cliff Drive, Suite 5A, Santa Cruz
(831) 462-5660
www.saveourshores.org

Save Our Shores is dedicated to the preservation of the environmental integrity of the Monterey Bay Marine Sanctuary through education, policy research, and citizen action. It provides volunteer opportunities through a Sanctuary Stewards Program, The Sanctuary Watch, and a used oil-pad program. Volunteering as a Sanctuary Steward involves an extensive training program, but the positions require only enthusiasm and a willingness to serve.

GOLF

M any visitors to the Monterey Peninsula have only one thing in mind: golf. Sure, they'll enjoy the scenery, the world-class restaurants, and the historic attractions. But not far from their center of attention at all times are those little white balls and long expanses of green.

It's no secret that the Monterey Peninsula is a golf mecca. Names like Pebble Beach, Old Del Monte, Spyglass Hill, and Spanish Bay are whispered with reverence. Many players wait their whole lives for a chance to play Pebble. Nongolfers may think it's crazy to spend hundreds of dollars for the experience of chasing a little white ball around the sand dunes and through the woods, but for devotees Pebble is a dream come true that spawns a lifetime of memories. And afterward the shots get longer, the putts truer, and the course more challenging and spectacular with each telling of the tale.

In this chapter we'll look at a host of public and semiprivate courses in and around the Monterey Peninsula. Some of the area's most familiar names, such as Cypress Point and Pasadera, aren't listed here because if you're not a member, chances are you won't be able to play. But in this chapter you're likely to find one or two unfamiliar names that offer an exciting and challenging round of golf during your stay on the Peninsula.

Before we start touring the courses, let's go over a few ground rules. Yardage for each course listed is from the men's white tees whenever they're available. The fees we list include the price for 18 holes and the cost of a cart. In most cases, carts are optional, and you can shave $15 to $30 off the price if you're willing to hoof it around the course on foot.

Green fees, ratings, and course conditions, of course, are subject to change. It is recommended that you schedule your tee times a week in advance, though you might be able to get on the less notable courses the day you decide to hit the links. For the Pebble Beach courses, make your plans as early as possible since prime times can be booked months in advance.

As a rule, the elements of nature will have a big impact on your golf game, particularly on the coastal courses. The rainy season will add a few water hazards, but most courses remain playable through the winter. Wind can be a huge factor year-round. You'll notice that a number of courses offer discount twilight fees, often as early as 1:00 P.M. But be aware that the wind typically picks up in the afternoon and can send your drives soaring and diving in unexpected directions on blustery days. For the best conditions, locals recommend an early or midmorning start. That being said, let's tee up the ball and get going. Here are the popular Peninsula courses to choose from.

COURSES

Monterey

Bayonet and Blackhorse Golf Courses
1 McClure Way, Seaside
(831) 899-7271
www.bayonetblackhorse.com
These two 18-hole courses at the former Fort Ord north of Monterey on Highway 1 are open to the public, providing a great alternative for local and visiting golfers. The two courses are set among the sandy hills and dunes overlooking Monterey Bay so they have excellent drainage and are open and very playable every day, rain or shine. Bayonet in particular is proving to be a local favorite. The par 72, 6,496-yard course provides an excellent

challenge. The long 631-yard, par 5 fourth hole and the 462-yard, par 4 fifth, with its uphill approach to a well-guarded green, present a skill-testing one-two punch. A round of golf costs $72 Monday through Thursday, $85 Friday, and $97 Saturday, Sunday, and holidays. Carts are mandatory on Saturday and Sunday before noon. Ask about reduced senior, junior, and twilight rates.

Blackhorse is a 6,175-yard, par 72 course. While Bayonet has the reputation as the better course, Blackhorse is one of the Peninsula's best-kept secrets for an enjoyable round. The views from the hills overlooking the Bay are spectacular, and the course presents a series of short but tough par 4 doglegs. Fees are $72 Monday through Thursday, $85 Friday, and $97 Saturday, Sunday, and holidays, with carts mandatory on weekends before noon.

Bayonet and Blackhorse share a driving range ($2.00 per bucket), a well-stocked pro shop, and the Bayonet Bar & Grill. Al Luna is the course pro, and golf lessons are available.

Del Monte Golf Course
1300 Sylvan Road, Monterey
(831) 373-2700
www.pebblebeach.com

Now more than a century old, the Del Monte Golf Course behind the Monterey Hyatt is the oldest continuously operating golf course west of the Mississippi. And it's a classic, too, designed by Charles Maud in 1897. Owned by Pebble Beach Company, Del Monte plays 6,069 yards of wide fairways lined with pine, oak, and cypress trees that make for a demanding par 72. The back nine features the 502-yard, par 5 13th hole with a tee shot over a deep ravine, followed immediately by the great 217-yard, par 3 14th with the green securely guarded by two imposing bunkers. Fees for Hyatt and Pebble Beach Resort guests are $80; nonguests can play for $90. Reduced twilight fees are available, so inquire about seasonal rates and hours. Carts are always optional. Neal Allen is the course pro, and group or individual lessons are available through the Pebble Beach Golf Academy. The Del Monte Golf Shop has great gift ideas for the duffers back home, and the Del Monte Grill serves great breakfasts and lunches in a beautiful setting. Locals will want to know about the annual membership plan, which provides reduced greens fees and tournament fun for a yearly fee.

Laguna Seca Golf Club
10520 York Road, Monterey
(831) 373-3701
www.lagunasecagolf.com

Known as the Peninsula's "Sunshine Course," Laguna Seca is a few miles inland from Monterey along the Monterey-Salinas Highway (Highway 68). Designed by the team of Robert Trent Jones Sr. and Jr., the 5,726-yard, par 71 layout is noted for its strategic bunkering. You'll need every club in the bag and every trick in the book to master this oak-studded and hilly course. Most challenging is the 511-yard, par 5 15th hole. It's a dogleg right, often straight into a stiff wind, with water hazards to the left, right, and front of the green. Fees are $65 daily with a twilight rate of $35 after 1:00 P.M. Carts are optional. The course pro is Jeff Hardy, and golf instruction is available. The clubhouse features a nice golf shop and a large restaurant with a full bar. Locals should ask about the many membership plans available that include privileges at Rancho Cañada in Carmel Valley.

Monterey Pines Golf Course
1250 Garden Road, Monterey
(831) 656-2167
www.montereypinesgolf.com

Formerly known as the U.S. Navy Golf Course, this well-maintained course is open to the public. Next to the Monterey Fairgrounds on Garden Road, it's right in town and provides a great golf value, especially for active and retired military personnel. The par 68, 5,913-yard course makes for a relatively pleasant, low-stress round. But before you conclude it's too gentle, get through the 18th hole, a four-handicap,

540-yard par 5 that may leave you heading to the clubhouse a little humbled. Active or retired military can play for $12. For Department of Defense personnel, the fees are $18 weekends. For you civilians, it's $24. Carts are optional. The course pro is Clay Murray, and lessons are available. There's a driving range ($1.50 and $3.00 buckets), the 19th Hole Grill that serves generous freshly made sandwiches, and a small golf shop sells what you need.

Pacific Grove

Pacific Grove Municipal Golf Links
77 Asilomar Boulevard, Pacific Grove
(831) 648-5777
www2.ci.pacific-grove.ca.us

Known affectionately as "the poor man's Pebble Beach," Pacific Grove Municipal Golf Course is right on the northern edge of the Peninsula, under the watchful eye of the Point Pinos Lighthouse. This 5,571-yard, par 70 course is actually two distinctly different sets of nines. The front nine is inland and offers nice green fairways, a few towering pines and oaks, and an achievable par on a solid day of driving and putting. But then it's time to cross Asilomar Boulevard and face the often-brutal coastal back nine. It's a links-style course deigned by Jack Neville, the original designer of Pebble Beach. The 10th hole teases you with a short and easy par 3, but then 11 heads directly seaward toward sand dunes, ice plant, thin fairways, and, if you're really lucky, howling gusts off the Pacific. You battle the bare elements of Point Pinos through the 16th and then have the pleasure of teeing off on the 17th over a small lake to a sloped green framed by thick cypress trees. A gently uphill par 4 finishes the course as you head back to the clubhouse. Greens fees are $32 Monday through Thursday and $38 Friday through Sunday and holidays. Twilight rates after 3:00 P.M. are $20. Junior rates of $15 are available for golfers age 17 and under. Carts are optional. Reservations can be made a maximum of seven days in advance. The course pro is Peter Vitarisi, and the pro shop and snack bar are conveniently situated between the first and ninth holes. A driving range is available, with balls at $3.00 a bucket.

Carmel

Carmel Valley Ranch
1 Old Ranch Road, Carmel
(831) 626-2510

Carmel Valley Ranch is a semiprivate course for members and guests of the Carmel Valley Resort, with an extensive reciprocal program for members of other clubs worldwide. The 5,563-yard, par 70 course is situated in the usually sunny Carmel Valley. The valley and hill terrain offer some great challenges, including the 402-yard, par 4 11th hole, with a 500-foot elevation tee looking down to a choice of two landing areas. Then you have to guide your approach shot to a small green protected by a pair of nasty bunkers. The short 138-yard, par 3 13th also has an elevated tee, but this time it's a blind tee shot to a green hidden below a grove of oak trees. Guests of the resort play for $150, while nonguests pay $160 Monday through Thursday and $180 Friday through Sunday. Carts are required and included in the greens fee. Harold Wells is the course pro, and five instructors provide lessons. A driving range is available to players free of charge. A nice pro shop and a great club grill are also on site.

The Golf Club at Quail Lodge
8205 Valley Greens Drive, Carmel
(831) 624-2888
www.quaillodge.com

The semiprivate Golf Club at Quail Lodge is open to members, resort guests, and members of other resorts that share a reciprocal program. The 6,140-yard, par 71 course is set in a beautiful location just 3.5 miles inland from the mouth of Carmel Valley. Among the favorite holes is the 161-yard, par 3 17th hole (which, by the way, provides a great view of Doris Day's

A small lake in front and a grove of cypress trees to the rear guard the 17th green at the Pacific Grove Municipal Golf Links. TOM OWENS

home). All you need to do is hit an hour-glass-shaped green surrounded on three sides by water and guarded by two mean front bunkers. Try it, you'll like it. Both the front and back nine come back to the newly renovated clubhouse, where you find a nice pro shop and snack bar. Greens fees for guests of Quail Lodge are $120 to $150. Reciprocal club members can play for $150 to $180. Twilight rates apply after 3:00 P.M. All fees include the cart, which is mandatory. The fee also includes a small basket of balls for the driving range. Extra baskets of various sizes are also available for a small charge. The driving range offers buckets of balls for $10 and $15. The course pro is Dave Anderson, and Quail Lodge is the home of world-renowned teaching pro Ben Doyle.

Rancho Cañada Golf Club
Carmel Valley Road, Carmel
(831) 624-0111, (800) 536-9459
www.carmel-golf.com
Rancho Cañada Golf Club in Carmel Valley

offers 36 holes of truly championship golf designed by Robert Dean Putman. The 6,126-yard, par 71 West Course is a beautiful and challenging layout. The extremely tight and narrow fairway on the 372-yard, par 4 15th hole is indicative of the challenges that await you. (As Sam Snead once quipped about the 15th, "I didn't know we'd have to play that hole single file.") Greens fees for the West Course are $80 daily, with a 1:00 P.M. twilight rate of $45. The 5,832-yard East Course may play second fiddle to the West, but it still provides an extremely challenging round, particularly on the back nine. You cross the Carmel River no fewer than five times completing this par 71 course. Of particular note is the 192-yard, par 3 13th hole that features a daring elevated tee shot across the river to the green below. Greens fees for the East Course are $65 and $35 for twilight hours. Carts are optional at both courses. If you plan on playing Rancho Cañada as few as five or six times a year, there are a number of

Golf in Carmel Valley offers warmer weather and less wind than the more well-known courses in Pebble Beach. MONTEREY COUNTY CONVENTION AND VISITORS BUREAU

annual membership packages that reduce the per-round cost significantly for play at either course as well as Laguna Seca in Monterey. Rancho Cañada has a nice driving range ($5.00 per bucket), an extensive golf shop, and a comfortable restaurant. Mark Stoddard is the course pro, and lessons are available.

Pebble Beach

Pebble Beach Golf Links
17-Mile Drive, Pebble Beach
(831) 624–6611, (800) 654–9300
www.pebblebeach.com
Welcome to golf heaven. There's probably not much we have to say to the serious golf nut about Pebble Beach Golf Links except "go play." Anyone who's ever watched the then-Crosby Clambake, now the AT&T Pebble Beach National Pro-Am, knows all about this world-famous course. But let's cover a few basics anyway. Designed by Jack Neville and Douglas

Grant (and first played in 1919), it's a 6,116-yard, par 72 course. But the numbers don't come close to telling it all. How do you describe the feeling of standing on the seventh tee? You're looking down 100 yards, seaward, to a postage-stamp-size, trapped-framed green perched on a rocky point that, depending on the wind, might take either a wedge or a 4-iron to reach. How do you measure the thrill of standing on a cliff above the Pacific Ocean ready to launch an approach shot 190 yards over the sea itself to the small eighth green surrounded by traps on three sides? Or of teeing up on the 209-yard, par 3 17th hole at Stillwater Cove, home to two of the most famous shots in U.S. Open history? (We're talking about Jack Nicklaus's famous tee shot in 1972 and Tom Watson's amazing chip-in from the rough in 1982.) How do you describe the view of the sea and The Lodge as you navigate the 548-yard, par 5 18th?

Now, for a few other numbers. Pebble Beach Resort guests pay $350 (with complimentary cart), while nonguests fork over $375 for this lifelong memory. Pebble Beach residents and club members pay $350. Caddies ($50 a bag plus gratuity) are highly recommended to help you get the most from your game. The driving range for Pebble Beach is off The Lodge grounds near the Pebble Beach Equestrian Center at Stevenson Road. The Lodge has a choice of shops, including The Golf Shop, and restaurants. The course pro is Chuck Dunbar, and the Pebble Beach Golf Academy provides public and private lessons. Make your tee time as soon as your visit to the Peninsula is firmed up. Otherwise, you may be in for a big disappointment.

Peter Hay Par Three
17-Mile Drive, Pebble Beach
(831) 625-8518
www.pebblebeach.com

Pebble Beach for $20 a round? Yes, it's true at the Peter Hay nine-hole, par 27, 819-yard course. It's not exactly the Pebble Beach Golf Links, but this compact course near The Lodge provides an inexpensive, approach-pitch-and-putt warm-up, or an enjoyable diversion all its own for the budget-minded. This is an especially good choice for newcomers to the game and for young ones learning the game. In fact, kids younger than 12 play for free when accompanied by an adult. Teens up to age 17 play for $5.00. And for adults it's only $20.00 a round. Former Pebble Beach pro Peter Hay designed the course.

Poppy Hills
3200 Lopez Road, Pebble Beach
(831) 625-2035
www.poppyhillsgolf.com

Deep in the Del Monte Forest, Poppy Hills is possibly the least known of the public courses in Pebble Beach. But this 6,237-yard, par 72, heavily wooded beauty is both breathtaking and heartbreaking, with its long, narrow fairways and difficult approaches. Designed by Robert Trent Jones Jr., Poppy Hills is the home of the Northern California Golf Association

(NCGA). You begin with a bang, a difficult 413-yard, par 4 with a thick grove of trees to the left that seems to act as a ball magnet. And the back nine starts with one of the best holes of all of Pebble Beach. The par 5, 472-yard 10th green is guarded by a beautiful lake strategically located to the front left, which just dares the best of golfers to try to make the green in two shots.

NCGA members play for $50 Monday through Thursday and $60 Friday through Sunday. Public greens fees are $125 weekdays and $160 weekends and holidays. Carts are optional. There is a driving range with $3.00 buckets and a well-stocked pro shop but no restaurant. The pro is Ken Woods, and the John Jacob School offers its top-notch training courses at Poppy Hills from May through November.

Spyglass Hill Golf Course
Spyglass Hill Road and Stevenson Drive, Pebble Beach
(831) 625-8563, (800) 654-9300
www.pebblebeach.com

Pebble Beach Golf Links gets top billing, but Spyglass Hill gives it a great run for the money as the top Peninsula course. Trying to pick the most popular hole on this par 72, 6,114 yard Robert Trent Jones Sr.-designed course with great ocean and forest views is difficult. You start on the first hole with a great 600-yard downhill to the Treasure Island green surrounded completely by sand. Then there's the demanding 468-yard Black Dog 16th hole, a par 4 dogleg. (All of the holes are named after a Treasure Island character or theme.) But talk to most golfers about the toughest hole at Spyglass, and they'll recall the eighth, Signal Hill, with its severe uphill climb to a sloped green protected by large bunkers. In fact, Signal Hill is rated among the PGA's Top 18 Toughest holes.

Greens fees for Pebble Beach Resort guests are $250, including complimentary cart. Nonguests pay $275, and carts are optional. Ask about seasonal twilight rates. The course pro is Bill Sendell, and Pebble Beach Golf Academy offers lessons.

Just because you didn't pack your clubs doesn't mean you can't play. Many courses and golf shops provide rental equipment.

The Links at Spanish Bay
2700 17-Mile Drive, Pebble Beach
(831) 647–7495, (800) 654–9300
www.pebblebeach.com

Those of you who dream of the challenge of an authentic Scottish links course will love The Links at Spanish Bay. Robert Trent Jones Jr., Tom Watson, and Sandy Tatum designed the 6,043-yard, par 72 course. This is a demanding course with 20-foot dunes, rugged native vegetation, and sand, sand, sand. Memorable holes include the 571-yard 14th, with a spectacular coastline view from the elevated tee, and the 414-yard 17th, which follows the gorgeous shoreline. On 17 you're tested with a 180-yard drive to an island fairway surrounded by trouble. Make that shot, and you approach the green over hilly dunes and six awaiting bunkers.

Fees are $215 with complimentary cart for Pebble Beach Resort guests and $240 for nonguests. Pebble Beach and Spanish Bay residents and club members pay $215. Carts are optional. Be sure to ask about the special twilight rate. The 24,000-square-foot clubhouse is the home of The Links pro shop, locker rooms, and a restaurant that overlooks the first fairway and serves breakfast and lunch. The course pro is Rich Cosand, and the Pebble Beach Golf Academy provides individual and group lessons.

DRIVING RANGE

Del Rey Oaks Driving Range
899 Rosita Road, Del Rey Oaks
(831) 394–8660

In addition to the driving ranges listed with the golf courses above, Del Rey Oaks Driving Range provides a great place to practice day or night, rain or shine. It fea-
tures covered as well as grass tees, bright lights for nighttime driving, practice bunkers, and an artificial green. A discount pro shop and snack bar are on-site. PGA professionals offer individual and group lessons. Buckets of balls cost from $4.00 to $7.00, and the driving range is open seven days a week until 9:00 P.M.

GOLF SHOPS

All of the golf courses listed in this chapter have their own pro shops that carry equipment, accessories, and apparel of varying quantities, qualities, and prices. Below are a few more local choices, ranging from discount golf stores to custom club designers. You might also want to check out the area's large discount stores (such as Kmart) and sporting goods shops (like Big 5) for bargain prices.

The Golf Mart
2040 Fremont Boulevard, Seaside
(831) 583–1000
www.thegolfmart.com

The area's newest discount golf store is also its largest. The Golf Mart boasts of 12,000 square feet of retail space, including an indoor driving range and the largest indoor putting green on the Peninsula. You'll find a wide selection of top brands at very decent prices.

Nevada Bob's Golf
399 Lighthouse Avenue, Monterey
(831) 372–5516
www.nevadabobs.com

Nevada Bob's is a discount golf store chain that carries a full line of golf equipment and accessories. If you need it, Nevada Bob's probably has it for a pretty low price. Free laser club fitting is available. It's open seven days a week.

Orlimar-Travaux
San Carlos Street and Fifth Avenue, Carmel
(831) 625–7115

For 38 years this has been home to

Orlimar custom fitted clubs. You'll also find a full line of custom men's clothing carrying such labels as Nicklaus, Norman, and Pebble Beach. Orlimar-Travaux is open seven days a week.

Riley Golf
2 Harris Court, Monterey
(831) 373-8855
www.rileygolf.com
Since 1980, Riley Golf has been designing and manufacturing personally fitted metal woods, irons, wedges, and putters for professionals and amateurs alike. Its new shop in the Ryan Ranch business park

also sells bags, instructional videos, and a line of apparel carrying the Riley logo. Riley Golf is open seven days a week.

Village Golf Shop
601 Wave Street, Monterey
(831) 624-5080
Known as "The Knickers Place," Village Golf Shop is the place to go to get your fashionable knickers and plus-fours. You'll also find accessories such as balls, bags, putters, shirts, gloves, hats, and shoes. Village Golf Shop is open seven days.

DAY TRIPS 🚘

This book is focused pretty firmly on the Monterey Peninsula, a small block of land of fewer than 30 square miles surrounded on three sides by the Pacific Ocean. That geographic fact is the primary reason people are drawn here. It's what accounts for the beauty of this chunk of forest-and-beach-covered rock jutting out into the sea. But turn around, away from the Peninsula, and the entire "Central Coast" of California (the semiofficial name for this part of the state) offers equally majestic scenery and equally pleasant diversions. Look south, and there is Point Lobos and Big Sur beyond. If a walk or even a drive through that section of God's green earth on a sunny day doesn't move you, maybe you're dead. Head east and you run into two distinct but very Californian valleys—the agricultural splendor of Salinas Valley and the wild west of Carmel Valley. And what lies north? Only a California beach-hugging trip through the fun and exciting metropolises of Santa Cruz and San Francisco as well as all the charming coastal communities and parks in between.

Day tripping is a favorite pastime of Monterey Peninsula locals, and all visitors of more than two days should partake in a jaunt around the region. Whether your pleasure is exploring the rugged beauty of Big Sur, riding a historic wooden roller coaster right on the beach, taking a steam-driven train through California redwood forests, or splurging on a day of shopping and dining in San Francisco, one of these day trips is just right for you. Let us present Highway 1 south through Big Sur, Highway 1 north to San Francisco, the Salinas Valley, and Carmel Valley.

HIGHWAY 1 SOUTH THROUGH BIG SUR

In 1966 Lady Bird Johnson stood on a stretch of Highway 1 south of the Monterey Peninsula and, as the nation's First Lady, dedicated it as California's first scenic highway. And little wonder why. The ribbon of asphalt and concrete that twists and turns approximately 130 miles from Carmel to San Luis Obispo winds through some of the most breathtaking scenery in the world.

Completed in 1937 after 16 years of backbreaking and dangerous labor, this stretch of Highway 1 is, at points, literally cut into the side of 1,000-foot cliffs. At other points, it sweeps down across tranquil coastal valleys only 50 feet above the surf. The numerous, sometimes mammoth bridges spanning the many creeks and rivers that dump into the Pacific are marvels of engineering. Yet they can't hold a candle to the natural splendor that waits around virtually every curve.

Anyone and everyone who comes to visit the Monterey Peninsula for more than a day or two owes it to themselves to visit the Big Sur coast. The approximately 27-mile drive from Carmel into the Big Sur River Valley takes less than an hour and is well worth the effort, even if it's only for a quick lunch or an immediate U-turn back to the Peninsula. The drive south on Highway 1 can be slow and treacherous or quick and carefree, depending on weather and traffic.

Rules of the Road

There are a few rules of the road we should point out before you begin your

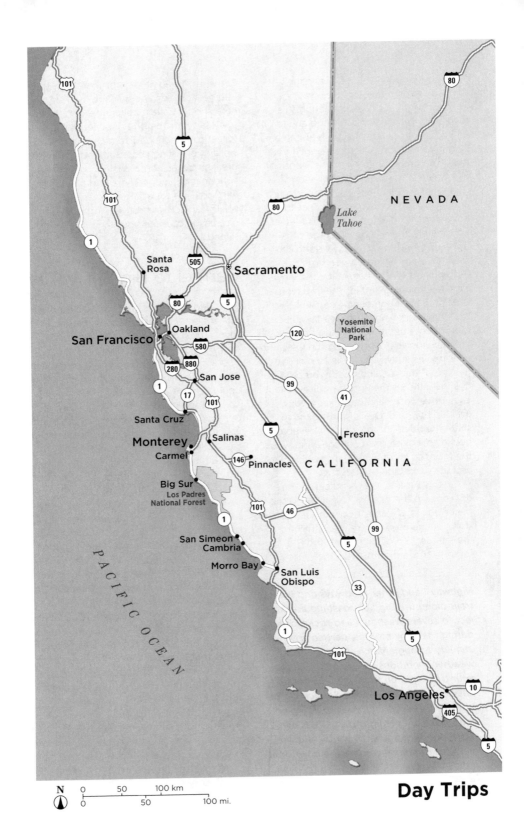

Day Trips

southbound journey. First of all, don't hurry, be happy! Enjoy getting there, and don't worry about the destination. A slow recreation vehicle lumbering up ahead or an impatient tailgater to the rear can easily get your blood pressure rising, if you let it. The great majority of this length of highway is a no-passing zone, and for good reason. Blind curves, steep grades, and heavy fog create hazards that turn ill-advised passing attempts into tragedies. Fortunately, there is no shortage of turnouts along the highway's edge. Use them! If Teddy Tailgater won't get off your butt, pull off to the side, enjoy the view for a few minutes and let the impatient idiot go bother someone else. Similarly, if the 15-miles-per-hour, refuses-to-pull-over motor home up ahead is filling up your entire windshield, destroying the view and your nerves, maybe it's time to pull over, get out of the car, and deeply breathe in this magnificent piece of paradise. Take it easy, drive defensively, and keep your eyes on the road. Our suggestion is to share the driving chores so that everyone gets a chance to gaze out the window at the majestic mountains, the crashing surf, and the deep blue sea beyond.

In this section, we've indicated the distance (to the nearest half-mile) to the major points of interest down the coast. Our mileage markers are measured from the intersection of Highway 1 and Rio Road near the mouth of Carmel Valley.

Highway 1 and other roadways and hiking trails along the Big Sur coastline are subject to severe washouts and rockslides during the rainy months, particularly January through March. Always check weather conditions before embarking on your trip south on Highway 1. Likewise, check with the U.S. Forest Service Office at (831) 667-2423 before embarking on long hikes or overnight trips. Trails can wash out during a harsh winter, and forest fires can make some areas downright inhospitable.

Set your mileage indicator to zero at the intersection, and the mileage marks noted here should be fairly accurate.

Ready for the ride of a lifetime? Don't forget to bring along some comfortable walking or hiking shoes, at least a windbreaker jacket, some drinking water and light snacks, your camera and plenty of film, disks, or tape, and, if you're susceptible to car sickness on winding roads, a big plastic bag and your favorite tummy remedy.

Carmel to Big Sur Valley

From Rio Road, our trip begins across a rather new bridge that spans the Carmel River. The old bridge was washed out only a few winters ago during major flooding, stranding those south of the river for weeks until a temporary crossing could be built.

At approximately the 1-mile mark of our journey on the coast side of the highway is Carmel Bay School, a preschool that's been attended by generations of Big Sur and Carmel children. If you turn into the parking lot at Carmel Bay School and turn right (north), you'll find a trailhead that takes you to a wonderful beach with fantastic views of Carmel, Pebble Beach, and Point Lobos. It's worth a visit if you're looking for a short and secluded hike to the beach not far from Carmel proper. Highway 1 then swoops down the hill to spectacular **Monastery Beach** (mile 1.5), part of Carmel River Beach. This is a very popular spot with experienced scuba divers, surfers, and beachcombers, not to mention myriad shorebirds. Please be aware that Monastery Beach has a severe drop-off. The surf, undertow, and riptides can be extremely hazardous. (This caution applies to virtually all of the open beaches along this coastline and will be repeated often in this chapter.) All but the best swimmers and divers are cautioned to enjoy the scenery from a safe distance.

Why is this stretch of sand and surf called Monastery Beach? The answer lies directly across the highway: the **Monastery of Our Lady and St. Theresa.** This monastery was built in the 1920s and continues to be home to an order of Carmelite nuns. There are no regular visitor hours, though the monastery occasionally opens for significant holiday services.

At mile 2 of our journey lies what has been called the greatest meeting of land and sea in the world. **Point Lobos State Park** is a 1,275-acre preserve, more than half of which is below the sea. In fact, it is the first undersea preserve in the United States. Simply put, Point Lobos is one of the most beautiful spots you'll hope to see, with more than 300 species of plants and 250 species of birds and animals populating a spectacular pristine coastline. Highlights include **Whaler's Cove,** with its 1860 Portuguese whaling station, and **China Cove,** an almost fluorescent aqua-colored bay on the south end of the park that's perfect for a picnic or, in warm mild weather, a quick dip in the cold crystal water. During whale-watching season (November through February), the **Cypress Grove Trail** to **Pinnacle Cove** makes for a great hike. Point Lobos is open daily from 9:00 A.M. to 7:00 P.M. (5:00 P.M. during winter months), with a $5.00 entrance fee per car ($2.00 with a senior). Bicyclists and pedestrians enter for free. For general information, call (831) 624–4909 or visit pt-lobos.parks.state.ca.us, for scuba information, (831) 624–8413 (see our Parks and Recreation chapter for additional details).

Beyond Point Lobos near the 3-mile mark is Carmel Highlands, an exclusive enclave of hillside homes and a scattering of small businesses like the **Sculpture House and Gardens Gallery,** Highway 1 and Fern Canyon Road, (831) 624–2476, www.sculpturecarmel.com, with its unique garden, indoor, and water sculptures. About 1.5 miles later is the coastal Yankee Point neighborhood (see our Real Estate chapter). This beautiful area is home to two of the Peninsula's finest hotels, The Highlands Inn and The Tickle Pink Inn (see our Hotels and Motels chapter).

Once past Yankee Point and across Malpaso Creek Bridge (mile 5), the coastline opens up into a panoramic wonder. In clear weather you can view miles of rugged shoreline stretching as far as the eye can see. This is the image of the Big Sur coast most people are familiar with, and it's your first chance to see the magnitude of the unspoiled splendor that still exists.

The next spot of note is a line of cypress trees clumped along the inland side of the highway at **Sobranes Point,** approximately the 7-mile point. This area is the starting point for the **Sobranes Canyon Trail,** which provides for a leisurely 1.5-mile hike to redwood groves along Sobranes Creek, affording nice views back to the coast. Farther up the canyon, the angle of ascent increases, creating a more rigorous hike. On the coast side of the highway are a few trailheads that lead down to the coast at Sobranes Point. Some trails can be quite steep, so caution is advised. This area is a favorite spot for local anglers and is also the northern point of the **California Sea Otter Refuge,** which stretches down to Point Sur.

Easier beach access is afforded farther south at **Garrapata State Park** (mile 9.5), (831) 624–4909. This is a great spot for beachcombing or a romantic sunset walk along the rugged coastline. Again, the surf is extremely dangerous, and surfing, swimming, and wading are highly discouraged. Inland you'll find hiking trails up to redwood groves among the park's more than 2,800 acres. About another 1.5 miles past Garrapata is your first great chance for a few creature comforts in this rugged country: **Rocky Point Restaurant** (mile 11). Here, you can enjoy a great breakfast, lunch, or dinner seven days a week from a wonderful vantage point overlooking the Big Sur Coast. A full menu of seafood and traditional American meals are served, and there's a full bar. Call (831) 624–2933 or visit www.rocky-point.com for hours and reservations, which are recommended for dinner (see also our Restaurants chapter).

At mile 11.5 is an inland turn to **Palo Colorado Canyon.** This road winds

For overnight campground reservations at the California State Parks along Highway 1, call ReserveAmerica at (800) 444-7275, or go to www.reserveamerica.com.

through a shady Big Sur residential area for the first few miles, then ascends sharply up the canyon to **Bottcher's Gap,** the site of a campground and several trailheads into the **Ventana Wilderness.** A popular day hike among the physically fit is a scenic 8-mile jaunt to the vistas of **Devil's Peak** and back. Spring and fall hikes are recommended, as winter rains and summer heat can make the trek very rigorous. For a more leisurely pace, try the hike down the fire road to the Little Sur River. A rustic campground about a mile down the road makes for a magical overnight trip. Parking at Bottcher's Gap is $5.00 daily.

Approximately 2 miles beyond Palo Colorado Canyon and Rocky Creek Bridge (mile 12.5) is one of the most photographed and recognizable bridges in America. **Bixby Bridge** (mile 13.5) was built in 1932 as one of the longest concrete arch span bridges in the world, with an arch of 320 feet and standing more than 250 feet above Bixby Creek. You probably recognize it from one of the seemingly hundreds of car commercials and movie scenes filmed here. For a real treat, park your car at the pullout just before the bridge and walk out to one of the observation alcoves that were built to take in the spectacular view. Pay attention to traffic, as the pedestrian path to the alcoves is quite narrow.

From Bixby Bridge, Highway 1 continues south around steep and winding **Hurricane Point,** one of the windiest sections of the Big Sur coast. Navigate around this treacherous point and feast your eyes on **Point Sur State Historic Park** in the distance, a huge outcropping of volcanic rock with the **Point Sur Lighthouse** (mile 19) perched some 360 feet above the

water. Point Sur Lighthouse, built in 1889, is now open for public tours on Saturday at 10:00 A.M. and 2:00 P.M., Sunday at 10:00 A.M., Wednesday at 10:00 A.M. and 2:00 P.M. (April through October), and Thursday at 10:00 A.M. (July and August). Monthly moonlight tours are also available from April through October. All tours are subject to cancellation due to inclement weather. Reservations are highly recommended, so call (831) 625-4419 or visit www.pointsur.org in advance of your trip. Meet your docent in the parking lot at the base of Point Sur's giant moro rock formation. The cost of the tour is $5.00 for adults, $3.00 for kids ages 13 to 17, and $2.00 for ages 5 to 12. Children younger than 5 get in free, but strollers are not permitted. Tours last three hours and include a rather steep half-mile hike with a rise in elevation of 360 feet.

The entrance to **Andrew Molera State Park,** (831) 667-2315, the area's largest state park at more than 4,800 acres, is at the 22-mile mark of our journey. This is a great spot for day hikes, with miles of trails along the 4 miles of coastline and up to 2 miles inland along the Big Sur River. There is walk-in, rustic camping on a first-come, first-served basis (no reservations accepted). The day use fee is $3.00. If you're staying overnight, there's a $1.00 per-person, per-night charge for up to three nights. Horseback riding is available from April until January through **Molera Horseback Tours,** (831) 625-5486, (800) 942-5486, www.molerahorsebacktours.com. Walk-ins are welcome, with rides starting at $25.

Adjacent to Andrew Molera State Park is the old **Coast Road,** an unpaved, sometimes narrow road that loops up through the woods and joins back to Highway 1 north at Bixby Bridge. The adventuresome with good tires and shocks on a sturdy vehicle will enjoy this alternate route back toward the Monterey Peninsula, but it's best to avoid it during the muddy rainy season (usually November through April). There is also a trailhead to the Little Sur River's south fork about 3.8 miles up the Coast Road from the southern entrance at Andrew Molera.

Big Sur Valley

Continuing south, Highway 1 now leaves the coastline and enters Big Sur Valley. The scenery changes dramatically from rugged coastline to idyllic forests of coastal redwoods, pines, sycamores, cottonwoods, maples, alders, and willows. The highway follows the Big Sur River as it meanders through the forest, and signs of civilization begin to appear on both sides of the road. Approximately half of the population along the entire Big Sur coastline resides in the Big Sur Valley. This area is also home to most of the area restaurants, inns, campgrounds, shops, and stores.

The first major establishment you'll come upon is the **Big Sur River Inn** (mile 24.5). Since the 1930s this venerable landmark has served as a popular meeting place for generations of locals and visitors. Today it offers lodging for overnight guests and a very popular restaurant for breakfast, lunch, or dinner. There's also an outdoor pool, and nighttime entertainment is provided on some weekend evenings. A favorite pastime on warm summer days is to enjoy a tall cold one and some delicious appetizers right in the middle of the Big Sur River. That's right: The Big Sur River Inn has outdoor seating smack dab in the middle of the docile river. Cool your tootsies and enjoy the scenery from the best seats in the house. For information, call (831) 667-2700, or visit www.bigsurriverinn.com.

Another spot worth mentioning if you're considering turning your day trip into an overnighter is the **Ripplewood Resort** (mile 25). Here you'll find 17 quaint cabins, nine of them right along the Big Sur River under a canopy of redwoods. Rates are reasonable ($99 to $125), and the serenity is unmatchable. Call (831)

667-2242 or visit www.ripplewoodresort.com for details.

Nearby are two other Big Sur landmarks: the **Big Sur Grange Hall** that serves as the community's town meeting hall and **St. Francis of the Redwoods Chapel,** with a unique glass wall that opens up to allow for religious services out under the redwoods.

Our next stop is **Pfeiffer Big Sur State Park,** (831) 667-2315. This 810-acre park provides a recreational haven for hikers, swimmers, sunbathers, anglers, and picnickers. The **Big Sur Lodge,** (831) 667-3100, (800) 424-4787, www.bigsurlodge.com, provides 61 guest rooms and a swimming pool, cafe (for breakfast, lunch, and dinner), gift shop, and country store. There are also more than 200 campsites and a large day-use picnic area with grills and tables. Giant coastal redwoods (reaching circumferences of up to 27 feet) provide a cool and sheltering canopy over the majority of the park, which provides miles of hiking trails. A favorite hike is the 0.7-mile trek from the lodge through the redwoods along Pfeiffer Redwood Creek up to 60-foot **Pfeiffer Falls.** Then follow the half-mile trail from the foot of the falls to the **Valley View Overlook,** which affords spectacular views of Big Sur Valley. The mostly downhill return trip from the overlook to the lodge is approximately 1 mile. You can encounter a variety of wildlife including squirrels, deer, quail, raccoon, fox, bobcat, wild boar, hawks, woodpeckers, and kingfishers. Call the park regarding fishing regulations for steelhead and rainbow trout. During the summer, the water temperature of the Big Sur River is often above 60 degrees, so bring your bathing suits. The U.S. Forest Service Office is within the park and provides the wilderness permits required for overnight backpacking into **Ventana Wilderness** and **Los Padres National Forest.** For park information call (831) 667-3100 or (800) 424-4787.

Farther south at about the 28.5-mile mark, you'll notice a rather nondescript,

poorly marked road that dips down off to the coast side of the highway. This is Sycamore Canyon Road, the route to **Pfeiffer Beach,** the most popular day-use beach in the Big Sur Valley area. This mostly single-lane road of a little more than 2 miles leads to a parking lot and a 150-yard path to a spectacular stretch of sandy coastline with dramatic rocks, arches, and caves. You might recognize it as the beach Richard Burton and Elizabeth Taylor cavorted on in *The Sandpiper.* Although Dick and Liz are gone, you will find surfers, anglers, tidepoolers, and probably lovers enjoying the scenic vistas. Beach access costs $5.00, and the park is open daily 9:00 A.M. to 8:00 P.M. (*Note:* You're likely to meet oncoming traffic on this narrow road. In California, uphill traffic has the right of way; downhillers must yield or back up to allow passing. Also, parking is limited to 65 vehicles.)

Meanwhile, back on Highway 1, it's time to check the gas gauge. If you're planning on continuing to the southern end of our journey, the service station at the **Cactus Cafe** is your last chance for fuel for 35 miles. We now approach two of the most luxurious resorts in Big Sur, practically across the road from each other at the 29.5-mile mark. On the ocean side, **Post Ranch Inn,** (831) 667–2200, (800) 527–2200, www.postranchinn.com, has been receiving rave reviews as one of the ultimate resort spots in the world since its heralded opening in 1992. The unique stone, glass, and wood architecture blends in with the spectacular scenery from a bluff high above the Pacific Ocean. The altitude of the room prices nearly matches the altitude of the bluff, but who's to say the experience isn't worth it? The **Sierra Mar** restaurant is seemingly perched on the edge of the world. When seating is available, a limited number of visitors can join the guests for a delicious lunch or continental Californian

dinner. Call the Post Ranch Inn for reservations. The **Post Ranch Mercantile** offers a variety of one-of-a-kind clothing, jewelry, and gift items.

Inland, **Ventana Resort,** (831) 667–2331, (800) 628–6500, www.ventanainn.com, is a local favorite, both for its luxurious accommodations (including fabulous clothing-optional Japanese hot baths) and its popular Cielo restaurant and bar with imaginative California cuisine for lunch and dinner (see our Restaurants chapter for more). The gift shop and boutique has a surprising selection of high-end goods for such a rustic location.

At the 30-mile mark, you'll find **Nepenthe,** (831) 667–2345, www.nepenthe bigsur.com. This legendary restaurant, built on a bluff 800 feet above the ocean in 1944 as a getaway cottage for Orson Welles and Rita Hayworth, is perhaps the most popular of all eateries among Big Sur day trippers. The coastline views on a bright sunny day or during the evening sunset are nothing short of stunning. There's ample outdoor seating to enjoy the vistas, and the food is downright tasty. The Ambrosia Burger with the homemade bean salad and basket of hot fries has been known to cause bliss, and vegetarians will be delighted with the menu too (also see our Restaurants chapter).

Just below Nepenthe at the parking lot is **The Phoenix Shop,** (831) 667–2347, with a great selection of gifts made by local artists. And directly over The Phoenix is **Cafe Kevah,** (831) 667–2344, a great choice for a quick pastry and coffee or soup and sandwich.

Heading south of Big Sur Valley, shortly past Nepenthe, Highway 1 leaves Big Sur Valley and again returns to the coast. Nestled at the mouth of Graves Canyon on the inland side of Highway 1 is the **Henry Miller Library** (mile 31). Miller lived, wrote, and painted in Big Sur from 1944 to 1962, and his story of the region is

[Facing page] *Built in 1932, Bixby Bridge is one of the most beautiful and most photographed bridges in the world.* MONTEREY COUNTY CONVENTION AND VISITORS BUREAU

contained in *Big Sur and the Oranges of Hieronymous Bosch.* The library was founded by Miller's longtime friend Emil White and features a fascinating collection of Miller's books, photographs, letters, art, and other memorabilia. The library is open every day but Thursday from 11:00 A.M. to 6:00 P.M. (Thursday through Sunday 11:00 A.M. to 6:00 P.M. in the winter) and schedules various exhibits, readings, concerts, and other special events year-round. Call (831) 667–2574 or visit www.henrymiller.org for details.

At 31.5 miles is **Deetjens Big Sur Inn,** (831) 667–2377, www.deetjens.com, a bed-and-breakfast inn with great rustic charm. Pioneers Helmuth and Helen Deetjen, immigrants from Norway, homesteaded this spot at Castro Canyon in the early 1930s and welcomed overnight guests traveling the coastal wagon road (prior to Highway 1). That tradition continues today as the Norwegian-style inn built with locally milled scavenged redwood is operated by the nonprofit Deetjen's Big Sur Inn Preservation Foundation. Breakfast and dinner are served for nonguests by reservation; call (831) 667–2378.

Two miles south of Deetjens is **Coast Gallery & Café,** (831) 667–2301, www.coastgalleries.com, the best known of the Big Sur art galleries. Housed in two giant, empty redwood water tanks, the gallery specializes in the work of local painters, sculptors, woodworkers, and other artisans. Around back is the **Henry Miller Gallery,** featuring a selection of watercolors, lithographs, books, and photos by the famous Big Sur citizen. There's also a great candle shop where you can watch a master candlemaker wax poetic.

Back on Highway 1, we continue south to a majestic stretch of coastline. At about mile 36.5 is beach access to **Partington Cove.** Look for an old dirt road that slopes directly to the beach and features some great secluded coves and tunnels. This spot was once an important shipping point for tanbark and timber. At the 38-mile mark is **Julia Pfeiffer Burns State Park,** a fabulous spot for quick and easy walks to some beautiful spots along the Big Sur coast. The most popular walk is along the trail that disappears into a tunnel under Highway 1 and emerges at **McWay Cove.** Here you'll find a splendid view of **McWay Falls,** which, at 80 feet, is said to be the tallest waterfall in California that drops directly into the Pacific. (Actually, it hits the sandy beach at low tide, but who's to nitpick?) The trail to the view of McWay Falls ends at a great little outlook that provides an unbelievable panorama of the coast back northward. It's a great spot for whale watching during December and January. You'll also notice ruins from the **Waterfall House,** which was home to Lathrop and Helen Hooper Brown, close friends of Julia Pfeiffer of the Big Sur pioneer Pfeiffer family. Inland at Julia Pfeiffer Burns State Park are nice trails through the redwoods, along McWay Creek, and up into the Santa Lucia Mountains. There are also picnic tables and restrooms for a nice luncheon stop.

South of Julia Pfeiffer Burns State Park, it gets a bit windier on Highway 1, and Big Sur becomes less populated. But there are still many highlights for those venturing onward. The first point of interest at mile 41 is the **Esalen Institute,** (831) 667–3000, www.esalen.org, one of the most notable venues of the "human potential movement" of the 1960s. Today Esalen offers many workshops and spa activities (it is on the site of the former Old Slate Hot Springs). Fortunately, the outdoor baths that were washed down the cliffs during the El Niño storms of the winter of 1998 have finally been restored. A hot soak in a bath seemingly suspended in the sky over the Big Sur coastline is a treat of a lifetime. Call regarding public access to the hot baths.

Ten miles farther at the 51-mile mark is Lucia, home of the **Lucia Lodge,** (831) 667–2391. The restaurant and cabins here are absolutely fantastic for those wanting to get away from it all. The cabins line a bluff overlooking a picturesque bay hundreds of feet below. The cabin farthest

Deetjens Big Sur Inn has been welcoming overnight guests since the 1930s, long before Highway 1 was built. © JULIE ARMSTRONG/MONTEREY COUNTY CONVENTION AND VISITORS BUREAU

out on the point is particularly nice for a romantic evening for two overlooking Lucia Cove and the Pacific.

At mile 52 is **Limekiln State Park,** (831) 667-2403. In addition to a fascinating half-mile hike up to the historic late 19th-century kilns of the Rockland Cement Company and a pretty waterfall along Limekiln Creek, the park provides coastal access to a beautiful beach. A pleasant picnic area and campsites are also available. The entrance fee is $3.00.

About a mile past Limekiln (mile 53 on our trip) is the **Immaculate Heart New Camaldoli Hermitage,** (831) 667-2456, www.contemplation.com, the first branch of the Benedictine order of monks in America. There's a gift shop that sells religious artifacts, books, and the Hermitage's famous brandied fruitcake and date-nut cake. (For those of you who don't make the trip this far south, these goods are also sold at Hermitage Shop in Carmel.)

Nacimiento-Fergusson Road

At mile 55 near Kirk Creek, you have your first opportunity since you passed Carmel Valley Road to leave Highway 1 and cross the Santa Lucia Range to the Salinas Valley. Nacimiento-Fergusson Road travels east over the 4,000-foot Nacimiento Summit before winding down the eastern slope through the **Fort Hunter Liggett Military Reservation** and onward to **Mission San Antonio de Padua,** the town of Jolon, and finally U.S. 101 at King City. The total trek from Highway 1 to U.S. 101 is 55 miles. Plan for about a one-and-a-half to two-hour drive over this narrow but paved road, which provides some great vistas back toward the coast, within the Santa Lucia Range, and overlooking the Salinas Valley. There are campgrounds with restrooms about 8.5 miles up the road from

McWay Cove is home to McWay Falls, said to be the tallest waterfall that drops into the Pacific Ocean in all of California. MONTEREY COUNTY CONVENTION AND VISITORS BUREAU

Highway 1 if you want to take a detour back into the Santa Lucias for a scenic vista and then return to the coast.

Continuing south on Highway 1 to mile 59 brings you to the quaint community of **Pacific Valley.** In addition to having a restaurant, market, and shop, Pacific Valley is home to the **Big Sur Jade Co. and Museum,** (805) 927-8655, which features some fine examples of the native jade. At mile 60 is **Sand Dollar Beach,** a favorite among beachcombers, scuba divers, surfers, picnickers, hikers, and hang gliders. This expansive stretch of sand makes for an enjoyable day in itself. A couple miles farther south is **Jade Cove,** reportedly the only known source of certain types of California nephrite and Pacific Blue jade. Rockhounds and divers owe it to themselves to make this little side trip to the water's edge.

The town of **Gorda** at mile 65 is your last best chance for diesel, gas, snacks, or a meal before continuing on down south about 25 more miles to perhaps the best known attraction of the southern Big Coast, Hearst Castle. The name Gorda comes from the Spanish term for "fat woman," which was the name given to the large shapely rock just off the coast.

The **Whalewatcher Cafe,** (805) 927-3918, is a favorite among Highway 1 regulars. Traditional American breakfasts, lunches, and dinners are accompanied by some fresh seafood dishes. Continue south past Soda Springs, Salmon Creek, and Ragged Point (all good scenic and hiking spots) and beyond the **Piedras Blancas** (white rocks) **Lighthouse** (in operation since 1874) to about mile 91 at **San Simeon.** That places you directly at the entrance to Hearst Castle. This is the ultimate destination for many visitors and a must-see for anyone interested in the style, architecture, and opulence of California's gilded age gone by.

Hearst Castle

Hearst Castle, (800) 444-4445, www.hearstcastle.org, was the summer home of publisher William Randolph Hearst, who began construction at what he commonly called "The Ranch" in 1919. The designer was famous San Francisco architect Julia Morgan, whose talents and patience were both severely tested on this monumental project. For nearly three decades, as the home expanded into its current 165 rooms (including 41 baths) and more than 125 acres of manicured gardens, terraces, paths, and pools, it was visited by the most famous names in world and Hollywood affairs. Especially impressive are the interior decor, antiques, and the many classic statues. Most of these largely European treasures in the house were unloaded from ships docked at San Simeon Pier and hauled up the hill to the castle. Today, there are a variety of tours of Hearst's La Cuesta Encantada (The Enchanted Hill), each offering a unique view of the estate. Tour 1, the so-called Experience Tour, is certainly the best for first-time visitors, providing access to the first floor of Casa Grande (the main house) with its famous Moorish twin towers, the spectacular gardens, and one of the three guesthouses. Tour 2 goes through the upper levels of Casa Grande (including the magnificent library), while Tour 3 takes you through the north wing of the main house and the Casa del Mar guesthouse. Tour 4 is an extended visit to the gardens and terraces and provides interesting peeks into the wine cellar and the dressing rooms of the Neptune Pool. All of the tours visit both the 104-foot-long, 345,000-gallon outdoor Neptune Pool and the 205,000-gallon, Venetian-glass-tiled indoor Roman Pool. Tours begin at 8:20 A.M., take approximately 100 minutes, and require plenty of walking, so wear those comfy shoes. Wheelchair-accessible tours can be arranged by calling (805) 927-2020 at least 10 days in advance of your visit. Entrance fees per tour are $12.00 to $18.00 for adults and $5.00 to $7.00 for youth ages 6 to 17. An evening tour with docents in 1930s period costumes is available in the spring and fall; it runs $24.00 for adults and $10.00 for children.

The coastline below Hearst Castle is a worthy destination all its own. There's **William Randolph Hearst Memorial State Beach,** (805) 927-2068, with swimming, fishing, picnic areas, and great views; the old **San Simeon Pier;** and **Sebastian's General Store,** a State Historical Landmark in the small town of San Simeon.

Cambria

Continuing south on Highway 1 to about the 101-mile mark, you reach the town of Cambria, originally settled in the 1860s by Welsh miners looking for copper and quicksilver. Often referred to as a more rustic version of Carmel, today's Cambria is a charming artist community made up of three distinct villages. The **East Village** is a quaint town of late 19th-century Victorian architecture, now home to restaurants, shops, galleries, and lodging. The **West Village** around Main Street also has enjoyable shops, galleries, and restaurants and is home to the Cambria Chamber of Commerce, (805) 927-3624, www.cambriachamber.org, which provides valuable visitor information. Finally, **Moonstone Beach** hugs the coast paralleling Highway 1 and is home to many bed-and-breakfast inns and other accommodations as well as great picnic spots at Leffingwell Landing and Shamel Park.

Others spots of interest include **Nit Wit Ridge,** a "found-material" mansion built by a local eccentric and now a historical landmark, on Hillcrest Drive north of Main Street, and the old **Cambria Jail House** on Main Street.

Inland from Cambria on Highway 46 are local wineries and tasting rooms. Highway 46 connects to U.S. 101 for a straighter and faster route back north to Salinas and (via Highway 68 West) the Monterey Peninsula.

Morro Bay to San Luis Obispo

Twenty miles farther south on Highway 1 is the town of **Morro Bay** (mile 121), situated at the heart of Estero Bay between the smaller towns of Cayucos and Los Osos. Morro Bay Harbor lies inside a 3-mile sandspit that provides protection for a thriving fishing community and recreational boaters. And standing like a guardian over the bay is 576-foot tall **Morro Rock,** one of the Nine Sisters volcano peaks that run toward San Luis Obispo. Today, this "Gibraltar of the Pacific" is a protected home for endangered peregrine falcons.

Morro Bay Estuary is a 2,300-acre tidal wetland park that provides for great hiking and wildlife watching. On the southeastern shore of Morro Bay is the **Elfin Forest,** an ecologically diverse parkland that is home to about 150 species of birds, mammals, and reptiles. There are also interesting middens throughout the parkland, evidence of the Chumash tribe that populated the area at one time. Nearby **Montana De Oro State Park** is 8,000 acres of shoreline and inland beauty with picnic tables and barbecue pits along the sandy beaches at Spooner's Cove. The active set will enjoy hiking, horseback riding, bicycling, hang gliding, fishing, tidepooling, or surfing in this park. The more citified visitors will appreciate the **Embarcadero,** a stretch of shops and restaurants along the harbor. From here you can visit a small aquarium or rent paddleboats to cruise the harbor.

From Morro Bay, we travel 14 miles inland to our final destination, the city of **San Luis Obispo** (mile 135). With a population of 45,000, this county seat is home to California Polytechnic State University and Mission San Luis Obispo de Tolosa. The downtown area is a lively, vibrant place with many outdoor cafes, coffeehouses, and specialty shops amid the picturesque Victorians and adobes. The Thursday night **Farmer's Market Street Fair** on Higuera Street is a local tradition with 5 city blocks of shops and booths selling fresh produce, flowers, arts and crafts, and great barbecued meats. The **Mission Plaza** area along San Luis Creek is home to a variety of special activities and festivals, so check out the local calendar of events available through the San Luis Obispo Chamber of Commerce and Visitors Center at 1039 Chorro Street, (805) 781-2777, slochamber.com.

From San Luis Obispo, the quickest route back to the Monterey Peninsula is to take U.S. 101 north to Salinas and then Highway 68 West back to Monterey. It's typically a two-and-a-half to three-hour drive, but it's quicker than the return trip on Highway 1. If you're considering spending the night, there are many nice spots within the city of San Luis Obispo. Or for a real local experience, follow U.S. 101 to **The Madonna Inn,** 100 Madonna Road, (805) 543-3000, www.madonnainn.com, a landmark for more than 40 years. Each of the inn's more than 100 rooms is uniquely decorated, including all-rock rooms with waterfall showers. Seeing is believing.

HIGHWAY 1 NORTH TO SAN FRANCISCO

North of the Monterey Peninsula, Highway 1 follows a storied and historic route along the scenic Pacific coast up to the grand city of San Francisco and beyond. Unlike Highway 1 South, which twists and turns like a pretzel through the rugged Santa Lucia Mountains of Big Sur, Highway 1 North is a relatively straight and gentle stretch of road. You pass through miles of

For up-to-date fishing and hunting information throughout the Santa Lucia Mountains, call the California Department of Fish and Game at (831) 649-2870 or visit www.dfg.ca.gov.

flat agricultural fields, small towns, historic cities, and gentle rolling coastlines.

The larger cities of Santa Cruz and San Francisco are in and of themselves substantial enough in history, charm, and splendor to warrant books all their own, and, indeed, many such books are available. So our quest here is not to provide you with all-inclusive, in-depth coverage of this long 100-mile-plus stretch of California Coast. Instead, we'll give you a general road map of points of interest on this splendid route and highlight some of our favorite spots along the way. Feel free to explore the many attractions and diversions we couldn't squeeze into this brief taste of Highway 1 north of the Monterey Peninsula.

To follow our approximate mileage markers, set your odometer on zero at the intersection of Highway 1 and Highway 68 east toward Salinas. Traveling north beyond Monterey and Seaside, you'll hit a stretch of tall sand dunes that obscure the view of the sea but provide a beauty all their own. This stretch of dunes is a favorite among hang gliders. At mile 4.5 we pass the entrance to the former Fort Ord and the current California State University at Monterey Bay.

Marina

Mile 7 up Highway 1 takes us to the bedroom community of Marina, population 25,000. Though not geared as a visitors' destination, there are a couple of potential diversions to point out. First is **Marina State Beach,** (831) 384-7695, a favorite spot among local surfers and hang gliders, at the west end of Reservation Road. Consistent wind and high sand dunes along the 170-acre park make for ideal hang gliding (or watching it), but swimming conditions can be dangerous due to a steep beach and heavy surf. A half-mile boardwalk provides for wheelchair access, and there is no entry fee.

Do you like to make a friendly wager on a game of cards? Marina is home to

Fort Ord, 5 miles north of Monterey on Highway 1, was largely closed in 1993. About 750 acres, including three housing areas and the post exchange and commissary, was annexed to the Presidio of Monterey. A majority of the land is now being used as home to California State University at Monterey Bay and, increasingly, sections are being developed for civilian housing.

two small casinos that offer games of chance and cocktail lounges. **Marina Casino Club,** 204 Carmel Avenue, (831) 384-0925, and **Mortimer's,** 3100 Del Monte Boulevard, (831) 384-7667, offer poker, Texas Hold'em, California Lowball, 21st Century Blackjack, and Pai Gow Tiles. Finally, recreational vehicle fans should certainly consider **Marina Dunes RV Park,** 3330 Dunes Drive, (831) 384-6914, offering 75 sites (60 with full hookups) and easy beach access for those morning and evening strolls.

Castroville

Back on Highway 1, we drive north of Marina through wide-open spaces and agricultural fields. You'll likely notice large clumping plants with long serrated leaves and possibly big green thistlelike blossoms standing out on long stems. These beauties are artichokes, and they put our next destination on the map. The town of Castroville is known worldwide as The Artichoke Capital of the World. Virtually the entire commercial artichoke crop in the United States is grown right here. The annual Castroville Artichoke Festival, held one weekend each August, draws huge crowds of fans who love their "chokes" boiled, deep-fried, barbecued, and every which way. Street vendors and restaurants serve up the thorny delicacies, while street parades and live music add to the festivities. To enter Castroville, take the Highway 156 exit at about mile 13 on our trip. Then exit immediately on Highway 183, also known as Merritt Street, the main drag through tiny Castroville. If it's not festival time, the town is pretty quiet, but there are a few restaurants worth noting. First, on the right as you enter town, is the **Giant Artichoke Restaurant,** Highway 1, (831) 633-3204, which serves the favorite thistle every which way but loose. Then there are two of the best greasy spoons in the area. **Bing's Diner,** 10961 Merritt Street, (831) 633-0400, offers great diner grub in an old streetcar. It's small and popular, so be prepared for a little wait. Then there is **Central Texan Barbecue,** 10500 Merritt Street, (831) 633-2285, many times voted the best barbecue in the area by local reader polls. You're also likely to notice a local gathering spot called **The Norma Jean Club,** named after the first Castroville Artichoke Festival Queen, who later adopted the screen name of Marilyn Monroe.

Past Castroville, Highway 1 narrows to a two-lane undivided road. Drive carefully with your headlights on through this 8-mile stretch, especially during foggy days and nights. There are plenty of slow-moving agricultural vehicles exiting and entering the highway, so be alert. At mile 16, enter the left turn lane to visit the charming fishing village of **Moss Landing.** A 90-degree left takes you to Potrero Road and the route to **Salinas River State Beach.** Here is where the Salinas River empties into the Pacific and where you'll find some great surf-fishing along the picturesque sand dunes. The park is open from sunrise to sunset daily with no entrance fee.

Moss Landing

By taking a 45-degree left from Highway 1 at mile 16, you enter Moss Landing Road, the route to the town of Moss Landing and its commercial fishing harbor. Moss Landing Road is a gold mine for junk store lovers and antiques shop aficionados. While unbelievable bargains are getting harder to find these days, you'll still discover some reasonably priced collectibles and fine antiques within some of the most rustically charming shops around these parts. Virtually any of the many stores in tiny Moss Landing can hold a hidden treasure, but some of our favorites include **Waterfront Antiques,** 7902 Sandholdt Road, (831) 633-1112; **The Wood Shed,** a tiny shop next door to Waterfront with no listed phone; **Little Red Barn Antiques,** 8461 Moss Landing Road, (831) 633-5583; and **Moss Landing Antique and Trading Company**, Moss Landing Road, (831) 633-3988. When it's time to eat lunch or dinner, Moss Landing is home to some wonderful fresh seafood restaurants. For lunch, **Phil's Fish Market and Eatery,** Sandholdt Road, (831) 633-2152, has marvelous fish and chips, chowder, and other simple seafood selections, with very casual indoor and outdoor seating. **The Whole Enchilada,** Highway 1 and Moss Landing Road, (831) 633-3038, does excellent Mexican seafood dishes (see also our Restaurants chapter). Farther north on Highway 1, at about mile 18, is a shop called **Little Baja,** (831) 633-2254, with a great selection of pottery and statuary from Mexico and elsewhere. Finally, Moss Landing is also home to the **Monterey Bay Aquarium Research Institute,** 7700 Sandholdt Road, (831) 775-1773, which holds a fascinating open house for the public each spring.

Elkhorn Slough

At mile 17 on Highway 1 near the large power plant in Moss Landing is Dolan Road. Turn east (right) here and travel 3 miles to Elkhorn Road. Turn left (north) and drive 2 miles to reach **Elkhorn Slough National Estuarine Research Reserve,** 1700 Elkhorn Road, (831) 728-2822, www.elkhornslough.org. Elkhorn Slough is what's left of an ancient river valley located at the apex of the Monterey Submarine Canyon. Today, the main slough channel winds 7 miles inland and feeds more than 2,500 acres of rich marsh and

Bargain hunters and collectors will have a field day in Moss Landing, a small fishing port that is home to dozens of antiques and junk stores. MONTEREY COUNTY CONVENTION AND VISITORS BUREAU

tidal flats. This is home to hundreds of varieties of birds, including pelicans, herons, and egrets, as well as countless fish, sharks, crabs, rays, sea lions, otters, land mammals, and insects. You'll find an informative visitor center, interpretive displays, and miles of well-maintained trails. The Reserve is open Wednesday through Sunday from 9:00 A.M. to 5:00 P.M. Docent-led walks are available at 10:00 A.M. and 1:00 P.M. on weekends (also see our In and Around the Water chapter). *Note:* **Elkhorn Slough Safari Nature Tours** offers 10-mile, two-hour guided tours of Elkhorn Slough on a 27-foot pontoon boat. Fares are $26 for adults and $19 for children age 14 and under. Call (831) 633-5555 or visit www.elkhornslough.com for seasonal schedules and reservations. The tour departs from the Harbor District parking lot off Sandholdt Road in Moss Landing. Advance reservations required.

Back on Highway 1, mile 18.5 brings us to Geiberson Road, the turnoff to **Zmudowski State Beach,** (831) 384-7695. This is one of the most secluded and least-used beaches in the area. It is a great spot for surf fishing and taking long romantic walks along the sand. Horseback riding is allowed along the beach, but not among the long rows of sand dunes that parallel the shore. Zmudowski State Beach also has a protected nesting ground for the snowy plover. The park is open from 6:30 A.M. to 7:30 P.M., and entry is free.

Watsonville

Leaving the Moss Landing area, Highway 1 stretches out through vast agriculture fields to the northern border of Monterey County. At mile 22, Highway 1 meets Salinas Road, an inland route to the Salinas

Insiders know that Highway 1 is ideal for any trip from Monterey to San Francisco. Compared to nerve-wracking freeway travel up U.S. 101, the scenery is superb, traffic is generally light, and it typically adds only 15 to 20 minutes to the journey.

Valley, and afterward widens back into a four-lane divided freeway. Here, we enter Santa Cruz County and the city of **Watsonville,** population 32,000. Watsonville is largely an industrial town serving the vast agricultural industry in the area, but it provides a few pleasant diversions for visitors. **Gizdich Ranch,** 55 Peckham Road, (831) 722–1056, www.gizdichranch.com, provides for a fun day of berry and apple picking. Load up with baskets of fresh strawberries, raspberries, olallieberries, or Watsonville's famous Pippin apples. Or you can buy homemade jams and pies and fresh-pressed apple juice. Each Memorial Day weekend the Watsonville airport is home to the **West Coast Antique Fly-In and Air Show,** (831) 496–9559. Antique aircraft and hot-air balloons fill the skies, providing an exciting and colorful extravaganza.

At mile 23.5 on Highway 1 is San Andreas Road, the exit to **Sunset State Beach,** (831) 763–7062. This is a more developed state park than most in the area, with 90 sites for overnight trailers and campers as well as day-use picnic tables and barbecue pits. The 3 miles of flat beaches are some of the area's best for swimming, and a lifeguard is on duty during the summer. Surf fishing is also popular and, when conditions are right, beachcombers often find an ample supply of shells and sand dollars for their collections. Sunset State Beach is open from 8:00 A.M. to sunset, with a day-use fee of $3.00 per vehicle. Call the California State Parks at (800) 444–7275 for overnight camping reservations (48 hours to seven months in advance).

Aptos

Mile 31 takes us to Larken Valley Road, the exit to **Seascape Resort,** 1 Seascape Resort Drive, Aptos, (831) 688–6800 or (800) 929–7727. Seascape is a luxury resort property that provides spacious accommodations, a great restaurant (Sanderlings), a splendid pool and spa, a tennis court, an exercise gym, and miles of scenic beaches. The **Aptos Seascape Golf Course** is adjacent to the resort. Day trippers should definitely keep Seascape in mind for their next weekend getaway in this neck of the woods.

At mile 32.5 we enter the unincorporated town of **Aptos,** a population-19,000 bedroom community of Santa Cruz. Aptos is home to **Cabrillo College,** 6500 Soquel Drive, (831) 479–6100, a two-year community college; and the charming shopping districts of Historic Aptos Village and Seascape Village. Mile 34 in Aptos brings us to the Seacliff Beach exit. **Seacliff State Beach,** (831) 685–6442, is an 85-acre park with a fascinating pier, partly made from an old 430-foot concrete ship from the World War I era, the *Palo Alto.* The boat was towed here and sunk to the sea floor in shallow waters in 1929 to be used as an amusement and fishing ship. Although the amusement business went broke after two years, anglers still find the ship and an added pier an excellent spot to spend a day fishing for perch, sole, flounder, lingcod, and halibut. This is a popular and sometimes crowded swimming beach, and there are picnic facilities and 26 developed sites for trailers and campers. A lifeguard is on duty for the summer. There is a day-use fee of $3.00 per vehicle, and overnight spots for self-contained vehicles are $18.00 per night.

Capitola Village

Mile 37 brings us to the exit for Capitola Village. Known as California's oldest seaside resort (dating back to 1869), Capitola Village is a charming beach town in a protected cove between two sea bluffs, with the Soquel River meandering to the ocean. The wharf and riverside area are full of small shops, art galleries, and sidewalk cafes, reminiscent of a European seaport. Upriver lies the well-known **Shadowbrook Restaurant,** 1750 Wharf Road, (831) 475-1222, with a private tram that takes you down a steep hillside to the entrance. Two annual festivals held each September are worth a mention. First is the **Capitola National Begonia Festival,** (831) 476-3566, featuring flower-draped floats drifting down Soquel Creek and a festive sandcastle contest on the beach. The second event is the **Capitola Art & Wine Festival,** (831) 475-6522, with sidewalk art exhibitions, live music, tastings from local wineries, and food booths from area restaurants.

Santa Cruz

At mile 40 we enter Santa Cruz, at population 51,000 the largest city on the Central Coast. This town is a daytripper's delight, offering a wealth of recreational and relaxation opportunities for the entire family. The beaches themselves are wideopen expanses of white sand, relatively warm waters, and great surf. **Natural Bridges State Park,** West Cliff Drive, (831) 423-4609, features awe-inspiring arches carved by wind and water from the soft sandstone as well as great spots for swimming, tidepooling, and picnicking. This is home each October to the **Welcome Back Monarch Butterfly Festival,** which, like Pacific Grove's Butterfly Festival on the Monterey Peninsula, greets the monarch butterflies that arrive each fall to spend the winter in this area. Surfers will also want to visit the **Santa Cruz Surfing Museum** in the **Mark Abbott Lighthouse,** West Cliff Drive, (831) 420-6281. The lighthouse overlooks the famous stretch of beach called **Steamer Lane,** the birthplace of mainland U.S. surfing.

The Great Dipper, a 1920s wooden roller coaster at the Santa Cruz Beach Boardwalk, is a National Historic Landmark. It's a must ride for coaster aficionados.

Downtown shopping on the **Pacific Garden Mall,** renovated after the devastating Loma Prieta earthquake of 1989, provides for a great afternoon or evening. Restaurants offer every type of food imaginable. Among local favorites are **India Joze,** 1001 Center Street, (831) 427-3554, which serves a tasty lunch and dinner menu of Indian and California cuisine; the **Library at Chaminade,** 1 Chaminade Lane, (831) 475-5600, for elegant evening dining; **The Hindquarter Bar and Grille,** 303 Soquel Avenue, (831) 426-7770, for hearty steaks, ribs, and seafood; **Oswald's,** 1547 Pacific Avenue, (831) 423-7427, for a charming bistro atmosphere with European flair; **Ideal Bar & Grill,** 106 Beach Street at Santa Cruz Wharf, (831) 423-5271, for a casual beachside lunch or dinner; and **Miramar Fish Grotto,** 45 Municipal Wharf, (831) 423-4441, for fresh seafood and a fantastic view of Lighthouse Point. There are many, many more fine restaurants in Santa Cruz, so don't hesitate to explore and find your own favorite.

For fantastic family fun in Santa Cruz we have three attractions to recommend. Kids' favorite, bar none, is the **Santa Cruz Beach Boardwalk,** (831) 423-5590, www.beachboardwalk.com, California's oldest amusement park right on the sand. The crowning glory here is the Great Dipper, a 1920s wooden roller coaster with a 70-foot ascent and tummy-tickling drops and turns. The Great Dipper and the Beach Boardwalk's 1911 carousel are both National Historic Landmarks. Other fun attractions include the bumper cars, Logger's Revenge water slide ride, and Neptune's Kingdome arcade. Plan on a whole day here, and take advantage of the Unlimited Ride wristbands, which go for around $25.

For something really different, visit **The Mystery Spot,** 469 Mystery Spot Road, (831) 423–8897, www.mystery-spot. com, Santa Cruz's answer to the Twilight Zone. Magnetic forces and gravity seem to have gone awry in the 150-foot-wide spot within a redwood grove in the hills about the city. Compasses go haywire. Things roll uphill. Optical illusions abound. The senses confound. Pure kitsch and pure fun, The Mystery Spot is a must-see for all of us who are a little off-center our-selves. Admission is $5.00 and free for those younger than five.

Our third family fun spot is **Roaring Camp & Big Trees Narrow Gauge Rail-road,** Graham Hill Road, (831) 335–4484, www.roaringcamprr.com, which is actually in the city of Felton in the Santa Cruz Mountains. This is a narrow gauge railway pulled by steam locomotives that chug through **Henry Cowell Redwood State Park,** down the San Lorenzo River Canyon and through Santa Cruz to the Beach Boardwalk. You can depart, spend some time at the Boardwalk, and return to Roaring Camp later in the afternoon. Chuckwagon barbecues are also offered. The cost of the ride to the Beach Board-walk is $19 for adults and $15 for children. Round-trip rides within the Santa Cruz Mountains are also offered for $17 and $12. Call for seasonal schedules. To find Roaring Camp, take Highway 17 north out of Santa Cruz. Exit in Scotts Valley on Mt. Hermon Road and proceed 3.5 miles to Graham Hill Road. Go ½ mile, and it's on the right.

Navigating Highway 1 north through Santa Cruz can be a little tricky. When you reach the Highway 17 interchange (a commuter route to San Jose and the San Francisco Bay area) at mile 40.5, the Highway 1 freeway ends. As Highway 1 drops into the surface streets of Santa Cruz proper, follow the signs to "Beaches and Ocean Street" if you're going to the Beach Boardwalk, wharf, or other water-front attractions. Follow the signs to Half Moon Bay and Highway 1 to proceed on our day trip north toward San Francisco.

At mile 42, Highway 1 takes a right-hand turn onto Mission Street and contin-ues through residential neighborhoods. (When you reach mile 43 at Laurel Street, notice the great farm-worker mural on the side of La Esperana Market.) At mile 44 is Bay Street, where a right-hand turn will lead you to the **University of California at Santa Cruz,** (831) 459–4008, www.ucsc. edu, home of the UCSC Banana Slugs and one of the loveliest campuses you can hope to find. This University of California campus is known for its liberal curriculum and relaxed campus atmosphere.

Between Santa Cruz and Half Moon Bay

At mile 45, Highway 1 exits residential Santa Cruz and opens back up to beauti-ful coastal views. Mile 46 brings us to **Wilder Ranch State Park,** an interesting beach park that was once a 4,000-acre ranch. Many of the historic 1870 ranch buildings are still there. A visitor center offering group tours is on-site; call (831) 426–0505 for information and reserva-tions. On weekends, ranch hands dress in Victorian costume and demonstrate blacksmithing, doll making, and other 19th-century crafts. Wilder Ranch is also a popular spot among local surfers. The day-use fee is $3.00 per car.

Mile 52 brings us to **Bonnie Doon Beach,** at the foot of Bonnie Doon Road. This area has traditionally been used by locals and UCSC students as a nude beach, so be prepared for sunbathers baring it all. Mile 53.5 brings us to charm-ing **Davenport,** population 200. Originally a small company town built around the Pacific Cement and Aggregates plant, Davenport is now a quiet getaway spot that offers a great stop for Highway 1 day trippers. The main attraction is the **New Davenport Cash Store, Restaurant and Bed & Breakfast Inn,** right on Highway 1, (831) 426–4122. At lunch the restaurant serves up great sandwiches made with delicious homemade bread. The hot dishes for breakfast, lunch, and dinner are also very fresh and tasty. The Cash Store inside the restaurant offers crafts from local artists as well as other interesting goods, while the bed-and-breakfast around back provides quiet and comfortable accommodations. Other stopping points in this tiny town include **Whale City Bakery Bar & Grill,** Highway 1, (831) 423-9803, for some coffee, croissants, cookies, or other baked goods for the road, and the **Pacific School Thrift Shop,** 81 Center Street, (831) 423-9338, where you just might find a great little bargain and vacation memento.

Leaving Davenport, Highway 1 hugs the coast, providing many spots for easy beach access. At mile 56, Scott Creek flows into the Pacific to create a freshwater marsh. The beaches have fascinating tide pools carved from sandstone, while the coastal bluffs are formed from ancient marine sedimentary rock that is 10 to 20 million years old. Waddel Creek and the "Skyline to the Sea" trailhead to **Big Basin Redwoods State Park,** (831) 338-8860, are at mile 61. You'll find a nature center and the beginning point of an 11-mile hike through the grassy Rancho Del Oso Canyon to the majestic redwood groves of Big Basin, California's oldest state park. It's a lengthy but moderate hike, with two trail camps along the way that can be reserved through Big Basin State Park headquarters. This canyon was explored by Captain Gaspar de Portolá back in 1769, and in 1862 it became home to what was to become the largest lumber mill in Santa Cruz County.

Año Nuevo State Reserve

At mile 62 we enter San Mateo County and at mile 63.5 reach **Año Nuevo State Reserve,** (650) 879-0227, (800) 444-4445, www.anonuevo.org. The 4,000-acre reserve is known worldwide by naturalists

as an important birthing and mating ground for huge northern elephant seals who arrive each December and stay through March. The large males can be up to 16 feet long and weigh three tons. The smaller 1,200-pound females typically give birth to pups within a week of their arrival. The mating typically begins in late January, and ferocious turf wars often erupt as the large bulls fight for dominance. Visiting Año Nuevo during the mating and young-bearing season is allowed only through 3-mile guided tours led by park rangers each weekend. During the rest of the year, you are free to explore this peninsula and its fascinating tide pools, which are abundant with life. Unusual tube masses, created by the abundant tubeworms, are often visible at low tide. The area is also mating grounds for harbor seals and long-necked cormorants. Smaller groups of elephant seals may return to molt as well. Shell mounds and other remnants of the Ohlone Indians who lived for centuries near this area can also be found. There is a $5.00 parking fee and a $4.00 per-person charge for the guided tour. Call (800) 444-4445 for reservations.

At mile 66.5, you'll find the **Costanoa Coastal Lodge and Camp,** (650) 879-1100, (800) 738-7477, www.costanoa.com. This is a fabulous overnight excursion into the tranquility of a lovely stretch of California coast and mountain. Accommodations include a 40-room lodge, cabins (wood and canvas varieties), and RV and tent sites. It's a great setup for hikers, adjacent to four state parks and 30,000 acres crisscrossed with bountiful foot trails. And after a big day of hiking, you can visit the spa for a whole-body massage—Swedish or shiatsu, your choice. Two nights here with a visit to Año Nuevo in between makes for a memorable weekend.

Mile 68 of Highway 1 brings us to the entrance to **Butano State Park,** (650) 879-2044, one of the area's nicest campgrounds, with 21 developed sites and hiking and cycling trails among redwood and fir forests that are home to purple calypso orchids. There is a $3.00 vehicle fee and a $15.00 to $17.00 per-night camping fee.

Near here is **Gazos Creek** coastal access. This pleasant, secluded spot, among grassy sand bluffs, is favored by surf-fishers and beachcombers. From the highway, you also get your first view of **Pigeon Point Lighthouse,** at mile 70 of our drive. Built in 1872 by the Coast Guard, the lighthouse is now operated by the American Youth Hostel Association and accommodates up to 50 visitors per night. Call (650) 879-0633 or visit www.pigeonpointlighthouse.org for information about accommodations, and call (650) 879-2120 for seasonal lighthouse tours, including newly offered night tours.

Mile 73 takes us to **Bean Hollow State Beach,** (650) 879-2170, a 44-acre beach known for its scenic vistas, secluded beaches, harbor seals, and lively tide pools. There is no entrance fee.

At mile 76.5 is the inland turnoff to **Pescadero,** a historic little town founded in the 1860s. About 2 miles up Highway 84, Pescadero makes for an enjoyable drive back into some idyllic countryside. For lunch, stop in at **Duarte's Tavern,** 202 Stage Road, (650) 879-0464, for its famous artichoke soup. Or stop by **Muzzi's Market,** 251 Stage Road, (650) 879-0410, to pick up some picnic fare for a drive on the back-country roads. **Memorial County Park,** (415) 363-4021, with its towering redwoods and scenic Pescadero Creek, makes for a great picnic spot. A limited number of campsites are also available.

Back on Highway 1, mile 77 brings us to **Pescadero State Beach,** (650) 726-8820. This 635-acre state park also provides for a nice picnic and tidepooling spot, with the Pescadero Marsh Natural Preserve right across the highway.

At mile 79, **Pomponio State Park,** (650) 879-2170, is yet another great lunch spot, especially if you are in need of some nice tables and barbecue pits. The sandy beach is also ideal for strolling and wading.

Mile 81 brings us to **San Gregorio State Beach,** (650) 879-2170, a 170-acre park where San Gregorio Creek empties into the Pacific. The estuary here is home to a variety of sea animals and birds.

Half Moon Bay

At mile 90 we reach civilization, the town of **Half Moon Bay,** population 10,600. Known as the Pumpkin Capital of the World, this is San Mateo County's oldest town, founded in 1846. It has a long history of agriculture due to its uniform mild climate and today is home to an abundance of both vegetable and flower growers. The big orange gourd, the pumpkin, remains king of the crops. Each October for the past quarter-century, this city has hosted the **Half Moon Bay Art & Pumpkin Festival.** The free-admission weekend event draws crowds from up and down the California coast, who enjoy the festivities on Main Street. Artist booths, live music, street performers, home-baked goods, and The Great Pumpkin Parade create a colorful scene. A giant pumpkin contest, a pumpkin-carving contest, and a haunted house are especially popular with the kids.

Half Moon Bay has visitor attractions during the rest of the year as well. At mile 92 near the Highway 92 East intersection is Kelly Avenue, the entrance to **Half Moon Bay State Beach,** (650) 726-8819. This is an ideal spot for sunbathing, beachcombing, picnicking, and horseback riding. Nearby, **Sea Horse Ranch,** 1828 Coast Highway, (650) 726-9903, and **Friendly Acres Ranch,** 2150 Cabrillo Highway, (650) 726-9916, provides horses and ponies to ride among 12,000 acres and miles of scenic beaches and coastal trails.

Hungry? We've got a couple of interesting choices here in Half Moon Bay and environs. At mile 95, **The Miramar Beach Restaurant,** 131 Mirada Road, (650) 726-9053, is a great seafood establishment that was originally a Prohibition-era roadhouse and bordello. Try the famous clam chowder. Or for something really out of this world, go on to mile 98.5 and the

Moss Beach Distillery Restaurant, (650) 728-5595, at 140 Beach Way. In addition to serving fine food, this establishment is known for a couple of tragic female ghosts who are occasionally spotted in or about the place. The Blue Lady, killed in an automobile accident back in the 1920s while on her way here to meet her lover, is said to be seen wandering the beach in her trademark blue dress. Another woman, who later threw herself off the cliffs and drowned herself in anguish over the same lover, has been spotted near the restaurant as well, dripping wet, covered with seaweed. The restaurant even holds special séance dinners in hopes of calling the two women from the other side. Bon appetit!

At mile 100 is **Montara State Beach,** (650) 726-8819. This area is known for its heavy surf and beautiful sandy beaches. While Montara is an experienced surfer's delight, beginning boarders and swimmers are advised to try a less hazardous spot. There is no entry fee.

At mile 101 of Highway 1, we reach a 3-mile stretch known as **Devil's Slide.** The winding, cliffside roadway is reminiscent of stretches of Highway 1 south at Big Sur, and, like Big Sur, is subject to landslides during the rainy season. In fact, during poor weather, it wouldn't be a bad idea to check with CalTrans, (800) 427-7623, and make sure this section of highway is open. If it's closed, take Highway 92 east back at Half Moon Bay to continue onward to San Francisco. Highway 92 crosses the Santa Cruz Mountains and hooks up with U.S. 280 north, which takes you directly into San Francisco.

San Francisco

We leave the Devil's Slide area at mile 104 and in ½ mile reach the town of **Pacifica,** a bedroom community of San Francisco. This tranquil little town is home to a few charming restaurants, including the cleverly named **Chez D Cafe,** 220 Paloma Avenue, (650) 355-2730, for coffee, baked goods, and light fare in the historic 1906 Anderson's Store building. Pacifica is also home to the **Sanchez Adobe,** 1000 Linda Mar Boulevard, (650) 359-1462. The oldest building in San Mateo County, it is now a fascinating museum that reveals local history and lore back to the local Native Americans and first Spanish settlers.

At mile 107, Highway 1 becomes a modern freeway for our ascent into San Francisco. As we enter the bustle of the city, Highway 1 merges temporarily with U.S. 280 North. As you enter San Francisco proper, Highway 1 then splits off to the left and takes you through Golden Gate Park, by the San Francisco Zoo, and over the Golden Gate Bridge to Marin and points north. U.S. 280 will take you to downtown San Francisco, the Bay Bridge, and over to Oakland and the East Bay.

To try and give justice to the city of San Francisco in this chapter would be an injustice. However, we would be remiss not to mention a few of the notable spots. For attractions, **Golden Gate Park,** Fell and Stanyon Streets, (415) 556-5801, and the **San Francisco Zoo,** Sloat Street and 45th Avenue, (415) 753-7080, are a real treat on a bright sunshiny day. **The Powell-Hyde Cable Car** line is a must, followed by a visit to the **Cable Car Barn and Museum** at 1201 Mason Street. **Chinatown** is a great eating and shopping experience, as are **Union Square** and **Ghirardelli Square.** A stroll through **North Beach** provides a real flavor for the city's Italian and Bohemian roots. **Coit Tower** has a spectacular view of the bay and marvelous interior murals. **Alcatraz Island,** of course, is a fascinating trip. Our list here could go on and on, and we haven't even mentioned the **Exploratorium** or the fabulous art museums.

If you're planning on spending the night, you have a wide range of choices. For the luxury of Nob Hill, it's hard to beat the **Mark Hopkins Inter-Continental,** 999 California Street, (415) 392-3434 or (800) 227-0200, with its spectacular Top of the Mark cocktail lounge; or the **Fairmont,** 950 Mason Street, (415) 772-5000 or

(800) 527-4727. At Union Square there are the **St. Francis,** 335 Powell Street, (415) 397-7000; and the extremely reasonable and charming **Chancellor Hotel,** 433 Powell Street, (415) 362-2004 or (800) 428-4748. Over near the Dragon Gates into Chinatown, the trendy **Hotel Triton,** 342 Grant Avenue, (415) 394-0500, is a fun choice. One of this Insider's favorite groups of hotels in the San Francisco Bay area is the **Joie de Vivre Hospitality** properties, (800) 738-7477. Each hotel is uniquely decorated, very comfortable, and reasonably priced. Near Union Square, they offer the arty **Hotel Rex,** 562 Sutter Street, and the cinematic **Hotel Bijou,** 111 Mason. Near Nob Hill, it's the French Country **Petitie Auberge,** 863 Bush Street, and the swanky and very English **White Swan Inn,** 845 Bush Street. If you enjoy the kitsch of a '50s style motel, try the fun and colorful **Phoenix Hotel,** 601 Eddy Street, near the Civic Center. Plus, the on-site **Bambuddha Restaurant and Lounge** serves up spectacular Californian, Asian-influenced cuisine in a can't-be-hipper atmosphere.

For restaurants, it's hard to beat the City by the Bay. If the sky is the limit, **Masa's,** 648 Bush Street, (415) 989-7154, has appeared at the top of many top 10 lists, in both quality and price. There are many good Italian restaurants populating North Beach and other areas, including **Pane e Vino,** 3011 Steiner Street, (415) 346-2111, and **Acquerello,** 1722 Sacramento Street, (415) 567-5432. For French, both the fancy **La Folle,** 2316 Polk Street, (415) 776-5577, and the more casual bistro-style **Fringale,** 570 Fourth Street, (415) 543-0573, come highly recommended. Other eclectic establishments in hip surroundings include **Flying Saucer**, 1000 Guerrero Street, (415) 641-9955, **Restaurant Lulu,** 816 Folsom Street, (415) 495-5775, and **Zuni Cafe & Grill,** 1658 Market Street, (415) 552-2522. And for

Chinese, virtually any of the many restaurants in Chinatown serve good, authentic, and affordable food.

For your trip back to the Peninsula, your best bet is to take U.S. 280 south to Highway 85 south to Gilroy. Then take U.S. 101 south to Prunedale, Highway 156 west to Castroville, and Highway 1 south to the Monterey Peninsula. An alternate route that typically has heavier traffic is to take U.S. 101 south to Prunedale, Highway 156 to Castroville, and Highway 1 to the Monterey Peninsula. Or read this chapter backward and backtrack your way back on scenic Highway 1.

SALINAS VALLEY

Steinbeck Country, Salad Bowl of the World, and the Other California Wine Country are a few of the names given to the Salinas Valley. This long expanse of rich agricultural farmland and fast-growing towns stretches about 100 miles along U.S. 101 from north of the city of Salinas to the San Luis Obispo County line. While not often considered a tourist destination on its own, the Salinas Valley offers some great day tripping activities for visitors and residents of the Monterey Peninsula.

The Valley is proud of its agricultural heritage and its important spot in California history as a major provider of food for a hungry state, nation, and world. By staging special events like September's **Salute to Agriculture,** an extensive program of tours and tastings, the Monterey County Agricultural Commission, Salinas Area Chamber of Commerce, and other local groups have made it a point to promote the Valley's key role in keeping America and the world stocked with fresh fruits and vegetables. Lettuce, broccoli, strawberries, tomatoes, sugar beets, spinach, and cabbage are only a few of the crops

[Facing page] *The Phoenix Hotel, one of the Joie de Vivre Hospitality properties in San Francisco, is a wildly painted, art-filled '50s-style motel near the Civic Center.* TOM OWENS

grown in this fertile valley. A group of wineries and vineyards that make up Monterey Wine Country Associates, (831) 375-9400, also plans tours and special events like the August Winemaker's Celebration and November's The Great Wine Escape Weekend to celebrate the expansive and growing wine industry. Check with the Salinas Area Chamber of Commerce, (831) 424-7611, for this year's schedule of special events and other day tripping opportunities.

The National Steinbeck Center

The National Steinbeck Center is a 45,000-square-foot museum and community center honoring Nobel Prize-winning author and native son John Steinbeck. Located at 1 Main Street in historic Old Town Salinas (only 2 blocks from Steinbeck's birthplace), the center features a unique array of interactive, multisensory exhibits that lets you experience the sights, sounds, and smells of the time Steinbeck roamed the Salinas Valley and Monterey Peninsula. Text and graphic panels, film clips, and audiotapes provide detailed information on the author and his works. You'll also find the world's largest collection of Steinbeck artifacts, such as original manuscripts, correspondence, unpublished works, and even Rocinante, the camper that was Steinbeck's home on wheels during his *Travels with Charley.* The newest addition to the center is the 8,000-square-foot "Valley of the World," showcasing the rich agricultural heritage and history of Monterey County and portraying Steinbeck's early years in the Salinas Valley as depicted in *The Red Pony, East of Eden,* and *Of Mice and Men.* Among the permanent exhibits are: "Cannery Row," revealing the sights, sounds, and salty smells of The Row and Doc's Lab, as captured in *Cannery Row* and *Sweet Thursday;* "Hooverville," the agricultural labor camp of tents and cabins described in *The Grapes of Wrath* and *The Harvest Gypsies;* and "Mexican Plaza," demonstrating Steinbeck's fascination with and admiration for Mexico's history, as brought to light in *The Pearl, Viva Zapata,* and *The Forgotten Village.* A changing gallery highlights special temporary exhibits, including the work of other California artists influenced by Steinbeck's work. The National Steinbeck Center's library contains an incredible collection of first editions, manuscripts, notes, audiotapes, and photographs that attract researchers and scholars from around the world. Visitors can view artifacts and gain access to Steinbeck's work at special CD-ROM stations in the Art of Writing room. A variety of special public programs keep the center fresh and alive for repeat visitors.

The **Steinbeck Festival,** held in early August every year, includes bus tours, lectures, films, and workshops. Call the center for information. The center holds numerous walking and bus tours to Steinbeck's birthplace and his gravesite at the Garden of Memories. It also hosts community events related to education, history, and the arts.

The National Steinbeck Center is an easy 20-minute drive from the Monterey Peninsula. Just take Highway 68 east to Salinas. The highway turns into Main Street in downtown Salinas. Proceed all the way to 1 Main Street in Old Town, and you're there. Steinbeck fans can expect to stay a good three hours viewing the multisensory exhibits. Admission is $10.95 for adults, $8.95 for seniors, $7.95 for youths 13 to 17, $5.95 for kids six to 12, and free for kids five and younger. Call (831) 753-6411 or visit www.steinbeck.org for details.

Wine Tasting

There are a number of routes one could take to sample the bountiful vintages of Monterey County's seven American Viticultural Areas (AVAs). In our Wine Country chapter, we've provided a list of some of the many tasting rooms throughout the County as well as a sample tasting route for your consideration. The Salinas Valley tasting tour is mapped out in the Wine Country chapter sidebar.

Pinnacles National Monument

About 35 miles southeast of Salinas lies Pinnacles National Monument, the remnants of an ancient volcano within the Gabilan Mountains along the eastern edge of the Salinas Valley. Hikers, rock climbers, cavers (spelunkers), and wildflower lovers will want to check out this unique geological and biological area. From the Monterey Peninsula, the quickest route to Pinnacles is to take Highway 68 east to U.S. 101 and then take U.S. 101 south to Highway 146 (about 25 miles south near Soledad). Follow Highway 146 east about 8 winding miles to the park's western entrance. (Pinnacles' eastern entrance, which is more hospitable to motor homes and trailers, is off Highway 25. From Salinas, go north on U.S. 101 to Highway 156 and then east to Hollister. From Hollister, head south on Highway 25. There is no road connecting the east and west sides of the park.)

Pinnacles features spectacular 1,200-foot spires, a unique chaparral ecosystem, and more than 30 miles of hiking trails. Picnic and barbecue areas are also available. While open year-round, the best time to visit is the spring wildflower season between March and May and the fall months of October and November. The summer can also be pleasant, but temperatures can reach 100 degrees and higher during heat spells.

The Pinnacle's talus caves are especially fun to explore. From the west side, visit the **Balconies Caves,** about 0.7 miles from the Chaparral Ranger Station. From the east entrance, the **Bear Gulch Caves** are a similar distance from the visitor center. Bring your flashlight, which is required,

or purchase one at the visitor center. Although the caves are relatively safe, caution is advised due to low ceilings, sudden drop-offs, and slippery-when-wet rocks.

Finally, rock-climbing at Pinnacles is best left to the pros with proper equipment. Rock climbers are asked to register at the visitor center and obey area closure signs posted at certain environmentally sensitive spots. For seasonal hours and road conditions, call Pinnacles National Monument at (831) 389–4485. Visit the Friends of Pinnacles Web site at www. pinnacles.org.

CARMEL VALLEY

In his story *The Old Pacific Capital,* Robert Louis Stevenson describes Carmel Valley as "a True Californian Valley." That description continues to ring as true as a dinner bell, with Carmel Valley serving as a California country counterpart to the Peninsula's cozy coastal town and village atmosphere. This unincorporated area is home to more than 12,000 residents and a wide range of native flora and fauna.

Expect sunshine in these wide-open spaces as you drive down the main highway artery of Carmel Valley Road, more formally known as Monterey County Highway G-16. A spring or summer day trip through the Valley is likely to provide views of brightly colored fields of wildflowers and rich green hillsides. Rich colors dominate the fall, as the sycamores, alders, and willows turn to golds and reds. Crisp blue skies with white fluffy clouds are a common sight during the chilly winter. You'll see ranches, farms, orchards, and vineyards as well as championship golf courses, rustic and regal resorts, and some great parks in which to enjoy the splendid setting. Drive some of the back roads and you may even encounter wild turkeys, California quail, gray foxes, and possibly a wild boar.

The lifeline of the Valley is the Carmel River, which flows 30 miles from the high canyons of the Santa Lucia Range out to the open sea. It is also the main source of drinking water for the entire Monterey Bay area, with reservoirs behind the Los Padres and San Clemente dams. The capacity of these dams is being severely tested by the area's ever-increasing population, and overpumping of the river aquifer has led to environmental damage. Controversy has reigned for years over the merits and curses of building larger dams with increased storage capacity to quench the area's growing thirst. But that's not our topic for today. Our goal is to provide an interesting, insightful, and relaxing tour of Carmel Valley.

We'll cover little more than 50 miles in our round-trip drive. Yet, at times you'll feel worlds apart from the Peninsula. Where Carmel Valley officially ends to the east is a matter of local debate. Some feel the Carmel Valley Village, about 14 miles inland, is the end of the trail. The approximately 64,000 acres that encompass the Valley from its mouth to the Village have been slowly and steadily divided into smaller and more populous segments since the 1830s, when large Spanish and Mexican land grants placed this entire wildland under private ownership, much to the dismay of the local Native Americans. Others feel that Carmel Valley's reach extends many miles farther east into the less populated canyons that eventually open up into the Salinas Valley near Greenfield. Regardless, our trip extends 23 miles out Carmel Valley Road and includes a scenic loop though the backcountry of Cachaqua Valley.

The Mouth of the Valley

We include general mile markers at major destinations along the way. Set your odometer at zero as you turn east onto Carmel Valley Road (G-16) from Highway 1 in Carmel. If you're traveling into the Valley during the summer months, be ready for some intense heat. Dress in layers, as the coastal mouth of the Valley can often be shrouded in chilly fog, while the inner Valley bakes under the hot sun. Ready?

From Highway 1 just south of Carmel proper, turn east on Carmel Valley Road. To the immediate right are Carmel Rancho Center, The Barnyard, and The Crossroads shopping centers. Here you can pick up those last-minute supplies you forgot to pack or get a ready-made lunch to take along on your trip. Two of our favorite choices for lunch or a snack are the **Bagel Bakery,** 539 Carmel Rancho Shopping Center, (831) 625-5180, and the **Power Juice and Food Company**, 173 The Crossroads, (831) 626-6577. Of course, once you see all the other specialty shops here at the mouth of the Valley, you just might forget about this whole idea of day tripping through the great outdoors and spend your entire day shopping.

Assuming you choose to continue on with your tour, you'll drive inland past open fields, Carmel Middle School, and three splendid golf courses. At approximately the 1-mile mark, you pass the two public Rancho Cañada Golf Club courses (see our Golf chapter). At about 2 miles, you reach Rancho San Carlos Road, the entrance to Carmel Valley Golf and Country Club, a private club for members and guests only. At the 3.5-mile mark is the Quail Lodge Resort (see our Hotels and Motels chapter), with its splendid accommodations and the award-winning Covey Restaurant (see our Restaurants chapter).

For those of you who left the golf clubs at home and are simply out for a leisurely drive, our first stop is at the Valley Hills Shopping Center, right next door to Quail Lodge past Valley Greens Drive. Hungry? For you morning folks, enjoy a great traditional country breakfast at **Katy 'n Harry's Wagon Wheel Coffee Shop,** (831) 624-8878. For 20 years, the Wagon Wheel has been serving hearty breakfasts of eggs, waffles, pancakes, French toast, and the like to a loyal following of locals and visitors. You might want to try the trout and eggs with a side of country potatoes or biscuits and homemade gravy. Lunch is served as well. If Mexican food is to your liking for lunch or dinner, the **Baja Cantina & Grill,** (831) 625–2252, with its outdoor fireplace deck and unusual automobile and filling station memorabilia is a bit farther back toward the rear of the shopping center. Walk off the hearty fare with a stroll through the **Tancredi & Morgen Country Store,** (831) 625–4477, and the other unique antiques and gift shops at the center.

Just past the Valley Hills Center, you'll find the **Earthbound Farm Produce Stand,** (831) 625–6219, featuring a nice selection of locally grown organic fruits and vegetables. This is a great stop for a few fresh car snacks or a picnic lunch. (During the summer and fall months, you'll likely find a number of fruit and vegetable stands along Carmel Valley Road, as local farmers sell their corn, pumpkins, melons, and other goods.)

Nearing the 4-mile mark at Cypress Lane is **Valley Hills Nursery,** (831) 624–3482. For you green thumbers, this is a great spot to pick up some beautiful begonias, fuchsias, azaleas, and those other luscious flowering plants that thrive in our cool coastal climate. At 4.5 miles, turn right (south) at Schulte Road and proceed about 1.5 miles to **Saddle Mountain Park,** (831) 624–1617, where you'll find some nice secluded campsites and picnic facilities as well as an outdoor swimming pool for day use. This is a good spot for kids who are itching to run, splash, and explore. Saddle Mountain has a challenging 3.5-mile trail that leads to a great view north over Monterey Bay toward Santa Cruz and south toward Big Sur. Right next door to Saddle Mountain is the **Riverside RV Park,** (831) 624–9329, in the event you're in need of a pleasant spot to park and hook up your recreational vehicle.

At the 5-mile mark you'll find the first of six wineries on our day trip. **Chateau Julien Wine Estate,** 8940 Carmel Valley Road, (831) 624–2600, www.chateau julien.com, is in—what else—a French-style chateau. The wines are very pleasant and include some interesting Italian grapes you aren't likely to find elsewhere in the

area. That includes Trebiano, Sangiovese, and a delicious, earthy Nebbiolo. Of course, you'll also enjoy the more traditional California selection of chardonnay (all barrel fermented), Riesling, Gewurztraminer (a not-too-sweet delight), sauvignon blanc, merlot, and cabernet sauvignon, as well as a unique Meritage white. For dessert, try the Carmel Cream Sherry or Aleatico. Wine tasting is offered daily, 8:00 A.M. to 5:00 P.M. Monday through Friday, 11:00 A.M. to 5:00 P.M. weekends, while tours are provided Monday through Saturday. When in town, inquire about the winery's special events, like the winemaker dinners and art festivals.

Mid-Valley

Next door to Chateau Julien is the **Flower Farm,** 9000 Carmel Valley Road, (831) 626–9191, where you can walk among the beautiful gardens and pick your own special bouquets. It's a memorable romantic treat for traveling twosomes. Six miles into our trip is the **Mid Valley Shopping Center,** another good supply stop for gasoline, picnic supplies—and a great cup of java at **The Carmel Coffee Roasting Company,** 319 Mid Valley Shopping Center, (831) 624–5934. They roast their own beans for a great taste and aroma. Immediately after the Mid Valley Center is Robinson Canyon Road. Turn right (south) to find **Carmel Valley Ranch Resort,** 1 Old Ranch Road, (831) 625–9500, with its championship private golf course for guests and members (see our Golf chapter). This expansive resort also offers 100 luxury rooms amid the rural charm of the Valley. Of great interest to many day trippers is **Carmel Valley Trail Rides,** (831) 625–9500, ext. 306, located right here at the Ranch Resort. Owned and operated by the Nason family, descendents of the Esselen Indian Tribe of Carmel Valley, Carmel Trail Rides offers one of the best opportunities to explore the Valley on horseback. Choose from a one-hour

Carmel Valley is wild, rugged country with poison oak, rattlesnakes, mountain lions, and other dangers. Have fun, but keep an eye on the kids and proceed cautiously when visiting the backcountry.

scenic ride, a two-hour oceanview ride, a three-hour sunset ride, or a three-hour picnic lunch ride. Prices range from $40 to $85. All-day rides are also available for $150 per person. Reservations must be made in advance. Riders must be at least seven years old and should wear long, loose-fitting pants and sturdy shoes.

About a mile out Robinson Canyon Road is **Korean Buddhist Temple Sambosa,** or "Three Treasures," 28110 Robinson Canyon Road, (831) 624–3686. To find the temple, turn right up the drive immediately after crossing the small bridge over the Carmel River and follow the signs. The original lavender temple, a Carmel Valley landmark since 1973, tragically burned in 1987. The temple is now housed in a modern, rather nondescript hall that belies the beautiful altar that awaits within. A traditional Korean roof and temple bell are also on the grounds above the Carmel River. The public is invited to Sunday services beginning at 10:30 A.M.

For a beautiful meandering drive through oaks and redwoods, continue farther south out Robinson Canyon Road. At about 10 miles out, you might even spot the remnants of Robert Louis Stevenson's cabin, where the author lived for a short period while recovering from a horseback riding accident. The cabin is within the 20,000-acre Rancho San Carlos.

Garland Ranch

Meanwhile, back at mile 8.5 on Carmel Valley Road is **Garland Ranch Regional Park,** more than 4,460 acres of beautiful scenery and great trails for hiking, horseback riding, and mountain biking. (You

have to make your own arrangements for horses or bikes.) The Carmel River runs the length of the park, which ranges in altitude from 200 to 2,000 feet. A nice easy walk is the 1.4-mile Lupine Loop, a springtime favorite among wildflower lovers. The 2.9-mile hike along the waterfall trail and shaded Garzas Creek is another favorite among local hikers, ending in a secluded redwood canyon. In the park you are likely to discover a wide range of wildlife, including California quail, great blue heron, red-shouldered hawk, wild turkey, blacktail deer, gray fox, brush rabbit, raccoon, bobcat, and the occasional mountain lion. (It's always a good idea to walk in groups and keep your eyes on the kids when venturing deep into the rugged hills and canyons.) The park is open year-round from sunrise until sunset, with docent-led nature hikes typically leaving from the visitor center at 9:00 A.M. Trail maps are also available at the visitor center inside the park. For information, call (831) 659–4488.

At the 10-mile mark of our trip, Laureles Grade Road intersects with Carmel Valley Road. By turning left (north) on Laureles Grade and driving 6 miles, you connect with Highway 68 near Laguna Seca, about midpoint between Monterey and Salinas. Just past Laureles Grade on the north side of Carmel Valley Road are a couple of great resorts that provide nice accommodations.

The first is **Bernardus Lodge,** 415 Carmel Valley Road, (831) 659–3131, www.bernardus.com, the latest high-end resort in the Valley. The lodge features 57 well-appointed rooms, a luxurious spa (ready for a grapeseed and red wine scrub?), swimming pool, tennis courts, croquet lawn, and a great restaurant with an amazing wine list.

Los Laureles Lodge, (831) 659–2233, www.loslaureles.com, is about a half-mile farther at 313 West Carmel Valley Road. It's a quaint 1930s-style country inn with a lot of white picket fence charm. Sitting poolside brings you back to a California country atmosphere of days gone by. The poolside bar and food service add to the laid-back atmosphere. And the indoor Los Laureles Bar is a nice spot for an evening cocktail in a warm atmosphere. For $5.00, day trippers can enjoy use of the swimming pool and bar, with an extensive lunch menu, while overnighters can enjoy relaxing accommodations and maybe a ride in the lodge's horse-drawn surrey.

An interesting slice of Carmel Valley history lies at about the 11.5 mark of our journey. Here you'll see the **Boronda Adobe,** built in 1840 by Don José Manual and Maria Juana Boronda. The story goes that after Don José was crippled in a bullfighting accident, Maria Juana Boronda began making cheese from an old family recipe in order to support the family. The cheese became very popular and, according to local lore, attracted the interest of noted Monterey businessman and dairy farmer David Jacks. Not one to miss a business opportunity, Jacks "borrowed" the recipe and soon began making his own "Monterey Jack Cheese." So, cheese lovers, here's the original home of that soft tasty white cheese made exclusively in California. (The adobe is still a private residence, so no tours are available.)

Looking for a secluded, affordable spot for a quiet overnight stay in Carmel Valley? At mile 12, turn left at Country Club Drive and head up 0.2 miles to **The Portofino Inn and Spa,** 10 Country Club Way, (831) 659–3486, (800) 568–6879, www.theportofinoinn.com. Formerly the Carmel Country Spa, this splendid retreat is currently being refurbished and converted from its former life as a "health farm." You'll still enjoy the huge swimming pool and Jacuzzi with deckside service, but the emphasis is now on relaxation rather than regimen. Day trippers can enjoy a day of swimming and sunbathing for $8.00 per person.

Back on Carmel Valley Road, at mile 12.5 (across from Ford Road) is the renowned **John Gardner Tennis Ranch,** 114 Carmel Valley Road, (831) 659–2207, which has been providing tennis instruction and accompanying creature comforts to Carmel

Valley for more than 40 years. There's not much here for day trippers, but overnighters can enjoy the accommodations with private patios and fireplaces, the pool and spa, and the healthy gourmet cuisine—whether they play tennis or not. The tennis lessons themselves range from one-day instruction to three-week tennis camps. For schedules and details, call (800) 453–6225 or visit www.carmeltennis.com.

Right next door to the tennis ranch at Ford Road is **Hidden Valley Music and Dance Center,** which hosts a year-round series of musical and theater performances, dance instruction (ballet, tap, jazz, and ballroom), and music seminar programs featuring internationally known artists. Call (831) 659–7442 or (831) 659–3115 or visit www.hiddenvalleymusic.com for schedules. Our travels farther east bring us to the heart and soul of the Carmel Valley.

Carmel Valley Village

At about mile 13 is **Carmel Valley Village** (or alternately, Madonna of the Village), the center of community life for most of the local inhabitants. The charm and unique character of this little piece of the Wild West shines through to visitors as well. One interesting bit of trivia that gives you an inkling of the Village's character is that the Carmel Valley county library is now housed in the former Buckeye Bar. Day trippers are encouraged to explore the Village and enjoy its wide range of shops, restaurants, and other attractions. We'll highlight a few of our favorite spots, but in no way should this list be considered all-inclusive. Explore!

Hungry? For breakfast, lunch, or dinner, there are a plethora of good restaurants throughout the Village. For real Carmel Valley cowboy character, try **The Running Iron,** 24 East Carmel Valley Drive, (831) 659–4633. It serves a hearty weekend brunch and daily lunch and dinner with a decidedly Western flair. Cowboy boots and other Wild West paraphernalia hang from the ceilings and

Picturesque Carmel Valley is a "True Californian Valley" that attracts many visitors as well as local artists during wildflower season. MONTEREY COUNTY CONVENTION AND VISITORS BUREAU

rafters throughout the restaurant. Burgers and steaks are emphasized (many locals prefer the traditional Lonesome Burger), but good seafood, more than 25 different sandwiches, and other fare are offered. And The Running Iron bar is a great down-home place to stop in for a beer and jaw a spell with the locals.

Wills Fargo Dining House and Saloon, Carmel Valley Road, (831) 659–2774, is a guaranteed winner for a delicious and festive dinner in the Village. At 5:00 P.M. the antique etched glass doors swing open, and you enter a decidedly Victorian-era room full of chandeliers, carved mahogany, crystal goblets, and other touches of elegance. The saloon mixes an "honest drink," and the butcher shop's certified Angus beef is cut and cooked to your specification. This is a steak and potato lover's delight, but you'll also find lamb, seafood, pasta, and other entrees as well as an ample children's menu. Friday and Saturday nights feature live music. Reser-

vations are advised.

If wine tasting is your pleasure, there are four great finds in Carmel Valley Village that are open daily. **Heller Estate,** 69 West Carmel Valley Road, (831) 659– 6220, www.hellerestate.com, offers some nice premium red and white wines produced entirely at its Carmel Valley Wine Estate in Cachagua Valley (where we'll visit a bit later). The grapes are grown with minimum irrigation thanks to ample hidden springs and without pesticides or herbicides other than sulphur dust. The white wines include chenin blanc, chardonnay, Cuvée Gold, and a late-harvest Johannisberg Reisling. The reds include cabernet sauvignon, merlot, pinot noir, and Meritage. The Village tasting room is small and modest, but the organically grown grapes result in premium wines that match up well with the best of Monterey County. Tasting hours are 11:00 A.M. to 5:00 P.M. daily.

Robert Talbott Vineyards, (831) 659–3500, www.talbottvineyards.com, opened its tasting room at 53 West Carmel Valley Road in 1999. The Talbott family offers five distinctly different chardonnays, from freshly fruity to intensely complex, and two nice pinot noirs—one for extended aging and one to enjoy immediately. If you're curious, yes, this is the same Robert Talbott that makes the splendid men's ties. In fact you'll find a Talbott Ties Factory Outlet just down the road at the Village Center. Tasting hours are 11:00 A.M. to 5:00 P.M. Thursday through Monday.

Bernardus Winery, 5 West Carmel Valley Road, (831) 659-1900, (800) 223-2533, www.bernardus.com, is housed in a rather plain building that was once home to a major bank. Inside, however, the tasting room is nicely decorated, making for a pleasant spot to enjoy some fine wines. You'll discover merlot, pinot, noir, chardonnay, and a unique Marinus Bordeaux blend red table wine, a Bernardus specialty.

Joullian Vineyards, 2 Village Drive, (866) 659-8101, www.joullian.com, opened its impressive tasting room in March of 2000. Joullian provides rich clonal selections of chardonnay, sauvignon blanc, cabernet sauvignon, and zinfandel, all grown exclusively in Carmel Valley's premium wine-growing region. The tasting room is open daily from 11:00 A.M. to 5:00 P.M.

A final Carmel Valley Village wine tasting room you should visit is **San Saba Vineyards,** 19 East Carmel Valley Road, (831) 753-7222, www.sansaba.com. Featured wines include chardonnay, cabernet sauvignon, merlot, and pinot noir. The tasting room is open Saturday and Sunday, 11:00 A.M. to 5:00 P.M., and in the summer Thursday and Friday 11:00 A.M. to 4:00 P.M.

Did you bring the whole family? The kids will undoubtedly enjoy some time at **Carmel Valley Village Park and Community Youth Center,** (831) 659-3983, along Carmel Valley Road east of Ford Road. Here you'll find large open spaces, picnic facilities, horseshoe pits, an activity house, a big outdoor swimming pool, and ample

playground equipment, including an old red fire engine.

East of the Village

East of Carmel Valley Village, the canyons and the road narrow, and the density of civilization decreases substantially. But there are still plenty of reasons (besides the beautiful scenery) to keep driving onward. At approximately mile 15 of our journey, Holman Road appears to the left (north). Up the road lies **The Holman Ranch,** a 400-acre, 1920s-era private ranch that today serves as a popular equestrian center for both English- and Western-style lessons and recreational trail rides. One-hour rides through the oak-studded hills are $40 per person, while a two-hour ride up a scenic ridge is $60. Pony rides are available for youngsters age five to 10, starting at $30, and specially arranged day rides are offered to expert riders for $100 and more. The Holman Ranch also hosts special events and theme parties. This private ranch doesn't accept drop-ins, so be sure to call ahead for reservations at (831) 659-2640. Visit them on the Web at www.theholmanranch.com.

At mile 16 is **Stonepine Estate,** 150 East Carmel Valley Road, (831) 659-2245, www.stonepinecalifornia.com, a former summer home of the famous Crocker banking family. Today, the 330-acre estate provides luxurious accommodations in the main house, Chateau Noel, and excellent equestrian facilities for guests.

Cachagua Valley

At mile 18 we leave Carmel Valley Road and turn right (south) on Cachagua (ka-shaw-wa) Road. Cachagua Road is about a 13-mile loop through the secluded Cachagua Valley that eventually reconnects with Carmel Valley Road about 7 miles farther east from our turnoff point.

After climbing over a ridge and passing a few residential neighborhoods, we enter Cachagua Valley. Our next stop at mile 23 is **Galante Vineyards,** 18181 Cachagua Road, (831) 659–2649 or 800–GALANTE. This is a spectacular little winery that's part of a 700-acre ranch (including cattle) and a huge garden of more than 12,000 rose bushes. The wines include tasty sauvignon blanc, merlot, and premium cabernet sauvignon. Tastings are provided by appointment only, so call ahead. Galante Vineyards also holds a summer series of outdoor concerts (with music, wine, and food) and other special events. Call for the current schedule or visit www.galantevineyards.com.

At mile 24 you'll find the small town of **Cachagua.** This little enclave has a simple country atmosphere that seems closer to the Appalachians than to Pebble Beach. The town itself offers friendly residents; the small **Cachagua General Store,** 18840 Cachagua Road, (831) 659–1857; and **Princes Camp,** 37200 Nason Road, (831) 659–2678, the local watering hole. Cachagua serves as the entrance point to a popular visitor destination, **Los Padres Reservoir.** Follow the signs through town and drive a half-mile to a parking spot next to **Cachagua Community Park,** itself a pleasant picnic spot along the Carmel River. From the parking lot, it's a half-mile hike to the lake, where trout fishing, swimming, and rowboating are allowed. From the reservoir there is a variety of hiking trails that lead into the Los Padres National Forest and Ventana Wilderness. This is a popular starting point for overnight backpackers heading toward Big Sur. Overnight backpackers should sign in at the Rangers Station at China Camp out Tassajara Road (see subsequent directions). For day trippers, a good day hike is along the Church Creek Trail above the dam.

Back at mile 24.5 on Cachagua Road is the COMSAT (Communications Satellite) Earth Station. This 34-ton, 10-story antenna dish is focused on a satellite more than 22,000 miles away and serves as a vital telecommunications link in

North America. Guided tours of the facilities are provided from 1:00 to 3:00 P.M. on Wednesday. Call (831) 659–2293 for information and reservations.

Drive 4 miles to the 28.5-mile point and Cachagua Road reaches the Tassajara Road junction. Up Tassajara Road about a mile is the town of **Jamesburg.** Like Cachagua, it's a small settlement without a lot of visitor amenities, but it's a good spot to pick up a quick snack or beverage.

From Jamesburg, Tassajara Road winds about 6 miles to **Chews Ridge,** a popular spot for camping and hiking and one of the few places around the Peninsula where you're likely to find snow after a cold winter storm. Hikers will enjoy exploring caves, some decorated with drawings and writings by Esselen and, later, Costanoan Indians. Here you will also find the **Monterey Institute for Research in Astronomy (MIRA)** observatory, (831) 883–1000. It's not generally open to the public, but a few special nighttime open houses are provided throughout the year. Call for details. **China Camp,** which offers overnight camping facilities, is a short drive farther down Tassajara Road. There's also a Ranger Station here for more information about the local facilities, backpacking routes, and hiking trails.

Past China Camp, Tassajara Road becomes more rugged and difficult to transverse without a four-wheel drive vehicle. Day trippers should likely avoid this section of the Valley unless they are specifically heading to the **Tassajara Hot Springs Zen Mountain Center** (see our Close-up in this chapter). Even visitors to the hot springs are advised to take advantage of the shuttle service offered to Tassajara.

From the Cachagua Road-Tassajara Road junction, it's just another 1.5 miles (mile 30) and you hook back to Carmel Valley Road. Turn left, and you have a 23-mile drive back to Highway 1 in Carmel. Turn right, and Carmel Valley Road takes you on a long and winding journey all the way to Salinas Valley near Greenfield. It's a lovely

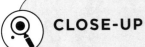

Tassajara Hot Springs
Zen Mountain Center

The Hot Springs of Tassajara have been drawing visitors in search of physical and spiritual well-being for centuries. At the end of Tassajara Road near the edge of the Los Padres National Forest, the rich mineral springs were used extensively by generations of local Esselen Indians and later became a hot springs resort for California settlers in the 1860s. According to an 1875 handbook issued by Monterey County, the Smithsonian Institution tested a sample of the mineral spring water and declared it "the richest spring then known in the United States."

Since 1967, Tassajara has been home to a Zen Buddhist monastery. From September through April, the monastery is closed to the public. But from May to August, Tassajara opens for a series of retreats, workshops, and work practice programs, as well as overnight accommodations and day use of the facilities. Day trippers can soak in the hot springs and bathhouse, swim in the warm-water pool, and stroll through the tranquil grounds between 10:00 A.M. and 9:00 P.M. daily. Reservations are mandatory. No food or towels are provided, so come prepared. The cost is $20 for adults and $10 for children. (For the full impact, it is suggested that you make your first trip to Tassajara sans kids.)

The trip to Tassajara is about a two-hour drive from Carmel Valley Village. The final 10-plus-mile leg up Tassajara Road is steep, winding, and bumpy—in fact, some passenger cars simply cannot make it. It is recommended, therefore, that you use The Stage, a Tassajara shuttle van that leaves the small town of Jamesburg each morning at 10:30 A.M. and returns at 4:00 P.M. each afternoon. The shuttle service costs $35 round-trip, and lunch is provided. For day trip and shuttle reservations, call (831) 659-2229.

If you're planning an extended stay at Tassajara, overnight accommodations range from $80 per person for simple dorm rooms to $150 per person for suites. There is also a variety of work programs to consider. A Guest Practice Program of three or more days ($50 per day) allows you to join the students and monks for zazen meditation, morning service, temple cleaning, and breakfast, followed by community work and lunch. The afternoons and evenings are then free for enjoying bathing, swimming, and hiking. Dinner is served in a common dining room. Work Practice Programs of five days or more ($70 for room and board for the first week) follow a daily schedule of meditation and work. And during the months of April and September, Work Periods provide the opportunity to receive free room and board in exchange for full working days of carpentry, painting, gardening, cooking, and general maintenance. Tassajara begins accepting reservations April 1. Call the San Francisco office of the Zen Buddhist monastery at (415) 865-1895 for reservations. Visit their Web site at www.sfzc.com.

Accommodations are comfortably rustic. There is no in-room electricity and only a single phone line, so be prepared to be isolated from the outside world.

30-mile drive but slow going with few signs of civilization until you reach Greenfield and U.S. 101. Assuming you're heading back to the Monterey Peninsula, wine lovers might want to consider going over Laureles Grade to Highway 68 and then proceeding west back toward Monterey. About 4.5 miles down Highway 68, you'll come to **Ventana Vineyards** tasting room, 2999 Monterey-Salinas Highway, (831) 372-7415, www.ventanawines.com. It's in the Old Stone House next to **Tarpy's Roadhouse,** just past the junction of Highway 218. The wide selection of featured wines include sauvignon blanc, pinot blanc, chardonnay, Gewürztraminer, Riesling, muscat d'orange, chenin blanc, cabernet sauvignon, merlot, cabernet franc, and syrah. The tasting room is open daily from 11:00 A.M. to 5:00 P.M.

If you forego the sidetrip over Laureles Grade, there is one more point of interest to mention, about 1.5 miles before you reach Highway 1. On the north side of Carmel Valley Road is a small monument to **El Encino del Descanso** (the Oak of Repose), where Native Americans stopped to rest on their burial processions up the valley. Today, you'll often find flowers left at a small shrine commemorating the dead.

Well, that's it for our day trip. Be sure to check out the **Carmel Valley Chamber of Commerce,** upstairs at 71 West Carmel Valley Road, (831) 659-4000, to discover the latest and greatest happenings in this always charming, sometimes wild and woolly neck of the Monterey Bay area.

RELOCATION

To live on the Monterey Peninsula has long been a dream of many who have visited. The scenery, the weather (if you can stand a bit of fog along the coast), the amenities, and the laid-back lifestyle have long made the Peninsula a first or second home of choice for those who can afford it.

That is the key phrase here—for those who can afford it. Living doesn't come cheap on the Monterey Peninsula. Home prices can be stratospheric. Services such as water, gas, and electricity continue to climb. Everything from gas prices to health care services seem high. And the opportunities to earn a good wage are scarce. Many jobs in the area are in the hospitality industry, known for its lower-than-average wages. And the recent economic troubles of California and beyond have forced national and international employers to move their offices and jobs elsewhere.

But you can still dream! For those lucky enough to land a good-paying job in the area, or for those retirees who can make it here on their sizable pensions, life is good. In fact, it's great.

So for you relocators or potential relocators, let's take a look at the local real estate market. Subsequent chapters in this book will examine retirement, health care, education, child care, media, and worship.

REAL ESTATE

When it comes to real estate on the Monterey Peninsula, the familiar adage rings true: location, location, location. With a unique perch on the scenic Central California coast, the Monterey Peninsula is and probably always will be premium real estate.

The gently rising terrain and native forests overlooking the Pacific Ocean provide spectacular views from virtually every corner of the landscape. With the dramatic rocky coastline and deep-blue sea vistas, ocean views are highly prized in this part of the country. In fact, property prices reflect both the quality and quantity of seaside scenic splendor that you can enjoy from your home and garden.

Then there are the homes themselves. Between its Pebble Beach estates, Monterey adobes, Pacific Grove Victorians, and Carmel cottages, the Monterey Peninsula offers a plethora of desirable architecture and lifestyles. And if it's wide-open space you yearn for, travel a few miles in any and all directions and you'll find it. From the Western ranch-style homes in Carmel Valley and the mountain-top cabins in Big Sur to the sprawling farmlands of the Salinas Valley, you'll discover plenty of room to roam. Though the focus of this chapter is the Monterey Peninsula itself, we cover the surrounding areas as well.

The highly desirable location and the inflexible laws of supply and demand have created a healthy real estate market that is annually near the top of the California scale in terms of price and appreciation. Even California's well-publicized, on-again-off-again economic problems over the last few decades and the mid-nineties near-closure of the area's largest single employer—the U.S. Army Base at Ford Ord—hardly put a dent in escalating real estate prices. These economic woes have brought temporary stalls and slight short-term dips, but those downturns seem to always be immediately followed by continued steady rises. Just when you think Peninsula prices can't get any higher, they do.

The reason for our healthy market is simple, really. There are only so many square feet on this relatively small headland surrounded on three sides by the Pacific Ocean. Plus, local conservation and preservation efforts, coupled with a limited supply of freshwater resources, have substantially checked the amount of new construction. Meanwhile, the desire to live on the Monterey Peninsula has only continued to grow as more and more areas of California fall victim to urban sprawl.

A recent phenomenon is the rapid influx of second-home buyers into the local real estate market. It is estimated that up to half of the home purchases in Carmel these days are by people buying a second home for a getaway retreat and eventual retirement spot. That trend has spread to Pacific Grove as well.

Lately, technology has also played a role in increased demand for real estate on the Peninsula. Over the past decades, employment opportunities outside the hospitality and agricultural industries have been fairly limited. But with the coming of telecommuting, more professionals whose skills are in high demand (many from neighboring Silicon Valley) have found they can live here and work for clients or employers elsewhere via modem, Internet, and fax.

In a nutshell, the combination of a great location, limited supply, and growing demand has created a residential real estate market where the price of entry begins at about $300,000 and rises from there to the multi-million dollar stratosphere.

What will $300,000 buy you in the area? Probably a plain-vanilla condominium or a modest one- or two-bedroom, one-bath home in need of repair. It's what local real estate agents call a "fixer-upper" or "charming starter home"—and it's likely off the Peninsula proper. Don't expect too much house or lot, but the views can sometimes make up for the lack of square-footage. Move up to the $400,000 range, and you've probably moved onto the Peninsula or added a third bedroom and/or second bath in the deal—or perhaps a better neighborhood or ocean view from your little bungalow. A price of $600,000 puts you in the range of a more substantial home and lot, including the many well-preserved Victorian or Monterey-style adobes, and

$800,000 starts moving you into the most desirable areas of Monterey, Carmel, and Pacific Grove and within the lower range in Pebble Beach. Beyond that, you're entering the near-oceanfront market of Carmel and Pacific Grove. Million-dollar-plus homes move you into the Peninsula's elite.

The lament of most outsiders who begin home shopping on the Monterey Peninsula is that they just can't buy nearly as much house here as they can back home. Unless you're moving from San Francisco, Manhattan, or some other high-priced locale, that's probably true. But what balances the cost equation is the natural splendor that lies outside your new front door.

NEIGHBORHOODS

In this section we'll provide a bit of insight into the neighborhoods that make up the Monterey Peninsula. Unlike many areas of today's California, where new housing developments with fancy Spanish names such as Hacienda Royale or Rancho Tranquil are springing up like wildfire, there hasn't been a substantial new subdivision of single-family homes on the Peninsula proper since the 1970s. A few multiunit townhome communities and condominiums have been built in the last two decades, the largest of which is the exclusive Residence at Spanish Bay complex in Pebble Beach. Plus, a few multiacre Pebble Beach estates have been subdivided into smaller parcels, where owners can design and build their custom homes. But new tract-housing subdivisions have been virtually nonexistent on the Peninsula proper for decades. So when we talk neighborhoods in this chapter, we're describing distinct geographic areas within Monterey, Carmel, Pacific Grove, and Pebble Beach where a particular style or age of home is prevalent. Sure, over the years remodels, rebuilds, and new structures have cropped up that don't fit the overall character of the neighborhoods described here. Still, this chapter should give you a general feel for the locales and might help you focus your search when looking for a home to purchase or rent. (All median prices in this chapter are for the year 2002.)

Monterey

Since the 19th century Monterey has been known for its distinct "Monterey Colonial" and traditional Spanish-adobe style. That architectural influence is still largely felt, even in many of the modern structures. Spanish and similar Mediterranean-style homes circa 1900 as well as circa 2000 can be found throughout the city. The best of this style of architecture generally begins in downtown Monterey and works its way uphill to the west. This area, known colloquially as Spaghetti Hill because of the predominance of Italian families who settled here during the heydays of the sardine industry of Cannery Row, features some fine examples of the Spanish and Mediterranean styles as well as many stately Victorians.

Toward the bottom of the hill, just above Pacific Street, many of the larger homes have since been converted into businesses and multiunit rentals. The higher you progress up the hill, the more residential the area becomes. Head even farther up the hill, above Veterans Memorial Park and below the Community Hospital of the Monterey Peninsula (CHOMP), and you enter the Monterey neighborhood known as Skyline Forest. Here you find newer homes and town houses set within the eastern edge of Del Monte Forest near Pebble Beach. The many tall pine trees tend to limit the amount of warm sunshine that comes through, and the shallow-rooted trees can cause occasional property damage when they come crashing down in the high-wind winter storms that can whip in off the Pacific. (This is a problem that occasionally plagues all forested areas of the Peninsula.) But the trees certainly add beauty and an air of tranquility to the Skyline Forest area. A trip down Skyline Forest Drive from Holman Highway (Highway 68) just north of CHOMP leads you into this neighborhood.

To the northwest of downtown Monterey, out Lighthouse Avenue past the Presidio and toward Pacific Grove, is the neighborhood of New Monterey. Located directly up the hill from Cannery Row, this area of town was populated by the many newcomers who migrated to Monterey during the peak of the fishing industry in the 1940s and early '50s. Strictly a residential area above Lighthouse and Hawthorne Avenues, New Monterey is a hodgepodge of mostly modest single-family homes, peppered with the occasional apartment house, rental duplex, or eye-popping Victorian. Many apartment houses populate the lower streets like Hawthorne Avenue and the main uphill drag of David Avenue, which separates New Monterey from Pacific Grove. Because of the hillside terrain, this area of town affords some of the nicest views overlooking Cannery Row and Monterey Harbor.

East of downtown Monterey toward the city of Seaside is an area of town informally known as "the sunbelt." This part of the Monterey is actually off the Peninsula proper and therefore out of the primary fog belt that extends across the tip of the Peninsula through Pacific Grove and Pebble Beach. The landscape in the sunbelt is a bit flatter and sandier than on the Peninsula, with fewer large Monterey pines and cypress. Homes here are generally less expensive than in other parts of Monterey, and the area has a substantial number of apartments and other rentals due to its proximity to the Naval Postgraduate School.

One neighborhood of note within the sunbelt is Del Monte Beach, a small group of homes and condominiums built on the sand dunes right above the shoreline. The views here are spectacular as you look out across the Bay northwestward toward Cannery Row and Pacific Grove. From Del Monte Boulevard, turn north on Casa Verde Way to enter the Del Monte Beach area.

An amazing aspect of the city of Monterey is that one neighborhood can be situated on a sandy shoreline while another can be nestled in a mountain forest. Jack's Peak, twin summits that rise more than 1,000 feet just a couple miles east of downtown, is home to some of the nicest and most expensive homes in the city. To get a taste of the area, take a drive out Aquajito Road, which forms a loop south of Highway 1 from Fremont Street at Monterey Peninsula College to Holman Highway (Highway 68) at the top of Carmel Hill. There are plenty of large estates on sizable lots here as well as rustic abodes nestled in narrow canyons along each side of the roadway. It's truly mountainous country living less than five minutes from downtown Monterey.

Two more highly populated neighborhoods are also situated in the foothills north of Jack's Peak. Called Fishermans Flats and Deer Flats, these subdivisions were originally built in the 1960s and later. They feature primarily three- and four-bedroom homes. A few have panoramic views overlooking Monterey Bay, while many others face the green hills and canyons of the local terrain. Downhill from both neighborhoods are Josselyn Canyon Road and Sylvan Road, which also have some nice homes in a semisecluded canyon running parallel with the Del Monte Golf Course. On the other side of the golf course lies La Mesa, a housing district for military personnel attending the Naval Postgraduate School.

The median home price in Monterey is $535,000. Entry-level homes near the $350,000 level are primarily in the sunbelt and New Monterey areas, while more expensive homes are generally clustered on the hills of downtown Monterey, Skyline Forest, and Jack's Peak.

Pacific Grove

Think of Pacific Grove, and you immediately think of Victorian architecture with its ornate gingerbread trim. These beautiful stately homes are still common around the downtown area, particularly along the major thoroughfares of Lighthouse, Central, and Pine Avenues. The Pacific Grove Heritage Society has been very active in ensuring the preservation of these homes, and you'll find the society's nameplates on many of the significant residences signifying the date of construction and the name of the original owner. The median price of a Pacific Grove home is $529,500. Because of its splendid location on the northern tip of the Monterey Peninsula, the median price would be higher except that the city was laid out with many small lots that can't handle much more than a small two-bedroom home.

North of Lighthouse Avenue and south of Lovers Point is a portion of town occupied by the original Pacific Grove Retreat. These tiny lots, most created as sites for temporary tent houses, are now packed tightly with some of the most picturesque Victorians in town. Elbowroom is at a premium, but the tight-knit neighborhood has great character, somewhat reminiscent of a small-scale San Francisco.

From Lovers Point, follow Ocean View Boulevard northwest along the coastline to find some of the most spectacular oceanfront property in the state. The famous purple carpet of flowering ice plant provides a breathtaking frame for a bay view that stretches all the way north to Santa Cruz. Prices on large homes here have surpassed the million-dollar range, but smaller beach houses are downright affordable compared to similarly situated properties in Pebble Beach and Carmel.

Just inland from this section of Pacific Grove is the neighborhood known as the Beachtract. Situated on streets named Surf, Shell, and Ripple are mostly 1950s- and 1960s-style tract homes of generally solid construction and prime location. "Bargains" of less than $600,000 can still be found in this area, but they're becoming rare as the Beachtract becomes one of the most desirable areas for newcomers who want to be close to the water but chose to avoid the really high-rent districts.

Keep following the coast out to the Peninsula's northernmost tip at Point

Victorian gingerbread trim adorns homes both large and small in the quaint town of Pacific Grove. TOM OWENS

Pinos and the shoreline winds south toward Pebble Beach. You're now in the area known as Asilomar, the name taken from the famous Asilomar Conference Grounds that's situated in the area. Stretching inland to Asilomar Avenue and its cross streets, this is a forested beach-front section of town noted for its tall Monterey pines and prolific deer population. (Gardeners here face a triple whammy of chilly fog, salty air, and hungry deer who seem to prefer the most colorful and costly store-bought plants to the natural flora.) The Asilomar section of Pacific Grove can be downright mystical on a fog-shrouded day. If you aren't an ardent sun worshipper and can withstand many cool foggy days, this section of town may be just right for you.

Two other neighborhoods of Pacific Grove deserve mention. One, called Candy Cane Lane, is situated east of Forest Avenue between Morse Drive and Beaumont Avenue. These primarily upper-middle-income family homes become a

winter wonderland each December as neighbors vibrantly decorate their houses, yards, and neighborhood parks in holiday decor. In fact, if you decide to purchase a home in this area, you'd better be prepared to join in the fun or be labeled a neighborhood Scrooge! The final Pacific Grove neighborhood of note is Del Monte Park, located at the top of David Avenue west of Congress Road. This district of 1950s and '60s tract homes is one of the more affordable spots in Pacific Grove with ample-size three- and four-bedroom homes. While lacking the Victorian charm of historic downtown, some of the houses here have nice views overlooking the Del Monte Forest of Pebble Beach and the Pacific Ocean beyond.

Carmel

With a median home price of $910,000, Carmel remains one of the most desirable areas of the Monterey Peninsula among

Carmel homes, like this spectacular stone cottage, add great charm to the seaside village.
TOM OWENS

well-to-do retirees who have vacationed here in the past and always dreamed of returning for good. The Carmel most of these visitors are familiar with is the collection of shops, inns, and restaurants on and around Ocean Avenue. Interestingly enough, Ocean Avenue also serves as a dividing line when describing the residential neighborhoods of Carmel. Most of the more prestigious Carmel addresses (that is, if they had addresses) lie in the area known simply as South of Ocean. This is the quaint Carmel of English cottages, English Tudors, Comstocks, and Cape Cod design. The homes range from cozy to palatial, but all share a common village ambience due to Carmel's abundance of trees, crooked streets, and general lack of street lights and sidewalks.

As a rule, the oceanview factor dictates property values, with homes along shoreline Scenic Road and on Carmel Point demanding the highest premium. Farther south in Carmel, beyond Rio Road and a bit inland, is the neighborhood known as

Mission Fields, which gets its name from the neighboring Carmel Mission. Here, outside of the village forest, you find the more traditional 1960s subdivisions of family homes. You can generally buy more home for the dollar in this section of Carmel, but we're certainly not talking low-rent district. One major precaution: During the 1990s, certain areas of Mission Fields were twice hit hard by flooding from the nearby Carmel River. Recent changes in the flood-control levees along the river have improved the situation somewhat. Still, before purchasing or renting a home in this neighborhood, check out its history regarding previous flooding.

Meanwhile, back north of Ocean Avenue is the neighborhood generally known as Carmel Woods. Here, the pine forest shared with neighboring Pebble Beach is denser and the terrain steeper than South of Ocean. Homes are also generally newer here, and the feeling is more rustic Californian than quaint English village. Parts of Carmel Woods lie outside the incorporated city, as does the High Meadow Drive neighborhood of larger homes and town houses located in the spacious foothills east of Highway 1 at Carpenter Street. Also along Highway 1 is the Carmel neighborhood of Hatton Fields. You'll find a number of California ranch-style homes in this hilly canyon area of gently winding streets. Farther east at the mouth of Carmel Valley is the neighborhood of Carmel Knolls. These fairly prestigious homes of modern design overlook the scenic valley and provide substantially warmer weather than Carmel proper.

Pebble Beach

For some, a Pebble Beach address is the epitome of "making it." Unarguably the most scenic area of the Monterey Peninsula, Pebble Beach is home to the rich and famous from around the world and features some of the most majestic estates on the West Coast. You can get a peek at the cream of the crop by taking the scenic 17-Mile Drive along the coast route from Cypress Point to Pebble Beach Golf Links. But spectacular homes are evident throughout the Del Monte Forest. The median price for a Pebble Beach home is $1 million. An ocean or golf-course view puts you in the $2-million-plus range.

The neighborhoods surrounding Pebble Beach Golf Links, Cypress Point Club, Spyglass Hill, Poppy Hills, the Monterey Peninsula Country Club, and Spanish Bay Golf Links all feature prestigious homes of various styles and vintages. The more modest homes, at least by Pebble Beach standards, include the inland areas near the Country Club Gate entrance and the neighborhoods below Forest Lake. Another neighborhood of note is atop the western slope of Huckleberry Hill near Holman Highway. Up here among spectacular views you'll find a swath of newer homes, many replacements for those destroyed in a devastating fire that swept through this part of the forest in the early 1990s.

Surrounding Communities

Those considering relocating to the area may find the Monterey Peninsula real estate market a bit too pricey. Fortunately, there are a number of surrounding communities that offer lower housing prices but the same great climate and, in some cases, ocean views. At the same time, some of the other off-Peninsula locales are just as pricey as the Peninsula but offer alternatives in terms of climate and/or terrain. Here are a few neighborhoods to consider.

BIG SUR

Author Lillian Bos Ross wrote that "Big Sur is a state of mind." It's also a beautifully rugged stretch of coastline that extends from the southern tip of Monterey County northward to Point Sur. While much of Big Sur is comprised of National Forest and other public lands, there are also privately owned homesites and ranches that provide inspirational solitude and privacy. Real estate prices are all over the map in Big Sur, with a median price of more than $1.6 million. Homes range from lean-to cabins located up barely passable dirt roads to hacienda estates in unbelievable settings and with all the comforts of city living. Regardless of which end of the spectrum they fall, Big Sur residents tend to be part of a tight-knit community of friendly semi-seclusionists. Highway 1 is the only route in and out of Big Sur, and its winter closure due to mud and rock slides is practically an annual event. With that in mind, planning to commute from a Big Sur home to a Monterey Peninsula job is an unpredictable proposition at best. But if you have that

Since street numbers and addresses are absent in most of Carmel proper, there isn't any mail delivery in town. Residents retrieve their mail from the post office, which has become a primary social center.

pioneer spirit, can make a living from your home, or are independently wealthy and not susceptible to cabin fever, there's hardly a more beautiful place on earth.

CARMEL HIGHLANDS/SOUTH COAST

Nestled in the northern reach of the Santa Lucia Range of Big Sur lie the Carmel Highlands. This civilized version of Big Sur sits high above Point Lobos Reserve and Yankee Point, approximately 3 miles south of Carmel. Made up primarily of million-dollar homes, it's becoming an upper-income alcove featuring fine residences with spectacular views. If you have the time after visiting Point Lobos, take a leisurely drive up Highlands Drive, Walden Road, or San Remo Road off Highway 1.

Below Carmel Highlands west of Highway 1 is a beachfront area known as South Coast because of its proximity to the Monterey Peninsula. Here on Yankee Point are some beautifully designed homes situated along breathtaking coastline. Homes are typically in the $2 million range and on par with Pebble Beach and Carmel coastal properties. A drive out Spindrift Road or Yankee Point Drive is well worth the time for house-hunters looking in this price range.

CARMEL VALLEY

Carmel Valley is the Wild West of the Monterey Peninsula area. Stretching inland from Carmel toward the Salinas Valley, it's a vast, largely undeveloped area with pockets of civilization dotting its valley floor and rugged hillsides. With a population of approximately 12,000, Carmel Valley is a mixture of exclusive resortlike properties, sprawling ranches, and cozy mountainside homes. At the mouth of the Valley lie the Carmel Knolls area and the Carmel Rancho district, with its modern homes and town houses and stylish shopping centers. Continue inland the next few miles along Carmel Valley Road, and you'll discover the golf resort communities surrounding Rancho Canada

Golf Course and Carmel Valley Golf and Country Club. Here are exclusive country club neighborhoods such as Quail Meadows and Summit at Carmel Valley Ranch.

Once east of the golf courses you enter the residential Mid Valley area, made up largely of residential family homes and small ranches along the Valley and more secluded neighborhoods up the narrow canyons. Robinson Canyon Road winds south through some beautiful countryside, eventually reaching Rancho San Carlos, a private development spread out over more than 20,000 acres.

Approximately 12 miles inland from Carmel is Carmel Valley Village, the heart and soul of this truly Californian community. Here, residential neighborhoods are nestled up scenic canyons and along the broad valley floor north of the Carmel River. South of the river, across Rosie's Bridge on Esquiline Drive, lies another residential neighborhood of both modern houses and rustic cabins situated along hillsides and large open-space meadows. East of Carmel Valley Village, the Valley narrows and the landscape becomes steeper and less populated. A few small communities, such as the gated Sleepy Hollow, are interspersed with sprawling vineyards and ranches. About 25 miles inland is the community of Jamesburg, located 3 miles up Crews Ridge Road. Homes here and farther out toward Carmel Valley Road to Salinas Valley are mainly rustic cabin-style structures, but larger homes and ranches dot the rural landscape as well.

The median price of a Carmel Valley home is $825,000, but property values vary widely. From the mouth of the Carmel Valley to Jamesburg, you'll find a friendly, tight-knit community with a Western flair that prefers the warm inland sunshine to the cooler, foggier coast. If that fits your lifestyle, Carmel Valley is certainly for you. Be aware that wildfires are a concern in the dry seasons, and the Carmel River is subject to flooding in the rainy season. While these events are certainly rare, pick your site carefully out here in the Wild West.

DEL REY OAKS

Incorporated in 1953, Del Rey Oaks is a small city of approximately 1,700 people and 300 acres landlocked between Monterey, Seaside, the Monterey Peninsula Airport, and the former Fort Ord Military Reservation. Canyon Del Rey Boulevard (Highway 218) between Fremont Boulevard and the Monterey-Salinas Highway (Highway 68) is the main thoroughfare through this bedroom community. Quiet neighborhoods of single-family homes and a few condominium projects populate the northern half of the city, while light-industry business parks make up the south end of town. In between, the Frog Pond Natural Area, a 17-acre seasonal freshwater marsh and nature preserve, is the home of the rare Pacific tree frog (see our Parks and Recreation chapter).

Homes in Del Rey Oaks are typically in the $400,000 to $450,000 range, with a median price of $435,000. Be aware that on-again-off-again talks of a large hotel project in Del Rey Oaks have been held in these parts. If such a project were to go through, it could change the sleepy nature of this corner of town.

MARINA

Located north of the former Fort Ord, approximately 9 miles up the coast from Monterey on Highway 1, is the City of Marina. Marina was originally laid out in 1913 as part of a real estate development among the sand dunes, with five-acre plots selling for $375. It later became a bedroom community for neighboring Fort Ord and today is home to 21,000 residents. Along with Seaside, Marina provides some of the most affordable family homes in the Monterey Peninsula area, with a median price of $369,000. The original section of town east of Highway 1 and south of Reservation Road is primarily of the 1950s and 1960s vintage, while newer tracts are located west of Highway 1 and north of Reservation Road. The Marina terrain is a bit sparse, located among the sandy dunes of this stretch of California coast, but the weather is exceptionally pleasant. Marina State Beach and Locke-Paddon Park provide fine recreation spots for family activities. Plus, Marina makes for an easy commute inland to Salinas and U.S. 101 by way of Reservation Road.

MONTEREY-SALINAS CORRIDOR

Follow Highway 68 out of Monterey east toward Salinas, and you're in the unincorporated Monterey-Salinas Highway corridor. Off this main east-west route to and from the Monterey Peninsula lie numerous canyons, primarily in the southern Sierra de Salinas hills. Up the canyons and along the hillsides, you'll find a variety of fairly recent housing developments of upper-income neighborhoods with names like Bay Ridge, The Villas, The Meadows, and Las Palmas Ranch. You'll find gated communities of single-family homes, town houses, and condominiums, some with country-club amenities such as golf and tennis. You'll also find older ranch-style and tract homes, a few with considerable acreage. Far back into the canyons of San Benancio and Corral de Tierra are working cattle ranches and large spreads similar to those of Carmel Valley, which lies just on the other side of the Sierra de Salinas range. These hills were the setting for John Steinbeck's *The Pastures of Heaven*. The median home price out in the Monterey-Salinas Corridor is $590,000. Those with a penchant for the sunny country-club style of living and who can benefit from a short commute to Salinas and other cities along U.S. 101 should definitely check out this area east of the Monterey Peninsula.

SAND CITY

With barely 200 permanent residents, Sand City is noted as being the second-smallest incorporated city in California. Primarily a commercial district wedged between Monterey, Seaside, and the waters of Monterey Bay, its 350 acres are, aptly enough, mostly sand. In fact, Sand

Location, location, location. Bayfront properties begin in the $1 million range across the Monterey Peninsula. TOM OWENS

City's sand business was at one time among the largest on the Pacific Coast. Today, however, the sand business has given way to light manufacturing and, more recently, retail businesses. A large center of discount chain stores was established here in the mid-1990s, and it continues to grow, making Sand City one of the busiest shopping districts in the area. Residential real estate in Sand City is made up of a handful of mostly modest homes inland from Highway 1. Some have nice Bay views; others share neighborhoods with commercial properties. Prices are generally in the $300,000–$400,000 range.

SEASIDE

Directly northeast of Monterey, Seaside is a substantial city of almost 10 square miles and more than 33,000 residents. Long serving as a bedroom community of its neighbor-to-the-north Fort Ord, Sea-side, incorporated in 1954, is the most ethnically diverse neighborhood in the Monterey Peninsula area and remains home to a population of retired military. When the army moved out and Fort Ord shut down as part of the nationwide round of military base closings in the early 1990s, dire predictions of economic disaster for Seaside hit the news. But out-side of a few closings of businesses directly dependent on the military, the city has survived remarkably well. Light industry, retail stores, hotels and motels, an array of ethnic restaurants, and a major auto center now provide a sound economic base for Seaside. This active commercial district is largely situated on the western side of town, along and between the major north-south thorough-fares of Del Monte and Fremont Boule-vards. East of Fremont Boulevard is mostly residential.

Seaside has the lowest-priced homes in and around the Monterey Peninsula.

The median price of $339,000 makes Seaside a popular entry point for relocating out-of-towners looking for the most house for the dollar. Favored neighborhoods are generally in the higher elevations along the eastern edge of town. Here, you'll find spacious homes, some with fabulous Bay views looking west toward the Monterey Peninsula. Homes farther west toward the flatter commercial district are generally less expensive but are typically smaller and don't afford the great views. By Monterey Peninsula standards, Seaside has had somewhat of a reputation as a high-crime area. Although problems with gangs and drugs in some of the lowest-income areas of the city cannot be denied, the city has gone through a quiet transformation in recent years. Since the closing of Fort Ord, crime rates have dropped significantly. Active neighborhood groups have reclaimed their streets and parks, and civic pride is on the increase. Economic prosperity has also received a big boost from new construction, such as the lavish Embassy Suites hotel near Laguna Grande Park. Seaside seems poised for a renaissance, and the low home prices now available have nowhere to go but up.

REAL ESTATE COMPANIES

There is no shortage of quality real estate companies staffed with experienced experts on the Monterey Peninsula. Carmel in particular has a number of notable real estate firms, including the oldest on the Peninsula. Most of these major real estate firms cover the entire Monterey Peninsula and surrounding areas. Some of the larger ones have multiple offices in more than one city. Therefore, we list these firms in alphabetical order rather than trying to segment them by locale.

Alain Pinel Realtors
Junipero Street and Fifth Avenue, Carmel
(831) 622-1040, (800) 933-1331
www.apr-carmel.com

Alain Pinel Realtors has more than 50 local agents, three of whom used to run local real estate companies of their own. Although specializing in homes in Carmel, Carmel Highlands, and Pebble Beach, the firm covers the entire Monterey Peninsula. Property management, long-term rental, and relocation services are provided. Local owners Robert and Judith Profeta have put together an experienced midsize agency, with branches in the San Francisco Bay Area.

Bratty Real Estate
574 Lighthouse Avenue, Pacific Grove
(831) 375-5173
www.brattyrealestate.com

Bratty Real Estate is synonymous with Pacific Grove. Established in 1957, this one-office, 10-Realtor agency is owned and operated by born-and-bred Pagrovians Bob and Dru Bratty. Although specializing in P.G., Bratty Real Estate covers the entire Monterey Peninsula. Property management and long-term rental services are provided, and the staff is well versed in the tax laws of 1031 "like kind" exchanges.

Burchell House Properties
Ocean Avenue and Dolores Street, Carmel
(831) 626-6461, (888) 441-6914
Lincoln Street and Sixth Avenue, Carmel
(831) 626-5045
www.burchellhouse.com

Established in Carmel in 1920, Burchell House Properties is the second-oldest continuously operating real estate business in Carmel. Still headquartered in its original location at Ocean and Dolores, which it used to share with Carmel City Hall, Burchell House is locally owned and operated and serves the entire Peninsula area from two Carmel offices. Its 22 agents are all licensed Realtors, and co-owner Gerry Hopkins says this medium-size boutique realty prides itself in using sophisticated technology to provide personalized service. Burchell House has a property-management division that specializes in long-term

The "Butterfly House" is a Carmel landmark, located on Scenic Drive with a view of Carmel Bay and Point Lobos. TOM OWENS

and vacation rentals. Uniquely, Burchell House also offers the services of a certified feng shui consultant. Feng shui is the ancient Asian art of balancing energies by aligning space design and furnishings.

Buyer's Real Estate
532 Abrego Street, Monterey
(831) 644-9312, (888) 644-9312
www.buyersrealestate.com
A real estate company that represents only buyers? Yes, it's Buyer's Real Estate, a five-year-old company run by Joel Denning. With only three Realtors on staff, they're small, but they don't take listings or offer property management services. Their sole focus is serving as a buyer's representative, covering the entire Peninsula and all price ranges. As an added value, they rebate 50 percent of their commission to the buyer at the close of escrow. They'll even give you free use of a moving truck after you purchase your new home!

Calandra Real Estate
708 Forest Avenue, Pacific Grove
(831) 372-3877, (800) 835-7705
www.calandrarealestate.com
Karen Calandra runs a small, two-Realtor office in Pacific Grove and takes pride in providing personal attention to her clients. She's even been known to help a new home owner hire a gardener, shop for furnishings, or interview a housekeeper. Founded in 1987, Calandra Real Estate covers the entire Peninsula and also represents properties in the Monterey Dunes Colony, a planned unit development north on Highway 1 near Moss Landing. Limited property-management and relocation services are provided to her clients.

Carmel Cottage Realty
Seventh Avenue and Lincoln Street, Carmel
(831) 625-1943, (800) 624-4331
www.carmelcottagerealty.com
With 20 years of experience, owner Terri

Gelardi takes pride in operating her small Carmel office in this era of large franchise real estate firms. As a licensed real estate broker, Terri and her four agents emphasize establishing long-term client relationships and then finding that something special within a given price range in Carmel or surrounding Peninsula communities. She invites potential relocators to drop by for a visit and a market overview, even if they're not quite ready to buy. And when it is time to buy, Terri can help you find just the right loan as well.

Century 21 Scenic Bay Properties
656 Munras Avenue, Monterey
(831) 648-7271, (800) 723-6887
www.c21scenicbayproperties.com

Owners Dick Kelly and Erling Andresen lead a team of (appropriately enough) 21 Realtors at Century 21 Scenic Bay Properties. Since 1985 the firm has offered a full range of single-family residences and condominium properties and provided complete investment, property-management, and relocation services to buyers and sellers across the Monterey Peninsula. Agents speak several foreign languages including German, Italian, Spanish, and Norwegian.

Chelew & Campbell Realty
1155 Forest Avenue, Pacific Grove
(831) 649-8888

Chelew & Campbell, a six-Realtor office owned by Rose Marie Coleman, has been selling real estate on the Peninsula since 1958. With more than 40 years of experience, Chelew & Campbell offers a full range of residential properties. Its property -management department features long-term rentals, including apartment houses. Relocation services are outsourced. Rose Marie invites visitors to drop by her Pacific Grove office with any real estate questions.

Coldwell Banker Del Monte Realty
Junipero Street and Fifth Avenue, Carmel
(831) 626-2221
3775 Via Nona Marie, Carmel
(831) 626-2222

Ocean Avenue and Dolores Street, Carmel
(831) 626-2224
Ocean Avenue and Lincoln Street, Carmel
(831) 626-2227
The Shops at the Lodge, Pebble Beach
(831) 626-2223
The Inn at Spanish Bay, Pebble Beach
(831) 626-2225
501 Lighthouse Avenue, Pacific Grove
(831) 626-2226
www.cbdmr.com

With seven offices and approximately 100 Realtors on staff, Coldwell Banker Del Monte Realty offers the combination of nearly 170 years of local experience with the resources of one of the largest real estate networks in the world. Pebble Beach pioneer Samuel F. B. Morse founded the original Del Monte Realty back in 1919, and the company established itself early on as a luxury-home specialist. Real estate giant Coldwell Banker purchased the firm in 1997 and, while continuing its Pebble Beach tradition, lists homes from $300,000 to $20 million across the Monterey Peninsula and surrounding areas. Coldwell Banker Del Monte Realty provides basic property-management assistance and is part of the national Coldwell Banker Relocation System. The extensive Coldwell Banker training program helps ensure that agents are well versed in the latest real estate trends and techniques.

Alan H. Cordan, Realtor
San Carlos Street and Fifth Avenue, Carmel
(831) 625-4393, (888) 333-7653
www.cordan.com

This is the epitome of a small personal-service real estate company. Alan Cordan has been active in the Monterey Peninsula market for 30 years and has operated his own firm since 1979. You won't find property-management or relocation services here, just the special attention of a dedicated businessman who can help you buy or sell a home. Alan specializes in homes at $500,000 or more in the Carmel and Pebble Beach area. Alan is a Certified Residential Specialist (CRS) and a Certified Real Estate Brokerage Manager (CRB).

The Monterey County Association of Realtors has an informative Web site with many real estate facts and figures. Visit www.mcar.com.

Fouratt-Simmons Real Estate
Court of the Golden Bough, Ocean Avenue and Lincoln Street, Carmel
(831) 624-3829
www.fouratt-simmons.com
Since 1946, Fouratt-Simmons Real Estate has been providing personalized service to the Monterey Peninsula. Owner Barbara Simmons and her 12 agents, all licensed Realtors, work to provide one-stop shopping for "castles to cottages" throughout the entire Peninsula and Carmel Valley. Located in the court of Carmel's historic Golden Bough Theater, Fouratt-Simmons has a full service property-management division offering long-term and vacation rentals. The company will even help you with escrow and financing.

Harbor Realty
299 Webster Street, Monterey
(831) 649-6860, (800) 449-6860
www.harborrealty.net
Harbor Realty has been serving the Monterey Peninsula since 1980. Today nine licensed Realtors averaging 10 years of experience can show you a wide range of residential and income properties, including apartment complexes. Locally owned and operated, Harbor Realty offers property-management and relocation services. It's a member of the Monterey County, California, and National Association of Realtors.

International Estates
Fifth Avenue and San Carlos Street, Carmel
(831) 626-5100
www.internationalestates.com
Specializing in luxury upper-end properties, International Estates has the distinction of being a Five Star-rated real estate agency. Owner Gayle Crusan has been serving the Peninsula since 1989 and has been rated among the top 5 percent in agent sales for the last five years. International Estates has eight Realtors, each representing their own listings throughout the Monterey Peninsula. They are full-service agents who attend all escrow signings. The company offers property-management services including long-term rentals as well as full relocation services.

The Mitchell Group Real Estate
El Paseo Courtyard, Dolores Street at Seventh Avenue, Carmel
(831) 624-0136
Dolores Street and Seventh Avenue, Carmel
(831) 624-6482
200 Clock Tower Place, Carmel
(831) 624-1566
312 West Carmel Valley Road, Carmel Valley
(831) 659-2267
1157 Forest Avenue, Pacific Grove
(831) 646-2120
www.mitchellgroup.com
The largest independent real estate firm on the Monterey Peninsula, The Mitchell Group has a staff of more than 100 licensed Realtors operating out of five busy offices. With a history that dates back to 1926, the Mitchell Group covers the entire Monterey Peninsula area, but partner Kent Nelson says the firm's specialty is waterfront properties from Pebble Beach and Carmel south to the Big Sur coast and large ranch estates out in Carmel Valley. The company provides full property-management services, including long-term and vacation rentals, and is an affiliate of Sotheby's relocation services. Mitchell Financial Services offers in-house mortgage lending, making this firm a truly full-service operation.

Pan American Real Estate
Fifth Avenue and Junipero Street, Carmel
(831) 624-3511, (800) 982-2763
www.panamericanrealestate.com

Pan American, with four licensed Realtors on staff, takes a unique approach to covering the entire Monterey Peninsula. Owner Joe Rousso assigns each agent to a distinct area of the Peninsula, making him or her a neighborhood expert. Pan American also has a licensed and certified appraiser on staff and provides complete estate appraisals and liquidations. You might find not only your dream home but also that antique bedroom set you've always been looking for. National and international relocation services are provided, as well as property-management services.

Tom Redfern and Associates
26350 Carmel Rancho Lane, Carmel
(831) 625-5200

If you're looking to purchase an apartment building on the Monterey Peninsula, Tom Redfern is your man. Specializing in apartment-house sales and exchanges, Tom Redfern and Associates is a small single-office, two-Realtor agency that focuses exclusively on this niche market. Tom has more than 25 years of experience in the area and a long track record of putting together transactions that provide optimum tax benefits and income opportunities.

RE/MAX-Realtors Monterey Peninsula
26362 Carmel Rancho Lane, Carmel
(831) 625-3535, (800) 698-3043
www.bertaronson.com

RE/MAX-Realtors is a large international real estate network with more than 2,500 offices worldwide. That network provides local franchise owner Bert Aronson with a wealth of resources from his Carmel office. With 24 licensed brokers on staff, RE/MAX covers the entire Monterey Peninsula offering both residential and commercial properties. Full property-management services are offered, including a separate vacation-rental division called Garden Court Vacation Rentals, (831) 625-1400. The office is part of the worldwide RE/MAX relocation network. Special features include loan-origination services and a training and education center that offers seminars on topics such as real estate investments.

John Saar Properties
212 Crossroads Boulevard, Carmel
(831) 622-7227
26135 Carmel Rancho Boulevard, Carmel
(831) 625-0500
www.johnsaarproperties.com

A former top-10 agent with a Northern California real estate franchise, John Saar left to form his own brokerage in 1997. Today he runs two Carmel offices with 16 Realtors. Saar has carved a unique niche in the Carmel and Pebble Beach market, providing out-of-towners with local representation in their search for a Peninsula home or investment property. Saar's marketing skills and high-tech, multimedia approach serves sellers well, too.

Greg Shankle Real Estate
261 Webster Street, Monterey
(831) 646-1401
www.gregshankle.com

Owned and operated in Monterey by the same local family since 1956, Greg Shankle Realty is an accomplished mid-size agency with 18 Realtors serving all of Monterey County. Ten of the agents are brokers and average more than 15 years of experience. The company is a member of RELO, an 1,100-member national network offering full relocation services. Owner Greg Shankle, a former member of the Monterey Peninsula Association of Realtors, reports that year after year his firm ranks at or near the top locally in successful transactions per agent.

RETIREMENT

Seniors living in Monterey County, having found such an ideal place to spend their golden years, feel blessed. Recent census data reveals that 10 percent of our more than 400,000 residents are older than 65.

In addition to the moderate clime, the Peninsula offers a realm of beauty not found elsewhere. The magnificent Monterey Bay, a National Marine Sanctuary, offers an ever-changing variety of scenery and seasonal changes.

A myriad of resources serves the growing senior population, providing a wealth of information and assistance and ensuring that Monterey County seniors feel welcome and well taken care of.

Today's seniors are experiencing better health and living longer. Walking along the beach, dining with friends, and enjoying the many social and cultural events are but a few of the activities on the Peninsula most seniors find especially satisfying. It is also a comfort to know that we have excellent medical facilities with many physicians to care for those who have health needs.

ACTIVITIES AND CLUBS

Listed below are some of the many agencies that provide services for the special needs of the senior population.

City of Monterey Recreation and Community Services Department
546 Dutra Street, Monterey
(831) 646–3866
www.monterey.org
The Recreation Department plans programs and leisure activities for seniors. Activities include sewing, crafts, exercises, golf lessons, dancing, and other specialized senior citizen classes.

City of Monterey Senior Center
280 Dickman Avenue, Monterey
(831) 646–3878
www.monterey.org
The newly renovated senior center is a multipurpose facility devoted primarily to senior citizen activities. Located in 1.2-acre Sholze Park, the center is also open to the general public for picnics and barbecues.

Oldemeyer Center
City of Seaside Community Services
986 Hilby Avenue, Seaside
(831) 899–6339
The Oldemeyer Center offers classes such as dancing, exercise, sewing, piano, and arts and crafts. This is the site for the senior nutrition lunch program. It also provides information referral services.

Sally Griffin Senior Center
700 Jewell Avenue, Pacific Grove
(831) 375–4454
www.sallygriffincenter.org
The Sally Griffin Senior Center offers a wide range of activities including fitness programs, entertainment, art shows, and special events. Educational topics include legal help, Social Security issues, and financial well-being. The continually updated schedule is posted on their Web site. The center also serves as the home of Meals on Wheels of the Monterey Peninsula.

SCORE
380 Alvarado Street, Monterey
(831) 648–5360
www.bayscore.org
SCORE (Service Corps of Retired Executives), a nonprofit association, provides free business counseling for small businesses. The counselors are all retired executives who volunteer their services.

AGENCIES AND SERVICES

Adult Protective Services
1281 Broadway Avenue, Seaside
(831) 899-8010
www.co.monterey.ca.us
Run by the Department of Social Services, this agency provides immediate response to emergencies. It provides goal-oriented services as well as information and referral to dependent adults and elderly persons in need of protection. The goal of the program is to prevent or remedy neglect, abuse, or exploitation of dependent adults and elderly persons who are unable to protect their own interests.

Alliance on Aging
2200 Garden Road, Monterey
(800) 510-2020
www.allianceonaging.org
The Alliance on Aging houses administrative offices for community programs such as senior employment services, health insurance counseling, senior homesharing, and tax counseling. It also provides referral information.

The Friendly Visitor Program, operated by the Alliance on Aging, links volunteers with isolated and lonely older people who need the emotional support of a friend in order to continue living alone. Telephone reassurance and limited amounts of escort driving are also provided.

In addition to providing information relevant to senior issues, this service also provides assistance in completing public benefit forms and tax returns. There is a bimonthly newsletter for Alliance members. When appropriate, it provides advocacy for seniors.

Area Agency on Aging
1000 South Main, Suite 211-A, Salinas
(831) 647-7899
www.n4a.org
This regional planning agency administers federal Older Americans Act funds and serves as an advocate for those age 60 and older.

Free watercolor, acrylic, and oil painting classes are offered for seniors every Monday at the Prunedale Senior Center. Participants must provide their own materials. For information call (831) 663-5023.

Counseling Center/Community Human Services
590 Pearl Street, Monterey
(831) 373-4775; (831) 373-4773,
24-hour crisis and referral line
This nonprofit organization provides individual, group, and family counseling on a sliding scale fee basis. Counselors are either interns working on a master's degree in marriage, family, and child counseling or social workers. Counseling sessions are held at the center, and appointments are necessary.

In-Home Supportive Services/Department of Social Services
1281 Broadway Avenue, Seaside
(831) 899-8010
The agency provides low-income elderly and blind or disabled persons of any age with nonmedical assistance so that they can safely remain in their homes. This includes domestic services, meal preparation, cleanup, laundry, shopping for food and other essentials, personal care, transportation for medical appointments, and protective supervision.

Meals on Wheels of the Monterey Peninsula Inc.
700 Jewell Avenue, Pacific Grove
(831) 375-4454
www.mealsonwheelsmonterey.org
This organization provides home-delivered meals to seniors and the disabled. The criteria for delivery are an inability to shop and cook for oneself. Meals on Wheels also provides a congregate lunch program with noon meals to seniors at Griffin Senior Center, 700 Jewell Avenue, Pacific

Grove; Monterey Senior Center, 280 Dickman Avenue, Monterey; Oldemeyer Center, 986 Hilby Avenue, Seaside; and the Marina Community Center, 211 Hillcrest Avenue, Marina. Senior center activities, services, classes, and information are also provided by the agency.

EDUCATION

Adult Literacy Program
(831) 899-0417

Trained volunteer tutors provide free, confidential one-on-one literacy tutoring to adults. Tutoring is available for both native and foreign-born speakers. Writing and spelling programs are set up to meet the needs of the individual. The one-on-one sessions are held at the Seaside Library, 550 Harcourt Avenue. A volunteer tutor takes part in a two-day workshop where technique, skills, and materials are provided. The tutor must be willing to commit four hours a week, two for preparation and two for the session.

Monterey County Free Libraries
26 Central Avenue, Salinas
(831) 424-3244
www.montereycountyfreelibraries.org

Established in 1912, the Free Libraries provide free access to information, educational, and recreational materials at 17 locations throughout Monterey County. The collection consists of books, books on tape, CDs, videos, newspapers, and magazines in English, Spanish, Vietnamese, and Korean. Youth and reference services, Internet access, and literacy programs are also offered.

The Gentrain Society sponsors 15 two-week courses per year in Western history, literature, drama, philosophy, religion, history, and art. College credit is offered. Classes are held Tuesday and Thursday at Monterey Peninsula College. For information visit www.gentrain.org or call (831) 646-4000.

Older Adult Program/Monterey Peninsula College
980 Fremont Street, Monterey
(831) 646-4058

Continuing personal-enrichment classes structured for seniors are offered at selected community sites and rest homes on the Monterey Peninsula. All classes are free, and registration takes place at anytime by attending the class.

Adult Schools

Adult education is a program of quality academic, vocational, and physical education based on the philosophy that increasing knowledge allows any subject to be enjoyed, pursued, accepted, or defended to greater degrees. The adult education program believes in the right of every adult in the community to gain an education regardless of age, heritage, disability, or background.

Programs for older adults are based on the following categories: scientific and human perspectives, fine and applied arts, cultural studies, mental fitness, and accident prevention. Course offerings include woodworking, where students repair or finish projects; open media art, which allows for creative expression through watercolor, ink, pastel, pencil, and collage; language programs such as French, German, Italian, and Spanish; physical fitness classes; communication improvement, where students use discussion and writing assignments to improve skills; and music appreciation.

Class fees average around $20 per seasonal quarter, depending on class materials. For information about the many classes offered by the area adult schools, call between 8:00 A.M. and 4:00 P.M. on weekdays.

Carmel Adult School
3600 Ocean Avenue, Carmel
(831) 624-1714
www.montereycountyadulted.org/Adult School/Carmel/CarmelAdult.html

Monterey Adult School
1295 LaSalle Avenue, Seaside
(831) 899-1615
www.mpusd.k12.ca.us/adultschool

Pacific Grove Adult School
1025 Lighthouse Avenue, Pacific Grove
(831) 646-6580
www.pgusd.org/pgaehome.htm

Salinas Adult School
20 Sherwood Place, Salinas
(831) 753-4260
www.salinasadultschool.com

EMERGENCY SERVICES

Dial 911 for any emergency call. Give the operator the location you are calling from and the nature of the emergency. If you are hearing impaired, emergency TDD service is available by dialing 911, then pressing the space bar until someone answers.

Emergency Disaster Services/Salvation Army
Monterey
(831) 899-4913
The Salvation Army is ready to respond to community need during emergency/ disaster situations. It has a mobile canteen ready to provide communication services, emergency food, counseling, or support services as needed.

Emergency Home Repairs Loan Program/ City of Monterey
669 Van Buren Street, Monterey
(831) 646-3721
www.monterey.org/housing/rehab.html
Low-income Monterey seniors receive top priority in obtaining a loan of up to $15,000 for emergency home repairs. The city staff supervise and pay the repair person(s) and inspect the repairs. The loans are made at 5 percent interest. No payments are made on the loan until the property is sold (deferred).

EMPLOYMENT AND TRAINING

Joblink/Older Worker Program
1976 Fremont Boulevard, Suite A, Seaside
(831) 899-8151
730 La Guardia Avenue, Salinas
(831) 755-5860
This program provides employment and training services at no cost to eligible older workers, age 55 and older, who want to work or re-enter the labor market.

Senior Aides/Senior Employment/ Alliance on Aging
2200 Garden Road, Monterey
(831) 655-1334
www.allianceonaging.org
Seniors age 50 and older can find work through this free employment service. It also provides part-time work assignments in nonprofit agencies for low-income seniors.

HEALTH SERVICES

Alzheimer's Association Helpline
182 El Dorado, Monterey
(831) 660-1993
This nonprofit organization offers support groups, peer counseling, information/ referral, a lending library, and Wander Protection Program.

Alzheimer's Day Care
Resource Center & Library
200 Coe Avenue, Seaside
(831) 899-7178
The Visiting Nurse Association provides adult day care for dementia-impaired adults, a support group for caregivers, and a lending library regarding Alzheimer's and other diseases common to the aging population.

American Lung Association of the
Central Coast
550 Camino El Estero, Suite 100, Monterey
(831) 373-7306
www.alaccoast.org
This organization was set up to help

improve the quality of life for those who suffer from respiratory disease. It promotes healthy lungs in a healthy environment. By thorough research it seeks to find answers regarding the prevention, cure, and control of lung disease.

American Red Cross
Dolores Street and Eighth Avenue, Carmel
(831) 624-6921
www.arccarmel.org

The American Red Cross is a humanitarian organization, led by volunteers, that provides relief to victims of disasters and helps people prevent, prepare for, and respond to emergencies. Volunteer health and safety instructors teach CPR/first aid, water safety, pet first aid, and babysitting.

Salinas Valley Memorial Hospital offers an extensive health resource on its Web site. MEDLINEplus features timely medical news, an encyclopedia of medical terms, drug information, physician referral, and much more. Visit www.svmh.com.

Blind and Visually Impaired Center
225 Laurel Avenue, Pacific Grove
(831) 649-3505

This center provides orientation and mobility instruction, teaches home living skills, gives Braille instruction, and operates a low-vision clinic. It also conducts exercise and ceramic classes. A weekly luncheon is hosted by the center.

Health Insurance Counseling and Advocacy Program
2200 Garden Road, Monterey
(831) 655-1334

This countywide service provides counseling and assistance regarding Medicare benefits, supplemental health insurance, Medicare Risk HMOs, and long-term care.

Hospice of the Central Coast
100 Barnet Segal Lane, Monterey
(831) 658-3737
www.chomp.org

Hospice, a service of Community Hospital of the Monterey Peninsula, is a team of medical professionals and trained volunteers who provide a wide range of services to patients and families who are facing end of life. The emphasis is on keeping patients at home whether they are pursuing aggressive treatment or are focusing on comfort measures. Services include skilled nursing care, symptom and pain management, medical social services, chaplaincy, home health aides, a pharmacy, support groups, volunteer support, and a free library that is open to the public.

Josephine Kernes Memorial Pool
15 Portola Avenue, Monterey
(831) 372-1240

This is a warm-water pool with individualized exercise swim instruction for mentally and emotionally disabled children and adults. Arthritis exercise classes are also held. A lift is available to assist nonambulatory people with getting in and out of the pool.

Monterey Bay Dental Society
2100 Garden Road, Suite B10, Monterey
(831) 658-0618
www.mbdsdentists.com

This organization provides free referrals to dentists who offer senior discounts. It also assists in patient-dentist conflicts.

Monterey Hearing and Balance Center
1077-D Cass Street, Monterey
(831) 375-5688

This full-service diagnostic center offers audiological testing with complete hearing evaluation, impedance testing, hearing-aid evaluation, balance evaluation, and consultation. Its state-of-the-art, advanced technology equipment provides accurate hearing-aid assessment and fittings. Insurance programs are accepted.

Visiting Nurses Association (VNA)
40 Ragsdale Road, Monterey
(831) 375-9537
www.ccvna.com

VNA, an affiliate of Salinas Valley Memorial Healthcare System, operates the SHARE Program, which meets the needs of adults who are physically impaired due to a stroke or head injury. Services include speech, physical, and occupational therapy. The Alzheimer's Program prevents or postpones institutionalization of adults who may be frail or have Alzheimer's or other dementia-related conditions. Extended Services Home Care is available 24 hours a day and provides personal care assistance with daily living needs.

HOUSING
Retirement Communities

Canterbury Woods
651 Sinex Avenue, Pacific Grove
(831) 373-3111
www.ehf.org/cw

Canterbury Woods offers private cottages and apartments on six acres in Pacific Grove. It provides a full range of services including housekeeping, linen service, and three meals a day served in the dining room. There is 24-hour security, and medical facilities are on-site. Activities include dancing, tai chi, and exercise classes.

The Park Lane
200 Glenwood Circle, Monterey
(831) 373-6126
www.hyattclassic.com

One of Hyatt's Classic Residences, The Park Lane is on 12 acres overlooking the Monterey Bay and surrounding forest. It offers a wide array of Hyatt-style services and amenities, including spacious balconies; beautiful grounds; choice of lunch or dinner daily; housekeeping; scheduled transportation; cultural, social, and educational programs; a fitness center and spa;

a library; and a putting green. Studios, one- or two-bedroom apartments, or garden chalets with elevators are available.

Forest Hill Manor
551 Gibson Avenue, Pacific Grove
(831) 657-5200
www.cnmh.org

Once a luxurious hotel, this facility offers studio, one-, and two-bedroom suites with various floor plans. The rooms have beautiful views of the Bay and forest. Amenities include weekly housekeeping and linen service, three meals daily, a 24-hour security staff, 24-hour licensed nursing staff, and van service. Forest Hill Manor also has an arts and crafts area, a woodworking shop, expansive gardens, walking trails, and three large libraries. Lectures, seminars, discussion groups, art exhibits, and local entertainment are commonly held on site, and day trips are offered.

Housing Services

City of Monterey
Corner of Madison and Pacific Streets, Monterey
(831) 646-3995
www.monterey.org

The City of Monterey offers a variety of services to older adults who are home owners and residents of Monterey. These include:

Mr. Fix-it Program
This program provides grants to a maximum of $950 for minor home repairs. Priority is given to low-income seniors. The city staff inspects, supervises, and pays repair persons.

Social Services Referral and Housing Oversight
Low-income Monterey seniors with housing-related problems can call for information, referral, and staff assistance.

Housing Rehabilitation Program

Giving priority to low-income seniors, this program provides loans for major repairs and renovations of up to $90,000 at 5 percent interest, with no payment until the property is sold or transferred. City staff inspects and supervises the project and pays the contractors.

Senior Homesharing Program/Alliance on Aging
2200 Garden Road, Monterey
(800) 510-2020
www.allianceonaging.org

The agency acts as a clearinghouse service to link people who offer living space in their homes or apartments with people seeking affordable housing.

LEGAL AND GOVERNMENTAL SERVICES

Conflict Resolution and Mediation Center
1900 Garden Road, Monterey
(831) 649-6219

This agency provides mediation and conflict services in the areas of landlord/tenant, neighborhood problems, youth, quality of life, and fair housing. It covers all forms of alternative dispute resolution, including arbitration services.

Eldercare Locator
(800) 677-1116
www.eldercare.gov

This Washington, D.C.-based organization provides information on a wide range of state and local services for seniors, including information on agencies that assist with housing issues, financial matters, legal aid, Alzheimer's disease, diabetes, and health care matters.

Lawyer Referral Service
Monterey
(831) 375-9889

For a $30 fee, the Lawyer Referral Service arranges a 30-minute consultation with an attorney with a practice in the required area of law.

Legal Services For Seniors
915 Hilby Avenue, Suite 2, Seaside
(831) 899-0492
21 West Laurel Drive, Suite 83, Salinas
(831) 442-7700
www.legalservicesforseniors.org

Free legal advice and representation is provided to persons age 60 and older through this program. The program has several outreach centers located throughout Monterey County. The priority areas are housing, public benefits (Social Security, SSI), elder abuse, consumer problems, and life-planning issues.

Monterey County Department of Social Services
1281 Broadway Avenue, Seaside
(831) 899-8001

This is the county government agency designated to administer a wide range of community and social service programs that use county, state, and federal funds. The two client-serving divisions within the government are income maintenance (commonly known as welfare) and social services, which encompasses services to adults, families, and children.

Social Security Administration
24 East Alvin Drive, Salinas
(831) 443-9195
www.ssa.gov

This office is administrator for Social Security benefit programs and Supplemental Security Income programs for the elderly, blind, or disabled.

PUBLIC LIBRARIES

The following public libraries offer a collection of books and materials in large print, reading aids, closed caption decoder, and TDD. The libraries provide special services to seniors including books on tape, aging and medical information, tax forms, videos, shut-in service, references, and referrals. They also have a special notice and information board for senior citizens.

Harrison Memorial Main Library
Ocean Avenue and Lincoln Street, Carmel
(831) 624-4629

Harrison Memorial Park Branch
Mission and Sixth Streets, Carmel
(831) 624-1366

Monterey Library
625 Pacific Street,
Monterey
(831) 646-3932
www.monterey.org/library

Pacific Grove Library
550 Central Avenue, Pacific Grove
(831) 648-5760
www.pacificgrove.lib.us

Seaside Library
550 Harcourt Street, Seaside
(831) 899-2055

TRANSPORTATION SERVICES

Monterey-Salinas Transit (MST)
1 Ryan Ranch Road, Monterey
(831) 899-2555
www.mst.org
MST provides fixed-route bus service
between cities on the Monterey Peninsula.
Discount fares are available for those age
65 and older and individuals with disabilities. Call for detailed route, schedule, and
fare information.

RIDES
Monterey County
(831) 899-2555
www.mst.org
RIDES is a transit service for seniors or
special-needs riders. It offers curb-to-curb
service anywhere in the county for $1.00
each way. Hours of operation are from
7:00 A.M. to 7:00 P.M. daily. It is best to
reserve your ride 24 hours in advance to
ensure service.

*The Books-by-Mail Program offers free
library services to those unable to get to
a library. To get a listing of available
books, call (800) 322-6884 or visit
www.montereycountyfreelibraries.org.*

Senior Taxi Scrip Program
City of Monterey, Monterey Senior Center,
280 Dickman Avenue
(831) 646-3878
Casanova Oak Knoll Park Center, 735
Ramona Avenue
(831) 646-5665
Hilltop Park Center, 871 Jessie Street
(831) 646-3975
Revenue Office, City Hall, Room 4,
Corner of Pacific and Madison Streets
(831) 646-3944
www.monterey.org
Operated by the City of Monterey and the
Yellow Cab Company, the Taxi Scrip Program provides seniors age 65 and older
who are residents of Monterey with discounted cab fare. Seniors pay $10 for a
$20 booklet of taxi scrip (coupons) at any
of the locations listed above. The scrip
can be used like cash for cab fare to
health care appointments, the pharmacy,
grocery stores, and other locations within
the city limits.

Veterans Van Service
445 Reservation Road, Suite E, Marina
(831) 384-0605
This service provides veterans with
transportation to and from VA centers
for health care. It also provides the
opportunity for spouses to visit
hospitalized veterans.

HEALTH CARE Ⓗ
AND WELLNESS

The Monterey Peninsula offers a kaleidoscope of health care options, from traditional to alternative medicine. Scores of physicians have set up private practices here, and medical specialists are in abundance in fields ranging from audiology to urology. Between Monterey County's three hospitals, there are two comprehensive cancer centers, a heart center, two neonatal intensive care units, and a number of highly-specialized departments and services. One hospital even has a working technology partnership with NASA. Several options are convenient for the out-of-town visitor in terms of drop in clinics or urgent care needs. Mental health facilities are also available, including those specifically tailored to recovery from substance abuse.

Alternative medicine plays a significant role in the area's health care scene, with disciplines represented in the fields of massage, physical therapy, chiropractic, iridology, meditation, herbology, aromatherapy, body contouring, yoga, acupuncture, nutrition, reflexology, and hypnotherapy.

Monterey County residents have access to free information lines that provide data on a number of medical topics; we list them along with general information about how to use the services and the subjects they cover. Finally, those traveling with a pet will appreciate the section we've added on emergency pet care.

HOSPITALS

Community Hospital of the Monterey Peninsula
23625 W.R. Holman Highway, Monterey
(831) 624–5311
www.chomp.org
With 174 beds, Community Hospital of the Monterey Peninsula is the nearest

acute-care hospital and is easily accessible from anywhere on the Peninsula. Accredited by the Joint Commission on the Accreditation of Healthcare Organizations, the hospital provides prevention, diagnostic, treatment, home health care, and end of life (hospice) services.

Patient rooms are private, and most feature a patio or balcony that looks onto beautiful and fragrant gardens. Through an endowment specifically for art and music, the hospital incorporates fine art and live music into the healing environment. In addition to inpatient, outpatient, and emergency care, a variety of services—education classes, diagnostic imaging, laboratory services, mental health and recovery programs, surgery, and radiation and chemotherapies—are provided here. The hospital also provides selected services at more than 15 satellite offices located throughout Monterey County.

The Family Birth Center, offering single-room maternity care, was built in 1996 and is adorned with many colorful paintings by Hank Ketchum, creator of Dennis the Menace. On its campus, the hospital operates a comprehensive cancer center with state-of-the-art diagnostic and treatment capabilities. A Library & Information Center, located in the lower level of the cancer center, provides books and tapes, computers with Internet access, and a librarian and volunteers who offer assistance.

Among the many specialized services offered by Community Hospital are a diabetes program, a blood center, a sleep disorders center, behavioral health services that include inpatient and outpatient mental health and substance abuse programs, hospice services, home health care, a breast care center, and rehabilitation services. The hospital provides classes, seminars, and screenings throughout the year. A wealth of information and links to other resources can be found on the hospital's Web site.

Natividad Medical Center
1441 Constitution Boulevard, Salinas
(831) 759–6517, (800) 821–2967
www.natividad.com

Natividad Medical Center (NMC), a county-owned and operated hospital with more than 150 beds, is located in a rapidly growing area of Salinas. Natividad is a full-service acute-care academic center staffed by full-time faculty and community physicians. The hospital, accredited by the Joint Commission on the Accreditation of Healthcare Organizations, is a local leader in managed-care programs with extensive outpatient services.

NMC, affiliated with the University of California at San Francisco School of Medicine, is home to the Family Practice Residency Training Program—postgraduate training for physicians specializing in the board-certified specialty of family medicine. It is the only academic medical center on the Central Coast. The hospital also has affiliations with Lucile Packard Children's Hospital, Stanford University, for operation of their adolescent medicine clinic; and with Santa Clara Valley Perinatologists to provide services for women with high-risk pregnancies, genetic testing and counseling, antenatal testing, and ultrasound.

The medical center offers the full complement of inpatient and outpatient diagnostic and treatment services including mental health and substance abuse programs. The Maternal/Child Health Center operated by NMC offers unique services including the Bates-Eldredge Child Sexual Abuse Clinic, a Breast Cancer Early Detection Program, and a Level II neonatal intensive care unit licensed by California Children's Services. It encompasses the Central Coast HIV/AIDS Pediatric Clinic in partnership with Stanford University and 13 pediatric subspecialty clinics.

Volunteering at one of the local hospitals **i**
is a great way for area newcomers to
meet people and get to know the Penin-
sula's communities. For more informa-
tion, visit the hospital Web sites or call
them at the numbers provided in this
chapter.

Salinas Valley Memorial Healthcare System
450 East Romie Lane, Salinas
(831) 757–4333
www.svmh.com

Salinas Valley Memorial Healthcare System, based in Salinas, is known for its commitment to employing the latest advancements in technology for prevention, diagnosis, and treatment of some of today's most challenging illnesses. In fact, this local hospital works in partnership with NASA on the Virtual Collaborative Clinic, among other technology developments that have health care applications.

Salinas Valley Memorial Hospital is a full-service acute-care facility, accredited by the Joint Commission on the Accreditation of Healthcare Organizations. In addition to a variety of highly specialized clinical departments providing inpatient and outpatient care, the hospital offers 24-hour emergency services, a Level II neonatal intensive care unit, medical and surgical care, a pediatric unit, and single-room maternity care.

Salinas Valley Memorial Healthcare System includes the Harden Regional Heart Center with state-of-the-art open-heart surgery facilities, private patient rooms, a catheterization lab, a special-procedure room, and a radiology suite.

Salinas Valley Memorial also operates a comprehensive cancer center, the highest designation available to a nonuniversity hospital. In May 2000 the hospital affiliated its cancer center with Stanford University Medical Center's Clinical Cancer Program, expanding the resources available to local people facing cancer.

The health care system also has affiliates that provide home health and hospice services, urgent care at several locations, and an assisted living facility, and is associated with the CSUMB Campus Health Center and Harden Medical Center. Throughout the year, the hospital provides a variety of education classes, seminars, and screenings, and is a Children's Miracle Network (CMN) hospital. CMN funds are used to support newborn and pediatric services at Salinas Valley Memorial, community outreach programs for children's health care, and individual children in need.

URGENT CARE CENTERS

Doctors on Duty
453 Canyon Del Rey, Del Rey Oaks
(831) 392-1790
501 Lighthouse Avenue, Monterey
(831) 649-0770
2260 North Fremont Street, Monterey
(831) 372-6700
3130 Del Monte Boulevard, Marina
(831) 883-3330
1212 South Main Street, Salinas
(831) 422-7777
1137 North Main Street, Salinas
(831) 757-1110
1505 Main Street, Watsonville
(831) 722-1444
Doctors on Duty, owned by Salinas Valley Memorial Health care System, provides urgent care, family health care, occupational medicine, and physical therapy. Physicians treat sports injuries and do physical exams (including immigration physicals), x-rays, and lab work. The clinics are open daily from 8:00 A.M. to 9:00 P.M. No appointment is necessary. The

clinics accept more than 100 insurance plans as well as major credit cards.

Monterey Bay Urgent Care Medical Center
245 Washington Street, Monterey
(831) 372-2273
Monterey Bay Urgent Care Medical Center, conveniently located near downtown Monterey and Fisherman's Wharf, provides prompt, walk-in urgent care seven days a week. Many of the physicians who work at this facility are also on staff of the emergency department at Community Hospital of the Monterey Peninsula. In addition to urgent care, the medical center staff offers family health care, occupational medicine, physical therapy, treatment for sports injuries, physical exams (including immigration physicals), X-rays, and lab work. The clinic accepts most health insurance plans and workers' compensation insurance plans, as well as major credit cards. Monterey Bay Urgent Care is open Monday through Friday from 7:30 A.M. to 6:00 P.M. and Saturday and Sunday from 9:00 A.M. to 5:00 P.M. No appointment is necessary.

HOME HEALTH PROGRAMS

Home health programs can vary widely in the services they offer. Services range from skilled nursing care, cardiac care, physical and occupational therapy, and mother-baby visits to assistance with daily living activities such as grooming and bathing. A sampling of organizations that offer home health programs is provided here and additional listings can be found in the local Yellow Pages.

Central Coast Visiting Nurse Association and Hospice
An affiliate of Salinas Valley Memorial Healthcare System
5 Lower Ragsdale Drive, Monterey
(831) 375-9882
957-A Blanco Circle, Salinas
(831) 758-8302
191 San Felipe Road, Suite H, Hollister
(831) 637-6724
www.ccvna.com

A special hot line, a service of the California Department of Managed Health Care, is available for people who need assistance solving a problem with an HMO. It's toll free at (888) HMO-2219.

Community Hospital of the Monterey
Peninsula Home Health Services
555 Abrego Street, Monterey
(831) 658-3939
www.chomp.org

Community Care
1900 Garden Road, Suite 280, Monterey
(831) 657-1999
21 West Laurel Drive, Suite 53A, Salinas
(831) 424-1455
www.communitycaremonterey.com

Country Home Care
995 Cass Street, Monterey
(831) 625-2284, (831) 771-1737 (Salinas)
www.countryhomecare.com

HOSPICE CARE

Hospice services are provided to people
with life-ending conditions and their families. For the most part, hospice care takes
place in the home and involves a team of
medical professionals and trained volunteers who provide a wide range of services
including pain and symptom management,
respite care, resource referrals, and counseling. Hospice care often enables people
to die with dignity in the comfort of their
home, surrounded by friends and family.

Hospice of the Central Coast
A service of Community Hospital of the
Monterey Peninsula
100 Barnet Segal Lane, Monterey
(831) 648-7744
www.chomp.org

Central Coast Visiting Nurse Association
and Hospice
An affiliate of Salinas Valley Memorial
Healthcare System
5 Lower Ragsdale Drive, Monterey
(831) 375-9882
957-A Blanco Circle, Salinas
(831) 758-8302
191 San Felipe Road, Suite H, Hollister
(831) 637-6724
www.ccvna.com

*For information on just about any health
topic, lists of physicians, resources available in the local communities, and calendars of health-related events and
activities, check out these helpful Web
sites: www.chomp.org, www.svmh.com,
www.natividad.com, and www.
montereymedicine.org.*

REFERRAL SERVICES
Physicians

Monterey County Medical Society
(831) 455-1008
www.montereymedicine.org

Chiropractic

Associated Chiropractic Referral Service
(831) 757-2319

Dental

American Dental Referral
(888) 657-6453
www.americandentalreferral.com

Dental Referral Service
(800) 577-7317
www.dentalreferral.com

Monterey Bay Dental Society
(831) 658-0168
www.mbdsdentists.com

Mental Health

California Psychological Association
(916) 325-9786
www.calpsychlink.org

*Visit www.chirodirectory.com to
research chiropractic resources.*

Health Information

Facts of Life Line
(800) 711-9848
www.ppmarmonte.org

A community service provided by Planned Parenthood, the Facts of Life Line provides free counseling weekdays from 9:00 A.M. to 5:00 P.M. Free taped messages can be heard 24 hours a day. Callers can hear messages on topics under the following categories: services provided by Planned Parenthood, family planning, pregnancy, prenatal care, childbirth, sexual abuse, sexuality, sexually transmitted diseases, and health care. When calling the Facts of Life Line, callers are guided through the system by a series of prompts.

ALTERNATIVE HEALTH CARE

If you prefer alternative healing systems, the range of services available on the Monterey Peninsula will please you. Whatever discipline you're leaning toward, the Yellow Pages of the phone book will be your guide to uncovering the alternative care approach you are seeking.

WELLNESS FOR PETS

Traveling with pets presents a whole set of challenges, but travelers can rest easy knowing that the following pet hospitals and clinics stand by to provide pets with the best possible care. All facilities listed are available for emergency services around the clock, seven days a week.

Animal Health Center
1261 B South Main Street, Salinas
(831) 422-7387
www.animalhealthcenterrx.com

The Animal Hospital at The Crossroads
Carmel
(831) 624-0131
www.carmelvet.com

Emergency Clinic and Critical Care Services
Ryan Ranch, 2 Harris Court, Suite A-1, Monterey
(831) 373-7374

Monterey Animal Hospital
725 Foam Street, Monterey
(831) 373-0711

Veterinary House Calls Clinic
Monterey, (831) 373-6948
Salinas, (831) 663-5523

EDUCATION

E ducation plays a significant role in the community of today's Monterey Peninsula. From a more than 150-year-old religious school to a barely seven-year-old state university campus to world-renowned foreign-language schools, the educational facilities on the Monterey Peninsula provide a wide range of scholastic opportunities for students of all ages. In this chapter we take a look at the public school districts, private schools, community colleges, technical schools, colleges, and universities that contribute so much to the vitality of the area.

PUBLIC SCHOOLS

Public school students and their parents on the Monterey Peninsula have experienced firsthand some of the same shortcomings that plague school districts up and down the state of California. Tight budgets and aging facilities have led to less than ideal circumstances for at least part of their children's educational experience. The Monterey Peninsula Unified School District, in particular, has faced serious budget deficits that forced closure of some schools and discontinuance of some special programs. That said, the public school systems of the Monterey Peninsula have done a commendable job providing quality educational opportunities for their students from kindergarten through high school.

Active parents volunteering their time to improve the school systems have much to do with the success stories in Monterey, Carmel, Pacific Grove, Pebble Beach, and neighboring communities. In addition to strong efforts by the local PTA programs, groups such as Monterey's Community Partnership for Youth, Pacific Grove's P.G. Pride, and Carmel's Padre Parents have rallied the commu-

nity to help compensate for budget shortfalls.

Local businesses and community organizations have also contributed greatly to the public school systems, particularly in the area of the arts. The nonprofit Monterey Jazz Festival provides musical instruments, sheet music, and docent training to middle and high schools throughout Monterey County. The AT&T Pebble Beach National Pro-Am raises substantial funds for local schools through its annual golf tournament. The Monterey Bay Aquarium and local museums create special educational programs otherwise unavailable to Peninsula youth.

The Peninsula is not an idyllic sanctuary free of drugs, guns, gangs, and other temptations that face youth nationwide. But it is comprised of a group of highly committed communities that realize the value of education to the present and future well-being of society. What follows is a brief overview of the three public school districts that cover the Monterey Peninsula and surrounding communities. Additional information can be obtained by requesting a School Accountability Report Card from any of the school districts.

Note: All of the school districts in this chapter use the State of California Standardized Testing and Reporting (STAR) Program for assessing academic achievement. For the first time in 2003, STAR utilized the CAT/6 scoring system, which measures and reports scores for the subjects tested at each grade level: reading, written expression, mathematics, and spelling for grades two through eight; reading, writing, mathematics, science, and social science for grades nine through 11. Scores are shown as a national percentile, with 50 percent the norm group average. (The scores presented here were the most recent as of August 2003.)

Carmel Unified School District
Carmel Valley Road, Carmel
(831) 624-1546
www.carmelunified.org

Carmel Unified School District (CUSD) serves the cities of Carmel and Carmel Valley as well as unincorporated areas down the Big Sur coast. CUSD is made up of three elementary schools, one middle school, one high school, and a continuation high school, with the district spending an average of $9,279 annually per student for educational staff, services, and materials.

Approximately 1,100 students from kindergarten through the fifth grade attend the three CUSD elementary schools. Class sizes are at or near the 20 student per teacher maximum set by the state except at the fourth and fifth grade levels, which average 25. CAT/6 scores for the three elementary schools were 67 to 76 percent for reading, 79 to 89 percent for math, 73 to 77 percent for language, and 65 to 74 percent for spelling.

Carmel Middle School has a population of 625 students in the sixth through eighth grades, with class sizes averaging 25 to 30 students. On the CAT/6 tests, middle school students scored 68 to 78 percent in reading, 67 to 74 percent in math, 65 to 73 percent in language, and 60 to 67 percent in spelling.

Carmel High School has a current population of approximately 700 students. Class sizes average 20 to 25 students, who now take advantage of computers and wiring for the Internet and cable television in every classroom. On the CAT/6 testing, ninth through 11th graders scored 58 to 62 percent on reading, 63 to 75 percent on math, 59 to 67 percent on language, and 66 to 75 percent on science. On the SAT, Carmel High 12th graders scored an average of 541 in verbal and a 554 in math.

Monterey Peninsula Unified School District
700 Pacific Street, Monterey
(831) 649-1562
www.mpusd.k12.ca.us

The Monterey Peninsula Unified School District (MPUSD) covers 67 square miles, including the cities of Monterey, Del Rey Oaks, Seaside, Sand City, and Marina as well as portions of unincorporated areas such as Pebble Beach. Twenty-four campuses comprise the district, including 13 elementary schools (kindergarten through grade five), four middle schools (grades six to eight), two high schools (grades nine to 12), and one alternative high school.

Total 2002–2003 enrollment in the 13 elementary schools was approximately 6,000. Current average class size in these schools is 20 students for grades kindergarten through three and 28 students for grades four and five.

Measured by the CAT/6 system, the 13 elementary schools in the district scored in the 35 to 47 percent range for reading, 36 to 49 percent in language, 46 to 61 percent for math, and 42 to 44 percent for spelling.

The four MPUSD middle schools' enrollment is at 2,400 with an average class size of 26 students. CAT/6 test scores ranged between 38 and 44 percent for reading, 36 and 44 percent for language, 34 and 41 percent for math, and 37 and 47 percent for spelling.

The two MPUSD high schools, Monterey and Seaside, are accredited by the Western Association of Schools and Colleges. In 2002–2003 they had a combined enrollment of fewer than 2,500 students with an average class size of 27 students. CAT/6 test scores for grades nine through 11 were in the 37 to 39 percent range for reading, 40 to 43 percent for language, 36 to 42 percent in science, and 33 to 35 percent in social science. Twelfth graders at Monterey High School had SAT scores of 524 for verbal and 540 for math; those at Seaside High School averaged 440 for verbal and 465 for math. Central Coast High School, MPUSD's continuation high school, provides an alternative school environment for students who have difficulty in the traditional high school setting.

Pacific Grove Unified School District
555 Sinex Avenue, Pacific Grove
(831) 646-6520
www.pgusd.org
Pacific Grove Unified School District serves the city of Pacific Grove as well as parts of unincorporated Pebble Beach. The district spends approximately $5,600 per student for educational staff, services, and materials. The district schools are comprised of two elementary schools (kindergarten to grade five), one middle school (grades six to eight), one general high school (grades nine through 12), and one community high school.

The two elementary schools in Pacific Grove—Robert Down and Forest Grove schools—have a combined population of more than 800 students in grades kindergarten through five. Class sizes average 20 to 28 students. The CAT/6 scores for the two schools averaged 65 to 70 percent for reading, 66 to 68 percent for language, 66 to 78 percent for math, and 49 to 63 percent for spelling.

Pacific Grove Middle School has 500 students with an average class size of 24 to 27 boys and girls. In CAT/6 testing, the sixth-through eighth-grade students scored in the 63rd to 69th percentile in reading, 64th to 80th percentile in math, 57th to 75th percentile in language, and 52nd to 63rd percentile in spelling. The middle school music program, particularly the Jazz Band, is top-notch, having done especially well in recent state competitions.

Pacific Grove High School has 500 students in grades nine through 12, with class sizes averaging 27 students. In CAT/6 testing the ninth- through 11th-grade students scored 60 to 71 percent in reading, 61 to 72 percent in math, 57 to 75 percent in language, and 56 to 71 percent in science. The 12th-grade SAT scores averaged 558 on verbal (481 state average) and 544 on math (493 state average).

Community High School provides an alternative for students who have not had success in a traditional school environment. It features a basic curriculum that emphasizes reading, writing, math, science, and art. Graduation requirements are the same as those at Pacific Grove High School. Community High School averages 35 to 40 students who are at various stages of their high school careers. Some may be simultaneously enrolled at Monterey Peninsula College, a two-year school. Class size averages 15 to 20. Students are required to be in school 3.5 hours per day. Independent study is emphasized.

PRIVATE SCHOOLS

All Saints' Episcopal Day School
8060 Carmel Valley Road, Carmel
(831) 624-9171
www.asds.org
In the sunny side of Carmel, All Saints' Episcopal Day School offers a rigorous academic curriculum within a Christian environment. Although the school has strong ties with All Saints' Episcopal Church, children from various religious backgrounds are admitted. Children as young as four years and nine months can take part in the school's Early Childhood Unit, a five-day morning program with an enrollment of 30 students. Schooling continues through the eighth grade, with an average class size of 21 to 24 students at the upper levels and 15 students at the kindergarten and younger levels.
Founded in 1961, All Saints' School places a strong emphasis on basic grammar, composition, math, and science, and all students study a foreign language (Spanish or French) beginning in the first grade. Latin is required of sixth through eighth graders. A strong fine arts program is also presented, including an annual Shakespeare production and an "Orchestras in the Schools" music program. The school hosts a series of "Visitors Days" for parents of prospective students in the fall and winter. Applicants must be in good academic and personal standing with their previous schools. Financial aid is granted on the

basis of economic need. All Saints' is a member of the National Association of Independent Schools and the National Association of Episcopal Schools.

Chartwell School
1490 Imperial Avenue, Seaside
(831) 394-3468
www.chartwell.org

The mission of Chartwell School is to educate children ages seven to 14 who have dyslexia and other specific language-learning disabilities so that they can return successfully to mainstream education. Founded in 1983, Chartwell provides a multisensory instructional program that includes language arts, language training, mathematics, fine arts, performing arts, science lab, and physical education. Class sizes at Chartwell are limited to nine students, with an average of seven. Parent workshops are also provided. Students entering their final semester participate in a formal transition program to prepare them for reentry into a traditional school system. A four-week summer program is also offered to students ages seven to 13. *Note:* At the time of this writing, Construction had begun on a new 28,000-square-foot facility located on 29 acres of the former Fort Ord army base, land donated by the Monterey Peninsula Unified School District.

Junipero Serra School
2992 Lasuen Drive, Carmel
(831) 624-8322
www.juniperoserraschool.org

Junipero Serra School is a kindergarten through eighth-grade Roman Catholic school located on the grounds of Carmel Mission. Founded in 1943, it is fully accredited by the Western Catholic Education Association and the Western Association of Schools and Colleges. Children from all parishes as well as non-Catholic children are admitted. Currently, the school has 165 students, with an average class size of 25. The academic program emphasizes religious education, family life,

language arts, science, health, social studies, math, Spanish, computers, music, physical education, art, and drama. A variety of extracurricular activities are provided, including choir, community services, journalism, and speech. Uniforms are required for all grades, and each family is required to contribute a number of hours to school service each year. Extended care is available after school hours for all grades, providing supervised homework, recreation, and arts and crafts.

Lyceum of Monterey County
1073 Sixth Street, Monterey
(831) 372-6098
www.lyceum.org

Lyceum of Monterey County is a creative program of instruction that offers 400 fun-filled classes to children from preschool age to high school. A private nonprofit organization founded in 1960, the Lyceum offers an incredibly wide variety of instructive programs in the arts, crafts, computers, sports, hobbies, humanities, life skills, science, and nature. Family programs are also offered. Programs can last from one day to one week and range in topic from surfing to babysitting safety to international folk dancing to computer-aided design. Kids from outside the county are welcome to join in during their stay on the Monterey Peninsula. Contact the Lyceum of Monterey Peninsula, and see what programs are being offered this year. The Lyceum also sponsors the annual Peninsula Spelling Bee for fourth and fifth graders and Monterey County History Day for middle school and high school students.

Monterey Peninsula Christian Preschool
520 Pine Avenue, Pacific Grove
(831) 373-1922

A ministry of Peninsula Christian Center, Monterey Peninsula Christian School is a preschool and extended-care program for children ages two through five. It offers a flexible schedule, provides a supportive learning environment, and teaches Christian values. The school is open Monday through Friday from 7:00 A.M. to 6:00 P.M., with a preschool program from 9:00 A.M. until noon. Children partake in outdoor play, games, arts and crafts, science and nature observation, music, and story time. Bible stories and verse memorization are included in the daily program.

Mothers' Morning Out
501 El Dorado Street, Monterey
(831) 373-1067

Provided by the First Presbyterian Church of Monterey, Mothers' Morning Out ministers to and provides a school curriculum for children ages two through prekindergarten, with three separate programs developed for different age groups. Children from age two through three years and five months attend the Little Critters school. The curriculum includes art, house play, a block area, manipulative materials, cooking experience, story time, science, outdoor play, and math readiness. The Main Room program for children age 3½ to five years old is offered weekdays from 9:00 A.M. until noon. The curriculum is similar to the Little Critters program except that language skills, such as letter recognition, are added. The prekindergarten program for children who will be eligible to enter kindergarten the following fall is offered from 1:00 to 3:00 P.M. Monday through Friday. The regular school session runs from August to May. There's a five-week summer program as well.

Pacific Oaks Children's School
1004 David Avenue, Building A
Pacific Grove
(831) 373-8853

A licensed, private, nonprofit corporation, Pacific Oaks Children's School provides preschool and kindergarten through second grade classes, as well as after-school programs for children five through 12 years of age. With a philosophy of learning by doing, Pacific Oaks offers preschool and kindergarten classes in language arts, math, social studies, music, art, science, nature, and physical education. The preschool operates year-round,

Monday through Friday from 7:30 A.M. to 5:30 P.M. Kindergarten meets during the regular fall to summer school year from 8:30 A.M. to 1:30 P.M., while first- and second-graders meet from 8:30 A.M. to 2:30 P.M. The after-school program highlights drama, art, music, and science. It meets after the regularly scheduled first-through fifth-grade classes of the Pacific Grove Unified School District.

Robert Louis Stevenson School
3152 Forest Lake Road, Pebble Beach
(831) 626-5200
www.rlstevenson.org

Founded in 1952, Robert Louis Stevenson School, or RLS as locals call it, is a coeducational boarding and day school on a beautiful 60-acre campus within the Del Monte Forest of Pebble Beach. Approximately half of the 500-plus ninth through 12th graders live on campus in six residence halls. Though nonsectarian, Stevenson School encourages its students to attend church as part of its quest to "educate the whole person" and offers vespers and Sunday Christian services at the school's exquisite Erdman Memorial Chapel.

Accredited by the Western Association of Schools and Colleges, RLS has a traditional college-preparatory curriculum. The Secondary School Admission Test (SSAT) is required for enrollment. Among 12th graders the mean SAT scores are 605 on the verbal and 621 on math. Advanced-placement courses are offered in art, English, foreign languages, American and European history, economics, mathematics, biology, chemistry, and physics. Average class size is 15 students.

Robert Louis Stevenson Lower and Middle School offers a range of academic choices for more than 200 students from kindergarten through eighth grade. Special programs are presented in art, dance, dramatics, music, and physical education.

San Carlos Regional School
450 Church Street, Monterey
(831) 375-1324
www.sancarlosschool.com

San Carlos Regional School was founded in 1898 and today serves students from preschool through the eighth grade. TOM OWENS

Established in 1898, San Carlos Regional School is an interparish Roman Catholic school that covers preschool through eighth grade. Accepting students of all faiths, its focus is providing Christian morals and basic academic skills in language arts, math, science, health, social science, Spanish, computer science, and physical education. Enrichment programs include field trips, retreats, service projects, and interscholastic sports. Current enrollment is approximately 300 boys and girls. Preschool is designed for children ages three to five, with each session limited to 15 children and two teachers. Uniforms are required for grades kindergarten through eight. Parental participation is vital, as each family is required to make a time and talent commitment to the school each year. San Carlos is fully accredited by the Western Association of Schools and Colleges. All homeroom teachers are fully credentialed. Extended-care services for grades kindergarten through eight run from 7:00 A.M. to 6:00 P.M.

Santa Catalina School
1500 Mark Thomas Drive, Monterey
(831) 655-9315
www.santacatalina.org

Santa Catalina is a Catholic school with a 150-year history in Monterey. Originally founded in 1850 by Mother Mary Goemaere, a Dominican sister, Santa Catalina School operates today as a coeducational lower school and an all-girl upper school. Both are on an expansive 36-acre campus that was once a Spanish hacienda estate. Santa Catalina School is accredited by the Western Association of Schools and Colleges and is a member of the California Association of Independent Schools and the National Association of Independent Schools. Santa Catalina Lower School provides a classic curriculum for students in preschool through eighth grade. The school emphasizes a strong foundation in the basic skills of language arts, social studies, science, and mathematics, along with religious instruction. Catholic students are taught the tenets of Catholicism, while others are instructed in interfaith classes that focus on values and world religions. Students add Spanish in grades four through eight. All classrooms are equipped with one or more computers that have Internet access. Santa Catalina Lower School participates in a local sports league with teams in basketball, flag football, soccer, tennis, and volleyball.

The all-girl upper school combines a rigorous liberal arts curriculum, modern educational technology, and solid Christian principles into a well-rounded high school experience. A student-to-faculty ratio of seven-to-one facilitates individual instruction, while faculty, dorm, and college admission counseling provide on-campus guidance. Performing and visual arts are emphasized, and a full inter-scholastic sports program offers seasonal competition. The 29,000-volume Sister Mary Kieran Memorial Library and a school-wide Internet and e-mail network promote studying. Residential dorms offer primarily double rooms, with girls changing roommates three times a year to promote new friendships. Student responsibilities and rights vary by class level. School clubs, voluntary service activities, and traditional off-campus events and excursions ensure that all students become an active part of the Peninsula community.

Serendipity Pre-School
1231 Seventh Street, Monterey
(831) 375-9743
A preschool program for children ages three up to kindergarten, Serendipity Pre-School focuses on developing reading, math, and science readiness skills, reinforced through art and music programs. The morning session runs from 9:00 A.M. until noon, while the afternoon session runs from 12:30 until 3:30 P.M. Before-school care is offered from 8:00 until 9:00 A.M., and after-school care is offered from 3:30 until 5:30 P.M. Extended preschool and day care are available for the full 8:00 A.M. to 5:30 P.M. schedule.

Preschool sessions begin with music and group time. The classes are then divided into the Rabbit Group and the Butterfly Group, based on maturity levels and other factors. These groups then rotate through a period of outdoor playtime and learning centers.

York School
9501 York Road, Monterey
(831) 372-7338
www.york.org
York School is an independent, coeducational college-preparatory Episcopal day school in the scenic foothills near the former Laguna Seca Ranch, a few miles inland from downtown Monterey. Serving grades eight through 12, York School enrolls just over 200 students with an average class size of fewer than 15. A rigorous college preparatory curriculum and an ambitious financial aid program attract a high-quality, culturally diverse student body. On the SATs, York students averaged 663 on the verbal section and 631 in math. More than 48 percent of seniors from the last seven graduating classes have been National Merit honorees. Accredited by the Western Association of Independent Schools, the National Association of Episcopal Schools, and the California Association of Independent Schools, York School awards grants and loans—totaling more than $650,000 in 2003—to approximately 37 percent of its students. As an Episcopal school, it emphasizes the development of moral and spiritual values in all aspects of student life.

COLLEGES AND UNIVERSITIES

California State University Monterey Bay
100 Campus Center, Seaside
(831) 582-3330
www.csumb.edu
When then-President Bill Clinton visited the brand-new California State University Monterey Bay (CSUMB) in 1995, it marked an important day for both the Monterey

Peninsula and the United States as a whole. For the nation, CSUMB represents a successful conversion of a former army base, Fort Ord, to a valuable civilian resource. For the Monterey Peninsula, the 21st campus in the California State University system represented yet another high-quality educational facility and hundreds of local jobs. From the humble beginnings of only 650 students that first year, CSUMB now welcomes approximately 3,000 full-time students each semester. By the year 2030, that population is expected to grow to 15,000. Many of these students are projected to attend the university off-campus and online as part of the California Virtual University system. The campus is already offering some technology courses entirely online. CSUMB is now accredited by the Accrediting Commission for Senior Colleges and Universities of the Western Association of Schools and Colleges. It offers 12 undergraduate majors and four graduate-level programs. The university grants both bachelor's and master's degrees in the arts and sciences as well as teaching credentials. Areas of specialty include human communication; visual and public art; world languages and cultures; education; CLAD/BCLAD teaching credentials; collaborative human services; global studies; liberal studies; management and international entrepreneurship; earth systems science and policy; telecommunications, multimedia, and applied computing; teledramatic arts and technology; social and behavioral sciences; marine science; and interdisciplinary studies. The majority of students, faculty, and staff live on campus, creating a unique residential atmosphere. More than 40 student clubs have been created, a testament to the close-knit community being established on this once sprawling army base 5 miles north of the city of Monterey.

The CSUMB Otters presently compete in the California Pacific Conference, participating in nine intercollegiate sports: men's basketball, soccer, golf, and cross-country and women's volleyball, basket-ball, golf, soccer, and cross-country. The campus prides itself on its full-service child care facilities for the children of students. This service offers daily or hourly child care for children ages six weeks to five years, as well as after-school care for kids in kindergarten through age 18. A babysitter referral service is also offered.

Chapman University, Monterey Campus
99 Pacific Street, Monterey
(831) 373-0945
www.chapman.edu

Chapman University, established in 1861, is an independent institution of liberal arts and professional training. With its main campus in Orange, California, it has operated its Monterey Academic Center since 1974, primarily to part-time students who are parents of young children and work full- or part-time. Chapman University offers undergraduate degrees in liberal studies, organizational leadership, and social sciences as well as master's degrees in education, psychology, and human resources. It also offers programs for teaching credentials. To help students balance the demands of job, family, and education, courses are offered in accelerated nine-week terms, one evening per week plus one Saturday class. Chapman University is accredited by the Senior Division of the Western Association of Schools and Colleges, and credits earned may be transferred to other colleges and universities.

Golden Gate University
500 Eighth Street, Marina
(831) 884-0900
www.ggu.edu

Founded in San Francisco in 1853, Golden Gate University is the fourth-oldest private university in California. The Monterey campus, one of 17 Golden Gate campuses in California and the Pacific Northwest, has been offering undergraduate and graduate degrees in business-oriented majors since 1971. Classes in Monterey are held on an eight-acre campus on the former Fort Ord military base. The Golden

State University Monterey Bay campus offers bachelor's degrees in business administration, accounting, and computer information systems. Master's degrees are offered in finance, human resource management, information systems, management, business administration, marketing, public administration, taxation, and other areas of business. The university is fully accredited by the Western Association of Schools and Colleges. Average class size is 16 students. Classes meet throughout the year in 15-, 12-, 10-, and 8-week formats. Full degree and certificate courses are available online in the Golden Gate Cyber Campus. Students can apply for, register for, and attend classes online, fully interacting with professors and other students. Other courses are offered on campus in intensive six-week sessions held Friday evenings and all day Saturday on alternative weekends.

Hopkins Marine Station
Ocean View Boulevard, Pacific Grove
(831) 655-6200
hopkins.stanford.edu/

Founded in 1892, Hopkins Marine Station is a marine biology research facility of Stanford University's Department of Biological Sciences and was the first marine laboratory established on the American Pacific Coast. Hopkins is ideally situated on Mussel Point, a rocky headland in Pacific Grove surrounded by the rich sea life of the Monterey Bay Marine Sanctuary. The facility is staffed year-round by approximately 20 resident faculty and support staff and is host to visiting researchers and graduate students. Both introductory and advanced marine and general biology courses are offered year-round to qualified students from any college or university. Special areas of study include cellular and developmental biology, immunology, neurobiology, comparative physiology, conservation biology, oceanic biology, marine botany, biomechanics, and marine ecology.

Monterey Institute of International Studies
425 Van Buren Street, Monterey
(831) 647-4100
www.miis.edu

Since 1955, the Monterey Institute of International Studies (MIIS) has served as a vibrant global village on the Monterey Peninsula, offering international courses and degrees to students seeking careers as bilingual, bicultural professionals. More than 700 students, approximately half being foreign students representing 50 nations, gather here to take advantage of four fully accredited graduate schools. MIIS offers master's degrees in international business administration, translation and interpretation, language teaching, commercial diplomacy, international environmental policy, international public administration, international policy studies, teaching English to speakers of other languages, and teaching a foreign language. A bachelor of arts honors program allows students with two years of undergraduate work to complete both their bachelor's degree in international studies and master's degrees in three years at the institute.

Summer and Winter Intensive Language Programs are provided in Arabic, Chinese (Mandarin), French, German, Japanese, Russian, and Spanish, as well as English as a second language. MIIS's Center for International Trade Strategy trains business executives on the intricacies of international commerce, while the Business and Economic Development Center, the Small Business Institute, and the International Trade Research Center offer international marketing assistance to businesses. The Center for Nonproliferation Studies is the largest private center in the world addressing international weapons proliferation and disarmament.

The school's library features books and periodicals in more than 30 languages. MIIS is accredited by the Western Association of Schools and Colleges.

COMMUNITY COLLEGES AND TECHNICAL SCHOOLS

Monterey College of Law
404 West Franklin Street, Monterey
(831) 373-3301
www.montereylaw.edu
Monterey College of Law (MCL) is a California State Bar-accredited community law school offering a four-year program of instruction leading to a doctor of jurisprudence degree. The school was founded in 1972 by local lawyers and judges with the goal of allowing residents to attend law school at night while continuing their daytime careers. Indeed, most of the students at MCL work full-time during the day while attending evening classes from 6:30 to 9:30 P.M. Fall and spring semesters last 16 weeks, while the summer semester is 11 weeks. Courses are taught by practicing attorneys and judges. The average class size is 45 students. In addition to being accredited by the State Bar of California, MCL is approved by the Council for Private Postsecondary and Vocational Education. The school reports that more than 70 percent of its graduates have successfully completed the bar exam and are admitted to practice law in California. However, the college has not sought accreditation from the American Bar Association. Therefore, graduates might not meet the necessary requirements to practice law or take the bar examination in other states.

Monterey Institute of Touch
27820 Dorris Drive, Carmel
(831) 624-1006
www.montereyinstituteoftouch.com
Monterey Institute of Touch offers both a 200-hour Certified Massage Practitioner program and a 500-hour Certified Massage Therapist program from its Carmel location. In addition, the institute offers a series of advanced workshops and seminars in massage techniques such as shiatsu, craniosacral, reflexology, and polarity. Some courses for massage practitioners are approved by the Board of Registered Nurses for earning continuing education units. The school emphasizes hands-on training and the latest advances in the holistic health care field.

Monterey Peninsula College
980 Fremont Street, Monterey
(831) 646-4000
www.mpc.edu
Founded in 1947, Monterey Peninsula College (MPC) is part of California's public community college system of 107 campuses throughout the state. Classes are held during two semesters (fall and spring) as well as a summer session, with enrollment reaching 10,000 to 12,000 students per semester. The average student age is 37 years, evidence of the school's significant 40-and-older population. More than 350 international students represent 46 countries at MPC. The 87-acre campus is minutes from downtown Monterey yet enjoys a decidedly rural setting. MPC's new 68,000-square-foot Library Technology Center includes 400 computer labs and expansive research facilities.

MPC confers the associate of arts degree in liberal arts and an associate of science degree in science, technology, and vocational fields. Its transfer program enables students to complete the first two years in preparation for moving on to a four-year college or university. Occupational education programs provide basic technical and professional curricula. MPC offers a full program of intercollegiate sports, including football, basketball, baseball, softball, and golf. The Maurine Church Coburn School of Nursing offers an associate of science degree. It is accredited by the National League for Nursing and approved by the California Board of Registered Nursing. MPC also has special accreditation and certifications from the California State Board of Dental Examiners, California State Fire Marshall, Commission on Dental Assisting of the American Dental Association, Commission on Police Officer Standards and Training, and the National Automotive Technical Education Foundation. MPC is

Workmen put the finishing touches on Monterey Peninsula College's 68,000-square-foot Library Technology Center, which opened in 2003. TOM OWENS

also home to the Marine Advanced Technology Education (MATE) Center, a national consortium of marine technology educational institutes.

MILITARY SCHOOLS

Defense Language Institute
Presidio of Monterey, Monterey
(831) 242-5104
www.dli.army.mil

In 1941 the U.S. Army established a secret school on the Presidio of San Francisco. Its mission: to teach the Japanese language to American soldiers of Japanese descent. In 1946 the school was renamed the Army Language School and moved to the Presidio at Monterey, where it expanded to teach more than 30 languages. That was the beginning of today's Defense Language Institute Foreign Language Center, now the world's largest language institute of its kind. The 395-acre campus, known

locally as DLI, is comprised of more than 750 classrooms, 21 language labs, and eight computer labs in seven distinct schools. More than 650 civilian faculty, 300 civilian staff, and 250 service members support the school. The primary mission of DLI is to teach the nation's military forces the foreign language skills needed to meet Department of Defense national security needs. In addition, the institute provides language training for other branches of the federal government and, since 1996, to civilians with U.S. citizenship.

DLI is accredited by the Community and Junior Colleges of the Western Association of Schools and Colleges and, in partnership with Monterey Peninsula College, offers associate's degrees in foreign languages. It offers basic through

---

The Defense Language Institute serves the entire Department of Defense and is the largest language institute of its kind.

advanced foreign-language studies with emphasis on intensive listening, speaking, reading, and writing development as well as the history, culture, and current affairs of the region where the language is spoken. Courses run 25 to 63 weeks, depending on language difficulty. The wide variety of languages offered will vary depending upon the present needs of the Department of Defense.

Aiso Library subscribes to hundreds of foreign-language newspapers, maintains 80,000 volumes of foreign-language books, and provides access to more than 5,000 foreign-language television programs.

Naval Postgraduate School
1 University Circle, Monterey
(831) 656-2441
www.nps.navy.mil
On the former grounds of Hotel Del Monte, Monterey's first world-class resort, Naval Postgraduate School (NPS) offers master's and doctoral degrees to members of all branches of the U.S. military as well as students from more than 25 foreign nations. In Monterey since 1947, NPS now serves 1,500 students on its 627-acre

The Naval Postgraduate School is located on the former grounds of the Hotel Del Monte, Monterey's first world-class resort. It is home to the splendid Arizona Garden.

campus. The curricula are designed to meet the defense requirements of the armed forces within the framework of a high-level academic institution. Each curriculum leads to a master's degree, while additional study in certain fields can lead to a doctorate. NPS ranks second of all colleges and universities in its number of alumni who have become NASA astronauts.

The 100,000-square-foot Dudley Knox Library houses approximately 400,000 bibliographic volumes in hard copy, 500,000 volumes in microfilm, and 1,200 journal subscriptions, making it the largest local research facility.

NPS takes an active part in the community by hosting a series of free Concerts on the Lawn, featuring popular classical selections by the Monterey Bay Symphony Orchestra. It also sponsors Discovery Day, a series of interactive science programs created by the academic faculty and targeted toward students between eight and 14 years of age. Finally, the school provides self-guided tour booklets of the former Hotel Del Monte and its fabulous Arizona Garden of specimen-size cacti and succulents. Rebuilt in 1926 after the second of two devastating fires, Hotel Del Monte (now called Herrmann Hall) serves primarily as offices and quarters for naval officers and is home to a small Naval Postgraduate School Museum.

CHILD CARE

hild care is a substantial industry in Monterey County. More than 11,000 Monterey County children spend at least half their day in a child care facility. Their parents work for the county, at restaurants, for private industry or the military, in hotels, or in the fields. The county has more than 800 licensed child care establishments: nearly 700 family day care homes and more than 100 centers.

The number of child care options hasn't kept pace with the rapid growth of the Monterey County work force, and welfare reform is expected to add to the numbers. In an effort to address child care needs, county and city officials, local businesses, and child care industry personnel have formed a partnership and are working toward a solution for the ever-increasing need for child care facilities.

As a result of child care challenges, some businesses in the Monterey Peninsula area have relaxed their policies on absence and tardiness and set up tax-credit programs to help employees pay for child care. A few companies provide benefits to help with the expense of child care. For example, upon discovering through a company study that their employees prefer to place their children in family day care homes, Community Hospital of the Monterey Peninsula set up 14 of them.

FAMILY DAY CARE HOMES

With nearly 700 family day care homes for children in Monterey County, it is impossible to list them all. In general, family day care facilities are less expensive than child care centers and have fewer regulations. Family day care homes for children may offer more flexibility in terms of schedules. For safety reasons, many family day care facilities are not listed in the phone book. Parents need to work with a referral service such as Children's Services International (see our listing in the "Resources" section).

All family day care homes must be licensed through the state and are required to provide their license number in all advertisements.

The license for the operation of a family day care home requires the following:

• The home must be kept clean and orderly with heating and ventilation for safety and comfort.

• It must have telephone service.

• The home must provide safe toys, play equipment, and materials.

• Any food brought from the child's home must be labeled with the child's name and properly stored or refrigerated.

• The home must be free of defects or conditions that might endanger a child.

• All in-ground swimming pools must have at least a 5-foot fence or covering inspected and approved by the licensing agency.

• Outdoor play areas must be fenced, or outdoor play must be supervised.

• An emergency card must be maintained with the child's full name, the phone number and location of a parent or other responsible adult to be contacted in an emergency, the name and phone number of the child's physician, and the parents' authorization for the licensee to consent to emergency medical care.

• Each family day care home must have a written disaster plan of action on a form approved by the licensing agency. All children, age and ability permitting, and all others in the household must be instructed in their duties under the disaster plan.

• The licensee must maintain either liability insurance, a bond, or a file of affidavits signed by each parent with a child

Parents and child care providers alike find Dennis the Menace Playground in Monterey to be a delightful play destination. MICHAEL CHATFIELD

enrolled in the home. The affidavit states that the family day care home does not carry liability insurance or a bond according to standards established by the state.

CHILD CARE CENTERS AND PRESCHOOLS

Nearly 200 child care centers and academic preschools exist in Monterey County. The Social Services Department inspects them annually to make sure they meet health and safety standards. Child care center employees are required to take the equivalent of three classes in early childhood development and to be annually certified in CPR and basic emergency procedures.

The requirements for operating a child care center or preschool match those for a family day care home but have additional requirements. When seeking a local child care center or preschool, you may want to consult the Yellow Pages of the phone directory. You can also contact Children's Services International (listed in our "Resources" section) for a referral.

RESOURCES

Children's Services International
344 Salinas Street, Salinas
(800) 273-0274
This organization provides information on child care, preschool, and family day care. It also offers a referral service for child care facilities.

Mexican American Opportunity Foundation
61 North Sanborn Road, Salinas
(831) 757-0147
www.maof.org
This foundation provides food to day care

centers. It also runs a state-funded child care center. To qualify for the child care center, parents must be in school or working at least six hours per day. The program is ideal for parents who need to further their education. The child care center is run by teachers, aides, and other workers. Breakfast, lunch, and an afternoon snack are served. The center has planned activities for the children, including learning activities, games, stories, and craft projects.

Monterey County Child Care Resource and Referral Program
622 East Alisal Street, Salinas
(800) 339-9306
Funded by the State Department of Education Child Development Division, this program offers free child care and resource referrals for families and child caregivers. They also provide technical assistance to caregivers and operate a toy lending library for licensed child caregivers. Information and services are available in English and Spanish. The program is a project of the Mexican American Opportunities Foundation.

Monterey County Family Child Care Association
P.O. Box 4122, Salinas 93912
(831) 442-2788, (888) 525-5006
mcfcca.org
This organization provides free referrals for child care in Monterey County and offers licensed family child care providers. They also serve as a resource and support network and offer training for care providers. Information and services are available in English and Spanish.

BABYSITTING SERVICES AND NANNIES

When visiting the Peninsula with children, it's still possible for parents to spend some alone time together by using a babysitting service. You can find a babysitter or nanny from either an agency or through the concierge at your hotel. Sitters or nannies will come to your hotel room or vacation rental. Some services also place full- or part-time nannies who live in or out of the home. We've listed a few local agencies that provide babysitting services.

A Mother's Touch
Monterey
(831) 644-0123
Established in 1998, A Mother's Touch provides nanny placement services as well as licensed child care at hotels, resorts, homes, and at their location year-round.

Sitters-by-the-Sea Professional Babysitting
Monterey
(831) 656-0107
Sitters-by-the-Sea provides nannies who are CPR-trained and bonded and conducts background checks on all employees. The nannies do on-site child care at your home, rental unit, or hotel. The company has served the Monterey Peninsula area since 1993.

VIP Child Care Services
(831) 659-2203
www.vipbabysitting.com
VIP provides babysitting for infants, children, and teenagers as well as custom children's programs for group events of 10 to 1,500 children. Their staff is insured, CPR certified, fingerprinted (with FBI background check), and registered with Trustline through the State of California. Their staff comes to your location prepared with art materials, games, and activity books for custom events. Reservations may be made 24 hours a day by phone or online.

Check online at mcfcca.org or call toll-free, (888) 525-5006, for free referrals to child care resources in Monterey County from the Monterey County Family Child Care Association.

MEDIA 📺

If you're looking for newsworthy items of local, national, or international significance, the media selections in Monterey County can provide you with the appropriate information. For a small market, the Monterey Peninsula has amassed media possibilities in everything from daily newspapers and syndicated news programs to Public, Education, and Government (PEG) Access channels and a Community Media Center.

NEWSPAPERS
Dailies

The Californian
123 West Alisal Street, Salinas
(831) 649-6626 from Monterey,
(831) 424-2221
www.californianonline.com
The Californian, a Gannett newspaper, has been a respected news source since 1872. Although the paper is based in Salinas, it has some presence on the Monterey Peninsula. Published weekdays and Saturday, the newspaper has a circulation of around 20,000. It provides coverage of countywide news with a primary emphasis on the Salinas Valley. From an editorial standpoint, the paper consists of national and local news, entertainment, features, sports, and classified sections. A pullout entertainment and dining guide, *411*, is published on Thursday. *The Californian* is available by subscription and at newsstands.

The Monterey County Herald
8 Upper Ragsdale Road, Monterey
(831) 372-3311
www.montereyherald.com
Since 1922, *The Herald* has provided news to residents of Monterey County. *The Herald*, a Knight-Ridder publication, is a

cousin of the highly respected and well-known *San Jose Mercury News*.

The Herald of today includes special sections for main national news, local news, sports, and classifieds. A "Living" section includes the syndicated columns of Ann Landers and Dr. Gott and a changing variety of features. Information on television programming and comics round out this popular section.

Each Thursday, locals and visitors alike check out *The Herald*'s pullout tab *Go!*, a weekly entertainment and dining guide that runs in the paper and is also distributed free as an independent publication. A Saturday *Real Estate* pullout runs with maps, open houses, and residential, commercial, and rental properties and is available free at newsstands.

The Herald, with a circulation of around 35,000, has the largest circulation of local daily newspapers. It is available by subscription and at newsstands.

Weekly and Monthly Papers

The Carmel Pine Cone
Fourth Street between Mission and San Carlos Streets, Carmel
(831) 624-0162
www.carmelpinecone.com
Published since 1915, *The Pine Cone* is a favorite of locals seeking news primarily about Carmel and immediately surrounding communities. This 25,000-circulation weekly is distributed at nearly 300 drop points in Carmel, Carmel Valley, Carmel Highlands, Pebble Beach, Monterey, Pacific Grove, and Big Sur. Highlights include local news, the fascinating (and often amusing) police and sheriff's log, an events calendar, a social column, fea-

tures on food and wine, a real estate section, and a good-size service directory.

Coast Weekly
668 Williams Avenue, Seaside
(831) 394-5656
www.coastweekly.com
This paper, with a circulation of more than 40,000, serves Monterey County in the areas of news and entertainment. The free publication comes out each Thursday and can be found at newsstands around the county. Best known for its "Hot Picks" arts and entertainment calendar, *Coast Weekly* is also considered by many to be a good alternative to mainstream media, particularly when it comes to local issues. Since its founding in 1988, the paper has received more than 50 local, regional, state, and national awards. One of the most anticipated issues is "Best of Monterey County," when readers cast their vote for their favorite businesses. It provides insider information on readers' top choices of local restaurants, entertainment venues, and service providers.

Visitors to the area will appreciate the stand-alone product *Best of Monterey Bay,* which recaps the results of "Best of Monterey County" and includes directories for various services, locations for entertainment, maps, and an annual calendar of events. This special edition is distributed at more than 100 locations, including area hotels, bookstores, and visitor centers.

Community Links
Pacific Grove
(831) 375-2026
www.communitylinks.net
This community calendar, printed monthly, works in unison with radio, television, and the Internet. The concept, created in 1997, is to inform readers about the events of Monterey County's community organizations. It is distributed monthly via *The Monterey County Herald;* heard daily on radio stations KAZU, KBTU, CD93FM, KMBY, KBOQ, and KRML, and on TV daily on KION, cable channel 2, and AMP channel 27.

Visitors and residents alike will find timely and detailed information on dining and entertainment for the week ahead in two free publications: Go! published by The Monterey County Herald and Coast Weekly. Both are released on Thursday and available at many stores, restaurants, and hotels throughout the area.

Around 35,000 are inserted into *The Herald* each month. An additional 10,000 free copies of *Community Links* newspapers can be found at Monterey county libraries and other locations countywide.

The Monterey County Post
225 Crossroads Boulevard, Suite 408, Carmel
(831) 624-2222
Controversy is the name of the game for this free, weekly, tabloid-size paper. The editors of the *Post* seek out tough issues and take sides in hotly contested local elections. Columnists pontificate on subjects such as jazz, Carmel politics, and furniture. *The Monterey County Post* has the distinction of being the only paper in the county with a weekly column written by a dog.

Peninsula Family Connection
612 Lighthouse Avenue, Suite 101, Pacific Grove
(831) 372-4996
This family-run, quarterly publication, billed as a "Comprehensive Guide to Family Fun on the Monterey Peninsula," has an annual circulation of 40,000. Local writers contribute articles on topics such as art, adoption, holistic living, pets, child development, and various aspects of parenting. A calendar of events provides information on local happenings that are especially suited to families. Listings of family-friendly restaurants and other businesses are also provided. The paper is free and available at libraries, bookstores, restaurants, family-oriented businesses, and social agencies.

MAGAZINES

Carmel Magazine
Carmel
(831) 625-9922
www.carmelmagazine.com
The covers of this high-quality, glossy, quarterly lifestyle magazine feature celebrities with local Carmel connections. Recent celebrities so honored include Brad Pitt, Robert Redford, Catherine Zeta-Jones, Ray Romano, and the former mayor of Carmel, Clint Eastwood. Regular features include art gallery showcases, restaurant reviews, topical features, and a regular column that profiles the dogs that Carmel businesspeople bring with them to work. The magazine is free at various businesses around town and is also available by subscription. A companion television show, *Carmel Magazine TV,* airs on local cable stations on the Monterey Peninsula and in Santa Cruz.

GuestLife Monterey Bay Magazine
Seventh Avenue between Lincoln and Monte Verde Streets, Carmel
(831) 626-5740
www.guestlife.com/monterey
This upscale annual tourist publication contains information on accommodations, shopping, culture, and cuisine. Its four-color, slick, and glossy appearance makes it an enjoyable read. More than 10,000 hotel rooms on Monterey Peninsula contain a hardbound edition of *GuestLife.* Local newsstands sell about 5,000 softcover editions throughout the year. About 30,000 separately bound softcover sections, Culture and Cuisine, show up at the local chamber of commerce, visitor center, galleries, restaurants, and at special events such as the AT&T National Pro-Am Tournament.

Monterey Peninsula Guide
Lincoln Street and Southeast Fifth Avenue, Carmel
(831) 625-6191
www.montereypeninsulaguide.com
Founded in 1980, this four-color magazine with an annual distribution of 60,000 is distributed through local hotels and motels, supermarkets and drugstores, and various bookstores. It's published annually and is replenished at distribution points throughout the year. Visitors receive a copy free in their hotel room, at the concierge desk, or at the airport. The magazine contains facts about the Monterey Peninsula, maps, a calendar of events, information on things to see and do, and feature articles on the arts, lifestyles, history, and golf. It also contains a lodging guide.

Monterey Peninsula Homes
Lincoln Street and Southeast Fifth Avenue, Carmel
(831) 625-6195
www.homesmagazine.com
Those looking to relocate to the Monterey Peninsula will want to pick up a free copy of this slick, glossy, four-color magazine that acts as an advertising aid for Realtors to promote their listings. The publication, first published in 1996, has a distribution of 30,000 and is published every five weeks. You'll find the magazine at participating realty offices and on media racks throughout the Peninsula, or it can be ordered online.

Monterey Land & See
Monterey County Visitors and Convention Bureau
150 Oliver Street, Monterey
(888) 221-1010
www.montereyinfo.org
This official Monterey County travel and meeting planner is sponsored by the Monterey County Convention and Visitors Bureau. The four-color publication contains a wealth of visitor information, area maps, and highlights of what to see and do in Monterey County. It also includes an extensive listing of area attractions, accommodations, restaurants, spas, sports and recreation opportunities, and wineries. An annual calendar of events gives specifics on recreational and cultural activities throughout the year.

Pacific Grove Directory
Pacific Grove
(831) 646-0351
www.bestofcal.com
This free guide for locals and visitors is a directory of accommodations, restaurants, shopping, trades, and personal services in Pacific Grove. There are also maps, interesting collections of historical information, community highlights, and information on Pacific Grove events. The circulation of 42,000 is distributed through the hospitality industry in Pacific Grove and Monterey as well as through the Pacific Grove Chamber of Commerce. It is also mailed to more than 8,000 homes and 1,000 businesses in Pacific Grove biannually. The directory is published quarterly.

TELEVISION

Peninsula-area viewers can access a variety of programming 24 hours a day through local cable, network, and specialty channels. Residents and businesses in Monterey are also served by Public, Education, and Government Access programming on several cable channels. Comcast is the current local provider of cable television. Those channel numbers are indicated in parentheses in the listings that follow.

KCBA Fox Channel 35 (3)
Salinas
(831) 422-3500
www.kcba.com

KION CBS Channel 46 (5)
(831) 784-1702
www.iknowcentralcoast.com

KGO ABC Channel 7 (7)
(415) 954-7777
www.abc7.com

KMST MCOE Channel 59 (26)
(831) 755-6424
www.monterery.k12.ca.us/kmst-tv

KQED PBS Channel 9 (9)
(415) 864-2000
www.kqed.org
KSBW NBC Channel 8 (6)
(831) 758-8888
www.theksbwchannel.com

KSMS Univision (Spanish) Channel 67 (4)
(831) 688-7200
www.univision.com

Cable

AMP (24, 25, 27)
2200 Garden Road, Monterey
(831) 333-1267
www.ampmedia.org
AMP (Access Monterey Peninsula) is a community media organization created to serve the public, educational agencies, and local governments in Monterey Country. This local nonprofit organization provides training and access to media technology for residents of Monterey County. AMP also airs programming 24 hours a day on channels 24, 25, and 27. Channel 24 features public access programming that showcases self-expression, from music, dance, poetry, and plays to religious, political, and social views. Channel 25 broadcasts programs about city services and public meetings; federal government programs including Navy/Marine Corps News, Army News, and Air Force Television News; and The Research Channel and programs of the University of California. Channel 27 presents community information in the form of looping bulletin board.

Comcast
120 Del Rey Gardens Drive, Del Rey Oaks
(831) 899-7100
www.cableistv.com
This is the major cable company serving the Monterey Peninsula. The company carries major networks such as ESPN, CNN, USA, and TNT. An optional pay-per-

view service can be set up on an automatic system that operates with a converter placed in the home. The monthly fee varies. Please call for more information.

RADIO

Radio fans won't be disappointed with the variety of station formats found in the Monterey Peninsula area. The selection includes those you'd expect and perhaps a few that will surprise you.

Adult Contemporary

KBAY 94.5 FM
(408) 287-5775
www.kbay.com

Christian

KLVM (KLOVE) 89.7 and 95.9 FM
(831) 663-6022
www.klove.com

Community/Public

KAZU 90.3 FM
(831) 375-7275
www.kazu.org
An informative radio station operated by California State University Monterey Bay. News and talk format, mostly provided by National Public Radio.

KSPB 91.9
(831) 625-8374
www.kspb.org
Commercial-free radio programmed by students at Robert Louis Stevenson School. Plays a broad range of musical styles and provides an interesting glimpse into the musical tastes of high school students. When not broadcasting live, the station airs the BBC World Service.

KUSP 88.9 FM
(831) 476-2800
www.kusp.org
In addition to NPR programming, locally produced programs feature classical, jazz, world, and roots music.

Country

KPIG 107.5
(831) 722-9000
www.kpig.com
Eclectic, offbeat, sometimes hilarious, but always entertaining, KPIG is truly one of a kind. A refreshing mix of musical styles is programmed by knowledgeable live DJs and touches on virtually every genre of American music. Thanks to a live Webcast, KPIG is the Internet's number-one radio station.

KTOM 100.7 and 100.9
(800) 660-5866
www.ktom.com
Contemporary country hits.

Jazz

KRML 1410 AM
(831) 624-6431
www.krmlradio.com
Straight-ahead jazz featuring local jazz aficionados.

Hispanic

KCTY 980 AM
(831) 757-5911
Regional Mexican music.

KRAY 103.5 FM
(831) 757-5911
Contemporary Hispanic music.

News/Talk

KGO 810 AM
(415) 954-8629
www.kgo.com
The 50,000-watt signal reaches Canada
and Mexico. San Francisco ABC flagship
station features talk show hosts with
guests of national renown. News and talk
24 hours.

KNRY 1240 AM
(831) 899-2600
www.knry.com
Nationally syndicated radio talk shows
share airtime with local, community, and
issue-oriented hosts.

KSCO 1080 AM/KOMY 1340 AM
(831) 475-1080
www.ksco.com
Talk radio.

Rock

KCDU 101.7 FM
(831) 658-5200
www.1017thebeach.com
Soft rock from the '80s, '90s, and today.

KHIP 104.3 FM
(831) 658-5200
www.thehippo.com
Classic rock.

KMBY 103.9 FM
(831) 658-5200
www.x1039fm.com
Alternative rock.

Soft Rock

KWAV 97 FM
(831) 649-0969
www.kwav.com

Top-40/Oldies

KDON 102.5 FM
(831) 649-5366
www.kdon.com
Contemporary hits.

KIDD 630 AM
(831) 649-0969
www.magic63.com
Music from the '40s through the '60s.

KOCN 105.1 FM
(831) 646-5105
Hits from the '60s and '70s. R&B and Old
School.

Urban

KBTU 93.5 FM
(831) 658-5200
www.935thebomb.com

WORSHIP

Religious worship was the foundation of early settlers and today continues to play a major role in the lives of Peninsula residents. The Yellow Pages directory yields nine pages of church listings—dozens of denominations, everything from A (Apostolic) to W (Word of Faith). This is, after all, California, and the tolerant, accepting attitude of Californians for all things unusual extends to the eclectic blend of religious beliefs and choices available here. Of course the traditional religious faiths are well represented.

The religious roots of the Monterey Peninsula began in 1770. Spanish King Charles III chartered missions in California for the purpose of establishing a presence in Alta California by religious conquest. In this way, Spain could take possession of the land before the Russians or the English could lay claim to it.

The Franciscans succeeded in founding 21 missions, with Father Junipero Serra overseeing the founding of the first nine. Serra's ambition, solely missionary, was to win the hearts of the Indians to Christ. With the exception of the San Francisco Mission, all of the California missions were established during the Spanish era. In 53 years, from 1769 to 1822, California was transformed into a Christian province by a handful of Spanish soldiers and a few Franciscan missionaries. The founding of Mission San Carlos de Borromeo de Monterey on June 3, 1770, shaped the little settlement called Monterey.

During Spanish rule the missions were the center of early California life. But after 30 years of being governed by the Spanish, Mexico gained its independence from Spain, and things changed in California. Under the rule of the Mexican government, the mission lands were taken from the church and sold at auction.

Until the secularization of the missions in 1842, the Church of Spain dominated the religious scene. Even after the missions were turned over to the Mexican government, a faction of people remained loyal to their Franciscan faith. The chapel in Monterey became the local parish church, and in 1850 it was designated the Cathedral of the Diocese of Monterey.

Methodists established a presence on the Peninsula in 1875 with the development of a religious camp meeting, the Pacific Grove Retreat. The Methodists didn't build churches in those early years because most of the meetings were held outdoors in the open air during summer months.

Other denominations were also attracted to the area, and Pacific Grove soon became known as the "City of Churches." Among the early faiths established were Episcopal in 1891, Congregational in 1892, Christian Science in 1905, Bethlehem Lutheran in 1925, and Seventh-day Adventist in 1928.

Many of the historical churches in Pacific Grove and other parts of the Peninsula were destroyed as they fell into disrepair. In the early days the churches were constructed quickly and cheaply, and the church leaders were more interested in building newer, more permanent structures than preserving the old ones. A few still remain and are a reminder of our religious heritage; we will briefly mention those who greatly influenced the spiritual development of the Monterey Peninsula.

ROYAL BEGINNINGS

The Royal Presidio Chapel, built in 1794, is the oldest building on the Monterey Peninsula and the oldest church in continuous service in California. The first two chapels were constructed of pole, brush, and mud, but the third was an adobe with foundations of stone and lime. It was named the Royal Presidio because it was the place where Spanish governors, representatives of the King of Spain, worshipped.

Today the church, located at 500 Church Street in Monterey, is listed as a California and National Historical Landmark. In 1968 it received the title "cathedral" by the Catholic Church, the smallest church to be so designated. The Royal Presidio Chapel is California's only extant presidio chapel and the last remaining structure of 18th-century Spanish origin.

MISSION MOVES TO CARMEL

Mission San Carlos Borromeo del Rio Carmel, founded in 1771 by Father Junipero Serra, was the second of the 21 missions founded in California. It was the first church to be completely built of adobe bricks. Ten years later, a sandstone church was built with stones quarried from the Santa Lucia Mountains in Carmel Valley. At that time the congregation was mainly Indian families.

After the missions were secularized in 1823 and the Franciscans were forced to leave, many missions fell into disrepair as looters stripped the missions of anything of value. The uninhabited Carmel mission was totally destroyed by vandals and lay in ruins for the next 50 years. In 1884 the restoration began with a new roof. Part of the quadrangle was restored and a memorial erected to the four padres buried there. The mission was completely restored in 1931 under the expert direction

of Sir Harry Downey. Pope John Paul designated the mission, in 1960, the status of a minor basilica. The Carmel Mission, located at 3080 Rio Road, is considered a Monterey County landmark.

PACIFIC GROVE'S FIRST CHURCH

Although the Methodists first established a religious encampment in Pacific Grove, they did not build the first church. St. Mary's by-the-Sea Episcopal Church, 146 12th Street, was the first church building constructed in Pacific Grove. It still holds services today.

St. Mary's was founded on March 25, 1886, by a small group of women who formed St. Mary's Guild. The church was built in 1887 on land donated by the Pacific Improvement Company. The Old English Gothic-style structure was modeled after an ancient church in Bath, England. The building size was doubled in 1911. Architect Lewis P. Hobart, who also conceived Grace Cathedral in San Francisco, devised this plan.

Several stained-glass windows in St. Mary's are of great historical interest. Bruce Porter of San Francisco designed the window over the main altar in 1894. It was created with more than 3,000 pieces of glass. Another, donated by Cyrus H. McCormick, was designed by Louis C. Tiffany and was placed in the church in 1922. Tiffany's window depicts pink foxgloves and white lilies. McCormick, of the millionaire McCormick Farm Implement family, married his wife at St. Mary's in 1889.

THE LITTLE WHITE CHURCH

The Christian Church of Pacific Grove, 442 Central Avenue, was established in 1894 by the "Willing Workers," a group of women who organized and laid plans for the church. They struggled for 10 years to raise

From the early California missions, a Zen retreat, and a Buddhist temple to the Jewish synagogue and a host of Catholic, Protestant, nondenominational, and nontraditional settings, a tour of the Peninsula's houses of worship is truly a walk down the path of history as well as an experience of diverse cultures from around the world.

enough money to build the church, holding fund-raising bazaars where handmade products and baked goods were sold.

In 1896 they purchased a lot from the Pacific Improvement Company for $1.00. The construction of the church, a low-budget plan, was completed that same year. Though simple, the church is quite elegant, a lasting testament to the women who willed the church into existence.

A CHURCH FOR HOTEL GUESTS

Visitors at the famed Del Monte Hotel found only one thing lacking—a church to serve their spiritual needs. C. P. Huntington and Charles H. Crocker (of the "Big Four"; see our History chapter) and the Crocker sisters, Miss Hattie and Mrs. Rutherford, became involved in the planning and support of the new church. Crocker obtained property adjacent to the hotel and donated it for the site of the new chapel.

Ernest Coxhead, an Englishman living in San Francisco, was the architect for the church. Coxhead was interested in the new "Arts and Crafts" style and felt it would be a good match for St. John's Episcopal Church. However, Huntington disagreed. He felt the church should adopt a typical English Norman style built in granite. The Crockers sided with

Coxhead, and the chapel was built with an exterior of redwood shingles.

The new chapel, open to all, was dedicated in 1891. At the service Bishop Nichols said, "This little Chapel-of-Ease is fitted for a unique piece of missionary work. Men and women will worship here who rarely attend divine services in our great city churches."

If you go to St. John's Episcopal Church, notice the elegant rood screen, donated by Mrs. Mary Morrison in 1932 and placed between the nave and the choir seating. Designed by Danish artist Robert Petersen, it has a graceful arch with a rood, or cross, at the top of the curve. Two swinging gates, each with a cross, complete the effect.

Through the years, St. John's has always taken a traditional stance, stressing Biblical faith and worship. After the demise of the Del Monte Hotel, it was moved in 1957 to its present location on Mark Thomas Drive.

FIRST BAPTIST CHURCH OF PACIFIC GROVE

The First Baptist Church, 246 Laurel Street, was the first African-American church on the Monterey Peninsula. Although it was organized in 1909, a church building wasn't erected until 1912. Many of its earliest members were from the Ninth Regiment of the U.S. Cavalry. The Ninth, stationed at the Presidio from 1902 to 1904, was an all African-American regiment of about 300 soldiers. They had been organized toward the end of the Civil War to fight the Indians. During their stay on the Peninsula, they were housed in tents in the area near where the Hopkins Marine Station now stands. This explains, in part, how an all-black church got an early start among the all-white population in Pacific Grove.

THE CHURCH OF THE WAYFARER IN CARMEL

The first church in Carmel originally met outside, under the trees on the corner of Dolores Street and Sixth Avenue. The year was 1904. In 1905 J. Devendorf graciously donated two lots he owned on Lincoln Street near Ocean Avenue and shortly thereafter the First Methodist Episcopal Church of Carmel was built and formally dedicated. The name of the church changed to the Carmel Community Church before it received its current name, the Church of the Wayfarer. The Wayfarer was a musical pageant written by one of the church members and, in the early 1940s when the name was changed, also reflected the international composition of the congregation.

The church was constructed with pieces of famous estates; the wood panels inside the church came from a house designed by Frank Lloyd Wright, and the tile on the floor was originally part of the Hearst estate. Take a minute to stop and look inside the wonderful old church as you visit Carmel, or attend a Sunday service if you prefer—all wayfarers past and present are welcome here.

TODAY'S RELIGIOUS SCENE

Visitors and locals alike refer to the Saturday religion pages in *The Monterey County Herald* for specific information regarding worship services. The religion pages offer information about special activities at individual churches, religious news, and columns by several local religious leaders. The Yellow Pages of the phone book contain listings of all the local churches. Many churches have display ads listing the time of their worship services.

Several churches broadcast services on local public access TV channel 24.

If you are visiting from out of the area, take the opportunity to attend a church service at one of our historical churches, alternative houses of worship, or community churches. From the oldest to the newest, Monterey Peninsula has a form of worship for everyone.

Many area churches are prized wedding spots. A clue that a celebrity couple is tying the knot lies in the paparazzi hovering overhead in helicopters. Local clergy are also happy to officiate at an alfresco ceremony at one of the Peninsula's picturesque coastal parks.

INDEX

ABOUT THE AUTHORS

TOM OWENS

A second-generation Californian, Tom Owens was born and raised in the suburbs of Los Angeles and moved up to the Monterey Peninsula in 1980. His first experience with the Monterey area was during his honeymoon in 1978, when he and his bride fell in love with Big Sur and the entire Monterey Bay coastline.

As head of his own marketing firm, Tom Owens Communications, Tom has an extensive background in magazine journalism, marketing, advertising, and public relations, covering everything from insurance to jazz. He is a communications arts graduate from California State Polytechnic University in Pomona.

Tom lives in Pacific Grove with his wife, Emily, and has two Peninsula-born daughters, Kate and Anna. Edie the dog and Gianni the cat round out the Owens household. Tom enjoys hiking. beachcombing, all kinds of music, and most kinds of travel.

MELANIE BELLON CHATFIELD

Originally from Michigan, Melanie traveled west in 1994 for a five-day vacation. Starting out in San Francisco, she and her friend Jan drove down Highway 1 to the Monterey Peninsula. One day later, she met Michael, now her husband, and decided to make Monterey her home.

At age 17, Melanie took a job with a bank in her hometown of Lansing. With the threshold for boredom of a two-year-old, Melanie worked in just about every department of the bank until she landed in the marketing department in 1979. There she found her calling and pursued her degree in marketing in the evenings. She moved to Kalamazoo and served as public relations manager for the banking

corporation until 1990. Seeking to flex her creative muscles, Melanie joined an advertising agency as a copywriter and public relations executive.

After moving to the Monterey Peninsula, Melanie started her own writing and communications business. Lured back into the corporate world in 1996, she worked as a staff writer for a corporation and then as community relations director for a local hospital. Since 1999, Melanie and her husband have worked together in their home office, where they provide writing and communications services for local and national businesses. They also write for lifestyle, health care, travel, and business publications. Along with writing, world travel has been a passion of Melanie's since she visited London with her senior class. She has scoured the countries of Europe during dozens of visits and explored terrain above and below the water (with the aid of SCUBA) on the Monterey Peninsula, and in southern California, Florida, Bali, Thailand, Mexico, The Bahamas, Honduras, and Italy.